Historical Dictionary
of
Canada

Barry M. Gough

The Scarecrow Press, Inc.
Lanham, Maryland, and London
1999

SCARECROW PRESS, INC.

Published in the United States of America
by Scarecrow Press, Inc.
4720 Boston Way, Lanham, Maryland 20706
http://www.scarecrowpress.com

4 Pleydell Gardens, Folkestone
Kent CT20 2DN, England

British Library Cataloguing in Publication Information Available

Library of Congress Cataloging-in-Publication Data

Gough, Barry M.
    Historical dictionary of Canada / Barry Gough.
      p.   cm.
    Includes bibliographical references.
    ISBN 0-8108-3541-X (alk. paper)
    1. Canada—History Dictionaries. I. Title.
F1026.G69   1999   99-25103
971′.003—dc21   CIP

∞™ The paper used in this publication meets the minimum requirements of
American National Standard for Information Sciences—Permanence of
Paper for Printed Library Materials, ANSI/NISO Z39.48–1992.
Manufactured in the United States of America.

To Robin W. Winks
American Scholar Extraordinaire of Canada

Contents

Editor's Foreword

It is easy to get the wrong impression about Canada. *A new country.* Perhaps compared to some in Asia and Europe. But it was first "discovered" a thousand years ago, and then again about five hundred years ago, and was gradually colonized and settled by outsiders for four centuries. However, before that there were the native peoples, some of whom remain. *Empty.* True, the present population is small for such a big place, but many people are concentrated in large, modern cities and most are urbanized. *A rather simple, homogeneous entity.* Hardly, for the population despite any melting-pot effect is rather heterogeneous and the provinces maintain considerable autonomy, some actually demanding more and one seeking independence. *A geographical appendage of its powerful southern neighbour, the United States.* Despite very close economic and other links, Canadians usually go their own way and have created a strikingly different society.

Canada is a very complex, and intriguing, nation which certainly deserves to be better known by foreigners and probably Canadians as well. That is the purpose of this *Historical Dictionary of Canada.* It presents the country, traces its history, takes a good look at the recent situation, and offers some insight into the future. It does so through concise and informative entries on significant persons, places and events, institutions, and ethnic groupings. Others deal with important political, economic, social, and cultural aspects. The broader context is described in the introduction and chronology. Admittedly, this book can only go so far. But it is a particularly good starting point because of a comprehensive and intelligently structured bibliography that can easily direct readers toward whatever subject may interest them.

To write such a book, it is obviously necessary to know Canada well. That first requirement is amply met by the author, Barry M. Gough, who has spent many decades studying Canadian history and politics and visiting different parts of the country. It is perhaps more important to develop a knack for explaining Canada to others. This, Dr. Gough has done as a professor of history and Canadian studies at Wilfrid Laurier University in

Waterloo, Ontario, and guest professor at various other universities. In addition to lecturing, he has written several books on Canada's history as well as numerous shorter works. This has given him more than enough opportunities to explain Canada to foreigners, and also to Canadians, which may actually be harder. This time Dr. Gough takes on a particularly broad range of subjects of interest to both publics and acquits himself very well.

Jon Woronoff
Series Editor

Acknowledgements

It is not possible to give thanks to each and every scholar, librarian, archivist, and institutional aide who has provided assistance for me over an academic career spanning three decades. My historical journey began early, with my father's abiding passion for his adopted country's history and geography and with my mother's keen awareness of roles that minority groups (often exploited, frequently ignored) played in the incalculable efforts in building the infrastructure of one of the world's preeminent and wealthy nations. Superb teachers in high school opened for me the complexities of constitutional development and disclosed a large teaching subject of lifetime activity. Professors at the University of Victoria and the University of British Columbia when I was an undergraduate offered only one advanced course on Canadian history; even so, Reginald Roy's and Margaret Ormsby's prescient inquiries into federal–provincial relations, sectional discontent, political pluralism, and above all, national development and international affairs opened wide vistas. They enlarged broadly a personal understanding of western Canadian history and national military affairs that have always been central themes of my own research. In later years in postgraduate study in the late 1960s, for me Canadian history as a specific subject took a more pronounced position in Canadian university curricula.

However, and this may now seem entirely strange, not until the mid-1970s and the T. H. B. Symons' report *To Know Ourselves: The Report of the Commission on Canadian Studies* (1975) did Canadian history become acknowledged as the main requirement for a university undergraduate history degree. Most practising historians of my age took few Canadian history courses. We now look with envy at the rich, varied backgrounds that our younger colleagues bring to classrooms and seminars. The fact of the matter is that our current age has had to frame a national history on the foundations of a very few scholars' pioneering endeavours. Among the deans of Canadian history I count the following as of particular value: Donald Grant Creighton, Harold Adams Innis, Gustav Lanctot, John Bartlett Brebner, W. L. Morton, C. P. Stacey, Michel Brunet, W. S. McNutt, Morris Zaslow, A. R. M. Lower, and Margaret Ormsby. It may date me when I cite these names, but they were of an earlier generation than mine. Even so, they set forth a foundation of national history based upon wide-ranging consensus that attempted to explain the national experience. It would take another generation after them and those who immediately followed them, such as myself, to pull down accepted remnants of the national historical edifice and in place build the foundations of a new history characterized by region and class, and when that had virtually run its course, by gender, race, and ethnicity.

In following these trends, preoccupations, and fashions, I can only say how grateful I am to the *Canadian Historical Review* for its ongoing bibliography of historical works and for its extensive book review section. These alone allow students of Canadian history a comprehensive place to begin the effective study of a subject that many feel has been hijacked by special interest groups.

As a subject of study, Canada presents undiminished opportunities for the historian of whatever inclination or desire—except, perhaps, tropical affairs. Far from being dull or irrelevant, Canada's history remains most promising for the study of racial accord, native affairs, regional diversity, economic challenges, patronage, social welfare experimentation, and nation-building. That Canada's history is so little known beyond Canada's boundaries cannot be blamed on the rest of the world alone. In large measure, Canadians have failed to broadcast the nuances of their remarkable (if complex) history. This book, which rests heavily on the previous work of others whose books are listed in the bibliography, is intended as a compendium of fundamentals and as a guide to a rich historical literature of a modern nation with a recent history of four centuries.

I must pay special thanks to research assistant Walter W. Sendzik for bringing this project through various stages. Bruce Hodgins assisted with historiography, Peter Russell with sport, and Terry Copp with Normandy. I also thank John McCallum of Wilfrid Laurier University's library for assistance in making the bibliographical search less arduous and at the same time more complete. Electronic means have been employed to good effect in the preparation of the bibliography. Cameron Croxall assisted with articles on Inuit subjects. Elsie Grogan provided superb word processing. I have relied heavily on W. S. Wallace's *Macmillan Dictionary of Canadian Biography* and Mel Hurtig's *The Canadian Encyclopaedia*, as well as other guides listed in the bibliography.

It must be said that Canada's is not a recent history and that each generation seems to prepare its own guides to national history and historical literature. Almost without fail I have attempted to keep this a modern study, with emphasis on the era since 1867 and particularly since 1914. The counsel of the series editor, Jon Woronoff, is greatly appreciated. I have the pleasure of thanking Robin W. Winks for suggesting that I undertake this book. If those who consult this work find their long-sought-after answers, and if their appreciation of the essentials of Canadian history is enhanced, I shall be grateful. Not least, if Canadians confused by their own perplexing national crisis shall have found some solace in the fact that their present state of affairs has been preceded by numerous variants of similar conundrums, I shall be eternally delighted. Notice of errors would be appreciated.

Barry M. Gough

Acronyms and Special Terms

ALTA	Alberta
BC	British Columbia
BCATP	British Commonwealth Air Training Plan
BNA	British North America
CBC	Canadian Broadcasting Corporation
CCF	Co-operative Commonwealth Federation
CEF	Canadian Expeditionary Force
CFB	Canadian Forces Base
CPR	Canadian Pacific Railway
CRTC	Canadian Radio and Telecommunications Commission
DEW	Distant Early Warning
DIA	Department of Indian Affairs
FLQ	Front de Libération de Québec
GATT	General Agreement on Tariffs and Trade
HBC	Hudson's Bay Company
HMCS	Her Majesty's Canadian Ship
JCPC	Judicial Committee of the Privy Council
MAN	Manitoba
MP	Member of Parliament
NAFTA	North American Free Trade Agreement
NASA	National Aeronautical and Space Administration (U.S.)
NATO	North Atlantic Treaty Organization
NB	New Brunswick
NDP	New Democratic Party
NFB	National Film Board
NFLD	Newfoundland
NORAD	North American Air Defence Command
NS	Nova Scotia
NWC	North West Company
NWT	Northwest Territories
OAS	Organization of American States

ONT	Ontario
PC	Progressive Conservative Party
PEI	Prince Edward Island
PJBD	Permanent Joint Board on Defence
PQ	Parti Québecois
QUE	Québec
RCAF	Royal Canadian Air Force
RCMP	Royal Canadian Mounted Police
RCN	Royal Canadian Navy
RE	Royal Engineers
RFC	Royal Flying Corps
RMC	Royal Military College of Canada
RN	Royal Navy
RNAS	Royal Naval Air Service
SASK	Saskatchewan
U.K.	United Kingdom
UN	United Nations
U.S.	United States of America
YK	Yukon

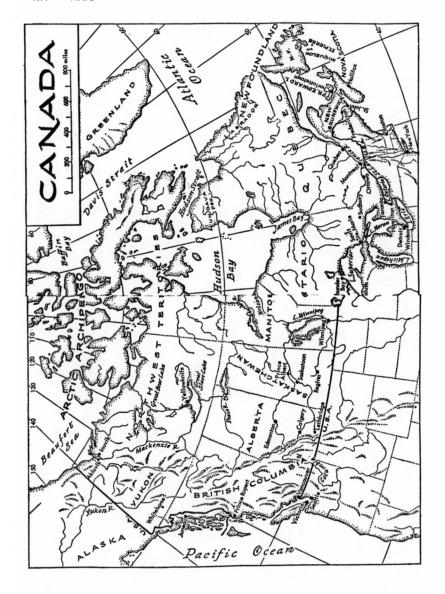

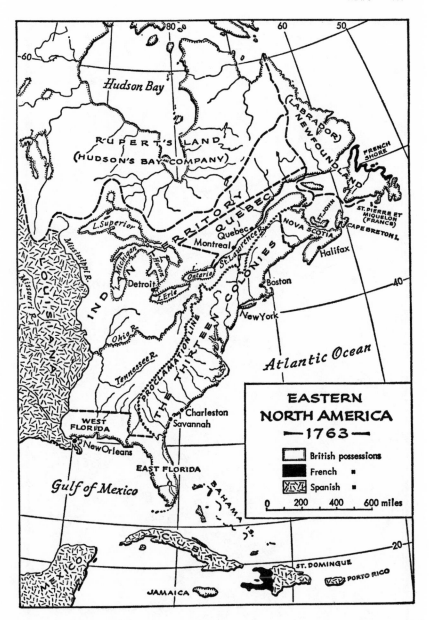

EASTERN NORTH AMERICA
—1763—

British possessions
French
Spanish

0   200   400   600 miles

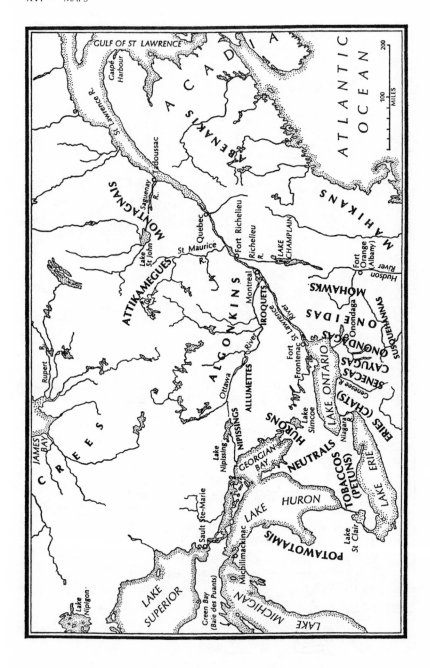

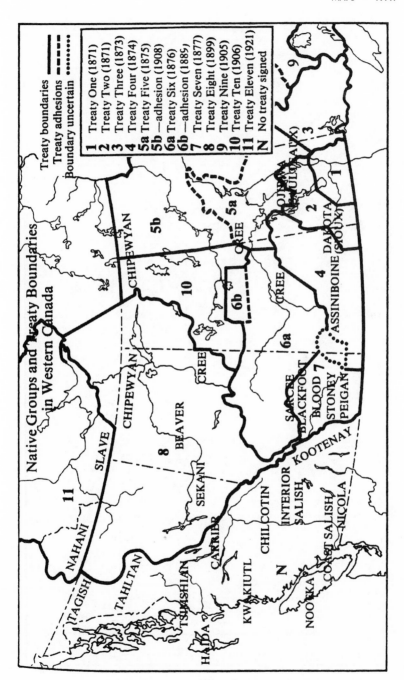

Native Groups and Treaty Boundaries in Western Canada

Treaty boundaries ———
Treaty adhesions ----
Boundary uncertain ·······

1 Treaty One (1871)
2 Treaty Two (1871)
3 Treaty Three (1873)
4 Treaty Four (1874)
5a Treaty Five (1875)
5b —adhesion (1908)
6a Treaty Six (1876)
6b —adhesion (1889)
7 Treaty Seven (1877)
8 Treaty Eight (1899)
9 Treaty Nine (1905)
10 Treaty Ten (1906)
11 Treaty Eleven (1921)
N No treaty signed

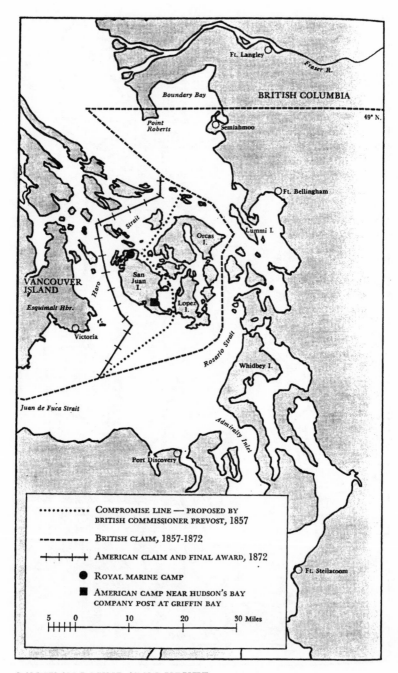

SAN JUAN BOUNDARY DISPUTE

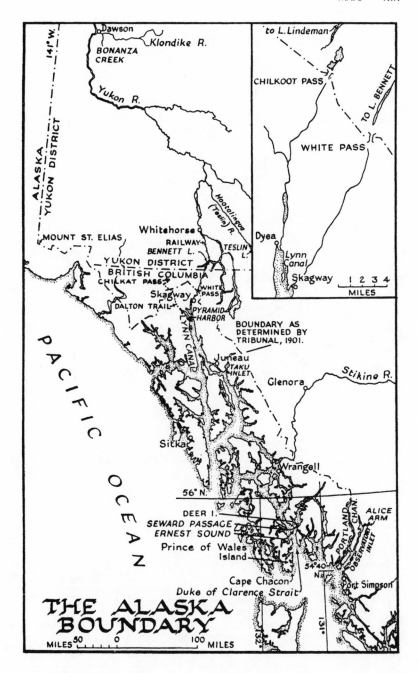

THE ALASKA
BOUNDARY

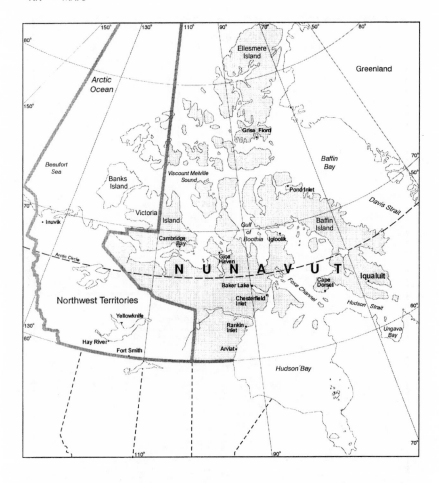

Chronology

c. 875 Celt-Irish monks from Iceland possibly settled on Cape Breton, absorbed into the Mi'kmaq population.

1004–1005 Leif Ericsson wintered in Vinland (L'Anse aux Meadows, NFLD).

1005–1008 Brother of Leif (Thorwald Ericsson) spent two winters in Vinland.

c. 1420 Basque whalers began to hunt in the Labrador Sea.

1494 Treaty of Tordesillas awarded Spain imperial control of Western Hemisphere.

1497 **June 24:** John Cabot or Giovanni Caboto landed on Cape Breton Island and claimed land for King Henry VII of England.

1504 First establishment at St. John's, NFLD. Norman fishing village established on Avalon Peninsula.

1534 **July 7:** First recorded exchange between Europeans and native peoples. Jacques Cartier traded for furs with the Mi'kmaq peoples. **July 24:** Cartier landed at the entrance to the St. Lawrence and claimed the land for King Francis I of France.

1558 First settlers arrived aboard the brig *Hawke* in Trinity, NFLD.

1603 Samuel de Champlain's first voyage to Canada.

1605 **Aug. 1:** The French colony of Port Royal established on the shore of Bay of Fundy.

1608 **July 3:** Champlain founded the settlement of Québec.

1609 First contact between the French in New France and the (Wendat) Huron peoples. **July 30:** Champlain assisted the Huron and allies in defeating the Iroquois on the shores of Lake Champlain.

1610   **June 14-19:** Champlain and Huron and Algonquin allies defeated an Iroquois party, Richelieu River.

1610–11   Henry Hudson in ship *Discovery* wintered in James Bay. Champlain sent Étienne Brûlé to winter among the Huron.

1613   **July:** Port Royal attacked and burnt by Samuel Argall, on orders from Governor Dale of Virginia; first English expedition against Acadia.

1622   **July:** First Scots colonists arrived in Nova Scotia.

1625   **June:** First Jesuit missionaries arrived in New France to bring Christianity to native peoples.

1629   **July 19:** Capt. David Kirke, an Englishman, captured Québec; subsequently, Québec with Port Royal was returned to France by Treaty of St. Germain-en-Laye, 29 March 1632.

1639   Smallpox epidemic swept through the St. Lawrence Valley. Algonquin and Huron nations suffered substantial losses.

1642   Fort Richelieu built to protect southern approach to Montréal.

1644   **March:** Settlers near Montréal defeated by Iroquois.

1653   Iroquois made peace with the French, bringing to an end the destruction of Huronia and the devastation of the Huron peoples by war (1642–49).

1660   **May:** Battle of the Long Sault, Ottawa River (near Hawkesbury), between 16 French led by Adam Dollard des Ormeaux and 44 native allies and some 800 Iroquois. All the French fighters in this battle were killed.

1663   Sovereign Council of New France created, and with it the first constituted civil and military government of the colony under specifically royal auspices and regulation.

1665   **June 30:** Carignan-Salières Regiment, 1,100 strong, arrived to defend New France; posts constructed.

1670   **May 2:** Gentlemen Adventurers of England trading into Hudson Bay (HBC) chartered by Charles II, subsequent to successful voyage of *Nonsuch* and establishment of Charles Fort.

1673   Construction of French fort at Fort Frontenac (Kingston, ONT) commenced.

1686   Expedition by de Troyes and Sieur d'Iberville marched overland to Hudson Bay and seized three HBC posts. **Nov. 19:** England and France agreed on neutrality pact to settle dispute over Hudson Bay.

1690 William Phips of Massachusetts led force to get Port Royal, which surrendered 21 May. Later proceeded to Québec, but Governor Louis de Buade Frontenac put up stout defence. D'Iberville, with three warships, entered Hudson Bay, raided Fort New Severn, and the next year returned to Québec with booty.

1692 Oct. 22: Madeline de Verchères led defence of family fort against Iroquois.

1696 July 4: Frontenac quit Montréal with 2,150 men to punish Iroquois for attacks on settlements.

1700 Sept. 8: Iroquois, Abenakis, and Ottawas agree to peace terms with governor of New France, Louis de Callières.

1701 Detroit established by Cadillac.

1702–13 Queen Anne's War (part of War of the Spanish Succession) brought many raids and massacres, and in 1710 the British conquered Port Royal, renaming it Annapolis Royal. In 1711 Adm. Hovenden Walker's Royal Navy expedition failed to reach Québec.

1713 Apr. 11: The Treaty of Utrecht signed by Britain, France, and Spain. Among other terms, the treaty recognized British sovereignty over Hudson Bay, Acadia, and Newfoundland. France retained New France, Île St. Jean (PEI), and the right to fish and use parts of the Newfoundland shore, "the French Shore."

1735 The great French fortress Louisbourg (begun 1719) completed on Île-Royale, Cape Breton. Then considered to be the strongest fort in America.

1749 July 9: Col. Edward Cornwallis established a British settlement at Chebucto, on the eastern shores of Nova Scotia; called Halifax.

1756 Britain declared war on France; beginning of Seven Years' War (known in the United States as the French and Indian War), essentially a war for Canada and to secure boundaries of the Thirteen Colonies. **Aug. 5:** French commander Louis-Joseph de Montcalm forced surrender of British garrison at Oswego; British lose command of Lake Ontario.

1757 Jan. 21: French defeated Maj. Robert Rogers and his Rangers near Ticonderoga in the "Battle on Snowshoes." **July/August:** French took Lake George and later Fort William Henry.

1758 July 26: British forces seized Fortress Louisbourg from the French. The capitulation was the beginning of the end for the French empire in

North America. **Sept. 13:** The British captured the city of Québec from the French after the battle on the Plains of Abraham.

1760 Sept. 8: Articles of Capitulation of Montréal established interim terms of conquest. **Sept. 9:** The French surrendered the city of Montréal, ending the French conquest of New France.

1763 Feb. 10: The British, French, and Spanish signed the Treaty of Paris. The treaty placed Canada under the sovereignty of Britain. As well, it outlined the boundary of Canada that included the Great Lakes basin and stretched west to the northeastern bank of the Mississippi River. **Oct. 7:** Royal Proclamation provided for the creation of the Province of Québec and recognized certain rights of native peoples.

1774 Québec Act passed by the British Parliament.

1775 Sept. 5: American forces led by Brig. Gen. Richard Montgomery and Maj. Gen. Philip Schuyler from Crown Point invade Saint Jean. **Dec. 31:** American forces led by Col. Benedict Arnold attempted to capture the town of Québec, but were unsuccessful.

1783 Treaty of Versailles, Article I, recognized a sovereign United States of America and defined first Canadian-American border.

1784 First Loyalists settled in Ontario; New Brunswick created as a province.

1788 John Meares, a British trader, arrived at Nootka Sound, the first of many sea-otter traders.

1789 Nootka Sound Incident, when Spanish commandant seized British shipping, forcing British diplomatic protests and threat of war. Spain backed down.

1791 June 10: Constitutional (or Canada) Act given royal assent in London for the creation of Upper Canada and Lower Canada, which was previously the Province of Québec.

1793 July 22: Alexander Mackenzie, first to cross the continent north of Mexico, reached Mackenzie Rock, Dean Channel, BC.

1811 May 3: HBC sold Lord Selkirk 116,000 square miles near and at the confluence of the Red and Assiniboine Rivers, for a colony.

1812 June 9: President James Madison of the United States declared war on Britain, which included Canada.

1813 **September:** Battle of Lake Erie (Put-in Bay) and subsequent retreat of the British Army to Moraviantown; death of Indian patriot and British ally Tecumseh.

1814 **July 25:** Battle of Lundy's Lane, Niagara Peninsula, perhaps hardest-fought campaign of the land war. **Aug. 14:** *Nancy*, famous ex-NWC schooner, lost to U.S. Navy at Nottawasaga, Upper Canada. **Sept. 11:** U.S. Navy defeats British forces led by General Prevost on Lake Champlain. **Dec. 24:** Britain and the United States signed the Treaty of Ghent to end the War of 1812.

1816 **June 19:** Massacre of Seven Oaks, Red River. Cuthbert Grant and associates killed HBC Governor Semple and 19 of his men.

1821 Merger of Hudson's Bay Company and North West Company under the name of the former.

1829 **June 6:** The last known Beothuk, Shawnadithit, died in Newfoundland. **Nov. 29:** The Welland Canal completed, bypassing the Niagara River and providing a waterway between Lake Ontario and Lake Erie.

1834 **Feb. 17:** Lower Canada assembly adopted the Ninety-Two Resolutions, demanding constitutional reform.

1837 **Nov. 16:** Patriot rebels in Lower Canada attacked British troops. Clash stemmed from the British government's attempt to run the province without the consent of the Assembly. **Dec. 5:** William Lyon Mackenzie led a rebel force in Upper Canada into Toronto with hopes of capturing the city. **Dec. 7:** Rebels, led by Mackenzie, defeated in a half-hour battle by British forces at Montgomery's Tavern, north of Toronto.

1839 **Feb. 11:** Lord Durham presented the British Parliament with his *Report on the Affairs of British North America.*

1840 **July 23:** An act of the British Parliament merged Upper and Lower Canada into one province called Canada. The new province was governed through a two-house system, an elected Assembly and an appointed Legislative Council, under an appointed governor general. **Aug. 10:** First manned flight, by balloon *Star of the East,* at Saint John, NB.

1842 **Aug. 9:** The Webster-Ashburton Treaty signed between Britain and United States. Among other provisions, the treaty set the boundary between New Brunswick and Maine, the dividing line being the Saint John River.

1843 **March:** Fort Camosun (later Fort Victoria), Vancouver Island, opened as HBC trading base on Northwest Coast.

1845 May 19: Capt. Sir John Franklin, RN, led his third expedition to search for the Northwest Passage. From this one, Franklin would not return.

1846 June 15: The Oregon Boundary Treaty was signed between Britain and the United States. It established the boundaries between Canada and the United States along the 49th parallel west of the Rocky Mountains, leaving Vancouver Island in British hands and the status of San Juan Archipelago uncertain.

1849 Jan. 19: Colony of Vancouver Island created by Royal Charter; HBC awarded Charter of Grant to develop the new colony. **Oct. 11:** Montréal citizens, including French Canadian liberals and English merchants, issued a joint manifesto urging annexation to the United States. Not successful.

1854 June 6: The United Province of Canada and the United States signed the first Reciprocity Treaty between the two countries.

1854–72 San Juan Boundary dispute results in British loss of San Juan Island to Washington Territory.

1861 Nov. 8: The *Trent* affair, prompting British naval and military reinforcement of Canada.

1862 Esquimalt, Vancouver Island, named British naval headquarters for Pacific Station.

1864 June 22: Tories and Reformers in the Canadian Assembly formed a coalition to unite British North America into one nation. The coalition was led by John A. Macdonald and George Brown. **Sept. 1:** Delegates from the Maritime Colonies and the United Province of Canada met in Charlottetown, PEI, to discuss union. **Oct. 28:** The delegates from Canada, New Brunswick, Nova Scotia, Newfoundland, and Prince Edward Island adopted the Québec Resolutions. The resolutions formed the first theoretical foundation for the creation of the Dominion of Canada.

1866 Mar. 7: 10,000 Canadian militia called out for protection against feared Fenian raids. **Mar. 17:** The Reciprocity Treaty of 1854 repealed by the United States. **May 31-June 2:** Battle of Ridgeway, ONT, forced Fenians to retire.

1867 Emily Howard Stowe became Canada's first female medical doctor. **Mar. 29:** British Parliament passed the British North America Act, providing for the union of New Brunswick, Nova Scotia, and Canada into a self-governing dominion called the Dominion of Canada. **July 1:** The British

North America Act went into effect with Sir John A. Macdonald as Canada's first prime minister.

1868   May 22: The Railway Act described the organization of railway companies, outlined regulations for operations, and provided possible subsidies for railways meeting certain government regulations.

1869   June 22: The Gradual Enfranchisement of Indians Act stripped native women of their status if they married non-Indians. Rupert's Land Act established temporary or provisional government of Rupert's Land and the Northwestern Territory when united with Canada, and called for a lieutenant governor to regulate the affairs under law for the peace, order, and good government thereof. **Oct. 11:** Led by Louis Riel, the Métis of Red River prevented Canadian surveyors from entering Métis territory. This was the beginning of the Riel Rebellion of 1869. **Nov. 2:** A Métis group led by Riel took control of Fort Garry.

1870   Mar. 2: Thomas Scott of Ontario, an Orangeman, executed by the Riel provisional government to show the Canadian government that the Métis of Red River had to be taken seriously. **July 15:** Manitoba entered the confederation. **Aug. 24:** The Métis of Red River fled as federal troops moved in to restore order. Riel fled to the United States.

1871   May 8: Treaty of Washington signed between Canada and the United States. The treaty, negotiated by a British commission, gave the Americans free access to Canada's inshore fisheries and provided no compensation for the Fenian raids on Canada. The only consolation of the treaty was that the United States recognized Canada's boundaries. **July 20:** British Columbia entered the confederation. **Aug. 3:** The first Indian treaty negotiated by the Dominion of Canada signed. Under the treaty, Ojibwa and Cree of southern Manitoba surrendered 43,250 square kilometres of their territory to the Crown. In return, they received reserves of land.

1872   Riel returned from exile to continue Métis crusade for rights. **Apr. 14:** Dominion Lands Act passed by the federal government. The act allowed the federal government to retain control of all public lands and resources in western Canada. **June 14:** Sir John A. Macdonald's Conservative government passed the Trade Unions Bill. Under the law, workers were allowed to be members of unions.

1873   May 23: The North West Mounted Police (later Royal Canadian Mounted Police) established by Act of Parliament. **July 1:** Prince Edward Island entered the confederation. **July 4:** Revelations of the Pacific scandal implied that Macdonald and his Conservative government took bribes from the Canadian Pacific Railway Company to secure a contract to build a transcontinental railway. **October:** Riel first elected to Parliament. **Nov. 5:** Macdonald and his cabinet resigned due to the Pacific scandal. The governor general placed Alexander Mackenzie and the Liberals in power.

1874   Jan. 22: The Liberals led by Alexander Mackenzie defeated Macdonald and the Conservatives in an election. Mackenzie formed the first Liberal government in Canada.

1875   Sept. 19: Supreme Court of Canada established. It did not become the final judicial authority in Canada until 1949. Until this time, the Judicial Committee of the Privy Council in London remained the ultimate authority.

1876   Apr. 12: Parliament passed the Indian Act. The act placed natives in a separate legal category as wards of the government. **June 1:** Royal Military College of Canada opened in Kingston, ONT. **Aug. 10:** Canadian Alexander Graham Bell invented the telephone.

1878   Oct. 17: Macdonald again became prime minister.

1879   Mar. 14: Conservatives passed the National Policy legislation.

1880   May 7: Indian Act of 1880 passed by the federal government. This act formally established the federal Department of Indian Affairs. **July 31:** Britain transferred sovereignty of the Arctic Islands to Canada.

1883   Nov. 18: Standard Time, originated by Sir Sandford Fleming, instituted in Canada.

1885   Mar. 19: Métis established a provisional government in the North West Territory. Riel was the leader behind the movement and president of the Provisional Government; Gabriel Dumont, its adjutant general. **Mar. 26:** Northwest Rebellion began between the Métis and Cree and the North West Mounted Police at Duck Lake, NWT. **May 12:** Canadian militia defeated Métis forces at Battle of Batoche, NWT, ending the Northwest Rebellion (Riel surrendered 15 May; Dumont escaped to the United States). **Nov. 7:** The last spike was driven by Donald Smith at Craigellachie, BC, thus completing Canada's first transcontinental railway. **Nov. 16:** Riel hanged in Regina for high treason for his role in the Northwest Rebellion. **Nov. 25:** Rocky Mountains Park (now Banff National Park) established by order-in-council. **Nov. 27:** Wandering Spirit and seven other rebel Indians hanged for murders at Frog Lake in April.

1886 July 4: The Canadian Pacific Railway's first transcontinental passenger train arrived in Port Moody, BC.

1887 Apr. 28: The North-West Territories Act specified that French be given equal status with English in the government and courts of the Northwest Territories. In 1892, the official use of French in recording and publishing the Assembly's proceedings was eliminated.

1891 Mar. 5: Macdonald led Conservatives to election victory for his last time. **June 6:** Death of Macdonald.

1893 Oct. 27: National Council of Women formed. **Nov. 27:** Montréal Amateur Athletic Association won the first Stanley Cup in hockey.

1896 July 11: Sir Wilfrid Laurier led the Liberals to election victory to become Canada's first French-speaking prime minister. **Nov. 27:** Clifford Sifton, minister of the interior, unveiled an immigration policy to populate the prairies and elsewhere in Canada. The policy favoured immigrants with farming experience. This was the largest immigration drive in the nation's history.

1897 Klondike gold rush in the Yukon.

1898 June 13: The federal government proclaimed the Yukon District a territory.

1899 Oct. 30: Canadian soldiers sailed for South Africa to fight in the Boer War with the British.

1903 Alaska Boundary Commission decided the boundary between Canada and Alaska. In certain provisions the decision favoured the United States. **Oct. 20:** Grand Trunk Pacific operated Canada's second transcontinental railway. Hailed as the first truly transcontinental railway, running from coast to coast.

1905 Sept. 1: Parliament gave Alberta and Saskatchewan status as provinces.

1909 British possession of Halifax and Esquimalt naval bases transferred to Canada. **Feb. 23:** First flight in the British Empire of a powered heavier-than-air flying machine at Baddeck, NS, by J. A. D. McCurdy.

1910 Apr. 20: Laurier's government passed the Naval Service Act. This marked the beginning of Canada's navy.

1911 May 2: Hydroelectric power from Niagara Falls officially inaugurated. **Sept. 22:** Sir Robert Borden became the prime minister as the Conservatives defeated the Liberals in the federal election.

1912 **Sept. 2:** The first Calgary Stampede.

1914 **Aug. 4:** Britain declared war on Imperial Germany; Canada automatically at war against Imperial Germany and the Central Powers.

1917 **Apr. 2:** Commencement of Royal Flying Corps training at Camp Borden, ONT. **Apr. 9:** Canadian Corps launched attack on Vimy Ridge. **Apr. 14:** Canadian troops succeeded in capturing Vimy Ridge. **Aug. 12:** Canadian flying ace Billy Bishop awarded the Victoria Cross for his victories in the air against German forces. **Aug. 28:** Parliament passed the Military Service Act. The bill defined six classes of men eligible for conscription. **Dec. 6:** A French munitions vessel exploded off the coast of Halifax. The explosion destroyed a large part of the city and killed more than 1,000 people. **Dec. 15:** Borden was reelected and formed a Union government that was pro-conscription. The cabinet consisted of both Conservatives and Liberals.

1918 **Apr. 1:** Conscription riots erupted in Québec as Québecois opposed the Union government's pro-conscription policies. **May 24:** Canadian women won the right to vote in federal elections. **June 5:** Canadian agreement with United States established air stations at Dartmouth and Sydney, NS, to carry out antisubmarine patrols. **Nov. 11:** World War I ended with Armistice.

1919 **Feb. 17:** The first French Canadian prime minister, Laurier, died. **May 15:** A general strike in Winnipeg began, lasting more than one month. **June 6:** Parliament passed Air Board Act, creating a board to control all aeronautical matters in Canada. **June 14-15:** First nonstop trans-Atlantic flight, by Alcock and Brown, from St. John's, NFLD, to Ireland. **June 28:** Canada as part of the British Empire signed the Treaty of Versailles with Germany to end the Great War.

1920 **Feb. 1:** The Royal North West Mounted Police and Dominion Police merged to become the Royal Canadian Mounted Police. **Apr. 3:** Parliament ordered the organization of the Royal Canadian Air Force. **July 10:** Borden resigned as prime minister and was replaced by Arthur Meighen.

1921 **Dec. 6:** Mackenzie King became prime minister as the Liberals defeated the Conservatives.

1922 **Feb. 11:** Canadians Dr. Frederick Banting and Dr. Charles Best discovered insulin for diabetes victims. **June 28:** National Defence Act passed, incorporating the Department of Naval Service, Department of Militia and Defence, and Air Board.

1923 Mar. 2: Canada and the United States signed the Halibut Treaty, the first commercial treaty negotiated without the participation of Britain.

1924 Apr. 1: The King's Regulations and orders for RCAF came into effect.

1925 Oct. 29: Liberals lost majority status. King remained prime minister, as the Conservatives and Progressives had insufficient seats to form a government. In theory, the Conservatives might have been the governing party, but the Progressives supported the Liberals, giving the Liberals a functional majority.

1926 June 29: King's Liberal government collapsed. King asked Governor General Viscount Byng to dissolve Parliament and call an election. Byng refused the request and asked Arthur Meighen of the Conservatives to form the government. **July 2:** After forming a government, Meighen was defeated on a no-confidence vote after just three days in office. **Sept. 14:** King led the Liberals to victory. He again became prime minister. **Nov. 19:** The Balfour Report was adopted by the Imperial Conference. The report recognized certain autonomous communities within the British Empire, including Canada.

1927 Mar. 2: Judicial Committee of the Privy Council awarded Labrador to the Dominion of Newfoundland, settling the dispute between Canada and Newfoundland. **Sept. 17:** Canada elected to a nonpermanent seat on the Council of the League of Nations.

1929 Oct. 29: Montréal and Toronto stock markets suffered worst crash in history. Canada entered into the Great Depression.

1930 Feb. 5: Cairine Wilson became the first Canadian woman to hold a seat in the Canadian Senate. **July 28:** Richard B. Bennett became prime minister as he led the Conservatives to victory over King and the Liberals. **Sept. 20:** Parliament passed the Unemployment Relief Bill. The bill focused on public jobs to reduce the effects of unemployment in Canada.

1931 Dec. 11: British Parliament passed the Statute of Westminster. The statute clarified powers between and among the dominion parliaments and allowed the dominions full legal freedom. Canada requested that British Parliament retain the power to amend the BNA Act.

1932 Aug. 1: The Co-operative Commonwealth Federation (CCF) was formed. A forerunner of the New Democratic Party, it was a socialist, political organization led by J. S. Woodsworth.

1933 Nov. 28: Newfoundland's Assembly accepted the Amulree Report. Its status of dominion was reduced to colonial status and Newfoundland was governed by a British commission.

1934 July 3: Parliament created the Bank of Canada.

1935 June 28: Bennett's Employment and Social Insurance Act received royal assent. The act was dubbed the "New Deal" since it was reminiscent of President Franklin Roosevelt's New Deal in the United States. **July 5:** Parliament passed the Canadian Wheat Act. The act brought into existence the Canadian Wheat Board. **Oct. 14:** Mackenzie King led the Liberals to victory over Bennett's Conservatives. **Nov. 15:** Canada and the United States signed a trade treaty to lower tariffs to allow for more economical access into opposing markets.

1936 June 23: The Canadian Broadcasting Act was assented to, creating the Canadian Broadcasting Corporation, a national, publicly owned television system (CBC created as a Crown corporation 2 November).

1937 Apr. 10: Trans-Canada Air Line Act passed, creating a national airline in Canada that was renamed Air Canada in 1965.

1938 Nov. 17: Canada, United States, and Britain signed a trade treaty to allow easier access into each country's markets.

1939 May 2: National Film Board established to promote Canadian filmmaking. **Sept. 10:** Canada declared war on Germany. **Dec. 17:** Canada signed an agreement with Britain to develop a massive air training scheme in Canada to produce qualified men for the RCAF and other British Commonwealth air forces.

1940 Mar. 26: King and the Liberals reelected with a majority. **Apr. 25:** Québec became the last province to give women the vote in provincial elections. **May 3:** The Rowell Sirois Commission completed its study of federal–provincial relations. It was a landmark study of Canadian federalism. **Aug. 18:** Canada and the United States signed a defence pact. The pact created a Canada–U.S. Joint Defence Board to deal with the protection of North America. **Dec.:** The first Canadian-built corvettes departed for Britain. As escorts, corvettes proved to be highly valuable in the Battle of the Atlantic.

1941 Dec. 7: Canada declared war on Japan.

1942 Feb. 26: Parliament ordered the relocation and internment of Japanese. **Apr. 27:** In a nationwide plebiscite the Canadian people voted in favour of conscription. **May 11:** A German U-boat attacked two freighters in the St. Lawrence River. This was the first enemy action in inland Canadian waters.

1943 Apr. 30: Rear Admiral Leonard Murray of the Royal Canadian Navy became commander-in-chief Canadian Northwest Atlantic with headquarters in Halifax. **July 10:** Canadian troops landed in Pachino, Sicily, and gained a hold on enemy-held territory. **Sept. 3:** The 1st Canadian and the 5th British Divisions landed in Reggio di Calabria, Italy. On 8 September Italy signed an armistice with the Allies.

1944 June 6: Canadian troops, along with British and Americans, landed on the beaches of Normandy. The landing, known as D-Day, eventually led to the fall of Germany. **Sept. 16:** Allied leaders met in Québec City to discuss the future prosecution of the war. The conference was attended by British Prime Minister Winston Churchill and U.S. President Roosevelt, and hosted by Canadian Prime Minister Mackenzie King. **Nov. 23:** Parliament passed the National Resources Mobilisation Act. Under the act Canada dispatched 16,000 conscripts to England.

1945 Feb. 21: Canadian troops captured the German defence complex, the Siegfried Line, one of the strongest German defence lines. **May 7:** German forces surrendered to the Allies. **June 11:** King and the Liberals reelected. **June 26:** Fifty nations, including Canada, signed the World Security Charter, creating the United Nations. **Sept. 2:** Japan formally surrendered, ending World War II.

1946 May 14: Parliament passed the Canadian Citizenship Act. The act classified a person born in Canada as a Canadian citizen to be recognized in all countries. Until this act, people born in Canada were recognized as Britons in other countries.

1947 Feb. 13: Imperial Oil Company discovered the Leduc oil field.

1948 Aug. 8: King announced retirement as prime minister and Louis St. Laurent chosen as successor. King had served as prime minister for the longest period in Canadian history.

1949 Mar. 31: Newfoundland and Labrador entered the confederation. **Apr. 4:** External Affairs Minister Lester B. Pearson signed an agreement creating the North Atlantic Treaty Organization, making Canada part of a military alliance with the United States, Britain, France, and other former European allies. **June 3:** St. Laurent and the Liberals returned at the federal election. **Dec. 16:** British Parliament passed a statute that provided Canada with the power to amend the BNA Act.

1950   June 30: Canadian government supported the UN policy in Korea as Canada provided units of the Royal Canadian Navy to Korea to participate in the military activities. **July 22:** Former Prime Minister Mackenzie King died.

1951   June: Indian Act revised by Parliament. Indian women married to non-Indian men were excluded from the provisions of the act. **June:** Massey Report completed on Canadian culture.

1952   July 27: Korean War ended. **Oct. 14:** External Affairs Minister Pearson elected president of the UN Assembly.

1953   July 13: Stratford Shakespearian Festival opened. **Aug. 10:** Liberals under St. Laurent defeated Progressive Conservatives under George Drew.

1954   Mar. 30: Canada's first subway opened in Toronto. **Apr. 8:** Construction of Pinetree radar line announced. **Aug.:** British Empire Games held in Vancouver, highlighted by the "Miracle Mile," when Roger Bannister and John Landy both ran the mile in less than four minutes. **Sept. 9:** Marilyn Bell, age 16, became first person to swim across Lake Ontario.

1955   Mar. 17: Montréal riot, after Canadiens' hockey star Maurice Richard was suspended. **May 5:** Canada and the United States signed agreement for the United States to build a Distant Early Warning network of radar in Canada's north and Alaska. Canadian Labour Congress formed.

1956   Jan. 10: Parliament passed Female Employees Equal Pay Act guaranteeing financial equality to men and women involved in identical or substantially identical work. **October:** Collapse of Hungarian uprising against Soviet authority. About 37,000 refugees arrived in Canada in 1956 and 1957. **Nov. 4:** The United Nations officially implemented a plan tabled by Secretary of State for External Affairs Pearson. The resolution called for emergency forces to be sent to the Suez Canal to help find a peaceful solution to the conflict. The idea of a peacekeeping force was the origin for Canada's many later peacekeeping missions.

1957   June 10: The 22-year federal reign of the Liberals ended as John Diefenbaker led the Progressive Conservatives to victory. **June 21:** Diefenbaker appointed Canada's first female cabinet minister, Ellen Fairclough. **Sept. 12:** Canada and the United States signed an air defence agreement for North America, creating the North American Air Defence Command (NORAD). **Oct. 14:** The former Canadian External Affairs Minister Pearson received the Nobel Peace Prize for his peace plan in the Suez Canal crisis.

1958 Mar. 31: Diefenbaker and the Progressive Conservatives reelected.

1959 Feb. 20: Avro Arrow project terminated, with loss of 20,000 jobs. **June 26:** St. Lawrence Seaway opened.

1960 Mar. 10: Parliament granted native peoples the right to vote in federal elections. **June 22:** Jean Lesage and the Liberals win Québec election, initiating the Quiet Revolution. **Aug. 10:** Diefenbaker's Bill of Rights, a statute specifying the rights of Canadians, became law.

1961 Aug. 3: The New Democratic Party was formed (replacing the CCF) and became Canada's third major federal political party. **Nov. 18:** Saskatchewan became the first province to adopt universal Medicare. **Dec. 31:** National Indian Council formed.

1962 June 18: Diefenbaker and the Progressive Conservatives reelected to a minority government. **July 1:** Medicare introduced in Saskatchewan and opposed by striking doctors. **July 30:** Trans-Canada Highway completed, reaching from the Atlantic to the Pacific. **Sept. 29:** The Canadian-built satellite *Alouette* launched into space by NASA. **Dec. 11:** Last hangings in Canada: Ronald Turpin and Arthur Lucas, Don Jail, Toronto.

1963 Feb. 4: House of Commons voted no confidence in Diefenbaker's Progressive Conservative government. Diefenbaker forced to call an election. **Apr. 8:** Pearson led the Liberals to power with a minority government. **April-May:** Québec separatists of the Front de Libération du Québec (FLQ) set off series of bombs in Montréal. Royal Commission on Bilingualism and Biculturalism began work.

1964 Dec. 15: Parliament adopted new flag for Canada—a single stylized red maple leaf on a white background between two red bars.

1965 Jan. 16: Pearson and U.S. President Lyndon B. Johnson signed the automobile pact. Under the pact American cars and car parts were allowed to enter Canada duty-free. **Nov. 8:** Pearson and the Liberals reelected.

1966 Dec. 21: Royal assent given to the Medical Care Act. The act provided Canadians universally with basic medical coverage.

1967 Apr. 27: Montréal hosted the world's fair, Expo '67. **July 24:** French President Charles de Gaulle visited Montréal and announced to the crowd, "Vive le Québec libre!"

1968 Apr. 20: Pierre Elliott Trudeau sworn in as prime minister after Pearson retired. **June 25:** Trudeau led the Liberals to a majority government. **Oct. 15:** René Levesque formed the Parti Québecois, its mission to proclaim a sovereign Québec.

1969 Feb. 1: Postal changes ended Saturday deliveries. **Sept. 9:** The Official Languages Act passed by Parliament. The act made both English and French the official languages of Canada.

1970 Oct. 5: In Montréal, the terrorist group FLQ kidnapped British Trade Commissioner James Cross. **Oct. 10:** The FLQ kidnapped the Provincial Labour Minister Pierre Laporte after the federal and Québec governments rejected demands of the terrorists. **Oct. 16:** Trudeau invoked the War Measures Act to counter the terrorist tactics of the FLQ. **Oct. 18:** Laporte found dead in the trunk of a car. The FLQ took responsibility for the murder. **Dec. 3:** Cross released unharmed by the FLQ.

1972 Sept. 28: Canada defeated the Soviet Union in an eight-game hockey series with a late goal in the final game by Paul Henderson. **Oct. 30:** In the election, Trudeau and the Liberals held power. The Liberals and Conservatives received the same number of seats.

1973 Dec. 12: Foreign Investment Review Act established an agency (FIRA) to screen foreign business activities and intended "take-overs."

1974 May 8: Trudeau and the Liberal minority government defeated in a no confidence vote: Trudeau forced to call an election. **July 8:** Trudeau and the Liberals reelected with a majority. **July 30:** Québec's provincial parliament passed legislation that made French the only official language of Québec.

1975 Mar. 24: Beaver adopted (but not followed) as symbol of Canadian Sovereignty Act. **July 30:** The Liberal government created, by statute, Petro-Canada Corporation as a result of the energy crisis that forced world oil prices to rise alarmingly. The company gave the federal government an avenue into the oil industry of the world.

1976 April: Eaton Company discontinued catalogue sales after 92 continuous years. **June 4:** Canada declared 200-nautical-mile coastal fishing zone. **July 14:** Parliament abolished capital punishment for all civilian offenses. **July 17:** The 21st Olympic Summer Games opened in Montréal. **Nov. 15:** Levesque and the Parti Québecois won provincial election.

1977 Aug. 26: Québec's provincial parliament passed Bill 101, creating the Charter of the French Language. The law forced all children to attend French school unless one of their parents attended an English primary school. **Sept. 6:** Highway signs changed to the metric system.

1979 **May 22:** Joe Clark became prime minister, as the Progressive Conservatives formed a minority government. **Dec. 13:** Clark defeated in a no-confidence vote and forced to call an election.

1980 **Feb. 18:** Trudeau elected as prime minister as the Liberals gained a majority. **Feb. 29:** Trudeau appointed Jeanne Sauvé as the speaker of the House of Commons, the first woman to hold the position. **Apr. 22:** Canada voted to boycott the Moscow Summer Olympics in response to the Soviet invasion of Afghanistan. **May 22:** In a provincial referendum pertaining to the separation of Québec from Canada, the people of Québec voted to stay with Canada by a margin of 59 percent to 41 percent. **June 27:** "O Canada" officially adopted as Canada's national anthem.

1981 **Sept. 23:** Québec banned public signs in the English language. **Nov. 14:** The Canadian-built Remote Manipulator System, better known as the Canadarm, used in space by the NASA space shuttle *Columbia*.

1982 **Apr. 17:** The new Canadian constitution became the law of the land as Queen Elizabeth II signed the royal proclamation. The new constitution was the final step in the patriation process. This new constitution included an amending formula to the British North America Act and provided the Charter of Rights and Freedoms.

1983 **Dec. 23:** Sauvé appointed governor general of Canada by Trudeau, again the first woman appointed to the position.

1984 **Feb. 29:** Trudeau announced his retirement after 16 years in office. **June 16:** John Turner selected as prime minister by the Liberal party following the retirement of Trudeau. **Sept. 4:** Brian Mulroney became prime minister as the Progressive Conservatives won a majority. **Oct. 5:** Marc Garneau became the first Canadian astronaut in space, as part of a NASA mission on the space shuttle *Challenger*.

1985 **Feb. 20:** The first solo flight of an American cruise missile took place over Canadian air space. **Aug. 11:** An American icebreaker, *Polar Sea*, passed through the Canadian Northwest Passage without permission of the Canadian government.

1986 **Mar. 17:** In Washington, DC, Prime Minister Mulroney and President Reagan signed an agreement to deal with acid rain. **May 2:** The world's fair Expo '86 officially opened in Vancouver, BC. **Aug. 4:** Canada imposed economic sanctions on South Africa as a measure against apartheid.

1987 **June 3:** Mulroney and the provincial premiers approved the Meech Lake Accord. Although signed, it needed to be ratified by the provincial governments. It subsequently failed. **Oct. 4:** In Washington, DC, Canada and the United States agreed on the terms of a free-trade agreement. **Nov. 1:** Founder of the Parti Québecois and former premier of Québec Levesque died.

1988 Jan. 2: Mulroney and Reagan signed the North American Free Trade Agreement (effective 1 January 1989). Although signed, the deal needed to be approved by both governments. **Feb. 13:** Calgary hosted 15th Olympic Winter Games. **Sept. 24:** Ben Johnson set a world record and won the gold medal at the Seoul Olympics; two days later he lost his medal after testing positive for steroids. **Oct. 26:** Canada was elected to the UN Security Council by the UN General Assembly for a two-year term. **Nov. 21:** Mulroney and the Progressive Conservatives reelected with a majority. **Dec. 15:** Supreme Court struck down Québec's French-only sign law. **Dec. 18:** Québec Premier Robert Bourassa used section 33 of the Canadian Charter of Rights and Freedoms (the "notwithstanding" clause) to enforce the French-only sign law in Québec.

1989 Dec. 2: Audrey McLaughlin became leader of the New Democratic Party, the first female to lead a national political party. **Dec. 6:** Montréal Massacre: in one of the most tragic events in Canadian history, 14 women were killed in Montréal by a gunman.

1990 Jan. 25: Andrew Thompson, deputy chief economist for the Royal Bank of Canada, indicated that Canada had entered a mild recession. **Jan. 29:** Ray Hnatyshyn sworn in as 24th governor general of Canada. **Feb. 7:** Ontario settled first land claim with native peoples in the Manitoulin Island area for $8.9 million. **Feb. 15:** Parliament passed a motion that upheld the principles of a bilingual Canada. **May 21:** Lucien Bouchard resigned as environment minister in the federal cabinet due to the failure of the Meech Lake Accord. **May 24:** In ruling the *Regina v. Sparrow* case, the Supreme Court ruled that native rights cannot arbitrarily be restricted or abolished by governments. **May 31:** Supreme Court ruled that governments cannot unilaterally ignore treaties with natives. **June 11:** Mulroney appointed Stanley Waters to the Senate. Waters was the first senator to be elected by the voters of Alberta. **June 22:** The Meech Lake Constitutional Accord failed to pass after three years of negotiations to try to bring Québec into the Constitution. **June 23:** Jean Chrétien elected as the leader of the federal Liberal party. **July 6:** NATO extended a hand of friendship to the European Eastern Bloc. **July 11:** Mohawks in Oka, Québec, erected barricades to protest the expansion of a municipal golf course on disputed land. In the melee, a Québec provincial police officer was killed. **July 25:** Lucien

Bouchard formed the Bloc Québecois with fellow-dissenting MPs from Québec. The mission of the new party was to lobby for the separation of Québec from Canada. **Aug. 7:** HMCS *Halifax*, a patrol frigate, launched from Saint John, NB, the first Canadian warship built in 20 years. **Aug. 9:** British Columbia reversed a 117-year-old policy by acknowledging aboriginal rights to title. **Aug. 13:** Gilles Duceppe became the first Bloc Québecois member elected to the House of Commons. **Sept. 6:** New Democratic Party of Ontario, led by Bob Rae, elected to a majority in Ontario. **Sept. 27:** The standoff between Mohawks and the police at Oka ended after 78 days. **Nov. 1:** Mulroney established a new forum to look at the future of Canada. The forum was chaired by former CRTC chairperson Keith Spicer. The forum travelled across Canada to allow the people to voice their opinions and ideas. **Nov. 29:** UN Security Council voted to authorize all necessary means to force Iraq out of Kuwait. The motion was sponsored by Canada, among other nations. **Dec. 17:** Senate gave assent to the Goods and Services Tax after a lengthy battle.

1991   Jan. 1: The federal Goods and Services Tax became law. **Jan. 22:** House of Commons passed a motion to go to war with Iraq as part of the United Nations Coalition. **February:** Canada began discussions with Mexico and the United States to form a North American trading bloc, NAFTA. **Feb. 27:** A cease-fire announced in the Persian Gulf War. **Apr. 15:** Canada agreed to send peacekeepers to the Iraq-Kuwait border for a one-year UN mission. **Apr. 17:** Canada sent monetary aid to Iran to help with the massive flood of Kurdish refugees. **Apr. 19:** NORAD agreement with the United States renewed for five years. **June 12:** Ovidi Mercredi, a Cree lawyer, elected by the Assembly of First Nations as the national chief. **June 18:** Québec government signed a landmark deal with the Barriere Lake Algonquin band that gave the band a say in the protection of its ancestral lands. This was the first deal in Canada that gave natives some control over traditional land. **Aug. 6:** Ontario signed a historic agreement with the First Nations that made the province the first in Canada to acknowledge native rights to self-government. **Dec. 5:** The Senate granted assent to a gun control bill that stiffened the regulations on buying and storing guns. **Dec. 16:** The federal government and the Inuit of the NWT tentatively settled a massive land claim deal to create a new territory called Nunavut.

1992   Miss Canada Pageant scrapped. **Jan. 15:** Canada recognized the Yugoslav republics of Crotia and Slovenia as independent states. **Jan. 30:** NASA's space shuttle *Discovery* returned to earth. Canadian Dr. Roberta

Bondar, one of the crew, became the second space pioneer from Canada. **Feb. 11:** GATT ruled in favour of Canada, ordering the United States to open up its beer and wine markets to Canadian products as part of NAFTA. **Feb. 15:** Kerrin Lee-Gartner won a gold medal at the Winter Olympics in Albertville, France, the first Canadian to win a medal in downhill skiing at the Olympics. **Feb. 21:** Canada joined a UN peacekeeping coalition force to enforce a cease-fire in the former Yugoslavia. Canada was one of the largest contributors. **Mar. 2:** Canada sent 100 troops to Cambodia as part of one of the largest UN peacekeeping forces in history. **Mar. 6:** Commercial salmon fishing in Newfoundland banned for five years to stop the depletion of the fish. **Apr. 16:** A UN report rated Canada as the world's best country to live in. **Apr. 22:** Gwich'in Natives of the Mackenzie Delta signed a major land claim settlement with the federal government. The group received monetary funds and land acquisitions. **May 4:** A plebiscite on a proposed boundary to create a new territory in the NWT called Nunavut approved by voters in the territory. **May 30:** Canada backed a UN trade sanction on Yugoslavia to attempt to halt some of the bloodiest fighting since World War II. **July 1:** Canada celebrated its 125th birthday. **July 28:** Trade Minister Michael Wilson received the approval of the federal cabinet to conclude a North American trade deal with the United States, and Mexico. Canada, Mexico, and the United States signed NAFTA, to take effect 1 January 1994, subject to approval by governments of each country. **Oct. 13:** Michael Ondaatje, Canadian poet and novelist, became the first Canadian to win the prestigious British Booker prize, for his novel, *The English Patient*. **Oct. 24:** The Toronto Blue Jays captured the World Series, the first Canadian team to win the award in baseball history. **Oct. 26:** The Charlottetown Accord was rejected in a nationwide referendum. **Oct. 30:** Inuit, federal, and territorial leaders signed a political accord for the division of the NWT and the creation of Nunavut effective 1 April 1997. **Dec. 15:** Canada sent troops under the UN flag to Somalia to assist in getting food to the starving. **Dec. 17:** Prime Minister Mulroney formally signed the North American Free Trade Agreement, with President Bush of the United States and President Salinas of Mexico. **Dec. 31:** Canada recognized the Czech and Slovak republics as independent states.

1993   Jan. 13: Major General Lewis MacKenzie announced his retirement from the Canadian Armed Forces after completing a mission that included leading a UN peacekeeping force of 1,200 in war-torn Yugoslavia. **Feb. 16:** The 1,200 troops of the 2nd Battalion of the Royal Canadian Regiment deployed into the devastated area of Sarajevo to escort UN convoys. **Feb. 25:** Trade Minister Wilson introduced legislation to implement NAFTA.

Mar. 27: The House of Commons passed the legislation that would bring Canada into the proposed NAFTA. **Mar. 29:** Catherine Callbeck became the first elected female premier of a province as the Liberals won a landslide victory in Prince Edward Island. **June 15:** Kim Campbell elected by the Progressive Conservative party to replace Prime Minister Mulroney as the leader of the party. **June 15:** Canada ended 29 years of peacekeeping service in Cyprus. **June 25:** British Columbian–born Campbell of the Progressive Conservatives sworn in as Canada's first female prime minister. **Aug. 31:** A 500-year-old way of life in Atlantic Canada ended as the federal government virtually closed the East Coast cod fishing industry due to a rapidly depleting stock. **Sept. 14:** Québec Premier Robert Bourassa announced his retirement from politics after a quarter of a century of political life. **Sept. 24:** The Canadian government lifted trade and investment sanctions against South Africa. **Oct. 25:** Chrétien led the federal Liberals to a landslide victory. The Progressive Conservatives were reduced to two seats and the newly formed Bloc Québecois became the Official Opposition. **Nov. 4:** Chrétien sworn in as Canada's 20th prime minister. **Dec. 2:** Chrétien agreed to bring NAFTA into effect 1 January 1994.

1994 Jan. 1: NAFTA came into effect, bringing Mexico into partnership with Canada and the United States to create the world's largest free trade zone. **May 10:** South Africa opened an embassy in Ottawa. **June 6:** Canadian war veterans marked the 50th anniversary of the D-Day invasion of Normandy along with other Allied forces on the beaches of Normandy. **June 20:** Canada resumed economic aid to Cuba. **July 14:** The Canadian government announced that it would not take part in an invasion of Haiti. **September:** In the Québec provincial election the Parti Québecois were elected. The election platform for the PQ was to proceed with the separation of Québec from Canada.

1995 January: Canadian Airborne Regiment disbanded. **March:** Spanish fishing vessel *Estai* seized on Grand Banks; in April the North Atlantic Fishing Organization acquired enhanced regulatory powers. Jacques Parizeau resigned as premier of the Province of Québec, and Lucien Bouchard announced intention to leave the House of Commons and seek leadership of the PQ. **Oct. 14:** Alexa McDonough chosen leader of Federal NDP. **Oct. 26:** Cree and Inuit of Québec, by referendum, rejected separation from Canada. **Oct. 27:** Montréal unity rally held. **Oct. 30:** "No" forces won Québec referendum by thin margin (50.6/49.4 percent). **Oct. 31:** Newfoundland passed constitutional amendment reforming schools system.

1996 Mar. 22: Nisga'a agreed in principle to land claim and self-government settlement. **May 28:** BC's NDP reelected under leader Glen Clark. **July 19-20:** Floods destroyed communities in Lac-St-Jean Saguenay; 10 killed. **September:** Guy Bertrand won right to seek injunction preventing any further referenda on Québec sovereignty. Québec government then declared courts to have no jurisdiction over such issues.

1997 May 31: Confederation Bridge between Prince Edward Island and New Brunswick opened. **June 2:** Liberals under Chrétien reelected in national election, with reduced majority (Liberals 155, Reform [Official Opposition] 60, Bloc Québecois 44, NDP 21, PC 20, other 1). **July 19:** Canadian fishing boats blockade an Alaskan ferry at Prince Rupert, BC; a diplomatic solution is reached by Canadian and U.S. representatives. **Nov. 17:** Hibernia crude pumped from Newfoundland's first offshore oil field. **Nov. 26:** Mr. Justice Horace Krever's report on "tainted-blood" supply inquiry filed in Parliament, showing neglect and mismanagement by authorities.

1999 January: Ice storm, called "storm of the millennium," hit eastern Ontario, southern Québec, Atlantic Canada, and New England, causing 24 deaths and at least $1 billion in damages. **Apr. 1:** Nunavut became a territory. **June 3:** Mike Harris's Conservative government reelected to continue the "Common Sense Revolution" (begun June 8, 1995).

Introduction

Canada is a North American country, state, and nation of primarily European background, population, economy, culture, and political organization. It is a European polity in the North American continent. It is one of the world's oldest democracies and one of the world's most successful federations. The last of the major self-governing states in the Americas to be decolonized, Canada has links to Europe, particularly to the United Kingdom, that remain deep and continuing. Today this is recognized in symbols of sovereignty, for the head of state is Queen Elizabeth II. The Crown is represented in Ottawa by the governor general of Canada and also in judicial and legislative practices. However, despite this constitutional link with an important past, Canada is governed at home by Canadians. Fiercely independent, Canadians have shaped institutions for their own needs. This is the story of Canada in the twentieth century.

Surrounded on three sides by great oceans—the Atlantic, Pacific, and Arctic—and bordering the United States on the south and in Alaska, Canada is a North American nation in northerly latitudes. Canada's climate varies from temperate in the south to subarctic and arctic in the north. Canada stretches from Middle Island, in Lake Erie, north to Cape Columbia, Ellesmere Island; and from Cape Spear, Newfoundland, to the Yukon-Alaska border. Canada has an area of 3,851,809 square miles, second only in extent to the vast territories of Russia. Canada shares an unfortified frontier of almost 4,000 miles with the United States. France's islands St. Pierre and Miquelon are the focus of the largely latent Canada-France maritime boundary dispute. Canada's area is diverse and varies from the high Arctic to the boreal or northern forest—all in northern latitudes, above 60 degrees north. From east to west, Canada also varies from the waters, islands, and peninsulas of Atlantic Canada—some of which are an extension of Appalachia—to the St. Lawrence Valley, the Great Lakes lowlands, the Canadian (or Laurentian) Shield, the Red River Valley, the Canadian plains and prairies leading to the foothills of the Rocky Mountains, the mountains of the Continental Divide, and the rivers, valleys and sounds, or fjords, of the

Pacific Coast or cordillera. Only 9 percent of Canada's land is arable. At one time Canada's forests were richer than they are now and in greater demand on the world markets. Today one-third of the world's pulp and paper is produced in Canada.

Rich in minerals (gold, copper, and nickel, to name but a few), Canada also has considerable deposits of potash and sulphur. Canada is blessed with abundant fresh water; indeed, one-seventh of Canada's landmass is water. In addition, Canada claims North America's greatest reserves of natural gas, principally in Alberta. It boasts extensive coal deposits and petroleum holdings (fluid and shale); petroleum also exists in offshore Newfoundland (Hibernia Field). Canada's wheatlands have a reputation as the granary of North America. Beef and pork industries are prominent.

Canada also has excellent harbours, of commercial and strategic value. Halifax on the Atlantic, Churchill on Hudson Bay, Vancouver on the Pacific are three such, to which might be added St. John's, Newfoundland; Montréal; Toronto; Thunder Bay, Ontario; and Prince Rupert, British Columbia. Canada's great rivers are the St. Lawrence, which drains the Great Lakes (all of which, excepting Michigan, are shared by Canada with the United States), the Mackenzie, the Nelson, the Saskatchewan, the Red and Assiniboine, and the Fraser. The Columbia River, important for hydroelectric power production, rises in Canadian lands (in southeastern British Columbia) before coursing through British Columbia, crossing the 49th parallel, and debouching into the Pacific Ocean near Astoria, Oregon. The Stikine River, which rises in the Yukon, flows to the Pacific through the Alaska panhandle.

Canada's population is approximately 30 million, making Canada only the twenty-ninth most populous country in the world. Canada has a population growth rate of 1.06 percent (1996 estimate). In terms of origin it is, in percentages: British 40; French 27; other European 20; indigenous Indian, Métis and Inuit 1.5; and other (mainly Asian) 11.5. In terms of religion, by percentage, it is (by 1991 estimate): Roman Catholic 45, United Church 20, Anglican 8, and other 27. Literacy is said to be 97 percent, perhaps the highest in the world.

Despite Canada's abundant size and its comparatively small population, Canada has a population that is immensely productive. On a per capita basis there is no more productive land or economy and no people more blessed in resources, space, and productivity. In comparison to other nation-states, Canada ranks seventh-largest among the world's economies, making Canada a member of the prized eight-nation economic giants known as the "G-8." Today's Canadian population is highly urbanized. The principal cities are Toronto, Montréal, and Vancouver. Cities of secondary importance in terms of size are Ottawa, Hamilton, Calgary, Edmonton, Mississauga, London, Halifax, and Winnipeg.

It has often been joked that Canada has more geography than history, though this is hardly true. However, it is correct that Canadian history, like Canadian geography, is little known—inside as well as outside the country. On the other hand, as much might be said of many other nations and countries. Canadian history differs from American or U.S. history and yet is a variant of the history of the Americas.

Canada's history is a vibrant, compelling one, dissimilar from any in the world. It features many unusual persons, various races and religions, businesses and empires, political parties and utopian experiments, and wars and social struggles. It is a microcosm of world history and of international affairs in modern times beginning with the Renaissance and Reformation. It dates to aboriginal times as well as to that of the Viking, Breton, and Portuguese mariners. Canada is arguably the most multicultural nation in the world and in that sense one of the youngest nation-states, and potentially the most promising. If outsiders consider Canadian politics and history dull, it is mainly because of a failure to appreciate the Canadian tendency towards accommodation and co-association. Conflict resolution is pervasive in Canadian society, and good manners and decency an invariable hallmark of personal relations.

FOUR CONTINUITIES OF CANADIAN HISTORY

Four continuities are to be discerned by students of the history of modern Canada. These are to be found throughout the national experience, although the relative degree of importance of these varies from time to time. Similarly, the degree of importance of these continuities can vary widely from province to province and from region to region.

Historical Continuity 1: Imperial Connections

The first continuity is the connection to and devolution from the British Empire. Inasmuch as the creation of Canada as a nation rests on imperial projection of European power, first by France (and marginally Spain) and second by Britain (triumphant in 1763 in consequence of the Seven Years' War), the relationships of French-speaking and English-speaking colonists to sovereign power and imperial structures of government headquartered in Paris and London have been profound and pervasive. Such influences, now diminished to mere vestiges, declined rapidly after 1931. They may be said to have concluded on 17 April 1982, when the British North American Act was patriated, an amending formula for that same act was effected for the first time, and the Charter of Rights and Freedoms was brought into being.

Until the "Quiet Revolution" of the mid-twentieth century, the Roman Catholic Church had a profound impact on the history of New France and Québec, especially in social integration and homogeneity and in education, social welfare, and health care. Until 1763 French imperial institutions dominated Canadian life in New France. Thereafter these continued as important legacies in civil law, landholding, and religious and educational institutions. Meanwhile, French Canadian society nurtured itself and expanded under a different, co-associational imperial power, that of Britain. Adherence to the tradition of a British imperial past may now be more sentimental than real. However, previous adherence to such values, particularly during the Boer War, First World War, and the Second World War, showed Canada and the United Kingdom as the closest of allies.

Historical Continuity 2: Two Founding European Peoples

The second continuity of Canadian history is the interrelationship—more specifically, the friction—between the English and French citizens in Canada. Separate entities developed side by side, although in business, government, and sport, alliances and mergers were a way of life. Hostilities emerged long after the 1759 conquest and became pronounced in the 1820s, leading to the Rebellion of 1837 in Lower Canada and its aftermath. Education and language legislation restrictions induced feelings of confinement and discrimination. The conscription (or draft) in the two world wars accentuated certain French fears that Canada was fighting British imperial wars. Later, rapid French Canadian population growth, gradual secularization of Québec, and growth of institutions in Québec (especially higher education) induced demands for greater powers for linguistic, educational, and provincial autonomy. The federal government responded with a policy promoting bilingualism and biculturalism.

In recent times, especially since 1976, discussion of separation has become an accepted part of Canadian political culture. However, more English-speaking people speak French than ever before, more school boards have "immersion" classes, and devolution of federal powers to provinces, including Québec, have negated many arguments for an independent Québec. However, the duality of the Canadian population is an ongoing feature of Canada. Not likely to disappear, the issue will reappear in different guises.

Historical Continuity 3: Federal–Provincial Relations

The third continuity of Canadian history is federal–provincial relations. The "Québec question" is one such major demonstration of the problem. Canada is a federation. That means that centralist views of what a federation is—or might be—will vary from peripheral views of the same arrangement. "Double-image" federalism often reflects strong federal and strong provincial (or territorial) intergovernmental arrangements. Just about every province has called for greater provincial powers. Québec's call is one variant of this; Ontario and especially Alberta and British Columbia have called for greater autonomy, especially over fiscal matters.

Historical Continuity 4: The United States as Canada's Neighbour

The fourth continuity of Canadian history is the nation's relationships to the United States. Living beside the world's most powerful nation has had a profound effect upon Canadian history. In colonial wars, especially in 1775 during the War of the American Revolution, and in the War of 1812, Canada was invaded by American forces. After 1814, the threat of American attack formed an important reason for British and Canadian defence preparations. The American Civil War and the Fenian problems of the 1860s presented numerous cross-border and diplomatic problems. Anglo-American difficulties invariably had a side effect on Canada.

By 1914 such threats had disappeared. Allies in two great wars and in Korea, Canada and the United States established joint defence arrangements after 1940. The economies and transportation infrastructures of the two nations are virtually merged, and this is evidenced in telecommunications, visual and print media, and automobile production. Still, Canada's foreign policy has attempted to steer an independent course as circumstances will allow. In the Vietnam War, for example, Canada maintained a neutrality. In peacekeeping, a separate and unique mode of foreign policy in keeping with United Nations objectives has been pursued by Canada.

PERIODS OF CANADIAN HISTORY

For convenience, the history of Canada may be divided into the following periods: the Colonial Era, to 1867; the National Era, 1867 to 1914; National

Consolidation, 1914 to 1945; and the Modern Era (in two parts: 1945 to 1982, 1982 and after). What follows are brief profiles of these four periods.

The Colonial Era to 1867

Prior to European exploration, Canada was inhabited by many different First Nations Peoples from coast to coast and in the Arctic. The native societies were far from primitive. At the time that Europeans began to explore Canada in about A.D. 1000, First Nations Peoples already knew much about the landmass of Canada. The natives adapted to the climate and weather of Canada. The natives of eastern Canada incorporated agriculture, fishing, and hunting into their ways of life; those of western Canada followed the migration patterns of the buffalo and other game. On the coasts, the natives relied on the seas as a means of subsistence. In their respective localities, they knew the rivers, lakes, and seas, and they had developed technological aids to assist in their travel. The birchbark canoe and the kayak are two important and well-known legacies, but to these could be added techniques for survival in the wilderness, such as tent making, berry collecting, and food dehydrating. Upon contact, European explorers were met by a culture that had adapted and incorporated the land into their daily lives. The explorers adopted many of these important aids to survival, and from natives they gained a greater degree of knowledge about the land they were exploring than they were prepared to admit in their writings.

The Colonial Era of Canadian history begins with the English claim to Newfoundland in 1583. Sir Humphrey Gilbert, who made the claim, found Spanish and Portuguese fishing boats in St. John's Harbour. British policy encouraged the fishery as a nursery of seamen, and until 1824 Newfoundland developed as an extension of metropolitan England. Settlement, though at first discouraged, brought desires for self-government, which was awarded by Britain in 1855. French claims to shoreline and inshore fisheries remained until 1906, but by 1713 English sovereignty was established over the island proper. The local indigenes, the Beothuk, died off by 1829, partly owing to diseases and to incursions by Mi'kmaqs from Acadia.

While Newfoundland was emerging as a fishing station, Nova Scotia and Prince Edward Island grew as places of colonization. Both began under the French flag and the French name for this colony was Acadia. However, over the course of the eighteenth century, ending in 1763, all of French territory in what is now Canada had come under British control. An important early colonization attempt by de Sieur Monts and Samuel de Champlain at Port Royal marked the first European agricultural settlement on what is now Canadian territory. Under James I, Sir William Alexander received a charter of grant to colonize Nova Scotia. In 1713, after colonial wars and pirate raids, Acadia passed into British hands—leaving Cape Breton and Île Saint-Jean (as Prince Edward Island was then called) under the French flag. Louisbourg was built as a French naval and mercantile base, and Halifax was founded as a British counterpart. In 1758 Louisbourg fell to British arms, and in 1763 British control was complete.

After the War of the American Revolution, Loyalists came in numbers to the mainland of Nova Scotia, and the province of New Brunswick was created to serve local needs. Prince Edward Island was established as a separate colony. Although much talk existed about a maritime union of these colonies, in association with Newfoundland, no such association came into being. Common needs for transportation and defence encouraged a closer association with the "Upper Provinces" of Québec and Ontario. However, strong particularities, oligarchies, and colonial capitals encouraged diversity, which remains as an important legacy of this period. Colonial culture remained closely tied to Mother England, though in some senses north–south links to New England contributed in another way to the separateness and diversity of these people in comparison to those of Newfoundland, Québec, or Ontario.

Québec is the oldest permanent European colonization in what is now Canada. In 1608 Champlain established a habitation at the narrows of the St. Lawrence River, Québec. From that day forth the community grew, though frequently by fits and starts, into the anchor of French empire in America. From earliest times the fur trade was the engine of the colonial economy, the lifeblood of banking, commerce, and relations with native peoples. English pirates held Québec from 1629 to 1632, and raids by English colonists and British forces attempted to wrest the colony of New France away from Versailles. Recollet, Jesuit, and Ursuline orders made important contributions to religious development in missionary areas as well as settled jurisdictions. Settlement was developed under rigorous administration, both corporate and civil. The seigneurial system was a form of regulated frontier development, designed to open new lands to colonization and to encourage family growth. The system was not feudal. It encouraged strong family land ownership and transfer, and it built a homogeneous society—a fundamentally important characteristic of the early history of Canada.

Not until 1763 did the king of France relinquish claims to sovereignty over Canada. Québec passed to British sovereignty. It is important to understand that Québec's subsequent prosperity and uniqueness depended on the duality of French Canadian resourcefulness and British security, for in the years after 1763 a benign British policy allowed for the continuance of French civil law and Roman Catholic practices (including tithing) while at the same time British military capabilities prevented armed American revolutionaries from capturing the colony in 1775 and 1777.

Throughout the first two centuries of Canadian history under European influence, native peoples played a significant role in the balance of power in North America. Native numbers suffered because of disease, displacement, and warfare; they also declined because of internecine rivalry and native diseases, many introduced before European contact. Natives traded for guns and ammunition, liquor, and beads and in consequence became dependent on European traders. In their treaty-making, agents of imperial powers did not always favour tribes. Indians were the key to the control of the empire of the St. Lawrence, the Great Lakes area, and the northwest trade beyond Detroit, Michilimackinac, and Grand Portage. In fact, Indians held the balance of power in the interior; they were a decisive factor in France's war against Britain in North America. When, about 1757, native allegiance generally transferred to Britain, France lost its valued native help in North America. Britain maintained that native alliance through the War of the American Revolution and the War of 1812. After 1815, as native military support was no longer needed, Indians ceased to have such value to the Crown.

In the War of the American Revolution Canada became the bulwark of the British Empire in North America. Halifax, and Nova Scotia generally, was a key "anchor of empire," so to speak. So were Québec and Montréal, which were heavily fortified. In Nova Scotia, which had many New England family connections, there was much residual affection for the revolutionaries of Boston and New York—but no general overt action against the Crown occurred. Nor in the province of Québec were there any risings against the Crown. Invasions of 1775 by Benedict Arnold and 1777 by John Burgoyne were checked or stalled. The war had important consequences: Loyalists came in heavy numbers to British North America, inducing constitutional change—the establishment of New Brunswick and Upper Canada (now Ontario) as colonies or provinces.

The War of 1812 saw a continuance of British dominance in Québec and the failure of assault from the United States. However, in the internal affairs of Québec two features are noteworthy: one, the evolution of the seigneurial system of landholding, a quasi-feudal arrangement that allowed for patterned communities; and two, the prevalence of the Roman Catholic Church and other French institutions, including language and schools.

Britain had no desire to live by the sword. As the French-speaking population grew, which it did rapidly in the early nineteenth century, so did indigenous desires for colonial self-government. Despite warnings of disaffection, the British ministry heeded not the rising storm signals and in 1837–38 the Lower Canada rebellion, the largest insurrection in Canadian history, brought some remedial results, including an investigation by a new governor, Lord Durham, into the causes of the rebellion. Eventually, in 1849 self-government was achieved by Lower Canada, or Canada East as it was then called. Meanwhile, Montréal and the province of Québec had grown into a powerful focal point of Canadian politics and financial affairs.

Ontario grew out of, or more correctly was separated from, the province of Québec in the year 1791. Loyalist settlers from the United States had settled lands on the north shore of the upper St. Lawrence and of Lakes Ontario and Erie. The freehold land tenure of Upper Canada set it apart from the seigneurial system of landholding in Lower Canada. In addition, Upper Canada had a primarily English-speaking populace which set it aside from that of Québec. Events of the War of 1812 reinforced anti-American sympathies among the population. Upper Canada became Canada West in 1840, and for a time Canada West and Canada East formed a sort of double government of co-association. Meanwhile British settlers, mainly from Ireland and Scotland, arrived in Canada West in large numbers, on assisted passages from Great Britain. "Late Loyalists" arrived from the United States, taking up inexpensive lands. Religious diversity replaced an older Anglican oligarchy, and the struggle for public lands and education took on nonsectarian dimensions out of necessity. Public schools and the university in Toronto (the colonial seat) responded to these nonsectarian requirements. British assisted-immigration from Ireland and Scotland, sometimes called "shovelling out paupers," brought thousands of immigrants to Canada, particularly Ontario, and mightily increased the non-Anglican nature of the original European population. Tensions between Roman Catholic and Protestant Irish were a by-product of this immigration. The first schools, public and private, were established in this period, and the first colleges and universities, too.

Throughout much of this era the commerce of British North America depended largely on resource extraction and staple trades. Key among these were furs, fish, timber, spars, gypsum, potash, and wheat. Later, shipbuilding became a major economy. Railroad and canal development encouraged Canadian exports. Halifax, Montréal, Québec, and Toronto all emerged as important entrepôts. Meanwhile, the Montréal-based North West Company (based on earlier practices of French traders) was succeeded by the

Hudson's Bay Company (founded 1670), and during the nineteenth century the fur trade persisted, though trade became more diversified by the company.

By 1867 British North America consisted of the following colonies or provinces: Newfoundland and Labrador, Nova Scotia, Prince Edward Island, New Brunswick, Canada East (old Lower Canada) and Canada West (old Upper Canada), and British Columbia. It also included Assiniboia and Rupert's Land. By this time forces mainly external to these provinces or territories were bringing about the reasons for a confederation of these parts, principally: (1) threat of American aggression after the American Civil War and the expression of continental integration known as Manifest Destiny; (2) the continuing reluctance of Great Britain to defend forever the territory of British North America and the desire to devolve such responsibilities upon the colonies; and (3) the need to encourage continental free trade (and prevent disputes on cross–border trade and fishing). In addition, internal reasons for effecting a confederation existed, including: (1) the need to overcome the difficulties of a double government in the United Province of Canada; (2) requirements to guarantee funding of an intercolonial railway linking Halifax with Montréal; and (3) general Canadian or British American control over local needs in transportation, finance, and economic regulation.

The National Era, 1867 to 1914

Four colonies made up the newly constituted Dominion of Canada in 1867—Nova Scotia, New Brunswick, Québec, and Ontario (the last two created from the United Province of Canada). The British North America (BNA) Act of 1867, a British statute, allowed for a strong central government to deal with national matters, but at the same time the constitution was to give expression to local matters. The Confederation of 1867 was not an end but a beginning, a blueprint for national expansion and consolidation. Section 91 of the BNA Act specified that the federal structure was for "peace, order, and good government." The dominion's first prime minister, Sir John A. Macdonald, never tired of stressing that Parliament and the central government were to have a commanding system in the new system. He and other Fathers of Confederation sought to avoid the weaknesses and mistakes of the United States's federal system by giving residual powers to the federal government. The Canadian Senate was established by this Act as a means of protecting the cultural identity and linguistic interests of a primarily French-speaking Québec and as a means to represent sectional and regional interests. Powers of appointing lieutenant-governors and Supreme Court judges (and also powers of disallowing provincial legislation) were vested in the federal government. The use of the English and French languages was guaranteed. In addition, provincial powers and controls over education were established, though remedial arrangements could be undertaken by the governor general in Council (Privy Council) if necessary. In other words, minority interests were to be protected, as were denominational affiliations and sectarian interests.

For a number of reasons Newfoundland, Labrador, Prince Edward Island, and British Columbia (all of them existing colonies) did not join the union at the outset. Reluctant to embrace the new scheme, it was only later, when circumstances (mainly fiscal and economic) required, did they join.

The principal territorial gain for the new Dominion of Canada was Assiniboia and the old Hudson's Bay Company territory of Rupert's Land. This territory was bought by Britain from the company and then transferred to the Dominion of Canada, the new Ottawa government paying the nominal transfer fee. By this arrangement, which ranks among the largest real estate deals in history, Canada acquired the Northwest Territories. Meanwhile, the Métis of Red River objected to Canadian assumption of control and rebelled against a lieutenant-governor sent to put up the Union Jack for Canada. Louis Riel, "the Father of Manitoba," eventually agreed to a new arrangement by which Manitoba became a province with representation in Ottawa. The balance of the Northwest Territories was administered directly by Ottawa through a nominated, later elected, council eventually established at Regina. The North West Mounted Police (later the Royal Canadian Mounted Police) was established to patrol the Canadian prairie and foothills west, to keep American whisky traders from debauching the natives, and to support the civil authorities in the regular settlement of western Canada. The Canadian Pacific Railway, the Dominion Lands Act, and the National Policy for Tariffs all encouraged the opening of "the last, best west," which by 1905 consisted of three provinces—Manitoba, Saskatchewan, and Alberta. The Northwest Territories and the Yukon existed in more northerly latitudes under Ottawa's immediate control. In 1885 the Mounted Police and the Canadian Army put down the Northwest Rebellion in the Upper Saskatchewan River Valley, bringing native (including Métis and Indian) resistance to an end. This pacification resulted in the trial and execution of Riel and shortly thereafter a general amnesty for Indian chiefs engaged in the rising.

British Columbia emerged from an old North West Company and Hudson's Bay Company background, and the earliest settlements date from the fur trade and missionary era. Heavily populated by natives, this area was a unique frontier, for its links were less transcontinental than they were by way of stormy Cape Horn. Until the railway era, commencing in 1885, British Columbia (as the province became) had a unique start. In 1849 Vancouver Island was established as a colony under Hudson's Bay Company proprietorship. In 1858 a separate colony called British Columbia came into existence for entirely different reasons than the settlement-based Vancouver Island. British Columbia was a gold colony. After colonial union some minor discussions were held on the subject of union with the United States. In 1871, British Columbia entered into terms of union with Canada, on promises of debt assumption and a regular railway communication with Canada. A sea-to-sea dominion was thus effected under this bold stroke, which was a triumph for Macdonald's government and, in the background, British imperial policy for the devolution of authority to the self-governing colonies.

National consolidation followed British Columbia's union, and in 1873 Prince Edward Island entered confederation with certain benefits including the promise of communication across the Strait of Northumberland. The National Policy encouraged east–west transportation links, the industrialization of Ontario and Québec, the opening of Canadian western lands, the policing of the prairie West, and the building of the national infrastructure in the face of steady American encroachments. It encouraged the concept of Canada among the varied peoples of British North America.

The two decades before 1914 were the period of great national growing pains. Problems that had to be faced were the liberalization of Québec politics (and the end of Roman Catholic dominance in secular affairs), the crisis of French language rights in Manitoba and the Northwest Territories, the struggle for control of the Yukon–Alaska border, and the fights between provinces (mainly Ontario, Manitoba, and Québec) and federal government over linguistic rights. As mentioned, one major crisis, in 1885, was the Saskatchewan rebellion or rising, when Métis and certain natives fought Canadian police and army and were put down.

In the latter part of this era Christian aid groups emerged, groups that we now classify under the heading of the Social Gospel. Dedicated to social regeneration and improvement, agents of the Social Gospel promoted a Christian cooperative movement that had strong utopian zeal and saw in Canada the possibilities for an ideal society. Taken together with the temperance movement, antinarcotics legislation, home and town improvements, scouts and guides, home economics, and public health, we see from this period important precursors of a state-dominated welfare state of the late twentieth century.

This era also saw the Canadianization of national institutions including the militia (not a reserve but a standing army), the garrisons at the Esquimalt and Halifax naval bases, and the statutory establishment of the Canadian Naval Service (in 1910). Canada sent a contingent to the Sudan and another to the Boer War. In addition, Canada took steps to field a Canadian Expeditionary Force, regarded as a remarkable national effort.

By 1914 Canada was a powerful self-governing dominion in the British Empire, regarded by many as "the Mother Dominion." Three national transcontinental railways existed, canals had breached navigational difficulties, and banks and financial houses had enlarged the mechanisms for such consolidation. Equally important, Canada had received countless immigrants, principally from the United Kingdom but also from Germany, Ukraine, and the United States. A nascent national society was being established, based on earlier colonial identities but now transcontinental in scope and in perspective. Registered native peoples came under a national Indian Act. Chinese and Sikh persons were in Canada in increasing numbers. Blacks in Nova Scotia, there since the era of the American Revolution, and also in Ontario, there since the days of the Underground Railway, formed conspicuous minorities. Above all, Canada was Britannic, non-American, and rather proudly independent even before "the Guns of August" created an altogether different, more horrific world.

Between 1897 and 1912, some 2,250,000 persons immigrated to Canada, and a like number would enter the country in subsequent years to 1930. Forty percent of these arrivals were of British stock. Other "new Canadians" came from the United States, Sweden, Finland, Iceland, Russia, Poland, Germany, Holland, and elsewhere. Most agricultural immigrants went to the prairies, where the population increased from 230,000 in 1891 to 1,327,000 in 1911. Alberta and Saskatchewan were created provinces in 1905, an index of their growing populations. It should be noted that many of the new immigrants were from industrial backgrounds. In fact, two-thirds of all immigrant males came from industrial experience. Thus general labourers or mechanics, clerks, traders, miners, and navvies working on railway construction also changed the Canadian population. Urban social ills inspired James Shaver Woodsworth, a Methodist minister, and many others to develop the Social Gospel. Asian immigration was tightly regulated by Ottawa and even by Victoria, the capital of British Columbia.

National Consolidation, 1914 to 1945

The themes of this period of Canadian history are intensely national rather than provincial, for it was during this era that national achievements and struggles assumed prominence in the overall history. War helped forge a nation. The two world wars brought in national mechanisms of control and mobilization, which now may be seen as coercive and forceful tendencies backed by legislation and regulation to put national needs first. Even in the interwar period, which is marked by the Depression, federal authority was employed to bring about the means of minimizing the effect of unemployment and dislocation.

Canada went to war upon the British declaration of war in 1914 but it remained Canada's choice as to the degree of participation in the war against the Imperial Germany and Austria-Hungary and their allies. One million Canadians donned uniform in that war, the Royal Canadian Navy came into its own, and Canadians served in number in the Royal Flying Corps. Canada's 1917 triumph at Vimy Ridge remains legendary; Newfoundland's sad human losses in other encounters are not forgotten (especially Beaumont Hamel in 1916 when the Royal Newfoundland Regiment was virtually annihilated). The Canadian economy, and the means of organizing it, became strong because of war. Pro-Empire sentiment superimposed itself on pro-Canadian perspectives and vice versa. Canada was a signatory, under the British Empire delegation, of the peace treaties. Meanwhile Canada had become a member of the British imperial war cabinet and had taken steps towards a redefinition of dominion status after the war. In 1931, by the Statute of Westminster, the autonomy of Canada was assured, as it was for the other self-governing dominions.

The 1920s were years of stunning economic growth. Trade with the United States increased dramatically. Canadians became more North American in outlook. They became less anxious than before to come to the aid of a Europe they thought should be able to look after its own affairs and police its own difficulties. Canada became a member of the League of Nations and the International Labour Organization conventions and promoted dominion autonomy in the British Empire.

The 1930s marked a significant departure from the previous decade. Unemployment, dust bowls, food kitchens, work camps, and the "On-to-Ottawa march" highlighted Canadian social and economic affairs. New political parties emerged: the Social Credit and Cooperative Commonwealth Federation (CCF) being most noteworthy. Even the Conservative federal government flirted with a thirties collective response, the "New Deal."

Canadian national institutions emerged during the interwar period. These include Trans-Canada Airlines (the forerunner of Air Canada), the Canadian Broadcasting Corporation, the National Film Board, and the St. Lawrence Seaway. Railway consolidation had already been effected under the title of Canadian National Railways. Unemployment Insurance was brought into being, and the Bank of Canada was established.

In 1939 Canada declared war on Nazi Germany and Fascist Italy and it did likewise in 1941 against Imperial Japan. For six years Canada fought a major war effort at home and abroad. Japanese Canadians were interned for two reasons: to protect Canada and to protect the Japanese from assault by other Canadians. Canada hosted the British Commonwealth Air Training Plan, assumed major responsibility for convoy and antisubmarine patrols in the northwestern Atlantic, and became a major shipbuilding power. In addition, Canadian troops raided Dieppe, landed at Sicily and Normandy, and liberated Holland. The RCAF engaged in strategic bombing against German targets. Canadian troops garrisoning Hong Kong were captured. Countless Canadians died in prisoner-of-war camps. At home the economic infrastructure of the nation grew by leaps and bounds, aided by American investment. Newfoundland bases came under United States control in exchange for financial relief for the United Kingdom. Joint boards of defence encouraged Canadian–American cooperation in armaments and war production. The Alaska Highway was built by the United States, with Canadian cooperation, for the purpose of providing supplies for its ally the Soviet Union in the war effort against Germany. By the time peace came in 1945 Canada was very much more continentalized, or Americanized, than ever before. British financial influence diminished shortly thereafter.

The Modern Era

In many respects the era after 1945 is marked as one of maturation and independence. Although some historians see this as an era of crisis, principally that of Americanization, it is now clear that Canadian institutions matured and developed to a degree that a Canadian cultural independence was assured.

Canada, 1945 to 1982

Most influential in all of this was the evolution of public school systems and curricula, increasingly based upon Canadian-produced learning materials. Canadian colleges and universities educated all professional requirements for the nation, with links to the United Kingdom, France, and the United States. In the 1960s the awarding of Ph.D. degrees became more general in Canada, though only in the more senior, and larger, universities. As of 1971 Canada had 66 degree-granting institutions of higher learning. The "baby boom," Sputnik era, and demand for public university education all were factors in this sensational growth of universities and colleges. Canadian publishing, long considered under siege from Americanization or British colonial literature and neglect, entered its classic era, and even though threats to such independence were seen from time to time, an indigenous publishing industry existed, especially in Québec, Ontario, and British Columbia. A national sentiment was encouraged by the Canadian Broadcasting Corporation. The Canada Council and the National Film Board, the Humanities Research Council of Canada, and the Social Science Federation made important contributions to identifying Canadian needs and concerns.

Many institutional changes came in consequence of the Royal Commission on National Development in the Arts, Letters, and Sciences (1951), better known as the Massey Commission. It announced a cultural principle of "Canada First." Its recommendations for founding a national institution (the Canada Council, 1957) and for the national funding of Canadian universities (effected 1957) were followed up by the federal government.

Americanization of Canadian universities, both feared and actual, resulted in the founding, by the Association of Universities and Colleges of Canada, of a Commission on Canadian Studies. Chaired by Trent University's founding president, T. H. B. Symons, the report *To Know Ourselves* (1975) urged increased attention to all aspects of Canadian Studies in universities and colleges, at home and abroad. The commission found general ignorance and, above all, neglect about "Canadian content" in curricula. *To Know Ourselves* coincided, quite generally, with a growing Canadian concern about the Americanization of Canadian periodical literature, films and television, and publishing. It also coincided with serious evaluations of the Americanization of the Canadian economy, which in turn resulted in the Foreign Investment Review Act (1973). Other reviews were undertaken, at various times, by Kari Levitt, Walter Gordon, and Herb Gray.

Institutions or measures to encourage the family, including Family Allowance, home economics, and public health administration made important contributions to the well-being of Canadian society that ought not to be overlooked. Public health and medical practices encouraged a far healthier population than that of a century before. Indeed, Canada made mighty advances in medicine, dentistry, public health, and better foods.

Medicare, or public medicine, was introduced first in Saskatchewan in 1944. By measures of other provinces and of the federal government this became, by 1966 and the empowering Medical Care Act, a national responsibility, universally guaranteed and portable. Similarly, for the ageing population, Old Age Assistance and then Canada Pension universal protection was put in place (Québec established a separate scheme). By 1970 Canada had an advanced and universal social security network which, for all its faults, was a model of its kind.

The population of Canada grew dramatically in this period and, towards the latter part of the century, particularly beginning in the 1980s, became more ethnically diverse. In 1945 the population of Canada was about 11 million; by 1998 the population approximated more than twice that number, 29 million. Whereas the growth immediately after 1945 arose from British, Dutch, German, Ukrainian, and other European peoples, by the end of the period under consideration the largest number of immigrants were Chinese from Hong Kong. Jamaicans and West Indians, East Indians, Africans, Vietnamese, and others have immigrated to Canada in large numbers. Persons from southern Europe and the Mediterranean have immigrated to Canada. Italians, Greeks, and Portuguese are the most conspicuous in terms of numbers.

In 1945, upon the return of peace, Canadians hoped and expected a return to normalcy. The Cold War, and the Gouzenko revelations of Soviet spying in Canada, jolted the public consciousness. No radical views dominated the political stage, and two-party politics were prominent on the federal scene, though the CCF and Social Credit did send vocal members of Parliament to Ottawa. No new federal parties were created during this period. In the federal election of June 1945 the Liberals under Mackenzie King were returned with a diminished but working majority. The sectional nature of Canadian national politics continued: All 65 seats in the Province of Québec were Liberal. The Progressive Conservatives in the House of Commons were largely from Ontario. The situation was much like 1921, when sectionalism was quite apparent.

From 1949, through three elections fought under Louis St. Laurent, the Liberals held power. In 1957 the Progressive Conservatives under John George Diefenbaker were elected, first by a minority, and then in 1958 by a stunning majority, and then again in 1962 by a reduced majority. Pearson formed minority governments under the Liberal banner in 1963 and 1965. One of his initiatives was to establish a Royal Commission on Bilingualism and Biculturalism, largely to appease Québec. New divorce legislation was introduced at this time.

Among the most important events of this era was the addition of Newfoundland and Labrador as Canada's 10th province. A colony since 1583, Newfoundland had rejected confederation in 1867 and 1894, and was granted dominion status during World War I. Financial difficulties during the Depression meant that the United Kingdom was forced to rescue Newfoundland from these, at the price of suspending self-government and placing Newfoundland in a form of control known as Commission. World War II gave Newfoundland enhanced strategic and economic value, and as part of the postwar decolonization movement, the United Kingdom worked for a way or means to liquidate obligations overseas. In 1945 future options were considered. After an election and two referenda Newfoundland and Labrador voted for confederation with Canada. On 31 March 1949 Newfoundland and Labrador became the 10th province of the Dominion of Canada. Canada assumed Newfoundland's public debt, paid annual subsidies and transitional grants, gave better welfare services (e.g., Old Age Pension), and introduced Canadian tariffs, which were higher than before. In 1962 the new province was given enhanced assistance, on the basis of a 1957 royal commission that found Newfoundland's needs even greater than envisaged.

Constitutional changes for the nation were noteworthy in this period. They may be briefly listed. In 1947 all appeals to the Judicial Committee of the Privy Council in London, hitherto the highest court of review, were terminated. Thus the Supreme Court of Canada became in all judicial matters the final court. In 1946 the Canadian Citizenship Act said that a Canadian was "a British Subject" as well as a Canadian citizen, with the latter put first.

In 1952, the first Canadian to become governor general of Canada, Vincent Massey, was installed, thus setting a precedent for Australia, New Zealand, and other dominions. To that point in time all governors general had been British-born, invariably soldiers, aristocrats, or other place holders.

Provincial politics in this era were marked by an emerging local and regional consciousness. It was strongly felt in Québec, where Jean Lesage and the Liberals ushered in the Quiet Revolution. Like many other premiers of that province, Lesage argued for an enhanced role for his province in decision-making and financial management. When René Levesque and the Parti Québécois were elected in 1976, a pro-sovereignist government was in place. The 1980 referendum followed, and with it, Prime Minister Pierre Elliott Trudeau's promise that there would be constitutional renewal for Canada. In other words, Québec's initiatives (which did not owe their uniqueness to one party or another) pushed Ottawa into a renewed attempt at resolving what was becoming a constitutional impasse.

British Columbia and Alberta were likewise demonstrative of their political aspirations. In British Columbia, W. A. C. Bennett's Social Credit party held power for virtually a generation (until defeated by the New Democratic Party in 1972). This right-of-centre coalition of Conservatives and Liberals was dedicated to commercial prosperity and keeping the socialists out of power. In Alberta, Social Credit and then the Progressive Conservatives, the latter under Peter Lougheed, had unrestricted parliamentary power based on several election victories. In both these provinces, great industrial development occurred: mining and forestry plus hydroelectric power in British Columbia; oil and natural gas extraction in Alberta. Thus, during the oil shortage crisis of 1973, when the federal government introduced the National Energy Policy, with stringent controls over the pricing and export regulations of oil and natural gas, Alberta—and the western provinces generally—were outraged at Ottawa's "interference." Whereas the provinces had enjoyed explicit control over natural resources since the 1920s, the federal government used constituted powers under trade and commerce provisions of marketing beyond provincial borders to implement the National Energy Policy.

In 1967 Canada celebrated the centenary of Canadian confederation. A World's Fair was held in Montréal, known as Expo '67. It highlighted many architectural wonders, including Habitat. Lester Pearson, who had succeeded St. Laurent as leader of the Liberal party but who had never won a majority parliament, supported Trudeau, then minister of justice, as head of the party. In 1968, under concepts of "Trudeaumania" and the slogan "A Just Society," the Liberals were returned at the polls with a commanding majority. Thus began Trudeau's 16 years as premier, an epoch only interrupted briefly by the victory of Joe Clark and the Progressive Conservatives in 1979. When Clark was defeated by a budgetary vote of no confidence and an election was called, resulting in Trudeau's return, "Welcome to the 1980s" was his memorable victory announcement.

Canada, 1982 and After

In national affairs this era has been one of acute stress in constitutional matters. Successive attempts to patriate the constitution (with an appropriate amending formula) were finally achieved by Prime Minister Trudeau on 17 April 1982. A Charter of Rights and Freedoms was brought into effect at the same time. The last vestiges of British legislative authority then disappeared, judicial links already having been broken in 1949. The monarch of the United Kingdom remains as the titular head of authority, represented by the governor general of Canada.

Major, dramatic shifts have occurred in federal politics beginning in 1982. Highlights include: the end of the Trudeau era and the short premiership of John N. Turner (1984); the long Progressive Conservative dominance of Brian Mulroney (1984–93) and its brief succession by Kim Campbell, Canada's first female premier (1993); and the victory of Jean Chrétien (1993) and his reelection (1997). Also of note was the birth of the Reform Party (Official Opposition status established by the election of 1997), the rise and influence of the Bloc Québecois (in the late 1980s and throughout the 1990s), and the near-destruction of the federal Progressive Conservative party in consequence of the 1993 election. Regional representation remained a marked characteristic of Canadian politics.

Québec governments since 1982 claim not to have been party to the 1982 arrangements. This matter is being tested in courts. In 1976 the election of the Parti Québecois under Levesque resulted in a 1980 referendum for sovereignty (or some such variant), which was defeated. Constitutional renewal under Trudeau was brought about in 1982. But by the Meech Lake Accord and the Charlottetown Agreement, these stillborn efforts to embrace Québec served instead to alienate Québec from the rest of Canada and vice versa. Unresolved issues of inclusion within Canada continue; so do certain claims and demands for independence by Québec. The future remains uncertain, though past experience demonstrates Québec's strong association with Canada and the flexibility of the BNA or Canada Act.

Canada's provinces, including Québec, have placed powerful demands upon the federal government, or the centre, for a devolution of authority. While federal powers have increased in such areas as health, family allowance, pensions, and unemployment insurance, provincial demands for greater autonomy have also grown. These pulls and pushes are constant aspects of national fiscal and taxation life, and they account for the difference that can be seen in the way Canada governs itself.

In foreign affairs, Canada's policies—as since 1945—have backed the following agencies or associations: the United Nations, especially its agencies of world health and peacekeeping; the Commonwealth of Nations (of which Canada is a senior partner); La Francophonie (of which Canada is likewise a senior partner); NORAD; NATO; and the Law of the Sea conferences. As a North American nation with frontiers on the Atlantic, Arctic, and Pacific, and as neighbour to the United States, Canada remains unavoidably caught up in all the major episodes of world history and affairs.

More recently Canada has joined the Organization of American States and NAFTA (North American Free Trade Agreement, with the United States and Mexico; with Chile as a special bilateral partner with Canada and the United States) and will emerge more as a Western Hemispheric member of the family of nation-states. The Pacific Rim remained, throughout these years, a place of constant and increasing opportunity, though by the late 1990s some Asian economies had proven to be not immune from crisis and bankruptcy. When Hong Kong reverted to the control of the People's Republic of China in 1997, Chinese immigration into Canada was diminished, though only slightly, and Vancouver real estate prices somewhat lowered. Since 1945, however, the tendency towards enhancing Asia-Pacific trade has been a prominent direction of Canadian policy and commerce. However, the United States remains the predominant business partner of Canada. In fact, initiatives by federal and provincial governments to increase trading arrangements with the European Union have not resulted in any great change in the traditional north–south trading relationships of Canada and the United States. As in the age of its founding, in the seventeenth century, Canada's economy depends above all on trade. As an exporting country (of resources, services, manufactured goods, and others) Canada's well-being remains at the whim and reality of world economic influences and conditions.

The Dictionary

-A-

ABORIGINAL RESIDENTIAL SCHOOLS. At confederation, two residential schools for aboriginal children existed. In due course, schools were built in every province and territory. Indian, Inuit, and Métis [qq.v.] children attended such institutions, sometimes under coercion of Department of Indian Affairs (DIA) authorities and the Royal Canadian Mounted Police (RCMP). By 1931 there were 80 such schools, three-quarters of which were in the four western provinces. The Roman Catholics ran 44, the Anglican Church 21, United Church [q.v.] 13, and Presbyterians 2. An estimated 100,000–125,000 native children passed through the system, which was closed down in the mid-1980s.

Based on an education philosophy of "resocialization" and preparation for enfranchisement, the scheme was essentially assimilationist. It involved the teaching of English and/or French where appropriate and indirectly involved the destruction or neglect of aboriginal languages and cultures; similarly, it assumed the supplanting of children's aboriginal spirituality with Christianity. Reports documented residential-school problems: in 1907 in 15 schools, 24 percent of children were found to have died while in the school's care. At Old Sun's on the Blackfoot reserve, Alberta, the figure was as high as 47 percent. Stark, physical abuse bordering on terror was reputedly the system in effect, according to the report of the Royal Commission on Aboriginal Peoples (1997). Incidents documented included whippings and other beatings, chaining and shackling, and incarceration. The success of the schools was questioned as early as 1913. The commission concluded that the residential-school system was "an act of profound cruelty" rooted in racism and intolerance. The commission blamed Canadian society of the era, Christian evangelism, and the policies of Canada's churches and federal government. Federal governments, repeatedly refusing to acknowledge responsibilities, maintain this as policy: treat each instance of abuse as an individual criminal act. In courts, allegations have been made against more than 100 persons; as of 1998, three have been convicted and many other cases are pending. In January 1998 the federal government made an official apology and announced funding of $350,000,000 as part of its "offer of reconciliation."

ACADIA. *See* Acadians; New Brunswick; New France.

ACADIANS. Initially residents of Acadia, a maritime portion of New France (q.v.), who in 1755 refused to take an oath of loyalty to the British crown. (In 1713, Nova Scotia had been acquired from France by Britain under terms of the Treaty of Utrecht [q.v.].) Most were embarked at Annapolis Royal, Minas (Grand Pré) and Chignecto. About 13,500 were shipped to American Southern colonies. Some returned after the peace between France and Britain; however, they found their lands occupied by New Englanders. More recently, *Acadian* refers to French-speaking persons of New Brunswick, who although a minority in that province, have linguistic rights guaranteed in the only officially bilingual province of Canada.

AGRICULTURE. The history of agriculture in Canada is defined by regional characteristics and historical circumstances (many external to Canada, such as war and depression). Unifying Canadian agriculture is the role of government and agricultural scientific experimentation. Indians of the lower Great Lakes were horticulturalists. Iroquois [q.v.] raised maize, squash, and beans and traded food for furs. In the Maritimes, settlers dyked marshlands and raised grain, vegetables, and livestock. Provisions were needed to feed navies and armies, and this spurred developments at Louisbourg and Halifax and elsewhere—in Québec, Montréal, Kingston, Penetanguishene, Port Maitland, and Victoria/Esquimalt. Agricultural grants were made, after 1763, to Prince Edward Island. Agriculture dominated much of the early development of the Maritimes. In Québec under the French regime, the seigneurial system was a government-regulated scheme of development. In Upper Canada the Crown was the central agency in surveying, selling, opening, and settling the land. In 1848, Vancouver Island, previously developed by the HBC-related Puget's Sound Agricultural Company, was opened to settler agricultural development. The Red River Settlement (1812–) was an agricultural project of philanthropist Earl Selkirk (q.v.).

In addition to climate, weather, and pestilential problems, early Canadian agricultural development was hindered by several problems: ravages of war, including crop burnings or destruction of shipments, competition from American farmers, inadequate infrastructure—especially canals—and secure markets. In 1846 repeal of the British Corn Laws removed the preferential status of BNA wheat, and prices declined. In 1854, by the Free Trade [q.v.] arrangement, Canadian farm products (as well as fish and forestry products) got reciprocal access to U.S. markets. Agricultural risings occurred in Upper and Lower Canada in 1837, though reasons other than agricultural issues (religion, class, privilege) underscored the reasons for revolt. BNA became a major producer and exporter of potash, potatoes, wheat, barley, and other grains, and apples. Cheese, milk, bacon, and other products became important for domestic and external consumption. Poultry production and selective beef breeding became important in the late 19th century. Lower Canada ceased to be self-sufficient in wheat and flour in the 1830s, growing increasingly dependent on Upper Canada, whose agriculture became diversified. In the 1920s, Québec's soil became exhausted due to lack of fertilizer. The Union Catholique des Cultivateurs (founded 1924) argued for better credit and protection. Crop rotation, field management, better equipment, separators, and refrigeration were catalysts. Urbanization created concentrated markets. Farmers' institutes and women's institutes promoted agriculture's importance and dignity. The Ontario Marketing Board was founded (1931) to promote long-range benefits. Wheat cultivation in the prairie provinces increased greatly—in 1916, 34 million acres were in use; in 1931, 60 million acres. Canada became in these years a prominent supplier of wheat and captured 40 percent of the world market. The Depression was partnered by the drought and pestilence (locusts). New means were sought for soil reclamation, irrigation and water conservation. Combine harvesting and electricity, mechanization, and cooperative farming also helped revive prairie agriculture. Wheat was crucial to the Allied effort in World War II.

Grain growers' associations in Manitoba and the Northwest Territories promoted ownership of inland elevators and cooperative marketing of grain. United Grain Growers derived from this. A radical wing of the prairie farm movement was led by Henry Wise Wood of the United Farmers [q.v.] of Alberta. Wheat pools were formed in the 1920s but collapsed in the 1929 depression. The Canadian Wheat Board (1935) was, in 1943, made the compulsory means of marketing Western wheat, and, in 1949, of Western barley and oats. The agrarian movements of western Canada had a profound effect on such matters as: western political identification (including resistance or objection to "Eastern interests"), new political parties (*see* Progressive Party; Social Credit Party; New Democratic

Party), temperance crusaders, 4H Clubs, women's suffrage, child welfare, rural education, and the union of Protestant churches into the United
Church of Canada (1925).

In British Columbia the Fruit-Growers' Association (1889) was the first
agricultural organization of producers; in 1913 the Okanagan Valley fruit
growers set up a marketing agency. British Columbia's Free Fruit Board extended these arrangements, in association with the co-op movement. The
Canadian Bureau of Agriculture was founded in 1852 to control livestock
diseases and prevent their entry into Canada. The Research Branch runs 35
experimental stations and establishments in various locations, including
Saanich, British Columbia; Indianhead, Saskatchewan; and Ottawa. Agricultural colleges in Canada include veterinarian departments in the University of Saskatchewan and Guelph University's Ontario Agricultural College.

AID TO THE CIVIL POWER. This is the customary legal process by
which municipal or provincial governments call upon the federal government for armed forces to preserve or restore order. In pre-Confederation Canada, British troops and gunboats provided aid to the colonial
governments. In 1868, the Militia Act first authorized the calling out of
Canadian militia (q.v.) in aid of civil power. In 1904, the act was amended
to include aid to municipalities, a provision exercised most often in labour
disputes. In 1924, the Mackenzie King (q.v.) government took the right
to call out the militia from the local magistrates and handed it instead to
provincial attorneys general. The province paid the costs involved. Since
the end of the Depression, there have been other instances of aid to civil
power. The right to call upon armed forces, now incorporated in the
National Defence Act, was exercised by the Québec government when
substantial units of the army were mobilized in August 1990 during a
land dispute with Mohawk near Oka. *See also* October Crisis; Oka.

AIR COMMAND. *See* Canadian Air Force.

ALASKA BOUNDARY. The dispute between the U.S. and Britain—and
later between the U.S. and Canada—centred on the boundary that begins at the 56th degree of north latitude and extends northwestward approximately 30 nautical miles inland until it intersects with the 141st
degree of west longitude and thence due north to the Arctic Ocean. The
dispute arose because contradictions and inaccuracies of the boundary
definition in the 1825 convention between Britain and Russia were also
incorporated into the boundary definition of the U.S.-Russian convention of 1867, which ceded Alaska to the United States.

Article III of the 1825 convention defined the boundary line, and Article IV qualified the definition. The two articles comprised part of Article I of the U.S.-Russian convention of 1867. Article III of the 1825 convention stated that the line was to begin at 54 degrees, 40 minutes north latitude between the 131st and 133rd degrees of west longitude at the southernmost point of Prince of Wales Island and "ascend to the north along the channel called Portland channel, as far as the point of the continent where it strikes 56th degree of north latitude." From this point the line was to run north along the summit of the mountains that lie "parallel to the coast as far as the point of intersection of the 141st degree of west longitude." From here the line was to run due north to "the Frozen ocean." Article IV qualified the definition by stating that Prince of Wales Island belonged to Russia (after 1867 to the U.S.). It further stated that when the line running along the summit of the mountains is "at a distance of more than ten marine leagues [30 nautical miles] from the ocean, the limit between British possessions and the line of coast which is to belong to Russia . . . shall be formed by a line parallel to the winding of the coast, and which shall never exceed the distance of ten marine leagues therefrom." The 1825 convention allowed British free navigation of rivers and channels that lie between the British possessions in North America and the Russian possessions from the 56th parallel of north latitude to the 141st meridian of west longitude.

The area described in the convention had not been surveyed. The convention, because of its double definition of the western limits of the Russian colony, could be applied to fix the line along the summit of the mountains or at 10 marine leagues from the coast—or a combination of both. There was also the question of whether the coastline followed the shores of an inlet or crossed the inlet's opening. The head of Portland Canal (originally known as Portland Channel) did not extend to the 56th parallel; therefore the exact location of the Portland Canal was open to question. These problems could not be decided until a survey was made.

As early as 1872 Britain and the U.S. made efforts to establish a joint commission for the survey of the disputed area. On 22 July 1892, a convention was concluded between these countries which provided for a "coincident or joint survey."

The need for settling the question became urgent when discovery of gold in the Klondike in 1896 brought thousands of U.S. and British subjects to the area. Conflict over customs jurisdictions, land claims, and enforcement of law made a solution imperative.

In 1898 Britain proposed that the boundary question be submitted to ". . . three Commissioners who should be jurists of high standing . . . to fix the frontiers at the heads of the inlets, through which the traffic for the Yukon Valley enters; continuing subsequently with the remaining strip or line of coast." Protocols of all the meetings were approved and accepted by both countries.

The joint commission, established as a result of May 1898 meetings, met at Québec. By early 1899 much progress had been made. The Alaska boundary dispute caused the collapse of the commission. U.S. commissioners proposed that this problem be set aside until the others were adjusted, but the British commissioners declined. The commission then adjourned until the boundary dispute was settled by the two governments.

Although discussions centring on the boundary line failed to provide a solution, it was necessary that the two countries come to a temporary settlement. In 1899, a modus vivendi fixed a provisional boundary above the head of Lynn Canal and across Chilkoot Pass and White Pass. The modus vivendi provided that the acceptance of the provisional boundary line would not "prejudice . . . the claim of either party in the permanent adjustment" of it. In 1903, the powers concluded a convention for the submission of the boundary question to a tribunal.

Members of the tribunal representing the U.S. were Elihu Root, Henry Cabot Lodge, and George Turner. Those appointed as the British-Canadian members were Lord Alverstone, Sir Louis Jetté, and A. B. Aylesworth. On 20 October 1903 the tribunal issued its decision. Jetté and Aylesworth refused to sign the award because they could "not consider the finding of the tribunal as to the islands, entrance to Portland Channel, or as to the mountain line, a judicial one." Neither country received all the territory it claimed.

With Lord Alverstone's decision to support the American position, Canada lost most of what it had claimed, though it received two islands at the mouth of the Portland Canal. The incident furthered Canadians' notions that they had to look after their own foreign relations and could not rely on the British in dealing with the Americans. By a convention signed 21 April 1906, commission duties were expanded to survey and mark the Alaska boundary line from Mount St. Elias on the 141st degree of west longitude to the Arctic Ocean. The original commission grew into the International Boundary Commission, United States and Canada (q.v.), and was made responsible for surveying and marking the entire land boundary line between the two countries. A comprehensive published report of the International Boundary Commission concerning the Alaska boundary line was published in 1952.

ALASKA HIGHWAY. Built in 1942–43 from Dawson Creek, British Columbia, to Fairbanks, Alaska, the Alaska (or Alcan) Highway was considered necessary by the United States because of the Japanese threat to Alaska. The idea of a land route to connect British Columbia and Alaska had been discussed by British Columbia, U.S. generals, and President Franklin Roosevelt. Canada maintained that a land link would increase American influence in British Columbia and make impossible Canadian neutrality in the event of a war between Japan and the United States. The attack on Pearl Harbor ended these concerns.

The road, stretching 2,451 km, was built by U.S. Army construction engineers in eight months at a cost of $148 million. The Canadian Army (q.v.) took over maintenance of the Canadian portion of the highway in 1946, and in 1964 this responsibility was assumed by the Department of Public Works.

ALBERTA. Named after Princess Louise Caroline Alberta, daughter of Queen Victoria. Although referred to as a prairie province, Alberta has a diverse landscape. Much of the province is covered in arable soil. The Peace River Valley is the northernmost permanent agricultural settlement in Canada. In contrast to the rolling plains of the other prairie provinces, Alberta has a natural border with British Columbia: the rugged and immense Rocky Mountains.

A large portion of Alberta was formally included in the holdings of the Hudson's Bay Company (q.v.) known as Rupert's Land. The native peoples that inhabited this area included the Blackfoot and the Sarcee in the south and the Cree, Assiniboine (q.v.), Slavey, and Beaver in the north. The Dominion of Canada (q.v.) acquired Rupert's Land from Britain in 1870. At this time, it became the Northwest Territories. In 1874, the North West Mounted Police (now RCMP) built Fort Macleod and began the process of establishing law and order in these frontier lands. In the late 1800s American cattlemen and British ranchers created great cattle kingdoms, giving birth to the largest livestock industry in Canada. In the early 1900s, the development of new fast-maturing wheat provided the incentive for a homesteading program. With the promise of free land and a better life, immigrants arrived from Europe, the United States, and other parts of Canada. In 1905, the Canadian government granted Alberta provincial status. In 1914 the first oil was pumped at Dingman; in 1947 oil was discovered at Leduc.

The economy of Alberta is resource-based and dependent on external markets. This type of economy exposes Alberta to extreme fluctuations. In the past, the arable soil of Alberta allowed for agriculture (q.v.) to be the dominant force in the economy. This has been supplanted by petroleum, mining, and manufacturing industries. Alberta has been able to undergo this change because it has the largest deposits of oil and natural gas in Canada and more than 70 percent of Canada's coal supplies. Most of the manufacturing industries are tied to the natural resources and construction industries. The natural beauty of the Rocky Mountains and the annual Calgary Stampede also provide a boost to the Alberta economy in the form of tourism.

The climate of Alberta is dry. This is due to the prevailing winds from the Pacific losing their moisture on the windward side of the Rockies. The summers are warm and the winters are very cold. However, in winter the temperature can rise very suddenly from a phenomenon known as the *chinook*.

The capital of Alberta is Edmonton. The provincial legislative assembly has 83 members. In the federal government, it has 21 members of Parliament and six senators. The area of the province is 661,190 sq km (6.6 percent of Canada). The flower of the province is the wild rose. The motto is *Fortis et Liber* (Strong and Free). The population is 2,592,300. *See also* Alberta Field Force; Blackfoot Confederacy.

ALBERTA FIELD FORCE. For three months in 1885 a unit of the Canadian forces known as the Alberta Field Force contributed to the quelling of the Métis (q.v.) and native rising in the Northwest Territories. Under the command of Thomas Strange, a retired British military engineer turned ranchman known as "Gunner Jingo," the locally raised force had as its principal mission the policing of native reserves. The force, which consisted of a motley assortment of cowboys, bank clerks, townspeople, scouts, and Mounties, travelled north from Calgary, then into Saskatchewan. They hunted for rebels and were exploited by settlers along the way. Among their important, though prosaic, duties was effecting the release of 40 hostages held by Big Bear's (q.v.) Crees. *See also* Northwest Rebellion (1885).

ALEXANDER, SIR WILLIAM [EARL OF STIRLING] (1567–1640), persuaded James I of England to approve a colonization scheme to create a New Scotland in the New World and received a grant of land with rights to create new baronets for this purpose. Colonization of Nova Scotia was unsuccessful both because of the difficulty in inducing settlers to go to the new land and because of the presence of the Acadians (q.v.) in Acadia. In 1632, as a result of the peace negotiated between France and England, Port Royal was returned to the French and the Scottish colony disappeared.

ALLAN, SIR HUGH (1810–1882). Founder of the shipping firm Allan Line. Allan was born in Ayrshire, Scotland, and arrived in Canada in 1826. In 1831, he entered a shipbuilding company, becoming a partner. The Allan Line was established in 1839. In 1852 the company won a healthy government contract for steamers on the St. Lawrence River (q.v.). Its vessels were also contracted for by government in the Crimean War and first Boer War. Allan was also one of the founders of the Canadian Pacific Railway (q.v.). In 1872 he won the contract to build the railway, but his contributions to coffers of the Conservative party of Sir John A. Macdonald (q.v.) were exposed to public scrutiny in what is known as "the Pacific Scandal" (q.v.). This caused the collapse of Macdonald's government and the contract too collapsed. Allan was knighted in 1874 for services to Canadian commerce. He died in Edinburgh.

ALLIANCES. Historically, since 1867 Canada has had two main alliances, in the early years with Britain and more recently with the U.S.

The alliance with the British began with the conquest of New France (q.v.) in 1759. As a part of the British Empire, Canada was involved automatically in Britain's wars. Wars between the United States and Britain were fought in Canada during the American Revolution and the War of 1812 (qq.v.). Britain stationed troops in Canada until 1870–71. Naval bases at Halifax and Esquimalt (q.v.) were maintained under British direction until the early 1900s. The alliance with Britain involved Canada in the South African War (q.v.) and both world wars (qq.v.). The contribution in the two world wars by Canada demonstrated the alliance between the two countries.

After World War II, Canada's alliance with Britain became overshadowed by the growing alliance between Canada and the United States. Unlike the familial alliance that Canada had with Britain, the American alliance was based more on security, trade and economics. During World War II, Canada negotiated the Permanent Joint Board on Defence (PJBD) with the United States to ensure the security of North America. The PJBD was renewed in 1947. In 1949 Canada joined NATO. Canada signed the North American Air Defence Agreement (NORAD) with the United States, 12 May 1957. These were security measures that aimed at protecting North America from the Soviet Union. Economically, the United States is Canada's largest trading partner and this also led to the North American Free Trade Agreement in 1988.

ALLINE, HENRY (1748–1784). American evangelist and founder of the "New Lights" sect, whose members are often called Allinites. He was the leader of the Nova Scotia "Great Awakening," a religious revival during the American Revolutionary period.

AMERICAN REVOLUTION, WAR OF THE. One of the most significant developments in the long history of Canada and, equally, of the Canadian-American border, the history of the American Revolution *as it relates to Canada* may be described, briefly, as follows. The roots of the issue date from the Proclamation of 1763 (q.v.), which defined British land policy for control of settlement west of the Appalachians (and was thus related to land exploitation and Indian rights) and British policies of taxation (which American colonists regarded as unjust and unconstitutional). Other causes of the revolution were the costs of garrisoning (the Quartering Act of 1765; extended 1774) and the Stamp Act (1765; repealed 1766). New political theories in the American colonies rejected the British Crown's rights of control of legislation, including taxation measures.

In 1774 the British government passed the Québec Act (q.v.), which reestablished Québec's western and southwestern commercial and territorial ambitions into the Ohio country and the Mississippi watershed. This conflicted with the western expansion plans of Virginia, Connecticut, and Massachusetts. Some American colonists thus classified the Québec Act as one of the "Intolerable Acts." In September 1774 the First Continental Congress resolved to declare British coercive acts as unconstitutional, to urge Massachusetts to take total control of taxation policy, to push colonial governments to form and arm their own militias, and to recommend economic sanctions against Britain. A plan for colonial union was subsequently considered; at the Second Continental Congress (May 1775) Québec was invited to join, the request speaking of Canadians as "fellow sufferers." Québec sent no representatives.

In 1775 American armies took many actions against British forces; the most notable involving Québec were: (1) capture of Fort Ticonderoga on 10 May and Crown Point on 12 May, (2) Brig. Gen. Richard Montgomery's expedition against Fort St. Jean (south of Montréal), which fort capitulated 2 November, and (3) Col. Benedict Arnold's expedition from Maine to the St. Lawrence (q.v.) opposite Québec. The officer commanding the British troops, Gen. Sir Guy Carleton (q.v.), withdrew from Montréal to Québec, leaving it uncovered; American troops then occupied Montréal 13 November. Arnold's troops joined with Montgomery's forces from Montréal, and launched a combined assault on Québec 31 December; it ended in disaster for American arms: Montgomery was killed, Arnold wounded, 100 killed or wounded, and 300 taken prisoner. Carleton lost 11 small river vessels and was himself nearly captured. The British defence of Québec was a stout one; American forces under Arnold maintained a weak cordon around it for the winter. American military plans had called for cross-border attacks against British garrisons and forts. However, British advantages included well-equipped and disciplined forces, naval power for supply and resupply, cooperation of Loyalists, and centralized fiscal power and influence. In 1776 France decided to come to the aid of the American colonists, but the alliance was not effected until 1778.

In the campaign of 1776 in Canada, American Gen. David Wooster took over command from Arnold, then cordoning off Québec. When British naval resupply arrived in the St. Lawrence and brought reinforcements to Carleton on 6 May, the American military leadership decided to abandon the siege of Québec. Carleton turned the American withdrawal into a rout. The Americans were defeated at Trois Rivières 7 June and fell back on Fort St. Jean, and thence to Ticonderoga in early July. Arnold and the Montréal garrison made their retreat to Ticonderoga, and they made preparations to retain control of Lake Champlain by building a fleet for that purpose. In the Battle of Valcour Island (11 October 1776), Carleton's fleet crippled Arnold's; two days later, at Split Rock, the American fleet was destroyed. Carleton then occupied Crown Point, later abandoning it and falling back to the security of Canada.

In 1777 the British force of Loyalists and Indians, 1,800 strong, advanced from Lake Ontario (Oswego) under Col. Barry St. Leger and besieged Fort Stanwix on the Mohawk River. Stiff fighting followed in the area of northern New York, and late that year Gen. John Burgoyne's army collapsed under pressures of British forces led by Gen. Sir Henry Clinton.

Meanwhile, the Thirteen Colonies declared independence 4 July 1776, but already, as noted above, American invasions of Canada had been mounted. Certain colonies, most notably Massachusetts, saw the Québec Act as enshrining popery on the banks of the St. Lawrence. But Massachusetts took no direct action in the invasion of Canada. Halifax, the guardian of Nova Scotia, was not attacked in this war.

There was no further fighting on Canadian soil, as the campaigns intensified in Virginia and North Carolina. Carleton succeeded Clinton as British commander in chief in North America and massed all British forces at New York. Preliminary articles of peace were signed 30 November 1782; on 4 February 1783 Britain proclaimed a cessation of hostilities.

The results of the war included: (1) Britain recognized the United States of America by the first article of the definitive peace treaty, signed 3 September 1783, (2) because neither Nova Scotia nor Québec had joined the revolution, they did not join the United States, (3) boundaries were set up by this treaty from the St. Croix River (dividing Maine and Nova Scotia), along the 45th degree of latitude west of the St. Lawrence–Atlantic watershed divide, through the St. Lawrence to and including the Great Lakes (exclusive of Lake Michigan), and from Lake Superior to the Mississippi River, (4) the U.S. right to fish in grounds of Nova Scotia and Newfoundland and liberty to dry and cure fish on unsettled shores of Labrador, the Magdalen Islands, and Nova Scotia, (5) recognition of debts due creditors of either country, (6) restoration of rights and property of Loyalists (q.v.), and (7) cessation of hostilities and evacuation of British land and sea forces.

Why did the citizens of Québec not rise against the British government, given the promise of the Americans as liberators? For one thing, British military might in the great garrison of Québec could not be overthrown. For another, the American invasions of 1775 were not well organized and they fought largely against professional armies. Equally important, the seignieurs, clergy and inhabitants of Québec did not seek to overthrow their British "masters." They preferred the status quo, did much business with the British defenders and the American invaders, and had no legitimate reason to throw off the mantle of the British Empire. The Québec Act, designed to encourage the loyalty and fidelity of the Québecois, had consequent benefit to the British Empire. Paradoxically, Canada remained British because its inhabitants were French.

Nova Scotia also rejected revolution. Halifax was a garrison town and a naval base, and this encouraged wartime business with Britain and the Empire and, further, made American attack unlikely. Many Nova Scotians (tied to Massachusetts and New York by blood ties) were sympathetic to the rebels but remained neutral. These "neutral Yankees of Nova Scotia" were caught in the middle—between sympathy for the American revolutionary cause and neutrality to the British imperial system at war.

Another result of the War of the American Revolution was the arrival on British soil of various Loyalists. In Nova Scotia they settled in the St. John River Valley (in 1784 this was proclaimed a separate colony; New Brunswick [q.v.]). In Québec they settled along the north coast of the upper St. Lawrence River and Lakes Ontario and Erie, as far west as Essex County. In 1791, in consequence, the Province of Upper Canada (q.v.) was established, the predominant feature of which was Loyalist political identity, where freehold land (as opposed to a seigneurial land holding system) became predominant.

More generally, the remnant of the British Empire in North America—British North America—was forged by the War of the American Revolution. The event strengthened royal, British imperial, and British executive governmental systems and identities. British North America retained the military structure that was so predominant during and even before 1776; rejected the concept of revolution; adhered to the idea of evolution; and provided a counterweight to U.S. tendencies to secure continental dominion in North America. In short, two countries were established by the war: the United States and Canada. This explains the long association of Canadians with imperial sympathies and colonial identities and latent enthusiasms for Canadian self-government and independent status in the British Empire and Commonwealth. It thus shaped Canadian support for such episodes as the War of 1812 (q.v.), the Anglo-Boer War, and World Wars I and II (qq.v.).

AMHERST, JEFFREY [BARON AMHERST] (1717–1797), was the British commander at the successful siege of Louisbourg (q.v.) in 1758 and was commander in chief in America during the Seven Years' War (q.v.).

ANNEXATION MANIFESTO. Signed in 1848, this document called for Canada's annexation to the United States as being preferable to the proposed union of the British North American colonies. The signatories included A. T. Galt (q.v.), Louis-Joseph Papineau (q.v.), and a number of Montréal and Québec businessmen. The economic and financial causes of this unsuccessful quest were many. Principal among them was the end of colonial preference in the British markets for Canadian wheat, timber, and flour products. Canadian trading was disadvantaged by free trade (q.v.) with Britain. The Annexationists argued that union with the United States would raise farm prices, lower import costs, and attract U.S. capital for Canadian industry. The Annexationists failed; French Canadians were thoroughly opposed and the American government showed no interest. The movement, largely republican in sympathy, encountered strong political opposition by the British American League and followers of Louis Hippolyte Lafontaine (q.v.). It died out in 1854, when the Reciprocity Treaty allowed free trade with the United States in products of farm, forest, and waters. *See also* Reciprocity.

ANTIGONISH MOVEMENT. Founded in the 1920s by Father Jimmy Tompkins and his cousin Dr. Moses Coady of St. Francis Xavier University, Cape Breton, NS, this movement encouraged cooperatives and formed the United Maritime Fishermen, based in Moncton. The Antigonish Movement aimed at solving credit problems and ending economic distress in Maritime communities. Notions of cooperatives pioneered in Nova Scotia have become familiar around the world.

ARGENTIA CONFERENCE. Also termed the Atlantic Conference, this meeting of U.S. President Franklin Roosevelt and British Prime Minister Winston Churchill took place aboard warships anchored off Argentia, Newfoundland, from 9 to 12 August 1941. The meeting produced the Atlantic Charter of war aims and sped the process of coordinating the still-neutral United States with the Allies' war effort. Canada was not separately represented at this meeting.

ARMS OF CANADA. The Coat of Arms of Canada contain the Arms of England, Scotland, and Ireland and the Arms of royalist France in the first and second divisions of the shield. These emblems show that the arms are derived from ancient kingdoms and also exemplify the fact that men and women of these countries contributed to the settlement and early development of Canada. The emblem of Canada in the third division symbolizes Canada's national sovereignty as a monarchy

AROOSTOOK WAR. In 1839, British and American forces converged on the Aroostook River region of the ill-defined Maine–New Brunswick border region. The main issues involved timber rights and the communication lines between the British provinces. In March 1839, a compromise was reached before serious conflict could occur. The border was finally settled in the Webster–Ashburton Treaty of 1842.

ASSINIBOINE. The Assiniboine ("the people that cook with hot stones"), a Plains tribe, inhabited the area that is now southern Alberta. The Assiniboine were enemies of the Blackfoot Confederacy (q.v.). They fought many battles for control of the Canadian prairies. After the introduction of European firearms, battles and hunting expeditions occurred more frequently. As well, a steady decline in buffalo resulted due to gun-carrying Assiniboine. In 1836, the Assiniboine were inflicted with small-pox. The population of the Assiniboine continued to decline after 1836, and many were later confined to reserves.

ATWOOD, MARGARET (ELEANOR) (1939–). Canadian novelist, short story writer, poet, and critic. Born in Ottawa, she graduated from the University of Toronto and Radcliffe College. Her first published work in 1966, *The Circle*, won the Governor General's Award. Her book *The Edible Woman* (1969), dealing with emotional cannibalism, provoked considerable controversy. In 1985, *The Handmaid's Tale* was short-listed for the Booker Prize, as was *The Cat's Eye* in 1989.

-B-

BAFFIN, WILLIAM (1584–1622). An English navigator and explorer, Baffin sailed to Greenland with an expedition in 1612. In 1615, he led another expedition to find the Northwest Passage to Asia. His name was given to Baffin Bay, which he explored in 1616, and to Baffin Island. In 1616, he became the first European to reach Ellesmere Island. Sir Clements R. Markham edited accounts of Baffin's expeditions and published them as *The Voyages of William Baffin* (1881).

BAGOT, SIR CHARLES (1781–1843). Governor general of British North America from 1841 to 1843. He followed Lord Sydenham as governor general and, because of poor health, Bagot allowed the leadership of the cabinet created by Sydenham to pass out of control. In 1842, he invited Robert Baldwin (q.v.) and Louis Hippolyte Lafontaine (q.v.) to form a ministry, thereby furthering the development of parliamentary democracy in Canada. These actions were repudiated by his successor, Sir Charles Metcalfe (q.v.). However, the precedents were established and responsible government (q.v.) became a reality under Lord Elgin (q.v.).

BALDWIN, ROBERT (1804–1858). Lawyer, politician, and celebrated reformer from Canada West. Baldwin combined forces with Louis Hippolyte Lafontaine (q.v.) to establish what became the Liberal party (q.v.) of Canada. With his father, Baldwin devised the theory of responsible government (q.v.), wherein the legislative assembly would control the list of persons working for the government ("civil list") and other financial measures. This met with resistance from Governors Sir Francis Bond Head and Sir Charles Metcalfe (q.v.). However, Sir Charles Bagot (q.v.) accepted Executive Council participation in the legislative government. Baldwin with Lafontaine resigned in opposition to Metcalfe's autocratic rule. In 1848, Baldwin and Lafontaine established what is called "the Great Ministry" and were party to the transition from imperial rule to colonial self-government, mainly on fiscal matters.

BANTING, SIR FREDERICK GRANT (1891–1941). Canadian physiologist, the discover of insulin. Born in Alliston, Ontario, Banting studied medicine at the University of Toronto and became a professor there in 1923. While working under John James Rickard Macleod on pancreatic secretions in 1921, he discovered (with the aid of his assistant Charles H. Best) the hormone insulin, a treatment for diabetes. With Macleod, he was awarded the Nobel Prize for medicine, which he shared with Best. In 1930, Banting established the Banting Institute in Toronto. In 1941, he was killed in a wartime air crash.

BARKER, WILLIAM GEORGE (1894–1930). Canada's most decorated war hero, "Billy" Barker, born in Dauphin, Manitoba, was an officer in the Royal Flying Corps (RFC) and was credited with 40 "kills" of German and Austro-Hungarian military aircraft in World War I (q.v.). He is best remembered for single-handed combat against at least 30 enemy aircraft, which won him the Victoria Cross on 27 October 1918. Barker became the first director of the Royal Canadian Air Force (RCAF). He was fatally injured when his Fairchild crashed at Rockcliffe Air Station, near Ottawa. *See also* Bishop, William ("Billy") Avery.

BATTLE OF THE ATLANTIC. At the beginning of World War II (q.v.), The British received two-thirds of their food supplies, 30 percent of their iron ore, 90 percent of copper ore, 90 percent of bauxite, 95 percent of petroleum, 100 percent of rubber, and 80 percent of their soft timber from abroad. If the supplies could not get through, the British would be unable to fight, and cutting those supply lines was a major aim of Germany. The Battle of the Atlantic was to determine the outcome.

German U-boats ranged the Atlantic Ocean in search of British and Allied merchant shipping. In the early stages, this tactic was effective in reducing the supplies to Britain. Although Britain developed a detection device, they had few ships that could fight the U-boats. Between July and December of 1940, U-boats sank 1.5 million tons of shipping. The Battle of the Atlantic began as a race between the German's ability to build U-boats and the Allies' ability to construct merchant ships; and also between the development of German undersea tactics and the Allies' ability to build escorts and to learn to defeat the U-boats.

The climax of the battle was 1943. The number of U-boats at sea averaged more than 100. The Royal Canadian Navy (RCN) was pulled out of the struggle due to ill-equipped escorts and below-standard training. As well, there was an air coverage gap off the coast of Greenland, although the RCAF Eastern Air Command provided exhaustive coverage out of Newfoundland. In February and March of 1943, 171 ships were sunk by U-boats. At the Atlantic Convoy Conference in Washington in March 1943, RCNs Adm. Leonard Murray took over the Canadian Northwest Atlantic Command. The Allies gained control over the Germans by gaining access to German codes in June 1941. As well, better-designed detection equipment, new weapons such as the hedgehog, better training, and the extension of escort and, eventually, air coverage across the North Atlantic turned the tide in favour of the Allies. In May 1943, the Allies sank 41 U-boats and continued to deplete the German submarines in the following months. By 1944, the RCN and RCAF had almost entire responsibility for the surface escort of convoys. The Battle of the Atlantic was an Allied victory. *See also* Canadian Air Force; Canadian Navy.

BC FERRIES. A Crown corporation of the Province of British Columbia launched in 1960 by the Social Credit government of Premier W. A. C. Bennett. Numerous difficulties with Canadian Pacific Coastal Steamships, including seaman strikes and corporate indifference to the Strait of Georgia crossings (Vancouver–Nanaimo and Vancouver–Victoria), led to this government intervention. BC Ferries began with two ships (designed for 106 1960 Buicks or equivalent), two terminals (Tsawwassen and Schwartz Bay), and 200 employees. By 1998 it had one of the largest ferry fleets in the world, with 4,000 employees and 40 ships serving 25 different routes, carrying over 22 million passengers and 8 million vehicles a year. BC Ferries concentrated on in-province marine travel (as opposed to trade with the United States). It pushed Black Ball Ferries, an American corporation, out of the Nanaimo–Vancouver run; in addition, it ended the Canadian Pacific Railway's coastal traffic. BC Ferries inherited Gulf Islands ferry routes of the Provincial Department of Highways. It developed (1) the Port Hardy, northern Vancouver Island, to Prince River "inside passage" run and (2) the mid-coast route linking the Port Hardy–Prince Rupert run to McLoughlin Bay, Bella Coola and in the Queen Charlotte Islands, Skidegate and Alliford Bay.

BEAVAN, EMILY SHAW (b.1820). Author and teacher, Beavan lived in New Brunswick for most of her life. In 1838, she married Dr. Frederick Beavan. While in New Brunswick she carefully recorded her observations of a settler's life, which were later published in England as *Sketches and Tales Illustrative of Life in the Backwoods of New Brunswick*. The book provides a good illustration about frontier life and more specifically the role of women. Although her personal life story has large gaps, her work has provided great insight into the early development of Canadian life.

BEGBIE, SIR MATTHEW BAILLIE (1819–1894). Known as "the Hanging Judge," Begbie was born in England, the eldest son of Col. and Mrs. T. S. Begbie. He was educated at St. Peter's College, Cambridge, and he was called to the English Bar in 1844. In 1858 he was appointed a judge to the Crown Colony of British Columbia (q.v.). Begbie was very important in preserving law and order in the new colony during the days of the gold rush. He had a decidedly tough-minded attitude to criminals, but he was generally fair and not really responsible for many hangings. In 1866, when the colonies of Vancouver Island (q.v.) and British Columbia were united, he became Chief Justice of British Columbia. He was knighted in 1875 and was still chief justice at the time of his death in Victoria.

BELL, ALEXANDER GRAHAM (1847–1922). Inventor of the telephone. Bell also formed, in Halifax in 1907, the Aerial Experiment Association whose *Silver Dart* made the first manned flight in Canada in 1909. Hydrofoil HD-4 is preserved in the Bell Museum at Baddeck, Cape Breton, NS.

BENNETT, RICHARD BEDFORD (1870–1947). Prime minister and later member of the House of Lords. Born in New Brunswick and educated in Nova Scotia, Bennett became a lawyer and then politician. He was MP for Calgary for the Conservative party. In 1927, he became the leader of the Conservative party. Bennett became prime minister in 1930 and held the position until 1935. While prime minister, he faced numerous challenges of the Great Depression. Autocratic in manner, he appeared insensitive to the suffering of the country. He convened the 1932 Ottawa Imperial Economic Conference, which facilitated means of bilateral Empire trade preference. As well, his government launched the Price Spreads Commission in 1934, which revealed retailers' exploitation of employees in department and chain stores. He proposed the Wages and Hours Bill and Unemployment Insurance. He also established relief camps for single men. He created the Bank of Canada and the CBC. Prior to the 1935 election, Bennett introduced the Canadian New Deal (q.v.). These measures were largely set aside by the Liberals or higher courts. He continued in Parliament as leader of the opposition until he retired in 1938, moved to Guildford, England, and was made a peer in 1941.

BEOTHUK. The term *beothuk* has been interpreted to mean "man" or "human beings." The Beothuk, located in Newfoundland, were commonly called "Red Indians" by European explorers because they smeared their bodies and clothes with red ochre. The language spoken by the Beothuk appeared to be two or three dialects of a common tongue. Beothuk numbered about 500 when John Cabot (q.v.) discovered Newfoundland in 1497. The Beothuk were shy of Europeans and were murdered at every opportunity by European traders. The Beothuk were also enemies of the Mi'kmaq (q.v.), who hunted them in the alliance of European traders. Essentially, the Beothuk were hunted to extinction. Many died from tuberculosis. The last Beothuk was Nancy Shawnadithit (q.v.) who died in 1829. With her death died the Beothuk people.

BERNIER, JOSEPH ELZEAR (1852–1934). Canadian explorer noted for his 12 voyages to the Arctic. Born in L'Islet, Québec, his father and grandfather had been sea captains, and Bernier began to command ships at the age of 17. During an expedition in 1908 and 1909, Bernier claimed all the islands in the North American region of the Arctic for Canada. This action asserted Canada's claim to the Arctic region and awakened the Canadian public to the importance of the far north. Bernier also made several voyages around the world.

From 1906 to 1909, Bernier made two voyages to a number of islands in the Arctic. During these journeys, he travelled through Lancaster Sound to the islands of Banks, Melville, and Victoria, and then to McClure Strait and Prince of Wales Strait. From 1910 to 1913, he led two expeditions in the Baffin Island area.

BETHUNE, HENRY NORMAN (1890–1939). Physician, born at Gravenhurst, Ontario. Bethune pursued a career in thoracic surgery. In 1935 he joined the Communist party (q.v.) and devoted the rest of his life to the anti-fascist cause, first in the Spanish Civil War, where he organized a blood transfusion unit, and then as a surgeon in China, where the Communists were battling the Japanese. Mao Zedong's book *In Memory of Norman Bethune* was required reading during the Chinese Cultural Revolution.

BIDWELL, MARSHALL SPRING (1799–1872). Politician and lawyer. Bidwell came to Canada from the United States with his father. In 1821, he was elected to the Legislative Assembly of Upper Canada (q.v.) in his father's place, but was declared ineligible because he was not a British citizen. After the law was changed he was reelected in 1825. He went on to become leader of the moderate Reformers. He fled to the United States, never to return, after he was wrongly accused of complicity during the Rebellion of 1837 in Upper Canada. *See* Rebellions of 1837.

BIENCOURT DE POUTRINCOURT ET DE SAINT JUST, JEAN DE (1557–1615). Lieutenant-governor of Acadia. He was the commander of Port Royal, the first settlement in Acadia. His desire to establish an agricultural settlement at Port Royal was thwarted by the conflicting aims of the French court of evangelization of the Indians and of his financial backers for profits from fish and fur.

BIG BEAR (1825?–1888). The most famous and influential of the Plains chiefs. Big Bear (or *Mistahimaskwa*) was half Ojibwa, half Cree, and led the largest band of Cree on the Plains at that time, about 2,000. He was noted for his ability to shoot accurately under the neck of his horse while riding at full speed. He worked for pan-Indianism, attempting to unite the natives in the face of White settlement. In 1876, he was a negotiator of Treaty Six and refused the terms because he saw the treaty as a forfeit of his people's autonomy. He was forced to sign the treaty in 1882 in order to receive rations for his starving people.

In 1885, Big Bear's people were thrust into the Northwest Rebellion (q.v.) by a few hot-headed members. This small number attacked and killed white settlers at Frog Lake on 2 April 1885 and attacked Fort Pitt. Although Big Bear desperately attempted to prevent the killings, he was forced to surrender to the RCMP on 2 July 1885. He was tried for treason and sentenced to three years imprisonment. *See also* Plains Cree.

BIGOT, FRANÇOIS (1703–1777?). Intendant (chief administrator) of New France, 1748–59. Bigot was born in Bordeaux. A lawyer and civil servant, he was appointed commissary at Louisbourg (q.v.) (1739). His misappropriation of funds may have caused the downfall of that place in 1744. His career in fraud was not over. Bigot became intendant of New France owing to patronage. He was in Québec 1748–59 and carried out the most astonishing frauds (in the merchandising of retail goods, furs, and provisions). Supplies for military uses and for the Indians were diverted to his profit. His corrupt administration paved the way for the collapse of New France. He was arrested in Paris in 1759 and was imprisoned. Ordered to make restitution, he was banished from the kingdom of France. He probably died in 1777 but the place of death is unknown.

BILINGUALISM AND BICULTURALISM, ROYAL COMMISSION ON. Sitting 1963–71 as a Canadian government inquiry, the commission was instituted by the Lester Pearson (q.v.) government in response to pressure in Québec for fuller use of the French language in Canada. It researched the origins of the problem and proposed more equitable measures between Francophones and Anglophones. The commission was chaired jointly by André Laurendeau, editor of *Le Devior*, and Davidson Dunton, president of Carleton University. The final report documented certain alleged disadvantages of French Canadians at that time, both culturally and economically by their origins. The commission's key recommendation was the adoption of French and English as the official languages in the federal civil service and bureaucracy. A strongly federalist document, the commission's report advanced the cause of a two-nation federation. However, partly in response, in 1972 a Ministry for Multiculturalism was established, primarily because of the pressure of Ukrainian and German Canadians.

The legacies of the controversial Bilingualism and Biculturalism Commission have been extensive. All English-speaking provinces instituted or upgraded regulations concerning French minority education, and they introduced means for enhanced French instruction including "French Immersion" or "French Core" curricula. Federal financial assistance encouraged these measures to be implemented. New Brunswick declared itself officially bilingual and remains the only official province or territory so legally designated. Ontario greatly extended French services. Supreme Court of Canada decisions restored French language rights previously legislated away in Manitoba and Saskatchewan. Institutional bilingualism was effected by Ottawa's Official Languages Act of 1969 (q.v.). An Official Language Commissioner was appointed. The commissioner did not address constitutional issues or problems and in that sense did not address separatist issues then advancing in Québec. Some observers now believe the report to have been ineffective in controlling Québec's search for autonomy. Québec's move to unilingualism in education is seen by countless non-French speakers in Canada as a violation of the spirit of bilingualism. In the meantime, many Canadian children and adults from coast to coast have embraced the concept of bilingualism in theory if not in practice, and Québec has many more friends in the rest of Canada than it will ever know. Certainly cultural diversity as a concept was strengthened by the commission.

BISHOP, WILLIAM ("BILLY") AVERY (1894–1956), was born in Owen Sound, Ontario, and attended the Royal Military College in Kingston, Ontario. He joined the Mississauga Horse, went overseas with the cavalry, and transferred to the Royal Flying Corps in 1915. He became an excellent gunner and pilot. On 2 June 1917, Bishop made a single-handed early morning attack on a German airfield where he claimed to have shot down three aircraft. This attack won him the Victoria

Cross to go with his Distinguished Service Order and bar, his Military Cross, and his Distinguished Flying Cross. He is credited with 72 confirmed aerial victories. He wrote *Winged Warfare* (1918) and *Winged Peace* (1944). *See also* Barker, William George.

BLACKFOOT CONFEDERACY. The name *Blackfoot* is a translation of the native term *Siksikauwa*, which refers to the moccasins that were blackened or burnt by prairie fires. The Blackfoot nation consisted of the Blackfoot proper, the Blood, and the Piegan tribes and was at one time the strongest, most aggressive native nation in the Canadian prairies. Their territory stretched from the Rocky Mountains well into Saskatchewan and from the North Saskatchewan River to upper Missouri in the United States. The language of the Blackfoot Confederacy was Algonquin. The Blackfoot were nomadic in lifestyle. The major hunting staple of the Blackfoot was the buffalo of the prairies. In terms of religion, they worshipped the Sun and Thunder, which were the manifestations of the Great Spirit. One of the most notable of the Blackfoot peoples was Chief Crowfoot. The Blackfoot Confederacy signed Treaty Seven with the Canadian government in 1877. Epidemics of smallpox in the mid-18th century and of smallpox and measles in the mid-19th century drastically reduced the number of Blackfoot in Canada.

BLACKS. Black experience runs through Canadian history. Highlights include: 1608, Mathieu D'Acosta served as interpreter for Sieur de Monts, Governor at Port Royal; 1628, a slave from Madagascar sold in New France; 1709, slavery declared legal in New France; 1782–83, 3,500 Blacks, most former slaves, arrived in Nova Scotia and New Brunswick; 1792, Black exodus of 1,190 from Halifax to Sierre Leone; 1796, 600 Maroons exiled from Jamaica arrived in the Maritimes (in 1800 they opted for Sierre Leone); 1814–15, 3,000 Black refugees of the War of 1812 (q.v.) settled in the Maritimes; 1858, some 600 Blacks from the United States arrived at Vancouver Island, and in Victoria, British Columbia, the all-Black Pioneer Rifle Corps receives recognition; 1901, Black population of Canada number 17,437; 1960, significant numbers of West Indian Black people began to arrive in Canada; 1970, more than 100,000 Black people in Canada. *See* Slavery. *See also* Cary, Mary Shadd; Hall, William.

BLAKE, EDWARD (1833–1912). Lawyer and politician, second premier of Ontario (1871), and federal MP in Alexander Mackenzie's (q.v.) administration (1873). Blake resigned in 1874 to promote the concept of Canada First (q.v.). He was a persistent reformer and Canadian nationalist. As Canada's minister of justice he obliged the British government to accept Canada's Supreme Court Act and to reduce the governor general's powers. He was the Liberal party (q.v.) leader from 1880 to 1887. Blake resigned from the party in 1891 due its reciprocity (q.v.) proposals. He left Canada in 1892 and went to Ireland where he became an Irish nationalist member of Parliament. He returned to Canada in 1906.

Blake was ambitious, long-winded, and dominant. He was the only leader of the Liberals never to become prime minster. However, he convinced others to join his party, most notably Oliver Mowat (his successor as premier of Ontario) and Sir Wilfrid Laurier (q.v.), a future prime minister of Canada.

BLUENOSE, one of the great classic sailing ships (q.v.) of all time, is Canada's (and Nova Scotia's) treasure of sailing history, appearing on every 10-cent coin. A marvel of design and performance, she was a 285-ton schooner (112 feet on the waterline in length; 27-foot beam; 15 feet, 10 inch, draft). She had two masts, her main topmast rising nearly 126 feet above the deck. She carried a total of 10,901 square feet of sail.

Fitted out for speed, *Bluenose* had to be a working vessel—a genuine fishing vessel such as those that worked the salt banks of Newfoundland—to qualify for the prized International Fisherman's Trophy (a series of races held in alternative years off Lunenberg, Nova Scotia, and Gloucester, Mass.). The trophy was offered by Senator William H. Dennis, proprietor of a Halifax newspaper. The architect was William J. Roue and the builders were Smith & Rhuland of Lunenberg. She won the trophy in 1921, the first year of her entry, and won successively for about two decades, causing rival American interests (who spent fortunes on new or improved designs) much frustration. A deep-sea sealer of fine qualities, she was driven aground and wrecked on Sable Island in 1926, but survived; she did similarly at Placentia Bay, Newfoundland, in 1930. In 1935 she was the official Canadian representative to the Silver Jubilee of King George V and Queen Mary and was reviewed at Spithead (Portsmouth, England) with the Home Fleet. Angus Walters was her great captain of record; his abilities saved her on at least one occasion. In January 1946 she was wrecked and lost off Haiti.

The loss of this famous "saltbanker" was a matter of great regret: brothers Brian and Philip Backman, authors of a book about the vessel, led a campaign to build another *Bluenose*; they were supported by Roue and Walters and many others. In 1961 a replica was commissioned. *Bluenose II* was launched 24 July 1963 at a cost of nearly 10 times the original. She remains in service and is the property of the Government of Nova Scotia.

BOER WAR. *See* South African War.

BORDEN, SIR ROBERT LAIRD (1854–1937). Eighth prime minister of Canada, 1911–20. Born in Nova Scotia, Borden became a lawyer and politician. Earnest and dutiful, he rose to the head of the Conservative party in 1901. He became prime minister subsequent to the election of 1911, defeating Sir Wilfrid Laurier's (q.v.) pro-reciprocity Liberals. A skilful political manager and a pragmatist, Borden forged alliances with anti-Liberal forces inside and out of Québec. He utilized the French nationalists' opposition to Laurier's Naval Service Act in 1910 to gain support in Québec. Pro-imperial and yet strongly national, Borden introduced a measure to provide funds for the construction of three dreadnought battleships for the Royal Navy. This was defeated by the Liberal-dominated Senate. He led Canada through all the difficulties of World War I (q.v.), including the raising of the Canadian Expeditionary Force (q.v.) to wage war against Imperial Germany and Central Powers, the Conscription Crisis (which left the country bitterly divided), and the introduction of the "temporary" income tax. His government passed the War Measures Act (1914) and the compulsory Military Service Act (1917) and nationalized the Canadian Northern Railway (q.v.), forerunner of the Canadian National Railways (q.v.), in 1919. As well, he led the Canadian delegation to the Paris Peace Conference in 1919. Borden stepped down as prime minister in 1920 and was succeeded by Arthur Meighen (q.v.). Borden wrote and lectured extensively on Canadian and Commonwealth theory and practice and was an architect of the later British Commonwealth of Nations (q.v.). An international statesman, he also advocated the League of Nations. *See also* Canadian Navy; Reciprocity.

BOURASSA, HENRI (1868–1952). Founder and editor of the Montréal newspaper *Le Devoir* and grandson of Louis Joseph Papineau (q.v.), Bourassa was a French Canadian nationalist who opposed Canada's involvement in British colonial wars. When Wilfrid Laurier's (q.v.) government committed troops to the Imperial struggle against Boer republics in southern Africa, Bourassa resigned his independent Liberal seat in Parliament and was returned by acclamation. He stood at the centre of French Canadian opposition to the Naval Service Act of 1910. He helped bring about Laurier's defeat in 1911. A vigorous opponent of Canada's involvement in World War I (q.v.), he nonetheless voiced no opposition to the official declaration of war. He became a social reformer in the 1920s and 1930s. He is regarded as a prominent, early voice for French Canadian identity in Canadian national affairs. *See also* South African War; Canadian Navy.

BOURASSA, ROBERT (1933–1996). A Liberal, Bourassa became premier of Québec in the election of 1970; at 36, he was the province's youngest premier. In the October Crisis (q.v.) of 1970, he requested the federal government to send troops in aid to the civil power (q.v.). He argued for Québec's separate status within the confederation. He agreed to the Victoria Charter (1971) proposed for constitutional change but could not win his cabinet's backing; this killed the proposal. In 1976 he resigned when the Parti Québecois (q.v.) won the provincial election. He was reelected Liberal party (q.v.) leader in 1983, won the election of 1986, and remained premier until ill health obliged him to step aside in 1993. His record has demonstrated his strong commitment to Québec within the Canadian confederation. In 1996, Robert Bourassa lost a long, courageous battle with cancer.

BOURGEOYS, STE. MARGUERITE (1619–1700). Canada's first woman saint, Mother Bourgeoys, was a member of the Congregation of Notre Dame. She was one of the first French females to set foot in Ville Marie, the fort on the St. Lawrence River (q.v.) which was to become Montréal (q.v.). She arrived in November 1653, age 33, following a three-month voyage that took the lives of eight of the 15 women and 108 passengers, most of them soldiers for the new colony. She was Canada's first teacher. One of her tasks was to care for the "King's Daughters" and prepare them for marriage to colonial soldiers. She is therefore known, in history, as Mother of the Colony. The King's Daughters were not Parisian prostitutes, as has been the popular belief, but daughters of officers killed in war, even nobles. Mother Bourgeoys died at age 80. The sisters had a portrait made of the dead woman, who had refused to be painted while alive. It is one of the most often-printed portraits of early Canada. The painting hangs in the mother house of the Congregation, which also houses her bones in a tomb.

BRÉBEUF, STE. JEAN DE (1593–1649). A Jesuit priest, Brébeuf was the founder of the mission to the Huron (q.v.). He was a great organiser and administrator. He mastered the Huron language. Brébeuf was exceedingly devout and accepted the vow never to refuse the grace of martyrdom. He was tortured and martyred by the Iroquois (q.v.). He wrote the lyrics to *The Huron Carol*. In 1930 he was canonized and in 1940 named the Patron Saint of Canada by Pope Pius XII. He was called "the giant of the Huron missions" and "the apostle whose heart was devoured." *See also* Ste.-Marie among the Hurons.

BRITISH COLUMBIA. Canada's westernmost province, located on the Pacific coast and cordillera. British Columbia is the third largest province in both population and area. A large portion of the province is dominated by the Rocky Mountains. For this reason, there is only a small amount of agricultural land, located in river valleys and deltas and mountain trenches. The many islands that lie off the coast are also part of the province. The majority of the population lives in the southwest corner of the province, including the cities of Victoria and Vancouver. Vancouver is the third largest city in Canada.

Historically, this region of Canada was inhabited by the Athabascan and Salish tribes of the interior and the Kwakiutl, Haida (q.v.), Nuu'chah'nulth (q.v.) (or Nootka), and Tsimshian (q.v.) on the coast—as well as others. The coastal tribes utilized the sea and its resources and developed canoes. Tribes of the interior were nomadic; they tended to travel the valleys in pursuit of game. Juan Pérez of Spain explored the coast for Spain but Capt. James Cook (q.v.) was the first explorer to land on the shores of the British Columbia, at Nootka Sound on 28 March 1778. Capt. George Vancouver (q.v.), RN, explored the region in 1792 and mapped the Pacific coast and the island that is named after him. In the 1800s, there were many disputes between the British and the United States surrounding the boundaries between the two countries. This was partly settled with the signing of the Oregon Treaty (q.v.) in 1846. This treaty gave the British control of the mainland north of the 49th parallel and all of Vancouver Island (q.v.). Vancouver Island obtained colonial status in 1849. In 1858, British Columbia became a Crown Colony. The two colonies were united under one colony called British Columbia in 1866. British Columbia entered Confederation in 1871 with the promise from Ottawa of a transcontinental railway to the Pacific. The promise was fulfilled in 1885 as the Canadian Pacific Railway (q.v.) was completed to Port Moody, British Columbia. Regular passenger service began in 1886.

Climate varies throughout the region. The southern coastal areas experience the mildest winters in Canada. The Rocky Mountains have a large influence on the climate. The region west of the mountains receives a large amount of precipitation. The regions east of the Coast Range receive less rainfall.

British Columbia is known for its abundance of natural resources. A large portion of the province is forested. Abundant rainfall and the warmer temperatures on the Pacific side of the mountains have produced the largest coniferous trees in Canada. In terms of arable land, Okanagan Valley is one of the biggest producers of fresh fruit in Canada. British Columbia also has large coal reserves and natural gas and oil fields. The mountainous region gives British Columbia hydroelectric capacity that is second only to Québec. Many industries in British Columbia are centred around the lumber and fishing industries. As well, shipping is a major contributor to the economy. Vancouver ranks as one of the world's premier container ports.

The legislative assembly of British Columbia has 69 members. Federally, the province has 28 members in the House of Commons and six senators. The provincial capital is Victoria. The population of the province is 3,376,700. *See also* BC Ferries, Nisga'a.

BRITISH COMMONWEALTH AIR TRAINING PLAN (BCATP). This scheme, arranged by agreement signed 17 December 1939 in Ottawa by the United Kingdom, Canada, Australia, and New Zealand, trained aircrew from Canada, Britain, Australia, New Zealand, and other Commonwealth countries, as well as some from the United States and occupied Europe, at air bases in Canada. The plan was introduced to the Canadian government by the British before the outbreak of war in September 1939. Prime Minister Mackenzie King (q.v.) accepted the idea after war was declared. Wanting to avoid a large army and the casualties sure to result when it went into action, King saw air combat as less costly in human lives.

The RCAF ran and controlled the BCATP and carried out the training, initially with the assistance of private flying clubs. By 1941 the plan was in full operation with 107 schools across Canada. By the time the plan was shut down at the end of March 1945, it had produced 131,553 pilots, navigators, bombardiers, wireless operators, air gunners, and flight engineers, of whom 72,835 were Canadians. The plan was a major Canadian contribution to the Allied war effort. *See also* Canadian Air Force.

BRITISH NORTH AMERICA ACT. *See* Constitution Act of 1867.

BROCK, SIR ISAAC (1769–1812). Born in Guernsey, Brock came to North America in 1802 and in 1811 was promoted to major general and made provisional administrator of Upper Canada. In the War of 1812 (q.v.), forces following his instructions attacked Michilimackinac and Detroit. He was present at the latter's surrender. British troops forced the American forces to reconsider areas of attack. In the battle for Queenston

Heights (q.v.), Brock was killed by an American sniper; a monument to Brock now dominates the battlefield at Queenston Heights.

BROWN, GEORGE (1818–1880). Known principally as a reformer and one of the Clear Grits (q.v.), Brown was a prominent Father of Confederation, editor of the Toronto newspaper *Globe,* and advocate of Canadian expansion in the Northwest. He argued strongly for "representation by population (q.v.)." He formed, with A. A. Dorion (q.v.), a short-lived government in the Province of Canada in 1858. He is best remembered for working with A. T. Galt, Sir John A. Macdonald, and Sir George E. Cartier (qq.v.) in a political coalition that prepared the confederation arrangement of 1865–67. In 1880, Brown was shot dead by a fired employee.

BRÛLÉ, ÉTIENNE (1592?–1633). An interpreter and explorer who lived with the natives and learned their language as a token of the alliance between the French and the Huron (q.v.). Brûlé explored the Huron country with Samuel de Champlain (q.v.) in 1615. He was much attracted to native ways. Brûlé explored much of the Great Lakes area. In 1618 he travelled through Pennsylvania to Chesapeake Bay, and in 1622 to Lake Superior. He was killed by Hurons near Penetanguishene, Ontario, in 1633.

BYNG (OF VIMY), JULIAN [VISCOUNT BYNG] (1862–1935), was a British cavalry officer who commanded the Canadian Corps during the battle of Vimy Ridge (q.v.). He became governor general of Canada, 1921–26. He was involved with Arthur Meighen (q.v.) and particularly W. L. Mackenzie King (q.v.) in the Constitutional Crisis of 1925–26, commonly known as the "King-Byng affair."

-C-

CABOT, JOHN [GIOVANNI CABOTO] (1450?–1499?). Explorer and mariner. Cabot made the first North American landfall by a European after the Norse, for England in 1497. Encouraged by Bristol merchants and Henry VII, he landed somewhere on Labrador, Newfoundland, or Nova Scotia shores. It is said that he landed, or made a landfall, at Cape Bonavista, Newfoundland. In his ship *Matthew* was probably his son Sebastian Cabot, likewise an explorer in search of the Northwest Passage and Cipangu, and 16 other mariners. John Cabot made a second voyage in 1498 but vanished. In 1497, he noted the then-abundance of cod and was convinced he had reached "the land of the Great Khan."

CAMERON, JOHN A. "CARIBOO" (1820–1888). Born at Summerstown, Glengarry County, Ontario, Cameron made a fortune in the Cariboo gold rush in 1862. His wife died there, and he returned to Glengarry County with her body to bury her in the Cornwall Township cemetery, as he had promised to do while she was alive. He lost most of his money in poor investments. In 1888, he returned to the Cariboo to try to recoup his losses and make another fortune. He failed and died there in the same year. "Cariboo" Cameron was buried in a cemetery in Camerontown, where he made his first fabulous strike.

CAMPBELL, KIM (1947–). Elected leader of the Progressive Conservative party in June 1993, Campbell became first woman prime minister when Brian Mulroney (q.v.) stepped down. Owing to inexperience in national politics and burdened with problems of persistent recession, her party was defeated in the election of October 1993. She resigned as party leader 13 December 1993.

Avril Phaedra Campbell, born in Port Alberni, BC, assumed the nickname Kim when she was 12. A student of political science at the University of British Columbia (UBC) and the London School of Economics in England, she specialized in Soviet affairs, becoming an opponent of Marxism. Sometime lecturer in political science before attending the UBC law school, she was elected to the provincial legislature in 1986. Campbell was elected to the House of Commons in 1988. She made a spirited defence of the U.S.–Canadian free trade agreement. She became, in turn, minister for northern development, justice, and national defence. In 1996 she was appointed Canadian consul-general in Los Angeles.

CAMP BORDEN. Located northwest of Toronto, Camp Borden was established in 1916 as a training base and named in honour of Sir Frederick Borden, minister of the militia and national defence. The base was used to train an assortment of personnel in the army and air force. In World War II (q.v.), some 185,000 men and women, soldiers and airmen, were trained at the camp. The camp is now known as CFB Borden. The establishment is the country's largest military trades training station.

CAMP X. Located near Whitby, Ontario, the "Camp X" trained spies and saboteurs during World War II (q.v.). Officially titled Special Training School No. 103, the camp prepared agents from a variety of nationalities for espionage and resistance work in Nazi-occupied Europe. The camp was also the location of Hydra, a super-secret communication network linking Britain, Canada, and the United States.

CANADA COUNCIL FOR THE ARTS, THE. Created as an independent organization by act of Parliament in 1957, in consequence of the Massey Report (q.v.), more correctly known as the report of the Royal Commission on National Development in the Arts, Letters, and Sciences, published in 1951. Under terms of the Canada Council Act, the object of the Canada Council is "to foster and promote the study and enjoyment of, and the production of works in, the arts." To fulfill this mandate, the Canada Council offers grants and services to artists and other arts professionals and to arts organizations. The council administers the Killam Program of scholarly awards and prizes and offers a number of other prestigious awards. The Canadian Commission for United Nations Educational and Scientific Organization and the Public Lending Right Commission also operate under its aegis.

The council has a chair, a vice-chair, and nine other members, all appointed by the Government of Canada. The council board meets three times a year in Ottawa and makes decisions on policies and programs developed by the council staff. The Canada Council relies on advice from artists and arts professionals; it also works cooperatively with federal and provincial cultural agencies and departments. The Canada Council answers to Parliament through the minister of Canadian heritage and is called upon periodically to appear before parliamentary committees. It makes an annual report to Parliament. In 1995 the new strategic plan, *The Canada Council: A Design for the Future,* was published.

The Canada Council, like the National Endowment for the Arts in the United States or the Arts Council in the United Kingdom, has played a vital role in the cultural development of the modern nation-state. This cannot be quantified, but among the important beneficiaries of the largesse of the Canada Council are the Stratford Festival, the Royal Winnipeg Ballet, the Canadian Opera Company, and countless less-well-known professional and amateur organizations. Also significant is the assistance given for publication of works in the humanities and allied fields.

CANADA EAST. *See* Lower Canada; Québec.

CANADA FIRST. The first, theoretically nonpartisan group dedicated to advancing the cause of national unity based on patriotism, Canada First was born of distrust of the Conservatives and Sir John A. Macdonald (q.v.). Its origins date from 1868, when five young men met in Ottawa to discuss questions of national unity: William A. Foster, a Toronto barrister; Henry J. Morgan; Charles Mair of Lanark, Ontario; Robert Haliburton of Halifax, son of the author Thomas Haliburton (q.v.); and Col. George T. Denison, later president of the British Empire League in Canada. All in their late twenties or early thirties, these men formed the Canada First party. Denison wrote: "Nothing could show more clearly the hold that confederation had taken of the imagination of young Canadians than the fact that, night after night, five young men should give up their time and their thoughts to discussing the higher interests of their country, and it ended in our making a solemn pledge to each other that we would do all we could to advance the interests of our native land; that we would put our country first, before all personal, or political, or party considerations; that we would change our party affiliations as often as the true interest of Canada required it." Until Canada had a patriotic spirit, they believed, no real progress could be made towards building up a strong and powerful community. History showed them, they said, that great countries were based upon a patriotic spirit. They therefore were among the first Canadian nationalists to understand that at that time confederation was a creation without a soul, without a spirit that animated the nation, without a national identity.

The five were actually "Ontario First" in many ways. They published a monthly *The Canadian Monthly and National Review* and a weekly *The Nation*. They attracted the Liberal Edward Blake (q.v.) to their group. They had an interest in enlarging the Canadian dominions to the west and to the north. They were attracted to the idea of West Indian union with Canada. They wanted electoral, ballot, and legislative reforms along Chartist and later Fabian lines. Minority representation, immigration, militia reform, and more economic management of public affairs were also preached. Finally, and here they were most successful, they sought the imposition of a tariff, a duty applied to certain imports that would make them so expensive as to encourage Canadian industry. The group eventually lost its momentum; Blake did not supply the hoped-for enthusiasm, and the national policy of the protective tariff was introduced by Macdonald's party in 1879, thus taking the wind out of the sails of the Canada First group, and their influence gradually died away. *See* National Anthem.

CANADA HEALTH ACT. More correctly known as the Medical Care Act (1966), this act owed its origin to the Saskatchewan experience: Saskatchewan's Co-operative Commonwealth Federation implemented a Medicare program in 1962. Advice to Ottawa was also provided by Justice Emmett Hall, who headed the Royal Commission on Health Services. This has been called Saskatchewan's gift to Canada. The Canada Health Act incorporated principles of comprehensiveness, universality, portability, and provincial administrative responsibility. National medical services insurance began in July 1968, with British Columbia and Saskatchewan qualifying immediately. By 1972 all provinces and territories had implemented some form of Medicare. The plan, according to the Canada Health Act, "is administered and operated on a non-profit basis by a public authority appointed or designated by the government of the province . . . that is responsible in respect of the administration and operation of the plan to the government of the province for that purpose." Under such a scheme, boards such as the Ontario Health Insurance Plan are partners with the federal Ministry of Health and Welfare, which seeks to maintain the universality of the program in Canada as a constitutional right and obligation.

CANADA WEST. *See* Ontario; Upper Canada.

CANADIAN AIR FORCE (CAF). The Canadian air services had their foundation in the highly publicized World War I (q.v.) exploits of Canadian air aces and the threat of U-boats on the Atlantic Coast. Nearly 20,000 Canadians served with the Royal Flying Corps (RFC) and the Royal Naval Air Service (RNAS). The government of Sir Robert Borden (q.v.) authorized the formation of the Royal Canadian Naval Air Service and the Canadian Air Force to cooperate with the Canadian Expeditionary Force (q.v.). Both of these services, however, were disbanded after the war. After World War I, an Air Board was set up to organize Canadian air administration. In 1922, the Air Board was absorbed by the Ministry of National Defence under the command of a director of the CAF who reported directly to the army chief of staff. However, it was found that a more extensive organization was required, and the Royal Canadian Air Force (RCAF) was founded in April 1924. The RCAF remained small between the world wars and carried out mostly civilian tasks. Only in 1928 were small numbers of combat aircraft purchased, and no first-line aircraft were operational in 1939 save a few Hawker Hurricanes.

One of the chief contributions of the RCAF in World War II (q.v.) was the British Commonwealth Air Training Plan (q.v.) to train aircrew for the war effort. Canadian schools graduated 131,553 aircrew of which 72,835 were Canadian. The RCAF expanded quickly, eventually to more than 250,000 personnel, of which 94,000 served overseas. RCAF squadrons participated in the Battle of Britain, the Desert Campaign, the Far East, the Battle of the Atlantic (q.v.), and the strategic bombing campaign over Germany. More than 17,000 RCAF crewman were killed during the war, 10,000 in Bomber Command alone.

The RCAF demobilised quickly after the war and by the end of 1946 numbered only 13,000 of all ranks. It received its first jet fighters in 1948, De Haviland Vampires. Although no RCAF fighter squadrons served in Korea, some officers flew with the United States Air Force. In the early 1950s, the Canadian government committed itself to the formation of an air division in Europe. Several fighter squadrons, consisting of Canadian-built Sabre fighters, were deployed in Europe and helped train allied air forces. Also, the Canadian-designed and -built CF-100 Canuck all-weather interceptor was operational and stayed in service until 1981. The fighter was built under the terms of NORAD for the joint Canadian-American defence of the aerospace of North American against Soviet bombers. However, brief prosperous days ended when the CF-105 Avro Arrow jet-fighter was cancelled by the Diefenbaker (q.v.) government in 1959. The Arrow had a unique design that was years ahead of its time. From then on, the RCAF would fly foreign-designed and -built aircraft.

In the 1960s, the RCAF purchased CF-104 Starfighters and retained a declining role in Europe. In 1968, with unification, the RCAF was amalgamated into the Canadian Armed Forces (q.v.), lost its formal title, and became Air Command. In 1984, the Progressive Conservative government purchased 140 CF-18 fighters to replace the force's ageing air fleet. By the late 1980s only two fighter squadrons were based in Germany, and by the end of 1993, both were gone. In the Persian Gulf War (q.v.), several Canadian fighter squadrons participated in patrolling the Persian Gulf to support UN ground forces. CF-18s were in operations in Yugoslavia, 1999. Air Command is a small, but a highly professional force ranked among the best in the world. The RCAF Memorial Museum (opened in 1984) is at CFB Trenton, Ontario. *See also* Barker, William George; Bishop, William ("Billy") Avery.

CANADIAN ARMED FORCES. The Canadian armed services have generally been small, highly professional forces that have been expanded in times of international crisis. Canadian soldiers, sailors, and airmen participated in both world wars, in Korea, and in all peacekeeping efforts under the auspices of the United Nations since 1945. Canada is one of the founding members of the North Atlantic Treaty Organization (NATO) (q.v.) and is partner with the United States in the North American Air Defence Command (NORAD) (q.v.). Until the end of the Cold War, the primary task of the Canadian Armed Forces was to help provide credible conventional forces in Europe and to participate in joint naval task forces in the North Atlantic. Currently, the Canadian Armed Forces employs over 83,000 officers and enlisted personnel on active duty while maintaining over 65,000 reservists on inactive status. Defence spending in 1992 was $12.42 billion. However, in recent budgets defence spending has been steadily decreasing and the active armed forces are due to number just over 60,000 by the end of the decade. *See also* Canadian Air Force; Canadian Army; Canadian Navy.

CANADIAN ARMY. The first militia (q.v.) formed on Canadian soil was implemented by Governor Frontenac (q.v.) in New France (q.v.) in 1669. After the conquest of the French colony by Britain in 1759–60, the British government maintained the militia system and called it to service in 1763 and again in 1775. Early militia were also raised in Nova Scotia, Newfoundland, and Upper Canada. Militia units fought in the War of 1812 (q.v.) and aided in the suppression of the 1837 rebellions (q.v.). The Militia Act of 1855 formalized the militia system in Canada West and East (present-day Ontario and Québec). The U.S. Civil War forced Canadian governments to take defence more seriously and, accordingly, the size of the militia was increased to 35,000 men. In 1866, 20,000 militia warded off Fenian raiders (q.v.) in 1866.

After confederation in 1867, the militia system was retained and increased to 40,000 in all arms. Two battalions of militia aided in putting down the 1870 Red River rebellion (q.v.). In 1874, the Royal Military College of Canada (RMC) was founded at Kingston, Ontario, and a permanent, professional force was established.

The suppressing of the 1885 Northwest rebellion (q.v.) triggered important changes and professionalization of the Canadian militia. One thousand men were sent to aid Britain's efforts in the South African War (q.v.) in 1900. Minister of Militia Sir Frederick Borden further reformed the militia, replacing a British general with the Militia Council and placing a Canadian, Col. W. D. Otter, as the first chief of the General Staff. In 1909, the Canadian militia was fixed to British standards in all aspects of modern developments, including staff structure.

In 1914, the permanent force numbered 3,000, with a further 60,000 militia. Upon the outbreak of World War I (q.v.), the Army was expanded greatly and five full divisions were sent overseas in the Canadian Expeditionary Force (q.v.). After the war, the army was reduced to 4,000 and it received few modern arms. Expansion began again in 1936 when militia units were rearmed. In World War II (q.v.), Canada mobilized over

750,000 men, and five divisions were sent overseas while three remained for home defence. Canadians fought in Hong Kong, in the Italian campaign, in the Dieppe Raid (q.v.), and in northwest Europe. In 1945, the Army's strength was fixed at 25,000. However, in 1951, it was once more forced to expand due to Canada's involvement in the Korean Conflict (q.v.). The standard of strength was raised to 52,000. Until very recently Canadian Armed Forces (q.v.) maintained a reinforced brigade in Europe. Since 1956 Canadian Forces have also maintained a very active and taxing role in peacekeeping. In 1993, more than 2,200 Canadian Forces personnel were deployed on peacekeeping missions worldwide, the most prominent being in the former Yugoslav republics. The Canadian Army contains many historic regiments and units, including the Royal 22nd, the Royal Canadian Regiment, the Princess Patricia's, Lord Strathcona's, the Royal Highland Fusiliers of Canada, and the Seaforth Highlanders.

CANADIAN BROADCASTING CORPORATION (CBC). Established in 1936 by act of Parliament to control broadcasting in Canada, succeeding the Canadian Radio Broadcasting Commission (1933–36), the CBC acted as a bulwark against intrusion of foreign elements and a sponsor of made-in-Canada programs, fostering a sense of national consciousness and bringing English- and French-speaking groups closer together. In 1968, the Broadcasting Act was passed, updating the role of the CBC. The act stipulated that the Canadian broadcasting system should be effectively owned and controlled by Canada so as to safeguard, enrich, and strengthen the cultural, political, social, and economic fabric of Canada. The CBC is publicly owned and an advocate of Canadian programs. CBC also operates northern native-language programs and CBC International.

CANADIAN COAST GUARD. The Coast Guard was founded as the Marine Branch of the Department of the Marine and Fisheries in 1867 in order to relegate maritime traffic and navigation in Canadian waters. The early Coast Guard operated several ships and aided in mapping navigational hazards and enforcing Canadian maritime jurisdiction. In 1936, the Coast Guard came under the control of the newly formed Ministry of Transport and was officially renamed the Canadian Coast Guard in 1962. Responsibilities include icebreaking on Canadian waterways, the St. Lawrence seaway system, search and rescue, ship inspections, and navigational aids. Currently, the Coast Guard is staffed by 6,200 employees in five regional offices, operates 56 oceangoing vessels, 35 helicopters, 74 small rescue craft, and four hovercraft, and manages tens of thousands of navigation aids and monitors maritime traffic around Canada's busy ports. In early 1998 the government announced its intention to purchase new Cormorant helicopters for the Coast Guard.

CANADIAN EXPEDITIONARY FORCE (CEF). The CEF was established when the Canadian government decided to send an expeditionary force of one infantry division to the aid of Britain after World War I (q.v.) erupted. A force of 31,000 men sailed from Québec in October of 1914 and, after extensive training on Salisbury Plain, England, were sent to France in 1915. By late 1916, the Canadian Corps of four divisions had earned a reputation as being ferocious fighters. In all, 619,636 served in the CEF. Exploits of the CEF furthered Canada's sense of identity. *See also* Canadian Army; Vimy Ridge.

CANADIAN NATIONAL RAILWAYS (CNR). A Crown Corporation created by the Unionist government of Sir Robert Borden (q.v.) in 1919. Between 1919 and 1923, the government consolidated a number of railways including the National Transcontinental Railway and the Intercolonial Railway. The organization of the company was complete by 1923. Canadian National played a role in the earliest development of government-owned radio broadcasting in Canada and the establishment of Trans-Canada Airlines (now Air Canada). *See also* Canadian Northern Railway.

CANADIAN NAVY. Canada's navy was created by the Naval Service Act of 1910. The Royal Canadian Navy (RCN) was to be managed by the Ministry of the Naval Service, a department of the Ministry of Marine and Fisheries, and be under the command of a Naval Staff of not less in rank than rear admiral. It was to fall under the command of the Admiralty in London upon declaration of war but would be administered from Ottawa. It was to use the main bases at Halifax, Nova Scotia, and Esquimalt, British Columbia. Two cruisers were acquired from the Royal Navy—HMCS *Niobe* for the Atlantic coast and HMCS *Rainbow* on the Pacific—principally for training purposes. The naval question of the era contributed to the fall of the government of Prime Minister Sir Wilfrid Laurier (q.v.) in 1911.

The RCN formed coastal patrols against U-boats during the World War I (q.v.), but most naval personnel—an estimated 10,000—served with its parent service, the Royal Navy. After 1918, the Navy faced severe fiscal restraints and was forced to fight for its existence. Despite cutbacks, Comm. Walter Hose (q.v.) established the Royal Canadian Naval Volunteer Reserve, which was to prove vital during the subsequent wartime expansion. Also in the 1930s, modern destroyers were purchased, giving the Navy new weaponry. In 1939 when World War II (q.v.) broke out, the RCN possessed 11 warships and 3,000 officers and men; by 1945 the navy had 365 ships in commission and 100,000 personnel. Canadian corvettes, such as HMCS *Sackville*, now a Canadian national naval memorial in Halifax, played a heroic, legendary role in convoy protection in the Battle of the Atlantic (q.v.). The RCN contributed half of the antisubmarine escorts in the North Atlantic and was responsible for the sinking of 52 German U-boats and one Italian submarine. The RCN also deployed forces to patrol the English Channel and to support the Normandy landings in 1944. RCN ships also served in the Mediterranean.

After 1945, the government of Prime Minister Mackenzie King (q.v.) decided to construct a balanced fleet, including naval aviation, to contribute to Canada's role in the North Atlantic Treaty Organization (q.v.). However, the antisubmarine role remained strong. Budgetary constraints in the 1960s and 1970s saw the elimination of the Navy's last aircraft carrier, HMCS *Bonaventure*, in 1970. The naval air arm was limited to helicopters embarked aboard newly built destroyers. As time wore on, defence budgets cut even deeper and no new ships entered Canadian service after 1974 until 1991 when the new patrol frigate HMCS *Halifax* and her 11 sisters were commissioned. The Defence White Paper undertaken by the Progressive Conservative government in the mid-1980s sought to change the face of the Navy by the possible purchase of 10 to 12 nuclear-propelled submarines from either Britain or France. However, the cost was too high for Canada to bear. Since the end of the Cold War, like other NATO navies, the Canadian naval service has been left searching for a role. During the Persian Gulf War (q.v.), several Canadian warships, including a destroyer tender, participated in the naval task force in the Persian Gulf, supporting the ground troops in Saudi Arabia.

In 1968, the Canadian Navy was unified with the other services into the Canadian Armed Forces (q.v.). The Navy became Maritime Command with its headquarters in Halifax and, since 1995, Ottawa. Maritime Command is a small, though highly skilled force which has established itself as a highly capable antisubmarine fleet. In recent years several pressing issues required attention, namely the replacement of the Navy's elderly *Oberon* class diesel submarines and the replacement of the ageing helicopter fleet. Hopes to replace the Sea King helicopters (for antisubmarine work) were dashed when the new Liberal government cancelled the planned purchase of EH-101 helicopters in late 1993. *See also Haida*, HMCS.

CANADIAN NORTHERN RAILWAY. Founded by William Mackenzie and Donald Mann in 1899, went from one line in Manitoba to a transcontinental railway. It was popular with farmers, who were granted low rates, and with Western provincial governments. Mackenzie and Mann eventually decided to expand to the Pacific coast and to Montréal, but incurred massive debts before World War I (q.v.). Ottawa bought out Mackenzie and Mann, and the railway became part of Canadian National Railways (q.v.).

CANADIAN PACIFIC RAILWAY (CPR). Under terms of union, a rail link was promised to British Columbia (q.v.) when it entered confederation in 1871. Start of the project was delayed by the Pacific Scandal (q.v.) in 1873, involving Sir John A. Macdonald's (q.v.) government. Alexander Mackenzie's (q.v.) Liberal government was financially strapped as it took office from the Conservatives in 1873. When Macdonald's Conservatives regained power in 1878, they turned to a new group of financiers to develop a company to build the rail line. The company became the Canadian Pacific Railway in 1881. In 1881 Canada gave the CPR $25,000,000 and 25,000,000 acres to facilitate completion of the transcontinental line. Under the guidance of William Van Horne, construction proceeded rapidly and by November 1885 the last spike (q.v.) was driven at Craigellachie, British Columbia. Montréal was thereby linked with Port Moody, British Columbia. The railway proved profitable from the beginning and became the basis for the Canadian Pacific enterprises in shipping, air transport, mining and smelting, telecommunications, land development, forestry, and other industries.

CANADIAN SECURITY INTELLIGENCE SERVICE (CSIS). *See* Secret Service.

CANOL PIPELINE. Canol is short for Canadian oil. Built 1942 to 1944 from Norman Wells, Northwest Territories, to Whitehorse, Yukon, to supply oil products in defence of Alaska.

CAPE BRETON ISLAND. Discovered by fishermen from Brittany during the French regime, Cape Breton Island was called Île Royale. In 1773 Highland Scots settlers arrived in the *Hector* at Cape Breton. Cape Breton was an independent British colony from 1784 to 1820, when it was united with Nova Scotia (q.v.). *See also* Louisbourg.

CARHAGOUHA. Fortified village of the Bear people of the Huron (q.v.) and site of the first Christian mass celebrated in what is now the province of Ontario, 12 August 1615. The site is estimated to be a mile or more northwest of the present village of Lafontaine, Ontario. The celebrant was Father Le Caron, S.J., and present at the time was the noted explorer Samuel de Champlain (q.v.). Another observer, Father Le Clerq, related that "the raising of the Cross, the sign of our redemption, was hailed with volleys of musketry and accompanied by acts of thanksgiving, the Te Deum being chanted for the first time in that barbarous country." *See also* Huronia; Jesuits.

CARLETON, SIR GUY [1st BARON DORCHESTER] (1724–1808). British soldier. Carleton served under James Wolfe (q.v.) during the Seven Years' War (q.v.) and fought on the Plains of Abraham in 1759. As governor of Québec in 1775, he successfully defended the city against the Americans under Benedict Arnold, whom he subsequently defeated again on Lake Champlain in 1776. Carleton was governor of Québec in 1775–77, 1786–89, and 1793–96. Architect of the Québec Act (q.v.), he was also governor of Lower Canada (q.v.) 1791–96. His efforts in Canada contributed to Britain's success in keeping Québec under British rule. *See also* American Revolution, War of the.

CARMACK, GEORGE WASHINGTON (1860–1922). Also known as "Lying George," Carmack is famous for discovering the first Klondike gold at Rabbit Creek (renamed Bonanza Creek), on 16 or 17 August 1896 (the Yukon celebrates August 17 as the anniversary of Carmack's discovery). He staked four claims on the Bonanza and recorded them at the North West Mounted Police Office at Fortymile. With him when he made his discovery were Skookum Jim Mason and Tagish Charlie, his Indian friends. Carmacks, Yukon, on the west bank of the Yukon River 176 kilometres north of Whitehorse, is named after him. He was born in Port Costa, Ca., and died in Vancouver, British Columbia, a relatively wealthy man.

CARR, EMILY (1871–1945). Artist and author. Born in Victoria, BC, Carr studied art for five years at the Westminster School of Art in London, England. She returned to Canada, opening a studio in Vancouver, and began to paint British Columbian landscape and native culture. In 1927, she exhibited some of her artwork in an exhibition of Canadian West Coast art in Ottawa. Later in life Emily wrote short stories about her adventures in native villages on the West Coast. Some of her books are *Klee Wyck, The Book of Small,* and *Growing Pains.* She became one of Canada's most famous artists and authors, and the subject of numerous biographies.

CARTIER, JACQUES (1491–1557). Mariner and explorer. Cartier examined the Gulf of St. Lawrence and the St. Lawrence River in three great voyages. In 1534, he circumnavigated the gulf. In 1536, he discovered the river as far as Hochelaga or Montréal, where he put up a cross. In his third voyage, 1541, this one in search of a mythical El Dorado, the kingdom of Saguenay, he added geographical knowledge of the area. Guided by natives such as Donnaconna (q.v.), and aided by their knowledge of how to combat scurvy and endure Canadian winters, Cartier charted the shores of eastern Canada for France and extended French and Christian claims there.

CARTIER, SIR GEORGE ÉTIENNE (1814–1873). Lawyer, politician, and an architect of Canadian Confederation. Cartier led the Bleu bloc of Canada East (Québec) and forged an alliance with John A. Macdonald (q.v.) in 1854, forming a government in the Province of Canada. Cartier recognized that French Canada's destiny lay in an alliance with English Canadians but, at the same time, believed that French Canadians needed (1) legislation to protect their culture and (2) economic improvement through transportation and commercial schemes. He was attorney-general for the Province of Canada and solicitor for the Grand Trunk Railway, and he advanced the cause of his people. In 1858 in the so-called "double shuffle," the Macdonald-Cartier ministry was reconstituted and remained until 1862. Cartier entered the Great Coalition of 1864 which advanced the confederation design. Cartier insisted on a bicameral legislative structure and saw an upper chamber, a Canadian Senate, as being necessary to protect French Canada's regional, linguistic, and ethnic needs. Macdonald reluctantly agreed. Cartier impressed upon French Canadians the need for their vote in confederation. However, many saw him as having sold out. He was defeated in 1872 during the patronage crisis over the Canadian Pacific Railway (q.v.). He died in 1873, the first great Québec federalist.

CARY, MARY SHADD (1823–1893). Editor and activist. Cary was the first black woman in North America to establish and edit a weekly newspaper. She was born in Wilmington, Delaware, and moved to Windsor, ONT, in 1851. In 1853, she established the *Provincial Freeman*. The newspaper covered all aspects of Black life in Canada.

CASGRAIN, THERESE (1896–1981). Feminist and reformer. Casgrain was born in Montréal and in 1921 started the campaigning in Québec for women's suffrage. In 1946 she joined the Co-operative Commonwealth Federation, serving as its provincial leader 1951–57. She was named to the Senate in 1970.

CHAMPLAIN, SAMUEL DE (1567?–1635). Mariner, explorer, geographer, and colonizer; called "the Father of New France." For 30 years Champlain painstakingly established France's presence in the New World. He explored the Bay of Fundy, the coast of Maine and elsewhere on the Atlantic coast, and the interior of the continent as far west as Georgian Bay and Lake Huron. He allied with certain native peoples, the Algonquins, against the Iroquois (q.v.). In 1608 he established a settlement at the St. Lawrence River narrows: Québec. He made his great western journey in 1615, to Georgian Bay in Lake Huron via the Ottawa and French Rivers. He secured an alliance with the Huron (q.v.). His charts, travel accounts, and histories are important contributions to learning. The greatest of French explorers in the early history of New France, it is surprising that his gravesite remains unknown in the city of Québec. His astrolabe is in Ottawa's Museum of Civilization.

CHARLOTTETOWN AGREEMENT. *See* Meech Lake Accord.

CHINESE. Profoundly important in building modern Canada, in terms of labour, capital, and professional and social institutions, Chinese first came to British Columbia during the 1858 gold rush. In 1860 about 7,000 lived in British Columbia. They came in increasing numbers during the construction of the Canadian Pacific Railway (q.v.). Most came as contract labourers. They came mainly from Guangdong province, near Guangzhou (Canton) and Hong Kong. After 1885 they were charged a "head tax." British Columbian and Canadian governments sought to restrict illegal immigration, particularly of Asiatics. On 1 July 1923, "Humiliation Day" in Chinese Canadian history, Chinese immigration was suspended altogether; this legislation was repealed in 1947. Chinese and East Indian Canadians gained the vote federally and provincially in 1947. In the 1980s Chinese came from Hong Kong in increasing numbers, and in 1996 became one of the top countries of origin of Canadian immigrants. Discrimination in education and the professions resulted in late entry. In 1957 Douglas Jung was elected the first Chinese Canadian MP. In 1991 there were 586,645 people of Chinese origin living in Canada. Chinese schools and benevolent societies exist in number.

CHRÉTIEN, JOSEPH-JACQUES JEAN (1934–). Lawyer and politician, Chrétien was first elected as a member of Parliament in 1963 as a Liberal.

He has served as a minister in charge of various departments, including Indian and Northern Affairs, Justice, and Finance. His budgets of 1978 were designed to encourage industrial growth and to fight inflation. In 1980, he successfully led Québec federal forces against René Levesque's (q.v.) Québec separatist cause. After Pierre Trudeau's (q.v.) resignation in 1984, Chrétien distanced himself from national politics and left public office. He was elected leader of the Liberal party in June 1990. On 28 October 1993, Chrétien was elected prime minister (Canada's 20th) as Liberals won a decisive victory. He was reelected 2 June 1997 with a reduced majority. His leadership style is avuncular but challenging.

CLARK, JOE (CHARLES JOSEPH) (1939–). Journalist, university lecturer, and politician. Clark was born in Alberta and elected a member of Parliament in 1972. He became leader of the Progressive Conservative party in 1976 and was leader of the opposition 1980–83. In 1979, he formed a short-lived government and became Canada's youngest prime minister. His party could not maintain the government on a fiscal bill, however, and he resigned office. His party lost the 1980 election to Pierre Trudeau's (q.v.) Liberals. He was defeated by Brian Mulroney (q.v.) in the desperate party leadership struggle of 1983. In 1984 he became secretary of state for external affairs and later served in the special role as constitutional advisor during the Charlottetown Accord arrangements.

CLEAR GRITS. Term given to a reform-minded political party mainly centred in southern Ontario in the 1850s. The Clear Grits were determined upon political reform and promoted the concept of representation by population (q.v.), "rep by pop." They also sought direct election to executive posts and secularization of the Clergy Reserves. This party promoted Canadian federalism and western expansion, and after confederation in 1867 formed a core of the Liberal party (q.v.). Important Clear Grits included George Brown and Alexander Mackenzie (qq.v.). *See also* Rouges.

COMMISSION ON BILINGUALISM AND BICULTURALISM, ROYAL. *See* Bilingualism and Biculturalism, Royal Commission on.

COMMISSION ON NATIONAL DEVELOPMENT IN THE ARTS, LETTERS, AND SCIENCES, ROYAL. *See* Massey Report.

COMMONWEALTH CONFERENCES. *See* Commonwealth of Nations.

COMMONWEALTH OF NATIONS. The Commonwealth of Nations derives from the British Empire, specifically the Second British Empire (the reconstructed British Empire after the War of the American Revolution [q.v.]). The British Commonwealth of Nations emerged as a result of colonial nationalism and the move towards responsible government (q.v.). By 1931 membership had become voluntary. In the interim, however, colonial autonomy had to be *won*, for London invariably wanted to maintain uniform control over shipping, tariffs, armed forces, constitutional arrangements, and foreign treaty-making. World War I (q.v.) produced a crisis: empire solidarity vs. colonial/dominion nationalism. At the Imperial War Conference in 1917, at Sir Robert Borden's (q.v.) initiative, it was agreed that a redefinition of the British Empire was necessary.

The beginnings of the process date from 1887. Anniversary celebrations of Queen-Empress Victoria's accession to the throne (1887 and 1897) offered opportunities to Britain and the colonial premiers to gather to discuss matters of mutual interest, especially trade, communications, and defence. These events were important in Canadian foreign policy making and in Canada's growth as an autonomous nation.

In 1907 a regular arrangement of intra-imperial consultation was agreed upon, with a secretariat and meetings every four years. Sir Wilfrid Laurier (q.v.) required that Canada have prior consultation before imperial commitment. In 1911, the state of European relations was the focus of Sir Edward Grey's address. In 1926, the Imperial Conference accepted the Balfour Report definition of the Empire Commonwealth of that era. The report provided the dominions with equal status, in no way subordinate to one another, and united by a common allegiance to the Crown. In the British Statute of Westminster (1931; q.v.) these principles were extended to British law and adopted, though not always immediately by the dominions.

In 1930, the Imperial Conference rejected Prime Minister R. B. Bennett's (q.v.) call for imperial preferential tariffs. In 1932, at the Ottawa conference (q.v.), only bilateral arrangements were agreed upon. New principles of the Commonwealth were adopted after World War II (q.v.), including antiracist government policies. Looking back over the history of the Commonwealth, Canada's role was prominent in these areas: responsible government, federalism, judicial interpretation, creation of a dominion navy, plurality of official languages, and international appointments (*see* Massey Report). Noteworthy, too, is the fact that the first secretary general of the Commonwealth was a Canadian, Arnold Smith. The Commonwealth of Learning, an institute of distance education and organized by the Commonwealth of Nations, is headquartered in Vancouver.

COMMUNIST PARTY OF CANADA (CPC). Founded in Guelph, Ontario, in 1921, the CPC exists in various guises, names, and factions. It was known as the Workers' Party in the early days. Locked up in Québec in 1937 and banned federally in 1940 under the War Measures Act (q.v.), the CPC nonetheless gave Canadian labour many leaders and was influential in the Canadian Congress of Labour. Among its most devout followers were Fred Rose, MP (convicted in the Igor Gouzenko [q.v.] spy case), long-time leader Tim Buck, and Dr. Norman Bethune (q.v.), active in the Spanish Civil War and Chinese wars. Beginning in the 1950s, revelations about Stalin, Soviet interventions in Hungary and Czechoslovakia, and Sino-Soviet splits led to continual disaffections, divisions, and defections. Revelations subsequent to the collapse of Socialist and Communist governments in Central and Eastern Europe and in the Balkans 1989–91 further discredited communism in theory and in practice. The CPC remains active in disseminating certain information about feminist, aboriginal, pacifist, and tenants' rights and interests.

COMPAGNIE DES CENT-ASSOCIÉS (Hundred Associates Company). Organized by Cardinal Richelieu in 1627, this French colonizing company aimed to settle 4,000 colonists in New France (q.v.) within a 15-year period. The government promised protection for three years. The company received a French monopoly of the fur trade (q.v.) and French claims to North America, from Arctic waters to the Florida Gulf. Pirates captured the first two fleets of emigrants. Québec fell to English forces in 1629. The charter was revoked in 1663 when Canada became a royal province. Only 2,500 settlers came out under the auspices of the Hundred Associates.

CONSTITUTION ACT OF 1867 (BRITISH NORTH AMERICA ACT). This act divided the Province of Canada into Ontario and Québec and added Nova Scotia and New Brunswick to form "one Dominion under the name of Canada." The act set out the nature and form of government, including a division of powers which gave the federal power distinct control, under Section 91, of "peace, order and good government." It allocated powers to federal and provincial governments. It also established minority language and minority education rights. As well, it provided for the admission to Canada of new provinces. Amended many times (*see* Constitutional History), in 1982 this act was incorporated into and updated as the Constitution Act of 1982 (q.v.). By establishing an amending formula, patriating the constitution, and adding a Charter of Rights and Freedoms, the constitution became, at last, a fully made-in-

Canada instrument of constituted government. *See also* Dominion of Canada.

CONSTITUTION ACT OF 1982. The most important modern measure of Canadian constitutional process of the 20th century, this statute (effective 17 April 1982) had three important results: it (1) "patriated" the British North America Act; (2) instituted the Canadian Charter of Rights and Freedoms; and (3) introduced an amending formula. The Constitution Act was passed by the Canadian Parliament and signed by the sovereign. Enabling legislation preceded it in the British Parliament, closing off completely any residual rights of imperial legislation over Canadian affairs.

Reaching the terms of a made-in-Canada constitutional reform was a hectic and divisive process. Not only did it pit the federal authority against the provinces but it also involved a struggle not only within Québec but between Québec at large and the rest of Canada. Court cases launched by provincial governments generally favoured the federal authority to reform the constitution unilaterally but also recognized provincial rights within the federation. Native voices and female militancy also helped shape the process, and terms of the charter recognized Indians, Inuits and Métis (qq.v.) as "aboriginal peoples" of Canada. Québec's non-agreement to the measure meant that constitutional discussions would continue, and to date there have been two abortive attempts: the Meech Lake Accord (q.v.) in 1987 and the Charlottetown Accord in 1992. *See also* Constitutional History.

CONSTITUTIONAL HISTORY. Building on existing arrangements in 1867, the British North America Act (or Constitution Act of 1867 [q.v.]) brought Ontario, Québec, Nova Scotia, and New Brunswick into a federation—the Dominion of Canada (q.v.)—effective 1 July 1867. Rupert's Land and North Western Territory were added in 1870, extending Canadian dominion to the continental divide north of 49 degrees north latitude, excluding the High Arctic (added 1880). Manitoba (1870), British Columbia (1871), and Prince Edward Island (1873) were later additions to the provinces of Canada. By the Constitution Act of 1870, Rupert's Land and the Northwestern Territory (subsequently combined as the Northwest Territories) were declared federal territories subject to Ottawa; also by this measure Parliament was empowered to create new provinces out of territories. By the Adjacent Territories Order (1880), all British possessions and territories in North America, specifically the High Arctic, were added to the dominion. By the Constitution Act of 1886, the territories were given representation in Parliament (q.v.). In 1898 Yukon Territory (q.v.) was created out of the Northwest Territories. In 1905 Alberta and Saskatchewan became provinces and Manitoba's borders were expanded.

Meanwhile, by the Parliament of Canada Act (1875), Parliament was empowered to determine its own rules, privileges, and powers regardless of whether they exceeded the powers of the House of Commons of the United Kingdom. By the Constitution Act of 1915, Britain's parliament, for the first time, amended Canada's constitution in response to a draft bill prepared at Ottawa. Previous amendments had been prepared in London. The 1915 act defined Western Canadian representation in the Senate and minimum provincial representation in the Commons. By the Constitution Act of 1930, Ottawa transferred to the four western provinces lands and natural resources withheld at the time of their admission into confederation. By the Statute of Westminster (q.v.) of 1931, equality of status among the dominions, including Britain, was acknowledged.

By the Constitution Act of 1940, authority to legislate on unemployment insurance was transferred from provincial to federal authority. This was the first change since confederation in the allocation of powers to federal and provincial governments.

In 1949, the Newfoundland Act brought Newfoundland and Labrador into the federation to become Canada's 10th province. In 1960 a statute of the Parliament of Canada effected the Canadian Bill of Rights. Opposed by provincial governments, many of its provisions have since been embraced by the Charter of Rights and Freedoms (1982).

In 1964, by the Constitution Act of 1964, Parliament was empowered with unanimous approval of the provinces to pass laws on supplementary pension benefits so long as they did not affect provincial legislation. This permitted creation of the Canada Pension Plan and the Québec Pension Plan.

The Constitution Act of 1965 required senators to retire at the age of 75, that of 1974 established new rules for House of Commons representation, and those of 1975 (No. 1 and No. 2) increased the number of senators by giving one each to the Yukon and the Northwest Territories.

In 1982 the Constitution Act of 1982 (q.v.) established an amending formula (severing Canada's last constitutional tie to Westminster) and the Charter of Rights and Freedoms. Recent attempts at amendments (the Meech Lake Accord (q.v.) in 1987 and Charlottetown Agreement in 1992) have proved unsuccessful. *See also* Parliamentary System.

COOK, JAMES [CAPTAIN COOK, RN] (1728–1779). English naval officer, surveyor, and explorer born in Yorkshire, England. In June 1757 Cook passed his master's examinations. A varied service of patrols, conquests, and surveys took him to Halifax, Louisbourg, Québec, and Newfoundland during and immediately after the Seven Years' War (q.v.). He charted the St. Lawrence River (q.v.), a service which allowed the expedition under Maj. Gen. James Wolfe (q.v.) and Vice Adm. Sir Charles Saunders to dislodge the French from Canada. Cook made charts of Newfoundland which facilitated the cod fishery of the Grand Banks and the security of traffic coming in and out of the St. Lawrence, whether through the Strait of Belle Isle in the north or Cabot Strait on the south. His *New Chart of the River St. Lawrence* was published in 1760, and his sailing notes were published in the famous *North American Pilot* (1775).

After two great voyages to the Pacific, in 1776 he accepted the challenge to find the Northwest Passage. Cook searched for the western entrance on the northwest coast of North America and attempted to penetrate to the north and east via the Bering Strait. From 7 March to 18 August 1778, Cook's ships charted the coast from Oregon to the Bering Strait. He spent most of April at Nootka Sound, Vancouver Island, where he and his men compiled accounts of native life. Cook sailed to Unalaska and through the Bering Strait, then returned to Hawaii to winter. On 14 February 1779, an encounter with natives there cost Cook and four marines their lives. The rest of the crew returned to England from one of the longest voyages of discovery in history. Cook is better known in England, Australia, and New Zealand than in Canada—but his contributions to Canadian exploration and hydrography were immense.

CO-OPERATIVE COMMONWEALTH FEDERATION (CCF). *See* New Democratic Party.

CREE. *See* Plains Cree.

CUNARD, SIR SAMUEL (1787–1865). Halifax-born founder of British and North American Royal Mail Steam Packet Company in 1839, which won lucrative Admiralty and postal contracts. Cunard Steamship Company, which dominated the Atlantic passenger trade, was founded in 1878.

CURRIE, SIR ARTHUR WILLIAM (1875–1933). Born in Napperton, Ontario, Currie was the first Canadian-born commander of the Canadian Corps in World War I (q.v.). He joined the militia (q.v.) in 1893, and by the outbreak of World War I in 1914 he was a lieutenant colonel. By 1915 he was commanding the 2nd Canadian Infantry Brigade, building a reputation for himself and his men. In 1917, he became a lieutenant general and Corps commander. Currie's most notable legacy was his leadership in the war's last hundred days in 1918. He led the Canadian Corps against the Germans, sustaining heavy casualties. The Canadian Corps made spectacular gains and inflicted heavy losses. Currie entered Mons, Belgium, at the head of his troops as the armistice came into effect. *See also* Canadian Expeditionary Force.

-D-

D'AQUINO, THOMAS (1940–). Possibly the most influential private citizen in Canada, D'Aquino was born in Trail, British Columbia, and educated at the University of British Columbia, Queen's University, and the London School of Economics and Political Science. He studied politics, international affairs, history, and law. One of Canada's foremost policy strategists and one of its effective ambassadors abroad, he first served as special assistant to Prime Minister Pierre Trudeau (q.v.) before working in London and Paris on strategic business problems. From 1975 to 1985 he ran a consulting firm on international banking, giving legal advice to various investors in Canada and abroad. In 1981 D'Aquino became president and chief executive officer of the Business Council on National Issues (founded in 1976 as the senior voice of Canadian business on public policy issues in Canada and internationally). He has headed the BCNI's numerous studies on Canadian competitiveness. He took a major role in the free trade (q.v.) debate, backing both Canadian-U.S. free trade and NAFTA. He also took a key stance in national debates on strengthening the Canadian constitution and in national and provincial debt reductions. An avowed federalist, D'Aquino argues for Canadian competitiveness in a global economy. He has, it is said by some, the capacity to make and break governments.

DAVIES, (WILLIAM) ROBERTSON (1913–1995). Novelist, playwright, essayist, critic, and Master of Massey College; born in Thamesville, Ontario. One of Canada's most famous international writers, Davies is best known for *The Deptford Trilogy: Fifth Business* (1970), *The Maticore* (1972), and *World of Wonders* (1975). His book *What's Bred in the Bone* (1985) was short-listed for the prestigious Booker prize.

DAVIS, JOHN (c.1550–1605). English mariner and explorer; the first European to discover Davis Strait between Greenland and Canada. Davies led the way for such explorers as Henry Hudson and William Baffin (q.v.). He was one of the most skilled navigators of the late 1500s. He invented a type of quadrant, a device used in navigation, and developed what became the standard ship's log.

From 1585 to 1587, Davis headed three expeditions in search of the Northwest Passage, a route through Canada to Asia. He discovered Davis Strait on his first trip. During his voyages, Davis explored the east coast of Baffin Island and the west coast of Greenland but did not find a route west. From 1591 to 1593, he tried to find a passage to Asia via the Strait of Magellan in South America. In 1605, he was killed by Japanese pirates.

DAWSON [formerly DAWSON CITY]. After discovery of gold at Bonanza Creek in 1896, a townsite was laid out at the junction of the Klondike and Yukon Rivers. The town was named for the director of the Geological Survey of Canada (q.v.), George Mercer Dawson (1849–1901). Dawson, declared the capital of the Yukon Territory (q.v.) in 1897, was supplanted by Whitehorse in 1951.

DE LA TOUR, MARIE JACQUELINE (1602–1645). Born in France, Marie married Charles de Saint-Aden de la Tour and lived in Acadia (now New Brunswick). She was the first European woman to settle in New Brunswick. With a small French garrison, she defended Fort la Tour against British soldiers courageously for four days, but was captured and placed in prison, where she died.

DIEFENBAKER, JOHN GEORGE (1895–1979). In June 1957 Diefenbaker led Progressive Conservatives to victory by a close margin. As prime minister, he called for another election and won by the greatest landslide in history.

Born 18 September 1895 in Neustadt, Ontario, his family moved to a Saskatchewan homestead when he was eight. In 1916 Diefenbaker received his M.A. in political science from the University of Saskatchewan. After serving in World War I (q.v.), he returned to the university for a law degree in 1919. He then resided in Prince Albert and became a criminal lawyer. In 1929 he married Edna Blower (she died in 1951; in 1953 he married Olive Palmer).

In 1940, Diefenbaker was elected to the House of Commons. In 1956 he became leader of the opposition. In the 1957 election, he became prime minister. In 1958, Diefenbaker campaigned against Liberal leader

Lester B. Pearson (q.v.). Diefenbaker inspired a "vision of a new and greater Canada," less economically dependent on the United States. Under his influence, the Republic of South Africa, because of its apartheid policy, was expelled from the Commonwealth of Nations. Reelected 1962 by a slim margin, Diefenbaker's government fell in 1963 on his refusal to accept nuclear weapons from the United States. Pearson became prime minister after the April elections. Diefenbaker remained opposition leader until 1967, when he was succeeded by Robert Stanfield. Diefenbaker was elected for a 13th term in the House of Commons in May 1979. He died 16 August 1979 in Ottawa.

DIEPPE RAID. On 19 August 1942, 4,963 Canadians of the 2nd Canadian Division, along with British commandos and a few American Rangers, landed at Dieppe, France. The result was a disaster with some 70 percent of the Canadians killed, wounded, or taken prisoner. It was the first major Canadian land involvement in World War II (q.v.). As well, it was the first amphibious landing on a large scale, a tactic which had not been attempted prior to Dieppe. The raid was a disaster because the Germans were alerted of the raid and were geographically advantaged. The lack of communication on the part of the Allied command furthered the demise of the raid. As the infantry landed on the beach at about 5:40 A.M., the Germans atop the cliff of the beach devastated the landing craft with machine gun and other fire and slaughtered those who got ashore. *See also* Canadian Army.

DOLLARD DES ORMEAUX, ADAM (1635–1660). Commandant of Montréal garrison. With 16 men, Dollard des Ormeaux fought Iroquois (q.v.) at Long Sault, Ottawa River, where he and his men died in a heroic struggle.

DOMINION OF CANADA. Established 1 July 1867 by the British statute known as the British North America Act (*see* Constitution Act of 1867). The original Dominion consisted of four provinces: Ontario, Québec, Nova Scotia, and New Brunswick. By the BNA Act, Québec and Ontario were created provinces. The 1867 arrangement marked the first phase of confederation. Subsequent additions of provinces were: Manitoba (1870), British Columbia (1871), Prince Edward Island (1873), Alberta and Saskatchewan (1905), and Newfoundland and Labrador (1949).

DONNACONNA (d.1539?). Chief of Stadacona until May 1536, Donnaconna felt wronged when Jacques Cartier (q.v.) erected a cross in

Gaspé Bay. Cartier took him, and Donnaconna's two sons, into exile. Donnaconna died in France.

DORION, SIR ANTOINE-AIMÉ (1818–1891). Politician; member of the Institut Canadien and the Parti Rouge. Elected to the Legislative Assembly in 1854, Dorion remained a member of the House of Commons until 1874. In 1858, he and George Brown (q.v.) formed the "Short Administration" and in 1863 he was the Lower Canadian leader in the Sandfield-Macdonald-Dorion government. Although originally opposed to confederation, he came to accept the idea. *See also* Rouges.

DOUGLAS, SIR JAMES (1803–1877). Fur trader, second governor of Vancouver Island (succeeding Richard Blanshard), and first governor of British Columbia. A "Scotch West Indian," Douglas was born in Demerara, British Guiana, the son of John Douglas, a Glasgow merchant with interests in sugar plantations and of a "free coloured woman." He received a good education in England and, at the age of 16, was apprenticed to the North West Company (q.v.). He joined the Hudson's Bay Company (q.v.) in the merger of 1821 and served in various places, including Fort Vancouver. In the service of the Hudson's Bay Company, from which he retired in 1858, he headed Company operations on the Pacific Coast for much of the 1840s and 1850s. He founded Fort Victoria, Vancouver Island, in 1843. Firm, vigorous and despotic, Douglas shaped the close relations between business and government that characterizes British Columbia history. He became governor of Vancouver Island in 1851, lieutenant-governor of the Queen Charlotte Islands in 1852, and governor of British Columbia in 1858. His new responsibilities for the Queen Charlottes and British Columbia were directly related to the discovery of gold. Douglas retired in 1863, and was created Knight Commander of the Bath. He toured Europe for a time and then spent the rest of his life quietly in Victoria with his Métis wife, Lady Amelia Douglas. He died in Victoria and was buried there in Ross Bay Cemetery.

DOUKHOBORS. Greek Orthodox sect believing in a communal, democratic, nonmilitaristic, and nonconforming lifestyle. The Doukhobors called themselves Christians of the Universal Brotherhood. Prominent in Russia in the 18th and 19th centuries, they rejected the authority of both church and state and were consequently persecuted under Catherine II. They settled near the Sea of Azov, established thriving agricultural communities, refused military conscription, and again were persecuted. Their leader, Peter Veregin, was exiled to Siberia. Befriended by Leo

Tolstoy, they emigrated to Saskatchewan (7,000 in 1898–99) and were joined by Veregin. Beginning in 1908, they spread to southeastern British Columbia. Divisions beset them, and nudist strikes and destruction of public bridges resulted in police action against them. Veregin was linked with a time bomb in 1924 and imprisoned and was succeeded by his son, also named Peter Veregin, who died in 1939. The second Peter recommended abandoning communal ways and adjusting to Canadian life. The Union of the Doukhobors of Canada was established in 1945; the radical wing, the Sons of Freedom became separate shortly thereafter.

DUMONT, GABRIEL (1837–1906). Born in Red River, Dumont, a great hunter and horseman, became a leader of the Métis (q.v.). He did not participate in the Red River Rebellion (q.v.) in 1870. Dumont became adjutant-general of the 300-man Métis Army in the Northwest Rebellion (q.v.) in 1885. He was steadfastly loyal to leader Louis Riel (q.v.) and believed in Riel's capacity to shape events. He used guerrilla tactics and surprise ambushes to secure victories at Duck Lake and Fish Creek, but at Batoche the Métis were overwhelmed by a large Canadian Militia (q.v.) force. Dumont fled to the United States, but returned after the amnesty of 1888.

DUNCAN, WILLIAM (1832–1918). Yorkshire-born lay member of the Church of England–affiliated Church Missionary Society. Duncan established the Metlakatla mission near Fort Simpson, British Columbia, in 1862. A social revolutionary and Victorian evangelical, he transformed Tsimshian (q.v.) culture. A dispute with the parent society and the Church of England led him to take some of his adherents to Annette Island, Alaska, 1887.

DUNLOP, WILLIAM "TIGER" (1792–1848). Born in Scotland, Dunlop arrived in Québec in 1813 and became an army surgeon in the War of 1812 (q.v.). He described his experiences at Prescott, Gananoque, Cornwall, Niagara, and the Penetanguishene Road in his *Recollections of the American War*, published serially in 1847 (and in book form 1905). He returned to England and then served in the British army in India (and is supposed to have tamed tigers with snuff—hence his nickname). Dunlop came back to Canada in 1826 with John Galt, a Scottish settlement promoter and poet, who played a conspicuous part in opening the Canada Company Tract in Western Ontario. Dunlop was "Warden of the Forests." He settled near Goderich on Lake Huron and became known locally as well as afar for his high good humour. He wrote for English and Scottish magazines. His *Statistical Sketches of Upper Canada* (1832) is his best-known work. He was a member of the Canadian Parliament 1841–46. In his last years he was superintendent of the Lachine Canal. He died at Lachine and was buried at Goderich.

DURHAM, EARL OF [JOHN GEORGE LAMBTON] (1792–1840). Governor general of Canada in 1838. Lord Durham was sent to Canada in the wake of the rebellions of 1837 (q.v.), but remained only a few months before resigning and returning to England. He wrote the *Report on the Affairs of British North America*, also commonly called Durham's Report (officially communicated to Parliament 11 February 1839), in which he proposed union of the two provinces and the granting of responsible government (q.v.).

-E-

EATON'S. Originally the Timothy Eaton Company, Eaton's may be said to date from 1869 when Irish shopkeeper Timothy Eaton bought out a small dry goods store on Yonge Street, Toronto. He set prices for all his goods, promising fair, affordable prices backed up by his guarantee: "Goods satisfactory or money refunded." In 1884 he introduced the mail-order catalogue (the mail-order business continued until 1976). By the time Timothy Eaton died in 1907, his company had opened a second store (in Winnipeg) and employed 9,000 people. The company was privately owned and the company's control passed down the family. Its history was shrouded in mystery. In the 1960s the company reached its zenith, with 30,000 employees. Eaton's lost much of its market share to Simpson's-Sears (later Sears), the Hudson's Bay Company (q.v.), Wal-Mart, Zellers, and others. In 1997 it sought bankruptcy protection, devised a major restructuring plan, and closed 22 of 86 stores in its first wave of closures. Several potential takeovers were considered.

In its time Eaton's was a Canadian institution, sure and confident. Timothy Eaton would not sell tobacco products in his stores, and curtains would be drawn on storefront windows on Sundays.

EDUCATION. The history of education in Canada is a main theme in Canada's political, social and economic development. During the French occupation in Canada, the process of educating was integrated into everyday life. The family was the basic unit in the social organization. Educational learning was conducted within this family unit. In the 17th and 18th centuries, a family depended upon each individual to make an economic contribution to the family. Therefore, skills such as farming and gardening were taught to children. In New France (q.v.), a large portion of the rural population could not read or write.

Towns and villages in New France developed formal education. The Jesuits (q.v.), Recollets, Ursulines (q.v.), Congregation of Notre Dame, and other religious orders provided elementary instruction in catechism, reading, writing, and mathematics. In the 1660s Bishop Laval (q.v.) founded the Semenaire de Québec, which later became Laval University.

After the Conquest of 1759–60, the British began to develop a school system that was outside the influence of religion, especially in Québec. The British viewed education as a tool of cultural change. As immigration increased in British North America, British statesmen in Canada increased efforts to assimilate immigrants and natives through education. By the 1840s, the foundations for present-day Canada's school system were being laid. Upper Canada College was founded in 1829. It remains a prominent independent school.

The industrialization of Canadian society impacted upon the development of the education system. Commercial and manufacturing developments spurred large increases in urban growth. Social leaders objected to idle children in city streets. Social promoters saw working-class idle children as a breeding ground for crime. They viewed education as a tool to teach social skills and argued that free schools would greatly benefit children by placing them in a setting that was conducive to social harmony. Schooling was intended to teach the shared values and mores of society. The creation of the public school system encouraged the development of the standardization of textbooks, teacher training, classroom organization, and curriculum.

With induction of public schooling, paid for through taxation, the number of students acquiring an education increased. Many children received educational training to the age of 16. The public school system, devised by school reformers such as Egerton Ryerson (q.v.), became the foundation of present-day English Canada's school system. *See also* Universities.

ELGIN AND KINCARDINE, EARL OF [JAMES BRUCE] (1811–1863). Governor general of Canada from 1847 to 1854. Lord Elgin was instructed to implement responsible government (q.v.) in Canada. He achieved this and sought to ensure a workable and equitable government by the inclusion of French Canadians in both government and civil appointments.

Lord Elgin faced two major crises while governor general. The first was the riot which followed the passage of the Rebellions Losses Act for Lower Canada in 1848. This riot resulted in the burning of the parliament buildings in Montréal.

The second crisis occurred in 1848 when a group of Montréal businessmen drafted the Annexation Manifesto (q.v.), which proposed annexation to the United States as the cure for the political and economic ills of the colony. A number of Tory members signed the document. Lord Elgin required those who held commissions from the Crown to abjure the manifesto or resign their offices.

He also saw the abolition of both clergy reserves and seigneurial tenure, as well as the successful negotiation of the Reciprocity (q.v.) Treaty of 1854.

ESPIONAGE. *See* Secret Service.

ESQUIMALT. The primary Canadian Pacific naval base, located in British Columbia. Esquimalt was discovered in the 1840s and used by ships of the Royal Navy. It served as headquarters of British warships in the eastern Pacific (c. 1862–1905) and had a graving dock (built 1887) and supply and repair facilities. *See also* Canadian Navy.

EVANGELINE. Fictitious heroine of Henry Wadsworth Longfellow's poem *Evangeline.* She epitomized Acadians (q.v.) in exile, expelled by the British as "security risks" in 1755.

EXPLORATION. Native peoples knew of their own locales, lakes, and watersheds. They aided Europeans in the exploration of Canada. Much of the exploration of Canada was undertaken by mariners in sailing vessels. This was true for the exploration of the Atlantic, Arctic, and Pacific coasts of Canada, and it was also true for the discovery of the Great Lakes. The interior was mainly explored by way of the canoe (and when necessary, overland in winter by snowshoe). Native technology and knowledge of techniques of winter survival aided Europeans in their discoveries.

In the modern era of Canada's history, exploration may be said to have begun with the Norse (q.v.), who visited the Eastern Seaboard in about the year A.D. 1000 and left behind, upon their withdrawal, the remnant of a settlement at L'Anse aux Meadows. St. Brendan might have discovered America and Prince Modoc may have done likewise, but these Irish and Welsh claimants, respectively, to priority of the discovery of America have not been substantiated in the written or archaeological record nor in any ethnological records. The Norse may be said to have left, in their sagas, the first record of exploration, but their literacy legacy is wildly unscientific. Christopher Columbus, the "Admiral of the Ocean Sea," is not known to have sailed in Canadian waters.

The first mariner to discover Canada in the early modern era, and to have left a record of achievement, was John Cabot (q.v.). In 1497, sailing for merchant adventurers of Bristol, backed by Henry VII of England, he made a landfall at (most likely) Cape Bonavista, though this is not established beyond a shadow of doubt. He discovered what he called, "New Founde Lande," hence the name Newfoundland. From this discovery dates the first English claim to sovereignty in North America. Follow-on discoveries by his son Sebastian were made. The discovery of cod on the Grand Banks was the greatest find of the Cabots.

In 1534, Jacques Cartier (q.v.), already an experienced mariner (he had sailed to Brazil and the Caribbean), made the first of three voyages to North America. He discovered the Gulf of St. Lawrence, Anticosti Island, Québec (or Stadacona), and Montréal (or Hochelaga). His three expeditions (1534, 1535–36, 1541) rank as splendid achievements of the Age of Discovery; they placed Acadia and Canada on the maps of the world, and they in turn showed the great river leading to the continental interior and perhaps to Asia. Cabot, Cartier, and many others hoped to find a route to Cathay and Cipangu. They and many others had to be disappointed in this. They found an empire totally different from that of China and Japan, though one of potentially equal if not greater wealth and power in the future. The dream of finding a Northwest Passage continued well into the 19th century.

French exploration of the continental interior is highlighted by Étienne Brûlé (q.v.), who explored Georgian Bay and Lake Huron; and by Samuel de Champlain (q.v.), who followed Brûlé into Georgian Bay ("the sweetwater sea," he called it) via the Ottawa and French Rivers. René-Robert Cavelier de La Salle, who explored the Mississippi and claimed Louisiana for France, sailed the Great Lakes in his *Griffon*, which was lost at sea in 1679, perhaps on Manitoulin Island. Jean Nicolet and Daniel Duluth are two French explorers who went to the western shores of the Great Lakes. Father Albanel, a Jesuit (q.v.), went overland from the St. Lawrence River (q.v.) to Hudson Bay. Fur Trader Pierre La Vérèndrye explored the heartland of the continent, the Red and Assiniboine waterways, and built fur posts in southern Manitoba.

Meanwhile, fur traders Pierre Radisson and Médard Chouart des Groseilliers, in the 1650s and 1660s had discovered the fur-bearing resources of the lands between Lake Superior and Hudson Bay, sparking off the founding of the Hudson's Bay Company (q.v.) in 1670. The company, by its charter, was obliged to prosecute further discoveries but tended to ignore this obligation. In the 1690s, however, it sent the boy explorer Henry Kelsey into the continental interior to draw off Indians for the northern trade on Hudson Bay. Kelsey was the first European to see the Great Plains. But until La Vérèndrye, already mentioned, pushed French trade and discoveries into the Red/Assiniboine area, the continental interior west of Lake Superior was unknown to the outside world.

The giants of Northwest discovery are: Peter Pond, who crossed Methye Portage into the upper reaches of the Athabasca River watershed (and who drew speculative maps); Sir Alexander Mackenzie (q.v.), who explored the Great River, later known as the Mackenzie River, and four years later went overland from Peace River to Dean Channel; and David Thompson (q.v.), the remarkable mapmaker and surveyor who discovered the headwaters of the Saskatchewan and Columbia Rivers. In 1806 Simon Fraser (q.v.) explored the river that bears his name. Samuel Black made discoveries on the Finlay and Yukon River (q.v.) areas. Many other "Nor'Westers" and HBC traders delineated the water systems of the West and North. These included, for the Arctic coast east of the Mackenzie River, Thomas Simpson and Warren Dease.

The search for the Northwest Passage continued. In 1778 Capt. James Cook (q.v.), RN, explored Nootka Sound, Vancouver Island, and Alaska. In 1792–94 Capt. George Vancouver (q.v.), RN, surveyed the Northwest coast, filling in the details on scientific charts. Spanish explorers Juan Pérez, Bruno de Hezeta, Jacinto Caamaño, Juan Francisco de la Bodega y Quadra, Alejandro Malaspina, and others did likewise for Spain but (unlike the British) did not choose to make public their charts and other findings.

Maritime fur traders such as John Meares explored parts of the coast; Meares left unreliable data based on his own dubious claims to primacy of discovery. Boston traders explored the Queen Charlotte Islands. Hydrographic surveying (first discovered by Pérez) by the Royal Navy in the 19th century completed most of the details of the Pacific coast of British Columbia.

From Hudson Bay, overland explorations were made by Samuel Hearne to the Coppermine River (1770). John Franklin (q.v.), RN, made three expeditions to northern Canada (1819–21, 1825–27, 1845–47). The

Northwest Passage may be said to have been discovered in all its completeness by Capt. Robert McClure, RN, when searching for the whereabouts of Franklin's third expeditionary party. The transit of the Northwest Passage was completed by Roald Amundsen in his vessel *Gjoa* in 1903–06. Vilhjalmur Stefansson (q.v.) made discoveries for Canada in the central and high Arctic (1913–17), extending Canadian claims there. Similarly, Joseph Bernier (q.v.) made maritime explorations of the northeastern Arctic. The Geological Survey of Canada (q.v.) completed much of the discovery of Canada in the later 19th and early 20th century. The Royal Engineers made discoveries of road routes in British Columbia. Canadian Pacific Railway (q.v.) surveyors explored passes in the Rocky Mountains for the transcontinental railway. Aerial photography was used to fill in many details to the map. Surveyors working for boundary commissions made many contributions to discovery in such places as the Alaska/Yukon border, the Great Lakes international boundary, and the Maine/New Brunswick border. *See also* Frontier; Fur Trade; Henday, Anthony.

-F-

FAMILY COMPACT. The socio-political elite of Upper Canada (q.v.). The term was coined by Marshall Spring Bidwell (q.v.), speaker of the House of Assembly in 1828. Members of the Family Compact had some, but not complete, family ties. The group controlled land grants, seats on councils, and seats in the legislature. They monopolized business and economic sectors of society and identified with the Anglican Church. The Family Compact was the target for reformers who (1) wished to secularize the Clergy Reserves and (2) sought financial support for public education (q.v.).

The Family Compact had the invariable support of the lieutenant-governor of Upper Canada. Reformers sought control of the "civil list," appointments on the public payroll. Protests sent to London were ignored or set aside. Agitation and armed rebellions in 1837 (q.v.) in Toronto and southwestern Ontario resulted in a triumph for the civil power. In 1838 Lord Durham (q.v.) was sent to the province and elsewhere in British North America to investigate the cause of grievances. The major reforms that were to come of the investigation were not instituted until the late 1840s.

FEDERAL-PROVINCIAL CONFERENCES. In 1887 the first of these conferences was held, convened by the premier of Québec, Honoré

Mercier. Resolutions passed called for an end to federal powers of disallowance and for increases in provincial subsidies. Numerous conferences were held subsequently, including, since 1960, annual meetings of provincial premiers. First Ministers Conferences now address mainly constitutional and economic considerations (including interprovincial tariffs).

FENIAN RAIDS. The Fenians, Sons of Ireland or *Sinn Fein* ("Ourselves Alone"), represented the Irish Republican Brotherhood, founded in New York in 1857. The movement espoused violence in order to achieve Ireland's independence from the British Empire. Once established in Canada, the Fenians intended to negotiate the independence of Ireland. Well financed, in 1865 the Fenians had $500,000 and 10,000 U.S. Civil War veterans enrolled. A wing of the Fenian Brotherhood led by William Roberts proposed attacking Canada. Michael Murphy of Toronto favoured an uprising in Ireland. In any event, a cipher telegraph sent to Murphy summoning him to join forces with a raid on New Brunswick was intercepted by authorities and he was arrested in Cornwall, Ontario.

Between the years of 1866 and 1870, the Fenians attacked a number of places in British North America. Fenians had limited success in their attacks on British North America. They captured Fort Erie but were forced to withdraw by the Canadian militia (q.v.) resistance. Other attacks occurred in Québec and New Brunswick but were unsuccessful. Due to these mounting attacks, the British and Canadian governments increased local defences and forces and the Royal Navy watched for gunrunners. Coming at the end of the U.S. Civil War, the Fenian Raids raised the issue of security with the Canadian and Imperial statesmen. The Raids resulted in the growth of the confederation movement, especially in the Maritimes.

It is believed that a Fenian murdered Thomas D'Arcy McGee (q.v.), "the pen of Canadian Confederation," in 1868.

FLEMING, SIR SANDFORD (1827–1915). In 1897, Fleming was knighted for his proposal outlining a worldwide uniform system for reckoning time. His concept of "standard time" brought him international recognition. A brilliant, energetic innovator, Fleming was a professional engineer, surveyor, mapmaker, engraver, and writer of note. Born in Kirkcaldy, Scotland, he emigrated to Canada in 1845, settling in Peterborough, Ontario. He moved to Toronto, where in 1849 he assisted in founding the Canadian Institute (for the promotion of science, history, and national achievements). Two years later he designed the first Canadian postage stamp (with the beaver as central motif). He was builder of the Intercontinental Railway. As chief engineer (1871–80) of the Canadian Pacific Railway (q.v.) he conducted surveys for a transcontinental route.

FORT FRANKLIN. A Dene community in the Inuvik Region of the Northwest Territories, Fort Franklin is at the southernmost limit of the Hare tribe's ancient territory. Once a North West Company and Hudson's Bay Company (qq.v.) trading post, it was a supply depot and winter headquarters for Sir John Franklin (q.v.) in 1825–27. Discovery of pitchblende at Port Radium and oil at Norman Wells in the 1920s made Great Bear Lake and River into vital trading routes. A Roman Catholic mission, Federal Day School, and reopened Hudson's Bay Company post were developments of the modern era beginning in 1949.

FORT GEORGE. A major fort on the Niagara frontier during the War of 1812 (q.v.), Fort George was important in British defences. Overlooking the American Fort Niagara across the Niagara River and commanding a view of the river, the bastion of the fort is its largest structure. Below the bastion were storehouses and wharves of Navy Hall, local headquarters for the Royal Navy (later the interim headquarters of the governor of Upper Canada [q.v.]). In May 1813 American artillery bombardment and naval gunfire reduced the fort to a smoking ruin. The outnumbered British garrison was obliged to withdraw. American army engineers refortified the spot and occupied it during the summer and autumn of 1813. In December the Americans abandoned the fort, burned the town of Newark, and retreated to Fort Niagara. The British then reoccupied Fort George and reestablished control on the Niagara frontier in that area. Fort George fell into ruins and was abandoned in 1820. The powder magazine (built in 1796) was the only fort building to survive the War of 1812 and the ensuing years of neglect. Meantime the British engineers constructed Fort Mississauga at the river mouth and Butler's Barracks on the plains to replace Fort George. A Parks Canada site, Fort George was reconstructed to its pre-1813 appearance and in 1950 was officially opened to the public.

FORT PROVIDENCE. Established 1786 at Wool Bay, Great Slave Lake, by Peter Pond of the North West Company (q.v.) as an outpost camp and reopened by Alexander Mackenzie (q.v.) in 1789, Fort Providence was a trading centre for the Copper (or Yellowknife) and Dogrib natives. It was abandoned in 1823. Its importance was that of a resupply depot and was intended as such for Sir John Franklin's (q.v.) first expedition to the Arctic coast (1819–22).

FRANKLIN, SIR JOHN (1786–1847). Royal Navy explorer. Franklin led expeditions to the Arctic region. In 1819, Franklin explored the mouth of the Coppermine River while leading his first Arctic expedition. He led his second expedition to the Arctic in 1825–26. In 1845, Franklin led the best-equipped expedition to enter the Arctic up to that time. He discovered a Northwest Passage, but he and his crew died during the expedition. Many expeditions were sent out to find Franklin and his crew, leading to a full exploration of the Arctic. A search party led by Sir Robert McClure, RN, crossed the Northwest Passage during an expedition from 1850 to 1854. Explorers eventually found evidence of Franklin's party and reconstructed some of his voyage. The remains of Franklin have never been found.

FRASER, SIMON (1776–1862). Fur trader and explorer. Born in Bennington, Vermont (then New York), Fraser worked for the North West Company (q.v.) and became a partner in 1801. In 1805, after the union of the NWC and the New North West Company (the XY Company), he assumed responsibilities for the area west of the Rocky Mountains. He hoped to find a route to the Pacific to reduce the transportation costs to and from the Far West. In 1808, he discovered the lower Fraser River but it proved to be too dangerous for transportation. He called central British Columbia "New Caledonia," for what he saw there during his explorations reminded him of how his mother had described Scotland to him. He served in the Stormont Militia in the Lower Canada Rebellion, November 1838. Near Beauharnois he damaged a knee severely in a fall. He was incapacitated and was reduced to penury. He died penniless and is buried in St. Andrews, Ontario.

FREE TRADE. Not a recent phenomenon in Canada–U.S. relations, the first reciprocal arrangements (in areas of seas, forest, and farm products) include: the Reciprocity (q.v.) Treaty (1854, abrogated by the U.S. 1866), and the intended (but unsuccessful), negotiated (but unratified) free trade accord of 1911 (Wilfrid Laurier's [q.v.] Liberals were defeated on this issue). In 1935, Canadian–U.S. negotiations received approval as the Canada–U.S. Trade Agreement Act (1936).

In the 1980s, the Progressive Conservatives promoted a new free trade agreement with the United States. The Canada–U.S. pact was signed by Prime Minister Brian Mulroney (q.v.) and President Ronald Reagan 2

January 1988. Mulroney argued that new markets would open to Canadian business in a global (especially U.S.-dominated) economy. Opponents, including organized Canadian labour, (rightly and correctly) fearing loss of Canadian jobs, and companies bitterly but unsuccessfully fought the measure. The Business Council on National Issues and its president, Thomas D'Aquino (q.v.), lobbied successfully in support of free trade. The Canada–United States Free Trade Implementation Act received assent 30 December 1988 and became effective 1 January 1989.

FROBISHER, SIR MARTIN (1535?–1594). One of the first English navigators to search for a Northwest Passage to India and eastern Asia, Frobisher became known as one of the greatest seamen of his time. He fought against the Spanish Armada and was knighted for his services. His three attempts to reach Asia by sailing west extended geographic knowledge. On the first voyage in 1576, he rounded southern Greenland, visited Labrador, and became the first European to sail into a deep bay on Baffin Island, which he thought to be a strait. This bay now bears his name. Frobisher took back to England the rock that some people thought was gold ore. This touched off a scramble to join in his second voyage in 1577. Frobisher annexed the country to England on this trip, and returned with 180 metric tons of rock. On his third voyage, in 1578, he sailed with 15 ships and 41 miners. He entered what later became Hudson Strait but made no further attempts at discovery. This time he brought back more ore which turned out to be of little value.

FRONT DE LIBÉRATION DE QUÉBEC (FLQ). A terrorist organization of revolutionaries, ultra-leftists and anti-capitalists, founded in March 1963. The FLQ consisted of cells. Some members had training with the Palestine Liberation Organization. Two of the movement's theorists, Pierre Vallières and Charles Gagnon, were arrested, sparking off the October Crisis (q.v.) of 1970. The tactics of the FLQ were bombing (mainly mailboxes), kidnapping, and murder. The escalation of violence in October 1970 led to the Québec Government requesting Canada to call in the Canadian Army (q.v.) in aid to the civil power (q.v.). The War Measures Act (q.v.) was implemented by the Federal Government. The FLQ was forced into submission, 20 people were convicted, and safe passage to Cuba was secured for several of the leaders. Vallières, author of *Nègres Blancs d'Amerique*, is considered the "philosopher" of the organization.

FRONTENAC ET PALLUAU, COMTE DE [LOUIS DE BUADE] (1622–1698). French army officer, appointed governor general of French possessions in North America in 1672. Frontenac had two lengthy terms as governor general, though in 1682 he was recalled briefly on the charge of misgovernment. He promoted stabilization and expansion of New France's frontiers and the growth of the Canadian fur trade (q.v.) based in Montréal. He built Fort Frontenac (Kingston) on Lake Ontario and a number of other fur trading and military posts. He enlarged New France's frontiers to the Mississippi Valley, launched raids on New England, resisted the English at Québec in 1690, and broke the power of the Iroquois (q.v.) in 1696. One of the most turbulent figures in the history of New France, he was the architect of French expansion in North America.

FRONTIER. In its earliest phase the Canadian frontier was an extension of British, French, and (on the West Coast) Spanish, Russian, and U.S. influences. Largely oceanic or maritime in nature, these frontiers became beachheads, with extensive links to the interior via rivers and lakes. New France's (q.v.) frontier was a trading and military projection of power. After 1763, the frontier was largely a British corporate arrangement with the chartered Hudson's Bay Company (q.v.) dominating northern waters and lands, and its monopoly area being Rupert's Land. From Montréal, by contrast, the rival Canadian based North West Company (q.v.) opened up an individualistic trading frontier, which ended in 1821 with the merger with the Hudson's Bay Company. In British Columbia, after an open zone frontier rivalry (involving Britain, Spain, the United States, and Russia), British corporate monopoly and colonization came in the form of the Colony of Vancouver Island (q.v.), established in 1849 under HBC auspices. In 1859 the HBC licence of monopoly ended, and British Columbia became an open frontier under British colonial control. American influences in the 1858 gold rush were thwarted by executive power and a show of armed force. Much the same occurred in the Yukon in 1898 with the Klondike Gold Rush. In 1869 in Manitoba and 1885 in Saskatchewan local resistance to Canadian authority ended with the armed closing of the frontier. If the U.S. frontier represents individualistic pursuit leading to democratic and populistic consequences, as Frederick Jackson Turner argued (now widely disputed), the Canadian frontier tends to be that of corporate and government dominance and of armed support for the civil power to keep foreign rivals out and to ensure what is called "peace, order, and good government." The northern extension of Canada's dominion throughout the 20th century represents a continuance of traditions developed under first French and then British auspices.

FUR TRADE. The staple of the early Canadian economy until the 1830s, when the sales of fur drastically dropped, the fur trade was central to Canadian prosperity. French companies held monopolies, which passed from hand to hand. By 1608 the trade was based in Québec, and the French had extensive links with the Huron (q.v.) and Algonquins. The Iroquois (q.v.), great fur trappers, attempted to interrupt the northwestern trade in the 1640s and succeeded. Comte de Frontenac (q.v.) stabilized the southern frontier, allowing the French to penetrate towards Hudson Bay, the Illinois country, and the Mississippi River. By 1759 the French dominated most fur-bearing areas of eastern North America except the northern American colonies of Britain. In 1670, the English Hudson's Bay Company (q.v.) received its charter from Charles II, creating its monopoly rights over Rupert's Land, virtually the Canadian northwest. The Montréal-based North West Company (q.v.), and its rival, Sir Alexander Mackenzie's (q.v.) XY Company, fought against the Hudson's Bay Company for many years. In 1804 the North West Company and the Sir Alexander Mackenzie Company merged. The North West Company merged with the Hudson's Bay Company in 1821.

Canadian business infrastructure including transportation, banking, finance, and currency was laid down in the 18th century due to the fur trade. Many urban centres of modern Canada, such as Montréal, Edmonton, and Victoria, had their origins as fur trading posts. Fur-trading explorers such as Samuel Hearne (q.v.), Sir Alexander Mackenzie, and Simon Fraser (q.v) recorded information about the North American landmass.

Historical scholarship now shows that the fur trade depended on native energies and commitments. Natives traded furs, principally beaver, for industrial materials, especially ironware, and for liquor and tobacco. Historical studies confirm that traders were obliged to meet native demands and that a partnership in trade existed. Other studies show a tendency towards a fur-holding monopoly, and this was true in the French and British periods. Liaisons between European traders and native peoples resulted in the evolution of the Métis (q.v.), or mixed bloods, now recognized within the terms of the Canadian Charter of Rights and Freedoms. A unique fur trade of Canada was the Northwest Coast trade in the sea otter, the pelts being sold by ship owners in Macao and Canton. In the 20th century, fur farming was extensive in Canada. Fur trading continues in Canada, but its size has been greatly diminished because of international pressure by animal rights groups and censure of the European Commission and Brigit Bardot.

-G-

GALT, SIR ALEXANDER TILLOCH (1817–1893). High-spirited and difficult businessman and politician. Before his election to the Legislative Assembly in 1849, Galt was involved in the promotion of the Grand Trunk Railway. He signed the Annexation Manifesto (q.v.) in 1849. Galt pressed for the federation of British North America as early as 1857, and in 1858 he joined the Cartier-Macdonald government on the condition that the government support federation.

As minister of finance, he introduced the Galt tariff in 1859. This was the first Canadian tariff barrier that affected British goods. Galt successfully defended Canada's right to set tariffs against the protests of British interests. He was also a delegate to both Charlottetown and the Québec conferences (q.v.) and played an important role in the drafting of the British North American Act. Galt retired as finance minister in 1868 and from Parliament in 1872, but was appointed Canadian high commissioner to London in 1880, a position he held until 1883.

GEOLOGICAL SURVEY OF CANADA. Canada's unremembered explorers are the Geological Survey of Canada, who set out to draw the complete map of Canada in the 19th century. The key figures were Sir William Logan, Alfred Selwyn, George Mercer Dawson, and Robert Bell. Not only were they mapmakers, and true successors to Champlain, Hearne, and Mackenzie (qq.v.), they were draughtsmen, photographers, natural history enthusiasts, ethnologists, and biologists.

In 1841 the Province of Canada (then comprising Ontario and Québec), interested in the flora and fauna of the land, granted funds to defray expenses of a geological survey of the province. Coal was then a major consideration, and Logan, educated in Edinburgh, had a background in coal and copper. He took up his duties in Canada in 1843, headquartered in Montréal. Geology and metallurgy went hand in hand, and the means of recording measurement was surveying and thus mapmaking. The preliminary findings were shown, in 1851, at the Crystal Palace Exhibition in London, an imperial and worldwide celebration of scientific findings. In 1856 Logan was knighted for his scientific contributions. He retired in 1869, leaving behind a great legacy, for indeed he had fulfilled his own instructions: that the findings were to have economic advantages. Mt. Logan, Canada's highest peak, is named for him.

Logan was succeeded by Selwyn, who led parties into the West, seeking out the mineral resources along the route of the proposed Canadian

Pacific Railway (q.v.). In the north, on the Barrens, geologist Joseph B. Tyrrell (q.v.) made important discoveries, which he thought of importance, for as he said the North was "less well known than the remotest districts of Darkest Africa." Tyrrell, also a historian and editor, wrote about Samuel Hearne, David Thompson (q.v.) and other explorers. Albert Low, later a director, explored Labrador and the Ungava Peninsula of northern Québec.

Dawson, later a director after Selwyn, was a geologist, botanist, anthropologist, photographer, diplomat, and poet. He visited the Queen Charlotte Islands and also made important investigations of the Yukon. Like other members of the Geological Survey of Canada he was well connected to the British scientific establishment. Dawson City (q.v.) was named in his honour. He made an important report on the Haida (q.v.); and published reports on Yukon native peoples as well as reports on the Kwakiutl and Shushwap of British Columbia. Bell was the great administrator, but he gave way to Low as director early in the 20th century.

Aerial photography aided the Geological Survey, as did the Great Depression, when more than 1,000 persons were detailed to work on the Survey. The search for minerals during and after World War II (q.v.) also spurred on the Survey. Throughout its history the Survey combined practicality with scientific excellence. It is the custodian of the geological heritage of Canada. It has international links with other northern, circumpolar, and Commonwealth countries. It is also engaged in environmental considerations. *See also* Exploration.

GILBERT, SIR HUMPHREY (1539?–1583). English scholar and soldier. Gilbert believed there was a northwest route by water across the North American continent that would lead to the East Indies. He wrote an essay about his theory in 1576. In 1578, Queen Elizabeth I gave him permission to sail in search of the passage. Gilbert returned to England after losing one of his best ships and one of his bravest captains. He set sail again in 1583 in command of another expedition. His half-brother, Sir Walter Raleigh, started with him. Raleigh and his crew turned back two days after they left Plymouth, but Gilbert kept on. He landed in Newfoundland and took possession of the land in the queen's name. On the way back to England, Gilbert and his crew were lost in a storm.

GITXSAN-WET'SUWET'EN LAND CASE. A claim by two native nations to the 58,000 square kilometres in the Skeena, Bulkley and Babine watersheds, some 700 kilometres north of Vancouver. The land covers 133 separate native areas. The case, brought by 51 chiefs, began in 1984.

It was rebuffed by Chief Justice Allan McEachern of the British Columbia Supreme Court in 1991. The British Columbia Court of Appeal rendered a split decision. In 1997, a Supreme Court of Canada unanimous decision overturned McEachern's ruling and ruled that aboriginal title to land had never been extinguished there. The ruling has wide implications for other areas in British Columbia and in the Maritimes where aboriginal title was never extinguished. The Supreme Court concluded that a new trial was necessary. It also ruled that oral history gives bands constitutional claim in the absence of treaties. In 1866 the natives resisted telegraph linemen, in 1872 blockaded a river against miners, in 1908 sent a deputation to Wilfrid Laurier (q.v.) in Ottawa, in 1927 tore up surveyors' stakes, and in 1986 began the Marshmallow Wars, chasing fisheries officers away with a hail of marshmallows. *See also* Nisga'a.

GOUZENKO, IGOR (1919–1982). A cipher clerk at the Soviet Embassy in Ottawa beginning in 1943, Gouzenko's defection in 1945 provided information on Soviet spying, the principal aim of which was stealing atomic bomb secrets. His revelations and documents revealed a major Soviet espionage ring in Canada. Ten persons, including Col. Nikolai Zabotin and atomic scientist Alan Nunn May, were sent to jail. He also implicated Alger Hiss, a U.S. State Department official, as a Soviet spy; this evidence proved inconclusive. Canada provided Gouzenko and his family with a home and new identity. A media commentator in disguise, he also wrote a book about his defection, *This Was My Choice* (1948). *See also* Secret Service.

GOVERNORS GENERAL. The office of governor general is Canada's oldest continuous institution, dating back to 1608, when Samuel de Champlain (q.v.) acted as governor of New France. Today, the governor general represents the Queen as Canada's head of state—opening Parliament (q.v.), swearing in Cabinet ministers, performing duties as commander-in-chief of the Canadian Armed Forces (q.v.), welcoming dignitaries from around the world, and bestowing Canada's highest honours.

Canada has never had a resident monarch, though the government of Canada is a "constitutional monarchy," that is, a parliament-controlled system with a monarch, or sovereign, as head of state. Since earliest French days, Canada has been under sovereign power, first French, then (beginning in 1760 with the Articles of Capitalisation) British. By various constitutional and statutory measures, Canada's separate status in the British Empire was established or achieved; in particular, by the Statute of Westminster (1931) (q.v.), Canada's equal status with Britain and other self-governing dominions and colonies was acknowledged by Britain. This statute came in consequence of a long, difficult road to autonomy. Beginning with the French era, Canada had governors or sometimes "commanders-in-chief" (see appendix C). When Lord Durham (q.v.) was appointed to the office, he was named governor general as well as commander-in-chief. The former title recognized the plurality of British North American colonies or provinces (Lower Canada, Upper Canada, Prince Edward Island, Nova Scotia, New Brunswick); the latter title reflected the military nature of the position. Notably most French and British governors were military personnel—invariably army. Beginning with confederation (1867), the position of governor general was recognized in the constitution. (For a list of governors general, see appendix A.) Beginning in the late 19th century, the British government appointed nonmilitary, or civil, persons to the post. The governor-generalship was one of the highest-ranking appointments in British imperial administration. The viceroyalty of India was more prestigious, and several Canadian governors general later went to New Delhi (and Simla). The long list of governors and governors general reads like an impressive who's who of the French and British aristocracy. With the Canadianization of the office (under Vincent Massey, 1952–59), diplomats and politicians have held the position. The last British officeholder was Field Marshal Rt. Hon. Viscount Alexander of Tunis, from 1946 to 1952.

The governor general of Canada resides in Rideau Hall in Ottawa. The office maintains a residence, or apartments, in the Québec Citadel. Rideau Hall is the governor general's working residence; it was built in 1838 by a Scottish stonemason. The governor general has a Foot Guard and band. *See* (chronologically) Champlain, Frontenac, La Galissonière, Murray, Carleton, Durham, Metcalfe. *See also* Parliamentary System.

GREAT WAR. *See also* World War I.

GRENFELL, SIR WILFRED (1865–1940). English-born medical missionary and author. Grenfell accepted the position of Superintendent of the Mission to Deep-Sea Fishermen. He began the Labrador Mission in 1892 and organized five hospitals, seven nursing stations, and three orphanages. He was knighted in 1927. He was author of numerous widely read books.

GROULX, ABBÉ LIONEL-ADOLPHE (1878–1967). Historian and novelist. Groulx portrayed French Canada and Québec's progress as a struggle against English domination. He celebrated the clerical and agrarian pasts of Québec. As a French Canadian nationalist, he portrayed the

Québecois as victims of British and Canadian imperialism. His most famous work was *Notre Maître, le passé* (1944).

GULF OF MAINE CASE AND AWARD. In October 1984 the World Court drew a boundary that divides one of the richest fishing grounds of the world. The boundary was drawn "for all uses," a noteworthy first. This was also the first time such a ruling obtained with respect to a 200-mile exclusive economic zone. In dispute since 1783, the Gulf of Maine fishery and the Georges Bank have valuable scallop yields, herring having been fished out or otherwise depleted and cod and haddock much reduced. In 1979 Canada and the United States entered into a 10-year management deal, at the same time referring the boundary issue to the World Court. Four judges, in their ruling, drew a 253-nautical-mile boundary in three segments (northeastern, joint coastal, and open water). Canadians tended to be more satisfied with the ruling, for Canada gained the prominent scallop-rich area of Georges Bank (though was not awarded all of Georges Bank). The United States requested a one-year moratorium on the introduction of the boundary; Canada declined.

-H-

HACKING, NORMAN (1912–1997). Premier marine journalist and pioneering maritime historian. Hacking was born in Vancouver and graduated in history (honours) from the University of British Columbia. For 30 years he was marine editor of the Vancouver daily newspaper *Province*. He served in Canadian minesweepers and corvettes during World War II (q.v.) with the Royal Canadian Navy Volunteer Reserve; he made 13 trips on North Atlantic convoy duty, attaining the rank of 1st lieutenant. "The Admiral," as dubbed by his chums, was a great supporter of Canadian naval historians, was devoted to the Vancouver Maritime Museum, and was a founding member of the Canadian Nautical Research Society. He is best known for his various histories of steam navigation on the British Columbia coast. His book *The Prince Ships of Northern British Columbia* (1995) recounts the history of Grand Trunk Pacific and Canadian National Railways seaborne operations. He wrote an unpublished autobiography, *Hacking Aweigh*.

HAIDA. The Haida tribe is located on the West Coast on the Queen Charlotte Islands (and on adjacent Alaskan islands). Their isolation on the islands and their dependence on the sea made the Haida great voyagers.

The large, deep canoes of the Haida were used extensively for raiding other tribes. Smallpox at the end of the 18th century and smallpox (again), alcohol, and venereal diseases in the 19th century depleted the population.

Haida, HMCS. Canada's most famous warship, built by Vickers-Armstrong Ltd. at Newcastle, England, launched 25 August 1942, and commissioned under the White Ensign 30 August 1943. This Tribal-class destroyer had a long and active service in Atlantic, Arctic, and English Channel waters during World War II (q.v.) and later in the Korean Conflict (q.v.), and elsewhere. Her "hottest" work was with the 10th Destroyer Flotilla in the English Channel. She was an escort for the Murmansk convoys. *Haida's* battle honours are: Arctic 1943–45, English Channel 1944, Normandy 1944, Biscay 1944, Korea 1952–53. Her first commanding officer was Comdr. H. G. DeWolf, C.B.E., D.S.O., C.D., RCN (later Vice Adm. DeWolf, chief of naval staff). She is berthed at Ontario Place, Toronto, as a floating museum and memorial to the Canadian Navy (q.v.) and merchant marine of the Second World War. *Haida* is the last of the famous Canadian, British, and Australian Tribal-class destroyers.

HALIBURTON, THOMAS CHANDLER ["SAM SLICK"] (1796–1865). Born in Windsor, Nova Scotia, Haliburton was an author, judge, and politician. He wrote many books, including *The Clockmaker,* or *Sayings and Doings of Samuel Slick of Slickville* (1836–40). He coined many sayings, including "barking up the wrong tree."

HALIFAX EXPLOSION. A collision between the French munitions vessel *Mont Blanc* and the Belgian Relief ship *Imo* on 6 December 1917 caused the munitions ship to explode. The explosion levelled the heavily populated northern part of the city of Halifax, Nova Scotia. The explosion was heard as far away as Prince Edward Island. The blast killed 1,600 people and wounded another 9,000. Prior to the blast, Halifax had been a major convoy port and naval base of World War I (q.v.).

HALL, WILLIAM (1829–1904). The son of former black slaves brought to Nova Scotia from Virginia during the War of 1812 (q.v.), Hall was born at Horton, Nova Scotia. He joined the Royal Navy in 1852. He won the Victoria Cross for bravery while serving with a British naval brigade at Lucknow, India, in 1857. He later lived at Avonport, Nova Scotia, where he died.

HEAD, SIR FRANCIS BOND (1793–1875). Lieutenant governor of Upper Canada (q.v.) 1835 to 1838. In this position in the years immediately preceding the Rebellion of 1837 (q.v.), Head's policies and hostility to reform assisted in creating tension between the factions. His action in sending almost all regular troops to Lower Canada (q.v.) in November 1837 was, by his own admission, designed to provoke a reaction. He was unable to handle the rebellion and was returned to England upon resignation.

HEARNE, SAMUEL (1745–1792). Explorer of the Canadian north. Hearne was born in London, England. At the age of 20, he joined the Hudson's Bay Company (q.v.) and was sent to a post (now Churchill) at the mouth of the Churchill River. In 1769 he examined the western coast of Hudson Bay, then travelled inland from the fort to the south of Chesterfield Inlet and to Dubawnt Lake. In 1770 he again set out, this time for the Coppermine River on the Arctic Ocean, returning home via Great Slave Lake. Hearne thus became the first white man to reach the Arctic overland from Hudson Bay. Hearne was the first explorer to give a clear account of the barren lands and of Inuit (q.v.) life in these latitudes.

In 1774 Hearne built Cumberland House, the HBC's first post in the interior, as a counter to North West Company (q.v.) expansion. In 1775 he became governor of Fort Prince of Wales; was captured by the French naval officer Comte de La Pérouse in 1782. He was taken to France, where he was released on condition that his account of his Arctic travels be published (it appeared in 1795 with the title *A Journey from Prince of Wales Fort to the Northern Ocean*). In 1783 the Hudson's Bay Company sent him out to reestablish a post at Churchill. He remained there until 1787, when ill health forced him to return to England, where he died. *See also* Exploration.

HENDAY, ANTHONY (?–1762). English fur trader and explorer in Canada. A servant in the Hudson's Bay Company (q.v.), Henday was the first white to visit the Blackfoot Confederacy (q.v.) and to report on their customs and habits. He left Hudson Bay in 1754 to travel to the Saskatchewan River (q.v.) and made important explorations in what is now the province of Alberta. *See also* Exploration; Fur Trade.

HENRY, REVEREND FATHER PIERRE (1904–1979). A missionary of the Oblate of Mary Immaculate (O.M.I.) order, Father Henry lived among the Inuit (q.v.) and built a stone church at Pelly Bay, or Arvilikjuak ("the big place with bowhead whites"). Joined in 1952 by Rev. Father Franz Van de Velde, the priests travelled, lived, and worked among the Inuit of the eastern Central Arctic until 1965. The Inuit called Father Henry *Kayualuk* because of his full red beard.

HERSCHEL ISLAND. The Yukon's only coastal island. It was known to the Inuvialuit as *Qilciqtatuk,* "island," but renamed (in 1826) Herschel Island by explorer Sir John Franklin (q.v.) for his friend, the astronomer Sir John Herschel (1792–1871). American whalers in search of bowhead arrived in the 1880s, and in 1894–95, when whaling was at its peak, 15 whaleships and 1,500 men and women wintered there at Pauline Cove. By 1907, the whale population exhausted, whalers ceased their appearance.

Meanwhile, Anglican missionaries established a mission (1897) and the Royal Canadian Mounted Police exerted sovereignty over the island (1903). European diseases, introduced by the whalers, diminished the Inuit population in the Beaufort area from 2,000 to about 200 at the time whaling ended. Herschel Island became a territorial park in 1987.

HIBERNIA. A petroleum field 315 kilometres east of St. John's, Newfoundland, discovered in 1979 and developed in the 1990s at great expense to governments and partner investors. The turbulent history of this megaproject is marked by the 1992 crisis, when Gulf Canada withdrew from the project. The government of Canada contributed $1 billion in grants and $1.8 billion in loan guarantees. Against pressure to halt the project, the government also became an 8.5-percent shareholder. Hibernia Management and Development Co. is the owner; its partners are Mobil Oil Canada (33.1 percent), Chevron Canada (27), Petro-Canada (20), federally owned Canada Hibernia Holding Corp. (8.5), and Norsk Hydro of Norway (5). The first crude was drawn 17 November 1997, thereby adding Newfoundland and Labrador to the Canadian oil-producing provinces (Alberta, Saskatchewan, British Columbia, and Ontario being the others). The first well produced 45,000 barrels per day, twice the estimate. Once 80 wells are drilled, over an 18-year lifespan, the daily average will be 135,000–170,000 barrels.

HINCKS, SIR FRANCIS (1807–1885). Reform-minded newspaper editor and railway tycoon. Hincks founded the *Canada West* newspaper in 1837. He joined forces with Louis H. Lafontaine (q.v.) in promoting responsible government (q.v.), opposed by Lord Sydenham. As premier of the Province of Canada in 1851, he proposed reciprocity (q.v.) with the United States and initiated negotiations. A key player in the Grand Trunk Railway, he left public office in 1854 because of dubious financial dealings. Hincks was minister of finance in Sir John A. Macdonald's (q.v.) first cabinet in 1869 and attended to banking and currency regulations. He left politics in 1874, retired to business, and published his *Reminiscences* in 1884.

HISTORICAL WRITING. The first Canadian histories were compiled in French by priests, lay brothers, and colony-builders, including Marc Lescarbot, Gabriel Sagard, and Samuel de Champlain (q.v.). Lescarbot is regarded as the first historian of Canada; his work was titled *Histoire de la Nouvelle France* (1609). Pierre-François Charlevoix, S.J., is credited with writing the first perspective on French development in Canada. His *Histoire de description générale de la Nouvelle France* (1744) was based on the *Jesuit Relations* — the collective name given to a series of reports sent by Jesuit missionaries in Québec to the Society of Jesus in Paris, some of which were published in 1858 (73 volumes, covering the period 1610–1791, were published between 1896 and 1901). Jesuits continued as the premier Canadian historians, a trend identified later in the work of the secular Québec national historian François-Xavier Garneau in the mid-19th century. These histories provide information about Canada's native peoples and habitations, and its geography, flora, and fauna; they also exemplify the zeal of the Roman Catholic Counter-Reformation. They are also pious attempts to justify French imperialism.

The first English-language histories of Canada date from the period following the Conquest of 1759, when the British gained control of French colonies in Canada. The war of 1812 (q.v.), fought between the British and Canadians and American invaders, accentuated the desires of Upper Canadians and Maritimers to write new histories of British North America. As the 19th century progressed, historians of what later became Canada glorified the British Empire and wrote what could be called Britannic Canadian history. W. H. Kingsford's 10-volume *History of Canada* (1887–98) is a comprehensive account of the political and constitutional development of diverse provinces prior to and following confederation, brought into existence by the British North America Act of 1867. J. C. Dent's *The Last Forty Years* (1881) eulogizes moderate reform.

Changing international relations and Canadian military activities overseas (first in the South African War, then in World War I [qq.v.]) accentuated Canadian nationalism. In addition, the economic development of Canada—in forestry, mining, agriculture, railways, and shipping—invited Canadians to rewrite their history in more structural terms. Joseph Pope edited the memoirs of Sir John A. Macdonald (q.v.). Oscar Douglas Skelton compiled lengthy biographies of two great Canadians: A. T. Galt and Sir Wilfrid Laurier (q.q.v.). W. P. M. Kennedy wrote pioneering histories of the constitution. Works on labour by H. A. Logan, on Canadian–American relations by H. L. Keenleyside, and on Commonwealth relations by R. G. Trotter and Chester Martin were part of the diversification of research that marked the 1920s.

In the years before and after World War II (q.v.), historiography blossomed in the writings of several well-known, colourful, and nationally committed—if divided—university teachers. These include Harold Adams Innis (q.v.), Donald Grant Creighton, Arthur R. M. Lower, Frank Underhill, W. L. Morton, C. P. Stacey (q.v.), and, towards the end of this era, Maurice Careless, Margaret Ormsby, William J. Eccles, Kenneth McNaught, and Peter B. Waite.

Innis was the most important scholar to write histories on the economic development of what became Canada. His works on staples and on communications are fundamental to an understanding of Canada's economic history and the nation's continuing difficulties as a world trader. Innis also wrote histories of the Canadian Pacific Railway (q.v.) and the cod fisheries. His most important book was *The Fur Trade in Canada* (1930). Innis claimed that the fur trade (q.v.) and its voyager canoeing and trekking routes marked out the future political boundaries of Canada. He also argued that because Canada's staples economy was dominant on a world stage, it would remain both northern and marginal. Innis also wrote histories about the pulp and paper industry and biases of communications. He highlighted the pervasive influence of the United States in Canada's more recent development. By his many works, exemplary as pioneering social science in Canada and reflective of American scholarly influences, Innis became recognized as a truly international scholar.

In his *Commercial Empire of the St. Lawrence, 1760–1850* (1937), Donald Creighton explained how a merchant class, based in Montréal, developed the infrastructure of the modern nation-state. Creighton extended his theme in *Dominion of the North* (1944) and *The Road to Confederation* (1964). Widely read by students, Creighton is regarded by some as the dean of Canadian historians. His two-volume biography of Sir John A. Macdonald—*The Young Politician* (1952) and *The Old Chieftain* (1955)—while overly eulogistic, is regarded as the finest political biography written. Creighton feared the aggressive power of the United States and stressed the national need for a centralized federalism and a powerful and continuing British conservative tradition; he was critical of French Canadian historical leadership and of English liberal continentalism. Creighton concerned himself with the rise and fall of "the empire of the St. Lawrence." Others refer to his concept as "the Laurentian thesis."

Arthur R. M. Lower became an expert on Canada's hinterland, on the history of Canadian forests and timber trades. His great whiggish text, *Colony to Nation* (1946), stressed moderate reform, North American nationalism, and the reconciliation of the two (French and English) linguistic communities. His *Canadians in the Making* (1958) pioneered Canadian social history.

While Innis, Creighton, and Lower and many others wrote history from an Ontario or Montréal perspective, Manitoba-born W. L. Morton stressed the importance of the Canadian North and the West, each with its own legitimate perspectives, in *The Progressive Party in Canada* (1950) and *Manitoba* (1957). With *Kingdom of Canada* (1963), Morton became the great "Red Tory" of Canadian scholarship, stressing Canada's unique experience as a Nordic people, different from the Americans, with a state interventionist economy and strong government support for weaker groups and regions. Métis (q.v.) and the French-speaking Canadians outside of Québec were his heroes; separatists and neoconservative continentalists, his villains.

Other writers followed to reinterpret Canada's past. Maurice Careless, in his biography of George Brown (q.v.) of the *Globe* newspaper, *Brown of the Globe* (vol. 1, 1959; vol. 2, 1963), and in other books, stressed the role of Toronto-led Upper Canadian reform in building the country and nurturing its economy. He also developed a thesis on multi-tiered metropolitanism, analyzing efficacy of regionalism and multiculturalism and showing futility of searching for a single Canadian identity or culture. Of note is Craig Brown's *Robert Laird Borden: A Biography* (vol. 1, 1975; vol. 2, 1980), on one of Canada's prime ministers. William Eccles, the greatest English-language writer on the French regime (his *Frontenac, the Courtier Governor*, 1959, for example), stressed France's geopolitical and military interest in North America, criticized Innis's staples approach, and later emphasized the ongoing role of native people. Margaret Ormsby turned her attention to British Columbia and the Pacific in *British Columbia: A History* (1958), while Kenneth McNaught stressed the strength of an English-based social democratic tradition in his *A Prophet in Politics: A Biography of J. S. Woodsworth* (1959). C. P. Stacey wrote of Canada's contributions in World War II; his *Canada in the Age of Conflict* (vol. 1, 1977; vol. 2, 1981) is the standard account of Canada's external relations to 1948.

The period prior to the centennial of Canadian confederation (1967) sparked a number of works. P. B. Waite compiled *The Life and Times of*

Confederation, 1864–1867 (1962) and W. L. Morton wrote *The Critical Years: The Union of British North America, 1857–1873* (1964).

Beginning in the 1950s, Québec secular historians, after the corporatist-clerical historiography of Abbé Lionel Groulx (q.v.), took an increasing interest in their own history. Particularly important are works by Michel Brunet, Gustave Lanctot, and Fernand Ouellet.

The quantity of Canadian historiography exploded in the 1970s and 1980s as history departments in the country's universities (q.v.) grew rapidly and new scholarly societies and journals were founded. Attention diversified and often became more fragmented, more regional, and more social-, class-, and gender-oriented. Gerry Friesen's *Canadian Prairies: A History* (1984) and Ken Coates's and William Morrison's writings on the Yukon and on other Northern themes, inspired by the work of Morris Zaslow, have reflected a growing consciousness of regional affairs. Similarly, the Atlantic Shipping Project, funded by the Canada Council for the Arts (q.v.) and based on British Board of Trade papers, examined the role of shipping and seaborne trades in the history of Atlantic shipping and ports. The history of the Maritime provinces has also been served by writers such as Ernest Forbes, Ken Pryke, George Rawlyk, Judith Fingard, and, earlier, W. S. MacNutt. Barry Gough wrote histories of Pacific Coast maritime activities. H. Viv Nelles, Christopher Armstrong, Michael Bliss, Peter Oliver, and many others have written widely on Ontario regionalism and resource problems. Gilbert Tucker, Gerald Graham, Desmond Morton, S. F. Wise, and Terry Copp made significant contributions to histories of the Canadian army, navy, and air force. Blair Neatby, Jack Granatstein, Robert Bothwell, and John English have written voluminously on mid-20th-century political and administrative problems and personalities.

Ramsay Cook and Susan Mann Trofimenkoff have written widely and brilliantly of French Canadian nationalism and cultural movements. Representative are Cook's *The Politics of John W. Dafoe and the Free Press* (1963) and Trofimenkoff's *Action Française: French-Canadian Nationalism in the 1920s* (1975). Historians have stressed the long story of aboriginal groups and their relationship with "settler" societies; these scholars include Bruce Trigger, Cornelius Jaenen, Barry Gough, Sylvia Van Kirk, Jennifer Brown, Robin Fisher, J. R. Miller, Olive Dickason, Brian Slattery, John Milloy, David McNab, and Bruce Hodgins. Douglas Cole and Trigger have made distinctive contributions to native studies and to cross-cultural history. Hodgins, with others, has also focused on the comparative aspects of federalist Canada and federalist Australia.

Historians such as Douglas McCalla have confronted and challenged the staples approach to Canadian economic history, substituting a concept of complex internal activity that generated growth from expanding commercial and agrarian roots. Carl Berger and many others have explored Canada's intellectual past, Greg Kealey and Bryan Palmer its working relations, Suzanne Zeller its scientific basis, and Cynthia Commachio aspects of family, gender, and politics. Popular historians include Farley Mowat, Pierre Berton, and Peter Newman.

HOODLESS, ADELAIDE HUNTER (1857–1910). Home economist and teacher, born near St. George, Ontario. After the death of her son from contaminated milk in 1889, Hoodless dedicated her life to teaching girls and women about the sciences of child care and home management. She has been recognized as sole or joint founder of the Women's Institute (1897), the National Young Women's Christian Association, Macdonald Institute, the National Council of Women in Canada, and the Victorian Order of Nurses. She died while giving a speech to the Federation of Women's Club.

HOPKINS, FRANCES ANNE (1838–1919). Hopkins was born in England into an artistic family. Her childhood was filled with refining her painting and sketching skills. She moved to Lachine, Canada (now Québec), with her husband Edward Hopkins. Not content with remaining at home, Frances travelled with French fur traders (*voyageurs*) on a number of occasions. These voyages led to her most recognized work, which centres on the lifestyle of the voyageurs. Her paintings are a combination of landscape and portrait art that captured the true nature of a way of life that was extinguished with the building of the railroads. Although her work is recognized by many, the artist behind the work has remained relatively obscure. In 1990, the Thunder Bay Art Gallery organized the first major exhibition of her works.

HOSE, WALTER (1875–1965). Canada's most famous sailor of the modern era. Hose transferred to the Royal Canadian Navy after long service in the Royal Navy, and he commanded HMCS *Rainbow* on the Pacific Coast and then trade defence patrols on the Atlantic Coast, 1917–18. As director of the Naval Service (1921–28) and later chief of naval staff (1928–34), Rear Admiral Hose established the Royal Canadian Naval Volunteer Reserve (with companies in all prominent Canadian cities), the value of which became obvious in the late 1930s and during World War II (q.v.). He was important in the survival of naval force structures and administration during the dark days of Canadian armaments and defence history. *See also* Canadian Navy.

HOUSE OF COMMONS. *See* Parliament; Parliamentary System.

HOWE, JOSEPH (1804–1873). Politician, journalist, and statesman. Howe was born in Halifax and became editor of the *Nova Scotian* in 1828. He served in the Colonial Assembly for many years until 1863 and was a firm advocate of responsible government (q.v.). He served as provincial premier, fighting confederation, but later joined the federal cabinet as secretary of state. He is known as "the tribune of the people."

HUDSON BAY, ANGLO-FRENCH STRUGGLE FOR. Hudson Bay, discovered by Henry Hudson in 1610, became later in the 17th century an English commercial and strategic waterway, a northern access to the continental interior. The Hudson's Bay Company (q.v.) was founded in 1670 to exploit the landing of trade goods to the Indians and the taking out of furs, principally beaver. The French came to contest this dominance. War occurred in 1686, and intermittent armed conflict continued to 1713, when by the Treaty of Utrecht (q.v.) the French reluctantly and after a great struggle acknowledged English title to Hudson Bay.

Highlights of the struggle include: the HBC's ketch *Nonsuch*, with trader Sieur de Groseilliers aboard, arrived in 1668, and her crew built Charles Fort at Rupert River (the first English post on Hudson Bay). Governor Charles Bayley, at the site of the future York Fort (later York Factory), formally claimed Rupert's Land for the Hudson's Bay Company in 1670. Jean Talon (q.v.), intendant of New France (q.v.), sent an agent, Jesuit (q.v.) Father Charles Albanel, to establish a mission on Hudson Bay and coax Pierre Radisson and Groseilliers to leave the HBC and join the French (1672, 1674). Bayley arrested Albanel in 1675 and sent him as a prisoner to England. Radisson and Groseilliers entered French employ in 1675. The HBC built additional posts (Moose Factory, 1673; Fort Albany, 1675; Old Severn, 1685). French authorities established the Compagnie du Nord and sent two ships into Hudson Bay with Radisson and Groseilliers aboard; a New England post was also established but the HBC took it, and Radisson and Groseilliers left the fur trade (q.v.). Québec and Montréal merchants pressured the government of New France to send an overland expedition to capture HBC posts, and this was effected by Capt. Pierre de Troyes in 1686 in a brilliant overland and frontier campaign which caught the English defenders unaware. Sieur d'Iberville (q.v.), who went overland with de Troyes, wintered on Hudson Bay 1686–87 but returned to Québec by sea in the captured vessel *Craven*. An English–French diplomatic wrangle followed. Iberville sailed for Hudson Bay and continued his successful war against the HBC. In 1690–96 occurred the Battle for York Fort, the HBC stronghold, but the French could not capture the post until 1694 (another Iberville triumph). York Fort was renamed Fort Bourbon. It went back again to English hands, only to have Iberville take it again in 1697. By the Treaty of Ryswick, York Fort was returned once more to the English; the French regained some posts captured by James Knight.

In the next war, the French attacked overland in 1709 in a major expedition (70 Europeans, 30 Indians) but the English garrison at Fort Albany, aided by a native informant, made a successful defence. The conflict ended in 1713 with the Treaty of Utrecht.

HUDSON'S BAY COMPANY (HBC). Given English royal charter 2 May 1670, the HBC devolved from French Canadian fur trading knowledge, native hunting capabilities, and English commerce. Headquartered in London, and after 1970 in Winnipeg, the HBC is the oldest business corporation in North America. The first governor of the company was Prince Rupert of the Rhine. Rupert's Land, the chartered area of monopoly, was named for him. This area does not conform exactly to the boundaries of northern and western Canada, but was defined as the lands drained by lakes and rivers flowing into Hudson Bay. The charter required the firm to search for a Northwest Passage, and the company's apparent inaction led to a government inquiry in 1749 and to subsequent expeditions. In 1811, Earl Selkirk (q.v.) was granted a large tract of land by the HBC to create the Red River colony. In 1821, the HBC merged with the larger North West Company (q.v.), based in Montréal, but the name was kept because of the previous charter.

After 1821, the HBC held an unrestricted monopoly and controlled fur trade (q.v.) harvests. On the frontiers of competition (in the Yukon, American Mountain West, and Pacific Northwest) the HBC fought to retain the lion's share of the trade. By licence the HBC gained a monopoly of British fur trading in areas west of Rupert's Land. In 1849 the HBC received from the British government a Charter of Grant to the Colony of Vancouver Island (q.v.), and the colony was for a time a company colony. In 1857 a British parliamentary inquiry recommended that Canada eventually be given control of HBC lands. The company was refinanced in 1860s, revolutionized and diversified, and soon became a real estate agency. Gradually its northern stores and its southern department stores became its merchandizing focus. The fur trade continued as its staple until the 1930s but oil and gas, railways, mining, and other pursuits advanced readily. Of importance to Canadian historical studies are the celebrated journal *The Beaver* and publications of the Hudson's Bay Record Society and Rupert's Land Historical Society.

HUGHES, SIR SAMUEL (1853–1921). Businessman and politician; born at Darlington, Canada West, and educated in Toronto. Hughes was elected to Parliament (q.v.) as a Conservative in 1892. A strong nationalist and imperialist, he became minister of militia and defence in Sir Robert Borden's (q.v.) government in 1911. His energy and drive led to vast improvements in the efficiency of the militia (q.v.). He was important in the mobilization of the Canadian Expeditionary Force (q.v.) in August 1914 for World War I (q.v.).

HURON. It is believed that the name Huron was derived from the old French *huron* (a bristly, unkempt knave). The Huron confederacy consisted of four separate tribes: the Bear, the Cord, the Rock, and the Deer. The name of the confederacy was *Wendat* ("Islanders" or "Dwellers on a Peninsula"). The confederacy acted as protective union against the Iroquois (q.v.). The strongest tribe was the Bear, which accounted for about half the population of the Huron at the time of European contact. The Huron were located in southern and southwest Ontario. They were farmers of the land: agriculture was the main tenant of their livelihood. The principal enemies of the Huron were the Iroquois south of the St. Lawrence River (q.v.). After the arrival of Europeans, the Huron suffered a large decrease in population due to smallpox and other diseases. The Iroquois took advantage of this and attacked the Huron with firearms bought from the Europeans. By 1648, the Iroquois had reduced the number of Hurons further, and many fled Ontario or became part of the Iroquois nation. Remnant groups survived. Prior to the Huron downfall, they were amicable traders with the Europeans and developed relations with the Jesuit (q.v.) missionaries from France. *See also* Huronia.

HURONIA. A term applied specifically to that peninsular portion of today's Ontario, adjacent to Georgian Bay, Lake Huron, which was the focus of the Jesuit (q.v.) missions to the Huron (q.v.) native peoples. The Huron traded with the French at Montréal. The Jesuits (and Recollets before 1632) worked to establish a systematic network of missions. Agriculture and fur trading (qq.v.) developed. Iroquois (q.v.) expansion into Huron areas or destruction of Huron trading parties led to a crisis in the 1640s and the collapse of Huronia as a Jesuit mission in 1649. Many Huron died; others went to Montréal or to lands in Ohio and Michigan, where they were known as Wyandots. Many live in Oklahoma today. Ste.-

Marie among the Hurons (q.v.), an Ontario-administered heritage museum near Midland, Ontario, has preserved the main features of Huronia's history. *See also* Brébeuf, Ste. Jean de; Carhagouha.

HUTCHINSON, BRUCE (1901–1992). Author, newspaperman, historian, and Canadian legend. The dean of Canadian journalism, Hutchinson worked first at the Victoria *Daily Times,* then became a regular columnist for the Vancouver *Sun.* He was editor of both these papers and, for a time, editor of the Winnipeg *Free Press.* He was born in Prescott, Ontario, but he spent most of his early years in Victoria's James Bay. He wrote of these early years in *The Far Side of the Street* (1976). After his early experience as a reporter and writer in Victoria, he went to Ottawa to work in the parliamentary press gallery, becoming well acquainted with national political affairs and international relations. He bought property in Saanich (Christmas Hill), which he used as a base of operations, and later acquired a summer property at Shawnigan Lake. He continued to write for most of his life. Chief among his books are *The Unknown Country, The Fraser, The Incredible Canadian* (about William Lyon Mackenzie King), *The Struggle for the Border*, and *Mr Prime Minister.* "I'll work for anybody but I'll only work out of Victoria." He received many awards, including an honorary doctorate from Yale University. In 1967 he was named to the Order of Canada (q.v.). A Liberal by persuasion, he was a passionate defender of Canada and felt the battle for unity was well worth the struggle.

HYDE PARK DECLARATION. In April 1941, Prime Minster Mackenzie King (q.v.) met with President F. D. Roosevelt at the president's home in Hyde Park, New York. The declaration signed there by the two men increased the amount of raw materials the United States would buy from Canada, and Roosevelt agreed that Britain's account would be charged under the Lend-Lease Act for industrial components sent to Canada for incorporation into munitions destined for Britain. This agreement eased Canada of financial worries for the remainder of the war and linked the economies of the two countries more closely together.

-I-

IBERVILLE, SIEUR D' [PIERRE LE MOYNE] (1661–1706). Soldier and fur trader. Iberville's heroic Canadian expeditions were primarily against the English forts in Hudson Bay. He captured York Fort in 1694 and recaptured it in 1697. He also took St. John's, Newfoundland (q.v.), in 1696. In 1697, in order to restrict the English settlement to the Atlantic coast, Iberville was sent south to find the mouth of the Mississippi River and establish a fort there. He named the area Louisiana.

IMMIGRATION. Highlights of the long history of immigration in Canada are as follows: After aboriginal arrivals (the first immigrants), French from Normandy, Breton, and Picardy planted the first main colonies in Acadia and the St. Lawrence Valleys. English and Scots settlements, as well as Irish and Welsh ones, also were established in the 17th century. By 1763 the immigrant population of New France (q.v.), including in-colony human propagation, brought the total to between 65,000 and 75,000. Loyalist (q.v.) immigration to Nova Scotia and Québec consequent to the American Revolution (q.v.) brought new communities to the St. John River Valley and to lands along the St. Lawrence River (q.v.), Lake Ontario, and Lake Erie. As a result, new colonies were founded: New Brunswick (1784) and Upper Canada (1791, q.v.).

The Hudson's Bay Company (q.v.) assisted immigration to Red River in the second decade of the 19th century but did not otherwise encourage colonization, especially at Vancouver Island (q.v.). The British assisted immigration of Scots and Irish from the 1820s through the 1850s, boosting the English-speaking populations of Canada. The Canadian Pacific Railway (q.v.) had an immigration scheme, and so did the Salvation Army (founded by William Booth in 1865) and other church denominations and groups. Barnardo Children from the United Kingdom were immigrants, too. Named after Irish social worker Thomas John Bernardo, 30,000 of these homeless or orphaned children from British slums were placed with Canadian families between 1870 and 1930. Under Clifford Sifton (q.v.), Western Canadian immigration was promoted to fill up vacant, agricultural lands. Between 1905 and 1912 nearly a quarter of a million homesteaders arrived in the prairie provinces, attracted by good land and promises of more. This brought many new communities from northern and eastern Europe, including Iceland, Ukraine, Belgium, Holland, and Germany. Chinese (q.v.) immigration to British Columbia began, essentially, with the British Columbia gold rush. It continued with the introduction of Chinese labour for the building of the Canadian Pacific and other railways. Japanese immigration to British Columbia began in 1877. Sikh immigration from the Punjab occurred beginning at the turn of the century. In May 1914, HMCS *Rainbow* was used in aid of the civil power (q.v.) at Vancouver to turn away 360 illegal Sikh immigrants aboard the Japanese ship *Komagata Maru*. About 4,000 Sikhs lived in British Columbia before their immigration was banned in 1908. Asian immigration was curtailed by "gentleman's agreement" with Japan or by legislation (such as the "head tax" on Chinese). In 1967 the last remnants of exclusion on the grounds of race were expunged from Canadian legislation.

After 1945 more southern Europeans immigrated to Canada, principally Italians and Greeks. France, after 1763, supplied hardly any immigrants to Canada or to Québec. In the 20th century the United Kingdom headed the list of countries supplying immigrants to Canada, followed by the United States. However, Statistics Canada reported that as of 1996 the number of European immigrants to Canada had fallen to less than 50 percent of the annual total. In 1996 there were 1,038,995 immigrants to Canada (of a population of about 30,000,000), of whom 10.5 percent came from Hong Kong, 8.5 percent from the People's Republic of China, and 6.9 percent from India. Others came from the Philippines, Sri Lanka, Poland, Taiwan, Vietnam, the United States (2.8 percent), and the United Kingdom (2.4 percent). It may also be observed that on the basis of the 1996 census, Britain and other European countries now account for 47 percent of the five million immigrants living in the country. This is the result of the growing influx of arrivals from Asia, the Middle East, Latin America and so forth. Half of all immigrants as of 1996 lived in one of three cities: Toronto, Montréal, and Vancouver, in that order. In the 1990s half of all immigrants go to Ontario, Canada's largest province. Thus 42 percent of Toronto's population is made up of immigrants, compared with one-third for Vancouver. *See also* Japanese; Ukrainian.

INDIAN KINGS. The so-called Four Indian Kings of Canada were four Mohawk sachems who went to London in 1710 to plead for the assistance of Queen Anne. They were feted, and they created a sensation in London. One of the chiefs was Brant, grandfather of the famous Joseph Brant. As a result of the Indians' petition to the crown, funds were provided for a chapel (the Mohawk Chapel, near Brantford), a Bible, and a silver communion service (later divided between the Grand River Reserve and the Deseronto settlement, Bay of Quinte). Missionaries were subsequently sent to the Mohawk by the Society for the Propagation of the Gospel in Foreign Parts, a London-based missionary society. The Indians' visit called attention to giving military and religious protection against the French in Canada. *See also* Iroquois.

INNIS, HAROLD ADAMS (1894–1952). Economist and historian, soldier and social scientist. Born in Otterville, Ontario, Innis wrote histories of staple trades and communications. He spent most of his professional life at the University of Toronto. Arguably the most famous Canadian academic of all time, he wrote widely on fur, wheat, railways, pulp and paper, and communications. *See also* Historical Writing.

INTELLIGENCE SERVICES. *See* Secret Service.

INTERNATIONAL BOUNDARY COMMISSION, UNITED STATES AND CANADA. The International Boundary Commission, United States and Canada, had its beginning with the appointment of the commissioners to survey and mark that section of the Alaska boundary (q.v.) line as fixed by the Alaska Boundary Tribunal in 1903. Legal authority for the International Boundary Commission was provided by a convention concluded in 1906 between the United States and Britain. This convention established a joint commission to survey and mark the boundary that begins at Mount St. Elias on the 141st degree of west longitude and runs due north to the Arctic Ocean. The commissioners who were conducting the survey under the terms of the award of the 1903 Tribunal were also appointed to conduct the new survey.

The duties of these commissioners were expanded by the treaty signed 11 April 1908 between the United States and Britain. This treaty provided for the resurveying and re-marking of the entire boundary between the United States and Canada except the boundary of Alaska. Each article of the treaty defined a specific section of the boundary, as follows: Article I, through Passamaquoddy Bay; Article II, from the mouth to the source of the St. Croix River; Article III, from the source of the St. Croix River to the St. Lawrence River (q.v.); Article IV, from the St. Lawrence River to the mouth of the Pigeon River; Article V, from Pigeon River to the Lake of the Woods; Article VI, from the Lake of the Woods to the summit of the Rocky Mountains; Article VII, boundary from the Rocky Mountains to the Gulf of Georgia; and Article VIII, from the 49th parallel of north latitude to the Pacific Ocean.

Each article, except Article IV, included a provision for the establishment of a joint commission to carry out the terms of the article. Article IV, which concerned the water boundary, provided for the surveying and marking of the boundary by the International Joint Commission, United States and Canada (q.v.). Although the treaty provided for the creation of seven commissions in addition to the Alaska commissions established by the 1903 Tribunal and the 1906 convention, the same persons were appointed to serve on all the commissions; thus, each country was represented by only one commissioner for the whole of the U.S.-Canadian boundary line. *See also* International Waterways Commission, United States and Canada.

INTERNATIONAL JOINT COMMISSION, UNITED STATES AND CANADA (IJC). The International Joint Commission, United States and Canada, was established under treaty between the United States and Great Britain on 11 January 1909. The commission has a threefold jurisdiction. Its authority is final in all cases involving the use or diversion of boundary waters of the United States and Canada, or rivers crossing the boundary; it investigates and reports on questions relating to conditions along the boundary, which may be referred to it by either of the two governments; and it may settle any question that the two governments agree to refer to it for that purpose. The commission was made a permanent court of arbitration by Article X of the treaty.

Cases involving matters of prime interest to states, provinces, and nationals have come before the commission for investigation, report, or decision. Among these cases are those involving the use of boundary waters, water levels of the Lake of the Woods, the practicability of improving the upper St. Lawrence (q.v.) for both navigation and water power, and damage to orchards by fumes from the smelter at Trail, British Columbia.

The commission is composed of three U.S. commissioners and three Canadian commissioners. *See also* International Boundary Commission, United States and Canada; International Waterways Commission, United States and Canada.

INTERNATIONAL WATERWAYS COMMISSION, UNITED STATES AND CANADA. In 1902 the U.S. Congress requested the president to invite Britain "to join in the formation of an international commission, to be composed of three members from the United States and three who shall represent the interests of the Dominion of Canada, whose duty it shall be to investigate and report upon the conditions and uses of the waters adjacent to the boundary lines between United States and Canada, including all waters of the lakes and rivers whose natural outlet is by the River Saint Lawrence to the Atlantic Ocean." The commission was to report on means to regulate water levels and diversion of water and on methods for improving and regulating navigation on boundary waters. The invitation tendered by the U.S. ambassador at London was accepted by the Foreign Office in 1903.

When the full commission met on 25 May 1905, it was agreed that the chairman of the U.S. Section would serve as chairman of the body at its meetings in the United States and the chairman of the Canadian Section would preside over meetings held in Canada. In interpreting the scope of the law, the British government preferred a broad interpretation that included almost all of the U.S.-Canadian water boundary extending from the Atlantic Ocean to the Pacific. The U.S. Section contended that the law restricted the commission to discussing matters pertaining only to that part of the water boundary that flowed into the St. Lawrence River (q.v.). In June 1905 the Canadian government instructed its representatives to proceed with the work of the commission within the scope prescribed by the U.S. Section.

In 1905 the commission defined 11 problems to be discussed. The problems concerned such matters as the uses of the waters of the Sault Ste. Marie and Niagara Rivers, differences in the marine regulations of the two countries, maintenance of effective water levels, illegal fishing, and construction of channels.

Until 1908 the International Waterways Commission functioned within the scope of the U.S. act of 1902 as agreed to by the British government. A treaty concluded on 11 April 1908 (*see* International Boundary Commission, United States and Canada) expanded the commission's duties. Article IV of this treaty empowered the six commissioners to "reestablish accurately the location of the international boundary line beginning at the point of its intersection with the St. Lawrence River near the forty-fifth parallel of north latitude . . . and hence through the Great Lakes and communicating waterways to the mouth of Pigeon River, at the western shore of Lake Superior." This section of the northern boundary was originally defined in the provisional treaty of peace of 1782, and most of the points of controversy were settled by the Webster-Ashburton Treaty of 1842.

The whole commission held its first meeting under terms of Article IV on 2 June 1908 at Buffalo, New York. On 15 August 1913, the International Waterways Commission "fixed and adopted" the boundary line as surveyed and marked. The final report was officially transmitted to the U.S. and Canadian governments on 29 April 1915. *See also* International Joint Commission, United States and Canada.

INUIT. An aboriginal people of Canada living in the eastern Northwest Territories, previously called Eskimos; their homeland is Nunavut (q.v.). The relocation experiment of several Inuit communities was organized by Canada's Department of Resources and Development and the Royal Canadian Mounted Police. The relocations were from Port Harrison,

Québec, to Grise Fiord (Craig Harbour) and Resolute Bay (1953–55). Others, some earlier, were to Devon Island (1934), Baffin Island (1926), King George and Sleeper Islands (1951–52), and Churchill (1953). Canadian government authorities—especially former commissioners of the Northwest Territories—have denied that the Inuit were "human flags" to re-enforce Canadian sovereignty in the High Arctic. Official records reveal the government's purpose was to overcome the "Eskimo problem"—unstable economy, poor health, and growing welfare dependency. Policy directives of the time aimed at self-sufficiency and the maintenance of traditional ways of life. Relocations were physically and emotionally difficult for the Inuit, who did not "volunteer." Inuit were not part of the general political discussions that led to their removals to high latitudes. It can be said that mutual consent was absent from the process. Trusteeship, and government obligation, propelled policy.

In subsequent meetings of the Royal Commission on Aboriginal Affairs, Inuit leaders and organizations have sought redress and an apology from the Canadian government.

IROQUOIS. The Iroquoian peoples speak a common language. The Iroquois Confederacy was located along the southern shoreline of Lake Ontario and the St. Lawrence River. Initially, the confederacy consisted of five nations: the Mohawk, Oneida, Onondaga, Cayuga, and Seneca. The largest tribe in the confederacy was the Seneca, but the most aggressive was the Mohawk. The Iroquois nation fought many bitter battles with other surrounding natives. The Iroquois nation prevented the French from expanding up the St. Lawrence River. After Samuel de Champlain (q.v.) led the Hurons (q.v.) and allies to a great defeat of the Mohawks on Lake Champlain in 1609, the Iroquois Confederacy became permanent enemies of the French and allied themselves with the British. In 1713, the Tuscarora nation from the Carolinas fled to Canada from white settlers. They were accepted into the confederacy, creating the present day League of Six Nations. They assisted the British in conquering New France. Many Iroquois warriors fought for the British in the War of 1812 (q.v.). The population of the Iroquois declined after contact with Europeans, due mainly to smallpox and bitter wars with the Hurons and French.

-J-

JAMES BAY AGREEMENT. A treaty signed in 1975 between Québec and Cree and Inuit (q.v.) living in northern Québec adjacent to James Bay.

The agreement transferred native rights from the Cree and Inuit to Québec in return for $225 million, hunting and fishing rights, and substantial self-government. The treaty was negotiated to permit the Québec government to build the massive James Bay Project (q.v.).

JAMES BAY PROJECT. A massive construction project to harness the hydroelectric potential of several river systems emptying into James Bay. The project was announced in 1971 by Québec Liberal Premier Robert Bourassa (q.v.). The project has diverted rivers, created one of the world's largest underground powerhouses, and built dams and dikes. In addition, the project has created numerous ecological problems that have affected the Cree and Inuit (q.v.), as well as the natural environment. Most of the power generated is sold to customers in the United States.

JAPANESE. The first Japanese emigrant (Manzo Nagano) settled in Victoria, British Columbia, in 1877, and by 1914 there were 10,000 permanent Japanese residents in Canada. They, like other Asians, faced discrimination. In 1907, at Canada's insistence, Japan limited male emigration to Canada at 400. In 1928 Canada restricted Japanese immigration to 150 per year. Legal Japanese immigration did not resume until 1967. In 1986, the census found 40,240 Japanese in Canada.

The Japanese define themselves in Canada as follows: *Issei*, those who arrived 1877–1928; *Nisei,* their Canadian-born children; and *Sansai*, the third generation, born in the 1950s and 1960s in Canadian society. Japanese immigrants came from various backgrounds and classes. The *Issei* were predominantly of peasant or fishing cultures. Those arriving after 1967 were educated members of industrial urban middle class.

Exclusion and discrimination marked Japanese progress in Canada. The Japanese settled in certain enclaves: Powell Street, Vancouver; Steveston; Mission City; Tofino; and Prince Rupert (all in British Columbia). In some locations they built schools, community halls, Christian churches, and Buddhist and Shinto temples. They formed clubs and cooperatives.

In 1942 the War Measures Act (q.v.) was invoked to order the removal of Japanese Canadians residing within 100 miles of the Pacific Coast. This was done for two reasons, the relative weight of which is indeterminable: protection of the white society from Japanese attack, and protection of the Japanese from white reprisals for events at Pearl Harbor, Hong Kong, Singapore, and elsewhere. Thus, 20,881 Japanese Canadians (75 percent were Canadian nationals) were moved to detention camps in eastern British Columbia, Alberta, and Manitoba. Property was expropriated and sold. Attempted deportations continued until 1946, when the process was stopped owing to mass public protest.

The *Sansei* have built a new kind of Canada for the Japanese. More than 75 percent have married non-Japanese. Owing to pressure from the National Association of Japanese Canadians, the Government of Canada, following the example of the United States, issued a formal apology and provided (partial) financial compensation.

JESUIT RELATIONS. The series of works familiarly known as the *Jesuit Relations* were annual reports from the Superiors of the Jesuit Missions in Canada to the Provincials of the order in France. In addition to their distinctly religious portions, they include much firsthand information about the natural resources of the regions that were the centres of missionary work; the manners, customs, and language of the Indians; the incessant intertribal wars of the Iroquois (q.v.) and other Canadian Indians; and the zeal and tribulations of the missionary priests. Occasional comments on relations with the English colonies in New England and the Dutch colonies of New York add to the value of the reports as source books for the early history of the areas under consideration.

JESUITS. The Society of Jesus, the Jesuits, played a profound role in Canadian religious and social history. Given the monopoly of conversion of the native "heathens" in 1632, the Jesuits took over from the Recollets the full control of the Huronia (q.v.) mission; the mission ended in consequence of the Iroquois (q.v.) wars. The Jesuits were also notably involved in the exploration (q.v.) of North America, Père Jacques Marquette being the most notable Jesuit explorer. The Jesuits assumed control of the religion of Canadian settlements, both urban and rural. Their seminary at Québec became Laval University, the first in Canada. Another prominent institution of higher learning was Loyola College, which in the 1960s became part of Concordia University, Montréal.

The Jesuits became prominent landholders in Québec and in some areas could control, under law, one-seventh of all lands. The order was suppressed in the late 18th century but was reestablished in Québec in 1842. In 1888, by Québec statute, compensation to the Jesuits for loss of these lands (sequestered by the Crown) was finally agreed upon. How to allot the compensation, which had to be spent on education, was a difficult question. In the end, $400,000 was the value set on these lands. The act granted $70,000 to the province's Protestant schools; the rest was divided within the Catholic community at the pope's discretion. In Québec this was a satisfactory solution. In Ontario, however, the Orange

Order was enraged, charging the Government of Québec with inviting the pope to intervene in Canadian affairs. The prime minister, Sir John A. Macdonald (q.v.), refused to disallow the act, coming as it did, he argued, within clear provincial powers (especially land regulation and schools). *See also* Brébeuf, Ste. Jean de; Ste.-Marie among the Hurons; Universities.

JOHNSON, EMILY PAULINE (1861–1913). "The Mohawk Princess," poet and performer. Johnson was a Mohawk, born in Six Nations Reserve near Brantford, Ontario. In an effort to make a living, she began a career of platform entertainment in 1893. On stage she recited her poems. Her popularity rose as she crossed Canada and the United States reading her poetry for entertainment. A book of her poems titled *Legends of Vancouver* was published in 1911.

JOLLIET, LOUIS (1645–1700). Explorer, fur trader, seigneur, and officeholder. Born in Québec and educated at the Jesuit (q.v.) college there, Jolliet abandoned ecclesiastical life for the fur trade (q.v.). He was the discoverer, with Père Jacques Marquette, S.J., of the Mississippi River in 1673; they navigated downriver to within 400 miles of the Gulf of Mexico. Marquette's narrative tells this story; Jolliet's was lost. Jolliet was granted Anticosti Island in the Gulf of St. Lawrence as reward. He settled there with his family. He also made voyages to Hudson Bay (1679) and Labrador (1694). In 1680 he was appointed royal hydrographer and royal pilot. In 1697 he obtained a seigniory, "Jolliet," in Beauce County, Québec.

-K-

KING, WILLIAM LYON MACKENZIE (1874–1950). Lawyer and politician. King was born in Berlin (now Kitchener), Ontario. He studied law in the University of Toronto and undertook postgraduate work at the University of Chicago and Harvard. An expert on labour relations and social theory, he became a Liberal member of Parliament (q.v.) for Waterloo North in 1908 and minister of labour (1909–11). Defeated in 1911, he was for a time a labour advisor to J. D. Rockefeller. In 1919 King rejoined politics and he became leader of the Liberal party (q.v.). He was elected prime minister in 1921 and served 1921–26, 1926–30 and 1935–48. His reign in office is the longest in Canadian history.

A great conciliator and master of brokerage politics, King fought against governor general Julian Byng (q.v.) in a celebrated constitutional struggle in 1925–26. He often was at odds with the provinces, but he agreed to the transfer of resource management to the provinces. As well, he established a Royal Commission of Federal–Provincial Relations (the Rowell–Sirois Commission).

Often seen as a socially irresponsible prime minister, King was actually a brilliant parliamentary strategist. An avowed nationalist and opposed to military armament, he objected to British imperial jingoism and feared American military and economic domination during World War II (q.v.). He strongly supported the concept of dominion autonomy within the British Empire. He met Hitler and told him that Canada would not stand idly by in the face of German aggression. He led Canada towards and into war, launched a military rearmament scheme, and worked with British Prime Minister Winston Churchill and American President Franklin Roosevelt on the North Atlantic schemes of wartime cooperation. In Canada, military production increased during the war, Japanese (q.v.) security risks were dealt with, and manpower shortages were rectified by the Military Conscription Act of 1944. All of these were controversial. King's slogan on the subject of conscription had been "not necessarily conscription, but conscription if necessary."

King had a strong interest in spiritualism (for which he was often ridiculed), had an unusual private life, and built a delightful retreat in Kingsmere, north of Ottawa, in Québec. He authored *Industry and Humanity* (1918; rev. 1935 and 1947). In 1948 he resigned from office. *See also* New Deal.

KOREAN CONFLICT. When North Korea invaded South Korea on 25 June 1950, the United States invoked the Charter of the United Nations and passed a resolution through the Security Council to aid Seoul in repelling the invader. Canada responded along with 15 other United Nations members to aid in the effort to stop North Korean aggression.

Canada sent destroyers to Korea (one of which was HMCS *Haida* [q.v.]) to aid in the naval support forces stationed there. The Royal Canadian Air Force provided an air transport squadron to assist the sending of supplies to UN forces on the peninsula; in addition, a number of Canadian fighter pilots flew with U.S. Air Force squadrons and were responsible for the destruction of North Korean aircraft. However, the largest contingent of forces was sent by the Army; more than 21,000 Army personnel served in Korea. Of the 490,000 UN casualties, 1,588 were Canadians, including 516 dead. Canadian troops performed very well and won distinction for stopping Chinese attacks at Kap' Yong in April 1951.

KREVER INQUIRY AND REPORT. The Canadian "tainted-blood" investigation (1993–97) and subsequent report. In July 1981, Acquired Immune Deficiency Syndrome (AIDS) was identified among homosexuals in Los Angeles; in July 1982, AIDS was identified among haemophiliacs and in blood transfusion recipients. In December 1989 the Canadian government announced compensation for haemophiliacs and blood-transfused people infected with human immune deficiency virus (HIV).

On 4 October 1993 Mr. Justice Horace Krever was instructed by Minister of Health and Welfare Mary Collins to investigate the contaminated-blood scandal. He was to investigate what went wrong with Canada's blood supply in the 1980s, when an estimated 1,400 people were allowed to contact HIV, and another 12,000 to become infected with hepatitis C, from blood or blood products. (These are conservative figures: Krever reported as many as 28,600 could have been infected through blood transfusions from 1986 to 1990.) Three-quarters of Canada's 2,500 haemophiliacs also have hepatitis C, owing to tainted-blood transfusions.

Hearings began in November 1993 and ended in December 1995. Krever's right to make findings of misconduct was challenged in court by the Canadian Red Cross Society, four pharmaceutical companies, most provincial governments, and many individuals who believed their reputations might be damaged if Krever were allowed to assign blame. The federal court ruled in June 1996 in Krever's favour (upheld by the federal court of appeal in January 1997). The Red Cross and two pharmaceutical companies continued the fight to the Supreme Court.

After 247 days of testimony, 1,303 exhibits, 474 witnesses (about half of them victims), and numerous attempts (consuming 18 months) by interested parties to change or alter the inquiry, Krever's report was completed and presented to Parliament 26 November 1997. It is estimated that the inquiry cost the taxpayers almost $57 million for the commission plus $10.5 million for government expenses. The Red Cross legal bills were at least $10.5 million in defence. The number of victims who died *during the course of the inquiry* is estimated at more than 400. Highlights of Krever's findings: serious neglect was exhibited by governments and the Red Cross; infections continued while governments and agencies diddled or obfuscated the process; there had been a decline in public policy processes and acceptance of responsibility. Krever recommended, among other things, that a Canadian Blood Services be established (the Red Cross had been suspended in this responsibility previously); blood should be available on a not-for-profit basis; and rigid, independent (that is, nongovernment) scrutiny was needed to screen products and processes. In 1989, the federal compensation plan was announced and in September 1993, provinces and territories announced compensation of $30,000 annually to victims of tainted blood. In 1999, victims of hepatitis C settled a $1.2 billion federal–provincial compensation deal.

KWAGIULTH. The Kwagiulth ("Beach on the Other Side of the River") occupied northern Vancouver Island from Johnstone Strait to Cape Cook and all the coast of the mainland from Douglas Channel to Bute Inlet, except for a small area that was dominated by the Bella Coola. Primarily fishing people, the Kwagiulth were reluctant to engage in the fur trade (q.v.).The Kwagiulth suffered severe population declines due to various European diseases in the 1800s. They are famous for the *potlatch* (gift giving) and winter spirit dancing (*hamatsa*). Among the most famous of these people are anthropologist George Hunt (who worked with Franz Boas) and great carver Mungo Martin (who was principal carver for Thunderbird Park, Victoria, British Columbia). Fort Rupert and Alert Bay, British Columbia, were two of their prominent new villages.

-L-

LABRADOR. Now part of the province of Newfoundland, Labrador lies on the mainland across the Strait of Belle Isle. Its long coast is heavily indented with inlets, many important in history as places for fishing, whaling, exploration, mining, missions, and other settlements. Part of the Canadian or Laurentian shield, Labrador has a rugged, mountainous, and isolated character which shaped its human history. Long occupied by native peoples (the earliest evidence dates to 7,000 years ago), it was possibly visited by the Vikings (L'Anse aux Meadows and Amour burial site) and is possibly the "Markland" of Viking saga fame (*see* Norse).

The modern era of Labrador history begins with Basque fishermen establishing a whale fishery at Red Bay. This occurred before Jacques Cartier (q.v.) explored the coast in the early 16th century. Portuguese explorers, who visited coastal Labrador and Greenland (500 miles distant), were interested in the fishery—and continued to fish these waters intermittently even centuries thereafter. One Portuguese explorer, João

Fernandez, a *lavrador* or "landholder" in the Azores, may be credited with the origin of the name Labrador. Early European occupation was predicated on the coastal fishery; this was fiercely opposed by the natives (who call themselves Labradormiut) and the Montagnais-Naskapi. The fishing population of Labrador was a floating one; the economy of Labrador was international. Newfoundlanders and English came to fish there, but so, too, did New Englanders, especially after the War of 1812 (q.v.). New places for the coastal fishery were required, and the Royal Navy undertook exploration of fishing grounds and harbours in the northern reaches of the coast.

Meanwhile, specific settlements had been established: Cape Charles, 1770 (by businessman George Cartwright); Nairn, 1771 (by Moravian missionaries); and Rigolet, 1843, and North West River, 1834 (by the Hudson's Bay Company [q.v.]). Explorations (q.v.) were undertaken by John McLean (HBC) in 1939, A. P. Low (geologist) in the 1890s, and V. A. Tanner (Finnish geographer) in 1937 and 1939. Other Moravian missions were established in 1784 and 1896.

Because of its remoteness, Labrador had little in the way of medical care, schools, or adequate housing. Wilfred Grenfell (q.v.), an Englishman, is credited with heroic activities to establish hospitals, schools, and orphanages there. He publicized the needs of Labrador in print and by lectures and raised funds for educational and medical needs in Labrador.

During World War II (q.v.) Goose Bay was built as a base and "staging ground" for an overseas Allied lift called Ferry Command. A U.S. Air Force base for many years thereafter, it also became a busy commercial airport on the North American–European route, said in the 1950s to be the second-busiest in the world.

In 1954 the Québec North Shore and Labrador Railway was completed, allowing the outflow of the interior's iron ore. Churchill Falls was developed as a large hydroelectric facility. The establishment of the boundary of Labrador with the province of Québec (1902–27) resolved the dispute involving Québec, Newfoundland, and Canada.

In 1949 Newfoundland joined the confederation, and when it did so its boundary in Labrador was confirmed. Newfoundland, then as now, claims the watershed of all rivers flowing into the Atlantic Ocean. Many Québecers argue that Labrador is included in "Nouveau Québec." Generally speaking, the boundary and watersheds issue is not settled and revives from time to time in respect to hydroelectric-use issues. Canada's relations with Québec and Newfoundland mean that third-party interests are invariably part of the equation.

LAFONTAINE, SIR LOUIS HIPPOLYTE (1807–1864). Politician and jurist, Lafontaine promoted responsible government (q.v.) and full French Canadian participation in Canadian politics of the colonial era. He entered politics in 1830. Along with Robert Baldwin (q.v.), he is credited with the effecting of responsible government, by which the legislature gained control of the civil list, or those persons on the public payroll. He followed Louis-Joseph Papineau (q.v.) in many respects; yet he was opposed to the call to arms of the Patriots in 1837. He journeyed to London to argue for constitutional reform.

As leader of Canada East's (q.v.) reformers Lafontaine joined forces with Baldwin and Sir Francis Hincks (q.v.) of Canada West and formed an alliance which became the majority party. Governor General Sir Charles Bagot (q.v.), in 1841, upon the union of the Canadas, accepted the power of this bicultural, reform-minded ministry, which is known as the first Baldwin-Lafontaine administration. Responsible government was gradually effected from 1846 to 1849. In 1848 Earl Grey, the colonial secretary, called on Lafontaine to establish a ministry; this he did with his partner Baldwin. This ministry is referred to as the second Baldwin-Lafontaine administration. This coalition ended in 1851.

Lafontaine was prime minister of Canada from 1848 to 1851. He introduced the Rebellion Losses Bill in 1848, the triumph of which proclaimed responsible government. He was chief justice of Lower Canada (q.v.) from 1853 until his death.

LA GALISSONIÈRE, MARQUIS DE [ROLAND-MICHEL BARRIN] (1693–1756). Naval officer and prominent commandant general of New France. Though only in Canada a short time (1747–49), La Galissonière was a strategic reformer. He knew the value of Canada to France and the French empire, and he pressed on the king of France the necessity of bolstering the defences of Canada. Among his suggestions were the strengthening of the regained Louisbourg (q.v.) and its defences, the bolstering of Fort St.-Jean on the Richelieu/Champlain River corridor, and the strengthening of other posts. La Galissonière saw Canada much as an imperial extension of France, and he believed that Britain would have to conquer Canada in order to defeat France in a future war. He sought to encourage settlement, particularly at Detroit, which he saw as a key post. He wanted the St. Lawrence River (q.v.) linked to the Mississippi River in a grand design connecting French settlements on the St. Lawrence to those on the Gulf of Mexico, especially New Orleans.

At 17 La Galissonière joined the French navy, and after a successful career he was sent to Canada at the age of 54 as "commander-in-chief" of the colony. Canada was then in great peril, for Louisbourg and Acadia had been lost to the British, the Gulf of St. Lawrence was infested with English privateers, Québec was under threat of invasion, and the alliance with the Indians was shaky. The western frontier was in difficulty, owing to the recent war. Like his predecessors he could not shake the French ministers, and the king, from their apathy. When he sounded the alarm, it is said, it rang timidly in the offices of Versailles. He fought an exhausting, successful naval battle against the British under Adm. George Byng at Minorca in 1756 and died shortly thereafter.

LAM, DAVID SEE-CHAI (1923–). An immigrant to Canada from his native China in 1967, Lam amassed a fortune in real estate. A founder of the Hong Kong Merchants' Association of Vancouver, he facilitated Pacific Rim investment in British Columbia. His own company is Canadian International Properties Limited. An energetic visionary, he and his wife Dorothy through their philanthropy have assisted universities, gardens, and research institutions. Lam was appointed lieutenant-governor of British Columbia in 1988 and served until 1995.

LAND COMMAND. *See* Canadian Army.

LAST SPIKE, THE. Donald Smith, later Lord Strathcona, drove the last spike of the Canadian Pacific Railway's (q.v.) railroad at Craigellachie in Eagle Pass, British Columbia, 7 November 1885. The first spike was made of gold and bent when Smith hit it with the hammer; it was replaced by one of iron. With this action, Montréal became linked to Port Moody by a rail line 2,891 miles long.

LAURIER, SIR WILFRID (1841–1919). First French Canadian prime minister. Laurier, a superb orator, served in the Assembly of Québec 1871–74 and then in the House of Commons until his death. A Liberal, he was appointed (1877) minister of inland revenue in Alexander Mackenzie's (q.v.) administration. He went into opposition in 1878. Chosen leader of the Liberal party (q.v.) in 1887, he became prime minister when his party won the election of 1896. Laurier was returned in the elections of 1900, 1904, and 1908 and was defeated 1911.

In the "age of Laurier," two million immigrants arrived in Canada, the West was further colonized, farming based on wheat and grains in the prairies developed, Alberta and Saskatchewan were created, and two transcontinental railways were built. Increases in mining, lumbering, and manufacturing in the other parts of the country also occurred.

Emphasizing the need for cooperation and compromise, as exemplified by the settlement of the Manitoba Schools Question, Laurier favoured close ties with the British government. After the dispatch of Canadian troops to serve in the South African War (q.v.), he sought to balance imperial cooperation with the assertion of Canadianism. He created in 1910 the Canadian Naval Service (*see* Canadian Navy). In 1911 he concluded a tariff reciprocity (q.v.) agreement with the United States. The election of 1911 brought Laurier's downfall. The reciprocity agreement was repudiated by Canada. Laurier supported Canada's entry into World War I (q.v.). He condemned conscription. He refused to join Sir Robert Borden's (q.v.) Union Government, formed in 1917.

LAVAL, FRANÇOIS-XAVIER DE MONTMORENCY (1623–1708). Apostolic vicar in New France (q.v.) from 1659 to 1674; bishop of Québec from 1674 to 1688. Ecclesiastical controversy surrounded Father Laval's appointment to Canada, and conflict over jurisdiction remained an issue throughout his term. A Jesuit (q.v.), he founded two seminaries at Québec (1663 and 1668) to supply priests for New France; they later became Laval University (*see* Universities). In 1663, when Louis XIV established the Sovereign Council, Monseigneur Laval became second most important figure in New France. He had constitutional powers to appoint Council members and award seigneuries. He condemned the sale of alcohol to natives, which put him in opposition to business interests in Montréal and elsewhere. He did much to establish the Church in New France and promote education, arts, and crafts.

LEVESQUE, RENÉ (1922–1987). Québec radio and television journalist, politician, and premier of Québec. Levesque resigned from the Liberal party (q.v.) and founded the Parti Québecois (q.v.) in 1968. He won a great victory in the Québec election in 1976, defeating Robert Bourassa's (q.v.) Liberals. Levesque pushed his party and province not only to greater autonomy within Canada but towards a goal of Québec sovereignty. He introduced electoral and labour reforms in Québec and advanced schemes for the expansion of Québec Hydro. He brought about measures to get better provincial control over foreign-based corporations. Levesque's government introduced Bill 101, a highly controversial measure, which legislated for a unilingual Québec. His government also introduced and lost (41 percent in favour, 59 percent in opposition) a referendum in 1980 concerning the separation of Québec from Canada. Levesque was reelected in 1981 and began a campaign for greater autonomy within the confederation, and in this he found allies among other provincial premiers, particularly Alberta's Peter Lougheed.

Prime Minister Pierre Trudeau's (q.v.) Constitution Act of 1982 (q.v.) did not win Levesque's support. In 1984 Levesque announced that he would campaign in the next Québec election without demanding independence from Canada, settling into a mode which, for a time, became the party's official platform: sovereignty association. Levesque's leadership was reaffirmed at a special convention in January 1985, but he resigned in June 1985. He authored a best-selling *Memoirs* (1986).

LIBERAL PARTY. One of the two original political parties in Canada, known commonly as "Grits." The Liberal party originated out of a union of Clear Grits (q.v.) and George Brown's (q.v.) independent reformers in the legislature of the Province of Canada in the mid-1850s. Links were gradually formed with Québec Rouges (q.v.), and after confederation, other opposition groups also found themselves coalescing with the Liberals. In 1873, Alexander Mackenzie (q.v.) became the first Liberal prime minister and retained that post until 1878. In 1896, Sir Wilfrid Laurier (q.v.) was elected the first francophone Liberal prime minister and began the reign of the Liberals in the 20th century. Under various Liberal prime minsters, Canada developed into a social welfare state. Prior to 1984, the Liberals held power for a large majority of the century. The Liberal party's success has come about through skilful leadership, pragmatism carried to its highest level, and a solid base in the province of Québec.

LOUISBOURG. A maritime base and fortress of France on Île Royale, Cape Breton Island, Nova Scotia, constructed after 1719. Louisbourg was intended to dominate the Gulf of St. Lawrence, both to guard the French possessions and to provide a base from which to raid sea lanes between New England and Britain. The fortress was called "the Dunkirk of North America," after the fortified seaport on the French channel coast. It was also called "the Gibraltar of Canada."

Despite its massive walls, the fortress was exposed to long-range artillery fire across the harbour and from the low hills to the fortress's west side. In 1745 it was attacked by a force of New England militia under Gen. William Pepperell from Boston and Royal Navy vessels under Adm. Peter Warren and was forced to surrender 17 June after six weeks. The fortress was returned to France by treaty in 1748. In 1758 at the outbreak of the Seven Years' War (q.v.), it was captured again by the British. It remained under the control of Britain after 1758. In 1759, Gen. James

Wolfe's (q.v.) force destined for Québec assembled here. In 1760 British army engineers demolished its defences. By terms of the peace in 1763, Britain retained Louisbourg.

LOWER CANADA. Québec (q.v.) became Lower Canada by the Constitutional (or Canada) Act of 1791. Included within its borders were all lands held under the seigneurial system. Strife between English and French continued intermittently for a number of reasons, political, social, and economic. In 1837 a rebellion broke out, but it was put down. With the Act of Union, Lower Canada became Canada East in 1841. In 1867 Canada East became the province of Québec. *See also* Rebellions of 1837.

LOYALISTS. American Tories who chose to leave the United States after the American Revolution (q.v.) ended in 1783, or who were otherwise evicted or deported. Many Loyalists went to Nova Scotia and Québec. In 1784 New Brunswick was established as a new colony, for here the Loyalists had settled in number and constituted the resident European population. In 1791, Upper Canada (q.v.) was created from the old Québec, for somewhat similar reasons. "Late Loyalists" refers to Americans who came to British North America after the first wave. United Empire Loyalists is a latter-day appellation, dating to the late 19th century, and is also an organization dedicated to maintaining the identity and memory of forebears.

LUNDY'S LANE, BATTLE OF. This battle took place 25 July 1814 and was one of the fiercest battles of the War of 1812 (q.v.). A mixed force of British regulars and Canadian militia (q.v.), led by the Canadian general Sir Gordon Drummond, fought American invaders under Gen. Jacob Brown at a location just west of the Niagara River and close to Niagara Falls. The fight lasted several hours until around midnight with a high number of casualties on both sides. Drummond's force compelled the Americans to withdraw to Fort Erie (which Brown had taken 3 July and defended against Drummond 15 August).

-M-

McCARTHY, D'ALTON (1830–1898). From an Ulster Protestant background, McCarthy established the Equal Rights Association, which sought to limit the use of French in Ontario schools and to end Ottawa's acceptance of French as an official language in the Northwest Territories. He was an ally of Sir John A. Macdonald (q.v.), but his call for the use of force to maintain Anglo-Saxon Protestantism destabilized the Conservative party, in particular those within it who favoured accommodation with French-speaking Canadian conservatives, the Bleus. McCarthy's campaign brought in the Manitoba Schools Act of 1890 (q.v.).

McCLUNG, NELLIE MOONEY (1873–1951). Suffragist, politician, and educator. McClung was born in Manitoba. She belonged to the Canadian Women's Press Club and the Political Equality League where she worked for female suffrage. McClung led a delegation representing women's groups before the Manitoba parliament to ask that women be given the vote in Manitoba's provincial elections. Actions such as this led to Manitoba granting women the right to vote and thus run for office in 1916. In 1921, McClung was elected as a member of the Alberta legislature. In government, McClung always voted for social-activist legislation. She went on to become the first woman on the CBC's Board of Governors. In 1938 she was one of Canada's delegates to the League of Nations in Geneva, Switzerland. She retired to and died in Saanich, British Columbia. *See also* "Persons Case."

McCRAE, JOHN (1872–1918). Born in Guelph, Ontario, McCrae became a specialist in clinical medicine and pathology at McGill University, Montréal. A volunteer medical officer (surgeon to 1st Brigade, Canadian Field Artillery) in World War I (q.v.), he also wrote poetry, his best-known work being "In Flanders Fields," first published 8 December 1915 in *Punch*. In 1997 his medals were acquired by patriot Arthur Lee of Toronto and given to McCrae House (now a museum), where he was born.

McDONALD, ALEX (18??–19??). Born in Antigonish, Nova Scotia, McDonald was also known as "Big Alex" or "the Moose from Antigonish" because of his size. He came to the Yukon after working 14 years in Colorado, where he mined silver, and in Juneau, Alaska, where he panned for gold. Although he had no money originally, he eventually owned 50 claims and also became known as "the King of the Klondike." For a few years after the discovery of gold, he was perhaps the wealthiest man in the Yukon. In 1899, he married Margaret Chisholm while he was in England. He died some years later, in a cabin on Clearwater Creek in the Yukon. At the time of his death, he was again impoverished.

MACDONALD, SIR JOHN ALEXANDER (1815–1891). Lawyer, businessman, and politician, Canada's first prime minister. Macdonald was born in Glasgow, Scotland, and moved to Kingston, Ontario, with his parents in 1820. His father operated a series of businesses in Upper Canada (q.v.), merchant shops in Kingston and in Adolphustown Township, and for 10 years the large stone mills at Glenora in Prince Edward County.

In 1830, at the age of 15, Macdonald began to article in the office of Kingston lawyer George Mackenzie. By 1835, he opened his own law firm in Kingston. As a lawyer, Macdonald quickly attracted public attention, mainly by taking a number of difficult and sensational cases. Though he lost as many as he won, he acquired a reputation for ingenuity and quickwittedness as a defence attorney.

Macdonald was also an active businessman, primarily involved in land development and speculation. Throughout the 1840s, 1850s, and 1860s, he bought and developed urban property, first in Kingston and subsequently in Guelph and Toronto. He also acted as an agent for British investors in Canadian real estate. He acquired directorships in at least 10 Canadian companies, in addition to the Commercial Bank and the Trust and Loan Company, and he sat on two British boards.

From an early age, Macdonald showed a keen interest in public affairs. In March 1843, already a well-known lawyer, businessman, and public figure, he was elected to the Kingston Town Council as an alderman. The following year, he was elected to the provincial legislature. He ran in Kingston as a Conservative, stressing his belief in the British connection, his commitment to the development of Canadian resources, and his devotion to the interests of Kingston. In his early years in the Legislative Assembly, Macdonald proved to be a genuine Conservative, opposing responsible government (q.v.) and the secularization of the clergy reserves because such measures could have weakened the British connection or the authority of the government. From the beginning, Macdonald's approach to politics was essentially pragmatic.

Macdonald was appointed a cabinet member in 1847–48, when he served for seven months as receiver general and for three as commissioner of Crown lands. In 1848, he resigned with the government to make way for the reform administration of Robert Baldwin and Louis Lafontaine (qq.v.). In 1854, Macdonald became attorney general for Upper Canada in the newly formed coalition government of Sir Allan Napier MacNab (q.v.) and Augustin-Norbert Morin. In 1856, Macdonald became, for the first time, leader of the Upper Canadian section of the government, replacing MacNab. While in office, Macdonald reformed the government to make it more efficient. The Civil Service Act of 1857 established the rule that each major government agency would have a permanent, nonpolitical head called a deputy minister. He shared the direction of the government and his party with a French Canadian leader, George Étienne Cartier (q.v.). The Macdonald-Cartier ministry undertook many legislative initiatives, including the Independence of Parliament Act (1857) and an act for registration of voters (1858).

In 1862, Macdonald went into opposition when the Militia Bill was defeated in the assembly. A constitutional committee of the legislature was formed with George Brown as the chairman. Macdonald was a part of this committee, which presented a proposal for a federal system of government for the two sections of Canada or for all of British North America. Macdonald had always preferred a highly centralized form of government. In 1864, Macdonald's Conservatives were joined by Canadian Reformers and Cartier's Bleus to form the "Great Coalition" for the purpose of creating a federal union of British North America.

Macdonald was the dominant figure throughout the events that led up to confederation in 1867. At the Québec Conference (q.v.), he was the principal spokesman for the Canadian scheme. He chaired meetings in London in 1866–67 and was active in the creation of the actual British North America Act (*see* Constitution Act of 1867). Britain recognized Macdonald's efforts. He was the only colonial leader to be awarded an honorary degree (from Oxford in 1865). He was given a knighthood (conferred 29 June 1867) and was selected to be the first prime minister of the Dominion of Canada (q.v.). The Department of Justice was the portfolio Macdonald chose in 1867 and the one he retained until his resignation of his government in 1873. The early session of the Canadian parliament showed Macdonald's centralized views about the assimilation of Nova Scotia, New Brunswick, and the Hudson's Bay Company (q.v.) territory. Indian affairs came under his purview.

The Pacific Scandal (q.v.) of 1873 forced the Macdonald government to resign from office. Macdonald's government was accused of using money from the Canadian Pacific Railway (q.v.) Company to finance the election. The allegations proved true; Macdonald was forced to resign his government from office, and Alexander Mackenzie (q.v.) and the Liberal party (q.v.) formed the new government. In the 1874 election, the Macdonald's Conservatives were badly defeated.

Macdonald and the Conservatives were returned to office in the 1878 election and held the position until 1891. In the new government, Macdonald took on the Department of the Interior portfolio. During this term in office, Macdonald had to confront Louis Riel (q.v.) for the second time as the Métis (q.v.) of the West confronted the expanding settlers again. Macdonald quelled the situation with force and Riel was captured and hanged for his part in the rebellion. Macdonald also dealt with the Manitoba school question in 1890. Macdonald decided that the constitutionality of Manitoba's abolition of public funding for Catholic schools was best left to the courts, not the House of Commons. Macdonald's last fight was the election of 1891. In this election he fought the Liberals over reciprocity (q.v.) with the United States. He led the Conservatives to another victory, but died shortly after on 6 June 1891. Sir John A. Macdonald was one of the main figures of Canadian confederation and arguably the most important politician in national history. He assisted greatly in shaping the political structure of Canada and insuring the longevity of the Dominion of Canada.

MACDONALD, JOHN SANDFIELD (1812–1872). Lawyer and politician. Born at St. Raphael, Glengarry County, Upper Canada (q.v.), of Irish background, Macdonald represented Glengarry and then Cornwall for most of his political career. He became solicitor general in the Baldwin-Lafontaine (qq.v.) government of 1849–51 in the Province of Canada. He was a Roman Catholic and a Reformer. Somewhat erratic and changeable in policies, he was also an adroit House leader.

Macdonald's political life reflected the turbulence of the constitutional government of that age. He advocated "double majority," wherein a ministry required the majority of seats from each of Canada East and Canada West. This necessitated both Protestants and Catholics within the majority party. Macdonald was prime minister of Canada from 1862 to 1864. He voted for a Separate School bill against the wishes of his Protestant supporters. His defeat in March 1864, and the failure of the Tache-Macdonald ministry in June of that year, resulted in the deadlock and the constitutional crisis from which issued confederation. An anti-confederate, Macdonald became the first premier of Ontario, 1867–71. He was defeated in the House by Edward Blake's (q.v.) Liberals in 1871, and he resigned from office.

McDOUGALL, WILLIAM (1822–1905). Lawyer, newspaper publisher, and politician, McDougall advocated the inclusion of the Hudson's Bay Company's (q.v.) Rupert's Land into the territories of the Dominion of Canada (q.v.). A Clear Grit (q.v.) and a Father of Confederation, he became upon confederation the minister of public works in Sir John A. Macdonald's (q.v.) cabinet. McDougall's newspaper campaign for the inclusion in Canada of Rupert's Land marked him as a Canadian imperialist and expansionist. He was one of the negotiators who contracted for the transfer of Rupert's Land into eventual Canadian possession. He was the natural choice to be governor of the Northwest Territories. In 1869, the Métis (q.v.) of the Red River erected a blockade to prevent his entrance to their assumed jurisdiction. This set off the Red River Rebellion (q.v.) in 1870. Discredited, McDougall gradually retired from office. *See also* Manitoba.

McGEE, THOMAS D'ARCY (1825–1868). Journalist and politician. McGee was the editor of the *Nation*, a radical newspaper in Ireland until the Rebellions of 1837, when he was forced to flee to the United States in 1848. He came to Montréal, where he published the *New Era* from 1857 to 1867. He was a member of the Legislative Assembly from 1858 until 1867, then in the House of Commons until his death. He was a member of the "Great Coalition," formed to promote confederation, and a delegate to both the Charlottetown and Québec conferences (q.v.). Known as a great orator, he promoted the "new nationality" and earned his place as a Father of Confederation. He was murdered in Ottawa by a Fenian (q.v.) in 1868.

MACKENZIE, SIR ALEXANDER (1762–1820). Fur trader and explorer. Mackenzie was born near Stornoway, Isle of Lewis, Scotland. In 1774 he emigrated to New York and then moved on to Montréal. In 1789 he made an exploratory expedition from Fort Chipewyan to the mouth of the Mackenzie River via the Slave River and Great Slave Lake. On 9 May 1793, aided by natives, he began, from Fort Fork, Peace River, his famous overland voyage to the Pacific from Lake Athabasca. His route was by the Peace, Parsnip, Blackwater (now West Road), and Bella Coola Rivers. He reached tidewater at Dean Channel, British Columbia, on 22 July. His expedition to the Pacific showed the intricacies and difficulties of travel in that latitude. Mackenzie's back-breaking transcontinental journey was the first crossing of North America by a white man north of Mexico, and it preceded the explorations of Lewis and Clark by more than 10 years.

In 1799, Mackenzie went to England, where his journals were edited and published as *Voyages from Montréal . . . to the Frozen and Pacific Oceans* (1801). He was knighted and returned to Canada, where he became involved with the XY Company, rivals of the North West Company (q.v.). He lived in Montréal and sat as a member of the Lower Canada (q.v.) Assembly 1804–08. He later retired to Scotland and lived at Avoch, Black Isle, Ross-shire.

MACKENZIE, ALEXANDER (1822–1892). Second prime minister of Canada. Scottish-born Mackenzie was a Sarnia stonemason and contractor and a Clear Grit (q.v.). He became leader of the Liberals at the time of confederation. When George Brown (q.v.) quit public life and Oliver Mowat limited his ambitions to Ontario politics, Mackenzie became the prominent national leader of the Liberal party (q.v.). He became prime minister in 1873 because of the Pacific Scandal (q.v.) involving the leaders of the Conservative party. He won a decisive victory in the 1874 election.

Generally opposed to the completion of the expensive Canadian Pacific Railway (q.v.), his inactivity resulted in alienation in British Columbia, which by terms of union was guaranteed a transcontinental railway connection. A believer in the concept of free trade (q.v.), he refused to raise the tariffs during the depression of the late 1870s. In the 1878 election, the Liberals were defeated. In the face of a rebellion within the party ranks, he resigned in 1880.

MACKENZIE, LEWIS W. (1940–). Born in Truro, Nova Scotia. Mackenzie served for 33 years in the Canadian Army (Land Command), including nine years in Germany with NATO (q.v.) forces and nine peacekeeping assignments in six different mission areas. He was commissioned in the Queen's Own Rifles of Canada in 1960. In 1990 he became only the third Canadian in UN history to command a UN mission (as commander of the Observer Mission in Central America). In 1992 Maj. Gen. Mackenzie was appointed chief of staff of the UN Protection Force in Yugoslavia. That same year he created and assumed command of Sector Sarajevo with a force comprising soldiers from 31 countries, of which the Canadian Battle Group was the largest component, opening the Sarajevo airport for the delivery of humanitarian aid. Mackenzie retired from Canadian Forces in 1993. That same year his best-selling personal account of his peacekeeping experiences, *Peacekeeper: Road to Sarajevo,* was published. Canada's most famous living soldier, he has been widely honoured for his distinguished services to the causes of peace and security.

MACKENZIE, WILLIAM LYON (1795–1861). Scottish-born radical and occasional republican, Mackenzie emigrated to Canada in 1820 and became publisher of the York (now Toronto) newspaper *Colonial Advocate.* He entered politics in 1828. Mackenzie attacked the "Family Compact" (q.v.), or governing clique. He neither understood nor supported "Responsible Government" (q.v.); instead, he adhered to the application of elective principle to Legislative Council. The basis of this principle was direct accountability of officials and executive heads sitting on council. In 1837 Mackenzie's "Declaration of the Toronto Reformers" sparked the Upper Canada (q.v.) Rebellion. The rebellion was small and easily crushed. Following defeats at Montgomery's Tavern and Navy Island, Mackenzie fled to New York State, where he was imprisoned for breach of neutrality laws. In 1849 he returned to Toronto under an amnesty and staged a comeback. He served as mayor of York and was for a time (1851–58) a member of Parliament in the Province of Canada.

MACLENNAN, HUGH (1907–1990). Novelist and professor. Born in Glace Bay, Nova Scotia, MacLennan wrote *Barometer Rising* (1941) about Halifax at the time of the great explosion (*see* Halifax Explosion), profiles of the rivers of Canada, and other works, including *Two Solitudes* (1945).

McLUHAN, MARSHALL (1911–1980). Communication theorist. McLuhan was born in Edmonton and died in Toronto. He studied at Cambridge University (Ph.D.) and became a professor of English in the University of Toronto in 1946. He was, in his lifetime, famous for studies of how mass media affects thought and behaviour. He is noted for the concept "the medium is the message." He regarded himself as a grammarian looking at media biases and messages. His revolutionary thinking did not catch hold in his native Canada, but he was discovered by scholars and media-watchers in the United States. About to decamp for the United States and the University of Pennsylvania, he was kept in Canada by the urging of the University of Toronto's administration, who established for him the Centre for Culture and Technology.

He studied in particular the electric media, which was competing with print. He argued that the integrating forces of electric media shifted the uses of information away from the study of detail and thence into the need to interpret the contexts of media form. He distinguished between "hot" and "cool" media, the former being, for example, print or radio and full of information, and the latter telephone or television and less so. The former, too, involved less involvement by the recipient than the latter.

McLuhan's books included *The Mechanical Bride* (1951), *The Gutenberg Galaxy* (1962), and *Understanding Media* (1964). Later works, some co-published, are *Through the Vanishing Point* (1968), with Harley Parker; *The Interior Landscape: The Literary Criticism of Marshall McLuhan* (1969); and *Take Today: The Executive as Dropout*

(1972), with Barrington Nevitt. This world-famous communications innovator received numerous awards and recognitions. He was Schweitzer Chair (1967) at Fordham University, New York. Controversial and ahead of his time, his understanding of the media and its messages is now recognized as a foundation for communications theory and communications studies.

MacNAB, SIR ALLAN NAPIER (1798–1862). Lawyer, businessman, and politician. As a lawyer in Upper Canada (q.v.) in 1826, MacNab began to build the connections that were to aid both his political and business careers. He was a member of the Upper Canadian Legislative Assembly from 1830 until the union of the provinces in 1840. He led the loyal forces in Upper Canada in the Rebellions of 1837 (q.v.), defeating W. L. Mackenzie's (q.v.) group at Montgomery's Tavern. He was a member of the Legislative Assembly of Canada from 1841 to 1857 and served as prime minister from 1854 to 1856.

MACPHAIL, AGNES CAMPBELL (1890–1954). Politician; first female member of Parliament. Born in Grey County, Ontario, Macphail was a teacher in small county schools in Ontario and Alberta. After the federal government passed legislation in 1918 that allowed females to vote and hold office, she was chosen to run for office in 1921 in the constituency of South-East Grey (later Grey-Bruce); she beat nine men for the position. Her grasp of the issues, her determination, and her appeal to audiences brought her victory and a place in the history books as the first female MP. After her first term, she decided to run as an independent. She won four more elections before her defeat in 1940. Although defeated federally, Macphail ran for a provincial seat and won in 1943. *See also* United Farmers.

MANCE, JEANNE (1606–1673). A lay nurse, Mance founded Montréal's Hôtel Dieu Hospital and was co-founder of that city (Paul Maisonneuve was the other). She dedicated herself to the settlers, the welfare of the colony's soldiers, and the good financial management (as treasurer) of Montréal. She died at the Hôtel Dieu, the hospital she founded more than three decades earlier.

MANITOBA. The easternmost of the three Prairie provinces in Canada. Manitoba has an Arctic coastline (Hudson Bay) and an ocean port located at Churchill. Manitoba is commonly referred to as the Land of 100,000 Lakes. These lakes were a creation of the ice age. The land is relatively level and all rivers drain into Hudson Bay. Manitoba is an onomatopoeic native word for the lake of the same name. The capital of Manitoba is Winnipeg (q.v.), named from the Cree word for "murky water."

Historically, Manitoba was inhabited by the Woods Cree, Plains Cree (q.v.), Assiniboine (q.v.), Ojibwa, and Chipewyan Indians. The early explorers of this region used the Hudson Bay to enter the area. British explorer Sir Thomas Button was the first white man to enter the region. He spent the winter at the mouth of the Nelson River in 1612–13. In 1670, Charles II granted the Hudson's Bay Company (q.v.) rights to trade furs in the territory drained by rivers flowing into Hudson Bay. The large territory became known as Rupert's Land. In 1812 the first farming settlement was established. Earl Selkirk (q.v.) acquired a land grant from the HBC and created the Red River Colony. In 1870, Canada purchased Rupert's Land. That same year, the Canadian government created the province of Manitoba in the Red River Valley. Opposition to the creation of the province occurred as the Métis (q.v.), of mixed native and French background, fought against the Canadian government. Two major rebellions (1869–70, 1885) by the Métis occurred in this region, both unsuccessful (see Red River Rebellion). Provincial boundaries were extended in 1881 and 1912 to create the present limits of Manitoba. By 1878, the railway had reached Winnipeg and many people were attracted to the area for its arable land. Many immigrants began settlements in the province once the Canadian government offered settlement packages in the late 1800s. In 1919, Winnipeg was the focal point of the Winnipeg General Strike (q.v.).

The winters in Manitoba are dry and extremely cold. In the summer, the temperature is warm and the climate relatively damp. The precipitation level is the highest of the three Prairie provinces in the growing season.

The economy of Manitoba is diversified. One of the major contributors to the economy is the agriculture (q.v.). The main crop is wheat. Hydroelectricity is readily available, and copper and zinc are mined in the area. Winnipeg is the focal point for national transportation systems, both land and air.

Manitoba has a 57-member provincial legislative assembly. Federally, Manitoba has 14 members of the House of Commons and six senators. The population of Manitoba is 1,100,700. See also Exploration; Fur Trade; Manitoba Schools Act.

MANITOBA SCHOOLS ACT. Provincial legislation, under section 93 of the British North America Act (see Constitution Act of 1867), passed in

1890 under a campaign of D'Alton McCarthy (q.v.) and the Equal Rights Association to advance the interests of nonsectarian public education. This was a reversal of denominational schools as guaranteed by terms of Manitoba's entry into Canada as a province in 1870. Outraged Roman Catholics in Québec brought a court challenge; however the Privy Council found in favour of the law. The Supreme Court of Canada called for remedial legislation within the boundaries of the BNA Act. The Conservative government introduced such a measure, but it died with the end of that ministry. Sir Wilfrid Laurier's (q.v.) government brought about agreement by negotiation. This allowed for denominational religious instruction where 10 or more students with a native language other than English could be formed. Separate schools were not reestablished.

MARITIME COMMAND. See Canadian Navy.

MASSEY REPORT. The *Report of The Royal Commission on National Development in the Arts, Letters, and Sciences* (Ottawa, 1951) is one of the great state documents of Canadian history—and stands beside Lord Durham's (q.v.) Report, the British North America Act (*see* Constitution Act of 1867), and the Statute of Westminster (q.v.) as a matter of high order. The royal commission was chaired by Vincent Massey.

Between 1949 and 1951, the commission exhaustively examined the nature and problems of Canadian life, including foreign cultural (especially American) influences. It recommended the establishment of the Canada Council for the Arts (q.v.) (done 1957) and enhanced government spending in the arts and cultural institutions, including libraries and archives. It also recommended inauguration of federal grants for higher education (instituted 1957). Some circles, very much a minority, interpreted these as federal intrusions in provincial responsibilities. The commissioners stressed that a national purpose could be achieved by fostering the arts. They stressed in the report's preamble "that it is desirable that the Canadian people should know as much as possible about their country, its history and traditions; and about their national life and common achievements; that it is in the national interest to give encouragement to institutions which express national feeling, promote common understanding and add to the variety and richness of Canadian life, rural as well as urban."

In brief, the commission recognized two essentials: "the will of our people to enrich and quicken their cultural and economic life" and "if we in Canada are to have a more plentiful and better cultural fare, we must pay for it. Good will alone can do little for a starving plant; if the cultural life of Canada is anaemic, it must be nourished."

MEECH LAKE ACCORD. A "closed door" constitutional amendment of 1987 that was rejected. This document intended to recognize Québec (q.v.) as a "distinct society." Requiring unanimous support of Canadian provinces, the measure failed in Manitoba on a procedural technicality and was not voted on in Newfoundland. The measure was introduced by the federal government under Prime Minister Brian Mulroney (q.v.) as an attempt to deal with some perceived unfinished business of the 1982 constitutional package (*see* Constitution Act of 1982). The accord's failure intensified Québec's alienation and dissatisfaction, and fuelled native, Inuit (q.v.), territorial, and female resentment concerning exclusion in discussions leading to the accord. An attempt to broaden the basis of constitutional reform known as the Charlottetown Agreement, balancing Québecois requirements with native demands and certain representation-by-population measures for Western provinces, was defeated by the Canadian electorate in the referendum of 26 October 1992 in a vote (overall national figures) of 44.6 percent Yes, 54.4 percent No.

MEIGHEN, ARTHUR (1874–1960). Born near St. Marys, Ontario, Meighen was a lawyer and politician. He was a member of Parliament (q.v.) in Manitoba and solicitor general in Sir Robert Borden's (q.v.) administration. A brilliant speaker, Meighen had a firm hand on policy formation. He played key roles in railway nationalization, conscription, and the Wartime Elections Act. He ended the Winnipeg General Strike (q.v.) of 1919 and used the Immigration Act and Criminal Code to deal with strikers who would face deportation or jail. In 1920, upon Borden's resignation, Meighen became prime minster. His unpopularity and his high tariff policy resulted in his government's defeat in 1921. He became prime minister again in 1925. Deserted by the Progressives during the constitutional crisis of 1926, he could not keep power. He lost a subsequent election to his archenemy Mackenzie King (q.v.) and the Liberals. He was replaced by R. B. Bennett (q.v.). In 1940 and 1944, he attempted political comebacks but failed.

MERCIER, HONORÉ (1840–1894). Popular politician who defended French Canadian rights, Mercier revived the Parti National in response to Louis Riel's (q.v.) execution in 1885. In 1887, as premier of Québec, he passed the Jesuit (q.v.) Estates Act. He called the first Interprovincial Conference in 1887. Mercier was removed from office in 1891 on charges of corruption, which were never proved.

METCALFE, CHARLES THEOPHILUS [BARON METCALFE] (1785–1846). An experienced colonial authority, Metcalfe served as governor general of Canada in 1843. Asserting the Crown's right to make appointments, his measures led Robert Baldwin and Louis Lafontaine (qq.v.) to resign in protest, and the assembly voted in their favour. Metcalfe dismissed the government, and in the subsequent election he campaigned for office and won by a slim majority. His feeble administration ended with his resignation in 1845. He was the last of his breed: responsible government (q.v.) followed in 1846.

MÉTIS. A people enshrined within the Charter of Rights and Freedoms (*see* Constitution Act of 1982) as aboriginal. Proud, desperate, and independent, they are the progeny of sexual unions of Europeans, chiefly Scots and French, with native women. Their culture blended French language and native skills. They lived near fur posts and became buffalo hunters and freighters. The Red River cart, a Métis creation, could carry 1,000 pounds of cargo and could double as a raft for river crossings. In the classic era of their history (circa 1800 to 1885) they formed a self-regulating community and are said to have had a utopian society organized around the buffalo hunt. They faced the industrial world and all its pressures (land hunger, railways, steamboats, homesteading, urbanization, government, police, and so on).

Métis played conspicuous roles in the emergence of self-government in Assiniboia, Manitoba, and in the Northwest Territories. Under Louis Riel (q.v.) and other leaders, they resisted Canadian authority in the Red River (1869–70) and Saskatchewan (1885) rebellions or risings. Excluded from Indian treaties, they lived dispossessed lives, and many retreated to northern locations or Indian reserves. A political renaissance greeted them in the late 1960s and after. They have strong provincial, territorial, and national organizations and are the only mixed-blood people to have distinct constitutional status in the world. In 1991 there were 75,150 Métis living in Canada. *See also* Dumont, Gabriel; Red River Rebellion.

MI'KMAQ. The name Mi'kmaq (formerly Micmac) translates to mean Allies. At the time of European contact the Mi'kmaq occupied the whole province of Nova Scotia, including Cape Breton Island and portions of northern New Brunswick and Prince Edward Island. They were a typical migratory people who lived in the woods in the winter and on the seashore in the warmer months. The dialect of the Mi'kmaq was different from that of the tribes around them, but it resembled the Algonquin dialect in the Great Lakes region. The customs of the Mi'kmaq drastically changed after contact with the Europeans. The tribe quickly adopted many of the customs of the Europeans into their daily lives. Throughout the wars in the 17th and 18th centuries, the Mi'kmaq were faithful allies to the French. The Mi'kmaq also participated in the extermination of the Beothuk (q.v.) in Newfoundland.

MILITARY. *See* Canadian Armed Forces; Canadian Air Force; Canadian Army; Canadian Coast Guard; Canadian Navy; Militia.

MILITIA. In Canada the militia has consisted of a part-time, volunteer, armed citizenry which acts as a defensive unit to defend the country and keep the peace. It has been viewed as a supplement to the regular, professional army. Militia are trained by regulars with the purpose of defending the country.

The Canadian militia dates back to the days of New France (q.v.) when a militia was organized to protect the colonists from natives. After the British conquest, the militia was continued by the British, but on a lower level since London stationed regulars in British North America. The militia fought along with the regulars in the War of 1812 (q.v.). After 1867, the Dominion of Canada (q.v.) continued the militia system. The militia was used in both the Red River Rebellion and the Northwest Rebellion (qq.v.).

In the 1880s the Canadian government attempted to develop a professional standing army. Training schools were established, and regimented training of militia volunteers was implemented to create a more effective and efficient militia. The militia performed well in the South African War (q.v.), considering the equipment problems. By World War I (q.v.), the militia was in the process of becoming a regular standing army. *See also* Canadian Army.

MISTAHIMASKWA. *See* Big Bear.

MOHAWK. *See* Iroquois; Oka.

MONTCALM-GOZON, LOUIS-JOSEPH DE [MARQUIS DE MONTCALM DE SAINT-VÉRAN] (1712–1759). Professional soldier. In 1756 Montcalm was assigned to North America to take command of all French troops there at the outbreak of the Seven Years' War (q.v.). Although outmanned and outgunned by the British, Montcalm managed to hold them in check by striking along Lake Champlain and denying access to the St. Lawrence Valley. In 1759, the British, led by Gen. James Wolfe (q.v.), laid siege to Québec City. Wolfe led his troops to the Plains of Abraham, where they were met by Montcalm. Montcalm ordered his men to attack, and the battle was lost. He died on the Plains of Abraham.

MONTGOMERY, LUCY MAUD (1874–1942). Author and educator. Montgomery was born in Clifton, Prince Edward Island. In 1906 Montgomery wrote her most famous novel, *Anne of Green Gables*. The book was published in 1908 by an American company and was an instant bestseller. She eventually wrote a total of 22 books. In 1923 she became the first Canadian woman to become a Fellow of the Royal Society of Arts in England, and in 1935 she was invested as an Officer, the Order of the British Empire. Lucy Maud Montgomery has become one of the most famous Canadian writers in history.

MONTRÉAL. Prominent in the history of Canada owing to its strategic situation where the Ottawa River joins the St. Lawrence (q.v.) and where the Richelieu River drains from Lake Champlain, Montréal was in times past head of navigation for ocean-going vessels. Co-founders of the settlement were soldier-administrator Paul Maisonneuve and nurse and treasurer Jeanne Mance (q.v.).

The financial and business centre of New France and later Lower Canada and the Province of Quebec, it grew on the basis of the fur trade (q.v.), banking, and brewing. Later it became an industrial and communications headquarters and a railway and shipping nexus of world prominence. It was the immigration entry point of millions of British and Europeans. In its early days it was the subject of Indian and American military raids. It was headquarters of the fur trade of the North West Company (q.v.) until 1821, when upon the amalgamation of this corporation with the Hudson's Bay Company (q.v.) the trade flowed more so through Hudson Bay. By 1825 its population was 22,540, making it Quebec's (q.v.) largest city. Its population grew rapidly and by 1911 was nearly 500,000.

In 1849 riots led to the burning of the parliament buildings of the United Province of Canada; rioters were furious at the passing of the Rebellion Losses Bill. The riot lasted two days and involved thousands of people. The destruction of Canadian archival records was huge.

Corporations made Montréal their headquarters. Railways and communications were key to development. Air Canada is headquartered here, and the region is important in the history of aviation. The International World Exposition EXPO 67 brought world attention to Montréal. Before the opening of the St. Lawrence Seaway (1959) Montréal was transshipment point for all goods coming into the Great Lakes; but shipping technology bypassed the city, leading to a decline in oceanic and railway commerce. The Roman Catholic Church played a prominent role in the history of Montréal, especially in higher education (Université de

Montréal and Loyola College, now part of Concordia University). McGill University, one of Canada's greats, was established here. Prominent architectural and cultural wonders include: Musée d'Art Contemporain, McCord Museum of Canadian History, and the Molson Centre, home ice to the world-famous Montréal Canadiens.

The election of the Parti Québecois (q.v.) in 1976 made the city an even greater battleground for French language primacy. It also resulted in the migration of many Montréalers to Toronto (q.v.) and elsewhere in protest to the French primacy language policies of the Province of Quebec, even the proscription of English on commercial signs. Prominent banks, including the Bank of Montréal, shifted their corporate headquarters to Toronto. The population of greater Montréal, by recent census, is 2.8 million.

MONTRÉAL MASSACRE. On 6 December 1989, a lone man named Marc Lepine entered the engineering wing of L'École Polytechnique in Montréal. He ordered female students to segregate themselves from the males. He shot 14 females dead, injured eight more (and four men when they attempted to intervene), and then turned the gun on himself. Later a letter was found on his person; it contained a hit list of 15 high-profile women. It is now understood that Lepine's rage was against women seeking out nontraditional careers and female leaders in society. The anniversary of this event has since become a day of awareness and remembrance. Tighter gun controls were a consequence of political action taken by citizens concerned that such an event must have no repetition.

MOODIE, SUSANNA (1803–1885). Susanna Strickland Moodie, who came from a literary English family, immigrated to Canada in 1825. She published her first book (poetry) in 1831. She married a British army officer, J. W. Dunbar Moodie. They settled briefly on a farm near Port Hope, Lake Ontario, but removed to 400 acres of backwoods near Peterborough. They cleared land for their farm. Major Moodie was called for active military duty to suppress the Rebellions of 1837 (q.v.). In 1839 he was appointed sheriff of Hastings County; accordingly, the family moved permanently to Belleville, the county seat.

Susannah Moodie became an active contributor to the literary journal *Literary Garland* of Montréal. She wrote much sentimental poetry and melodramatic fiction, popular in its time. Her personal trials and experiences in Canada, however, mark her out as a major early novelist of Canada. Most noteworthy among her writings is *Roughing It in the Bush* (1852). This book has given her a secure place in literary history for the colonial era; it is a vigorous, authentic, and humorous account of frontier conditions in Upper Canada (q.v.). She also wrote *Life in the Clearings* (1853). Her sister Catherine Parr Traill won fame for her Canadian botanical studies and for her juvenile fiction of animal life.

MOSAIC, CANADA AS A. This concept or theory of ethnicity received currency in the 1960s as a contra-distinction to the melting-pot concept thought to exist in the United States. Dating from the 1920s, this pluralism of Canadian society attracted many writers, especially sociologists. John Porter's *Vertical Mosaic* (1965) suggested that the mosaic impeded upward mobility of ethnicities other than French and English and thereby promoted conservative traits.

MULRONEY, (MARTIN) BRIAN (1939–). The son of Irish immigrants, Mulroney studied law and became a labour lawyer in Montréal. He contested unsuccessfully Joe Clark's (q.v.) leadership of the Progressive party in 1976. President of the Iron Ore Company, he closed down plant operations in Shefferville, Québec. In 1983 Mulroney replaced Clark and shortly afterwards entered Parliament as an MP. In 1984 he won a majority electoral victory and became prime minister. Reelected in 1988, he resigned abruptly in 1993.

Mulroney brought forth two unsuccessful attempts at constitutional change: the Meech Lake Accord (1987, q.v.) and Charlottetown Agreement (1992). He brought Canada into the North American Free Trade Agreement with the United States. His government introduced the Goods and Services Tax. Largely discredited for patronage appointments and massive deficits, he left his party virtually in tatters. Named in an Airbus kickback scheme, he was not proven guilty (there was no trial), and he received an official apology from the minister of justice, Alan Rock, and damages.

MURPHY, EMILY FERGUSON (1868–1933). Politician and writer. Born in Cookstown, Ontario, Murphy wrote a variety of books about her adventures in Europe and Western Canada. The character Janey Canuck, referring to the common Canadian nickname, Johnny Canuck, was created by Murphy. She moved to Alberta with her husband and began a career of lobbying the government for social reforms. She worked to pass the Dower Act, allowing a wife to retain one-third of her husband's estate during his life and after his death, and the Children's Protection Act, to shelter abused children. With her in-depth knowledge of the law, Murphy was appointed the first woman magistrate in the British Empire to preside over women's court, in 1916.

One of Murphy's most historic contributions was the "Persons Case" (q.v.), her challenge of the British North America Act pertaining to the meaning of the word *person*, which was then interpreted as not including women. With Nellie Mooney McClung (q.v.), Irene Marryat Parlby, Louis Crummy McKinney, and Henrietta Muir Edwards, Murphy took the case to the Supreme Court of Canada. The court decided against the women, who then appealed to the Privy Council in England. The Privy Council announced that women were persons. Murphy dedicated her life to the improvement of the status of women in Canada, with great success. *See also* Social Gospel.

MURRAY, JAMES (1721–1794). Army officer and governor of Québec from 1760 to 1768. Succeeding James Wolfe (q.v.) as commander of the British army during the invasion of New France (q.v.) in 1759, Murray was made military governor of Québec in 1760 and in 1763 became civil governor of the province. He modified the policy of anglicization imposed by the Proclamation of 1763 (q.v.), allowing the retention of the French language and law and the Roman Catholic religion.

-N-

NATIONAL ANTHEM. Until 1 July 1980 the national anthem of Canada was "God Save the Queen." On that date "O Canada" was officially adopted as the national anthem by the Parliament of Canada. It was the work of Calixa Lavallee (1842–1891), who was prominent among the pioneer composers since the times of French and British colonization. It was first performed 24 June 1880 at the Skaters' Pavilion in Québec City. The words were written by Judge Adolphe-Baile Routhier and were designed to exhibit the great history of Canada, the pride, dignity and importance of patriotism; and the inheritance of Canada's lands and resources for the present generation and those of the future. The work is a 28-bar march in 4/4 time. The first stanza is:

> "O Canada, our home and native land,
> True patriot love in all our sons command.
> With glowing hearts we see her rise,
> The true north strong and free.
> From far and wide, O Canada,
> We stand on guard for thee.
> God keep our land, glorious and free.

O Canada, we stand on guard for thee.
O Canada, we stand on guard for thee."

NATIONAL RESEARCH COUNCIL OF CANADA. Established in 1916, the National Research Council of Canada has been the country's leading research and development organization. It functioned in its early days in an advisory capacity to government and was much involved with science in the service of war. In the early 1930s new laboratories were established in Ottawa. Just as much of the early research was related to military needs, so too was the research during World War II (q.v.), when it grew rapidly in consequence of needs to benefit Canada's war effort and that of its allies. Basic and applied research in science and engineering was undertaken in the 1950s and 1960s, and assistance for aid to industry was undertaken in the 1970s and 1980s. From the mid-1980s the National Research Council concentrated on partnerships and strategic contributions to technological advancement and wealth creation. Specialized agencies and services have grown out of the council, including the Defence Research Board, National Science Library [now Canada Institute for Scientific and Technical Information], Medical Research Council, Natural Sciences and Engineering Research Council, Atomic Energy Canada Ltd., and Canadian Space Agency.

An agency of the Government of Canada, the National Research Council reports to Parliament through the minister of industry. It is governed by a council of 22 appointees. Its mission is to support national science and engineering activities, perform and stimulate investment in research and development, and develop vital expertise and knowledge. Its diverse facilities and programs are used by thousands of scientists, engineers, and research organizations. It has an information arm, Canada Institute for Scientific and Technical Information, which offers one of the largest collections of scientific, technical, and medical information. It also has a publishing arm, NRC Press, one of Canada's leading publishers of scientific journals. It has, too, an Industrial Research Assistance Program and a Canadian Technology Network.

NATIVES. *See* Assiniboine; Beothuk; Blackfoot Confederacy; Haida; Huron; Inuit; Iroquois; Kwagiulth; Mi'kmaq; Nisga'a; Nuu'chah'nulth; Plains Cree; Tsimshian. *See also* Aboriginal Residential Schools; Big Bear; Constitution Act of 1982; Donnaconna; Gitxsan-Wet'suwet'en Land Case; Indian Kings; Métis; Nunavut; Oka; Pemmican; Pontiac's War; Shawnadithit; Tecumseh; Thanadelthur.

NATO. *See* North Atlantic Treaty Organization.

NEW BRUNSWICK. One of the Maritime provinces, bordered by Québec, Nova Scotia, the state of Maine, and the Atlantic Ocean. A narrow land bridge, the Isthmus of Chignecto, connects Nova Scotia with New Brunswick. Most of the interior plateau is forest-covered. The St. John River valley is rich in fertile soil.

The original inhabitants of New Brunswick were the Mi'kmaq (q.v.) in the east and the Maliceet along the St. John River valley. Prior to being named New Brunswick, the region was a colonial establishment called Acadia. Samuel de Champlain (q.v.) established the original settlement on St. Croix Island. The French settled the area and developed fur trading (q.v.) relations with the natives. Control of Acadia alternated between the French and the British for nearly two centuries. In 1755, the British forced the inhabitants of the colony to swear an oath of allegiance. In 1763, the British gained control of the colony with the signing of the Treaty of Paris (q.v.). When the United States gained independence from Britain, many Loyalists (q.v.) crossed the border from Maine to New Brunswick. This resulted in the area being made a province of Britain in 1784, called New Brunswick. The name comes from the family name of King George III. In 1867, New Brunswick was one of the charter members of the confederation.

The population of New Brunswick largely comprises the descendants of the Acadian (q.v.) settlers from the French period and the Loyalists who came to the province after the American Revolution (q.v.). The large proportion of French-speaking inhabitants led to the province becoming officially bilingual.

The climate of New Brunswick is diverse. The northern interior experiences severe winters, while the coastal areas are influenced by the moderating sea.

The forests of New Brunswick are the province's largest natural resource. A majority of the forest is softwood, making it suitable for paper production. The fishing industry is also a major supplier in the economy. The province has some deposits of silver, lead, zinc, coal, and potash. The main agricultural (q.v.) production is potatoes. The pulp and paper and the food processing industries are the main components of the manufacturing sector.

The capital of New Brunswick is Fredericton. The New Brunswick legislative assembly has 58 members. Federally, the province is represented by 10 members in the House of Commons and 10 in the Senate. The population of the province is 731,000.

NEW DEAL. By 1935, Canadians, dissatisfied with the slow economic growth—and the continuing depression—cried out for a new policy of action. R. B. Bennett (q.v.) and the Conservative party answered with Canada's New Deal. Bold in concept and scope and inspired by its American counterpart, it was a collectivist onslaught against industry and finance. It sought to improve the social state of the masses; to gain government economic controls over trade, markets, owners, and producers; and to institute social legislation for the protection of the unemployed. It was presented when the sands of time were running out on the Conservatives, who hitherto had generally followed traditional policies of creation and retention. Its co-author was W. L. Herridge, Bennett's brother-in-law, and Canada's minister in Washington. Herridge observed F. D. Roosevelt's New Deal at first hand and wrote, "This is the end of an economic era. Capitalism will never again work in the old way. The only system which can work hereafter is the system controlled and guided by the state."

In early January 1935, Bennett announced in five radio broadcasts to the nation that society was to be overhauled from top to bottom. There would be a "new deal" for everyone. His program sought social security laws, labour statutes, and economic controls. He intended to implement the findings of the Price Spreads Commission against price-fixing and to repair the economy along lines of greater social justice and distribution of national income. Legislation passed at the parliamentary session included the Minimum Wages Act, the Limitation of Hours of Work Act, the Unemployment and Social Insurance Act, and the Natural Products Marketing Act.

The 1935 election was fought over these issues. Mackenzie King (q.v.) and the Liberal party (q.v.) promised reduced tariffs, a trade treaty with the United States, marketing reforms, new unemployment insurance, and securities control. This policy was far less daring than Bennett's and, coming from a reform party, it was more credible. "King or Chaos" was a useful Liberal slogan that year. The Conservatives were roundly defeated. King took the New Deal legislation to the courts. The Judicial Committee of the Privy Council found most of it to be *ultra vires*, or beyond the authority of the federal Parliament, on grounds that it affected the property and civil rights of the provinces. This was another example of the Privy Council adopting an interpretation of the constitution unfavourable to strong central government. Accordingly, it can be seen as a victory for "provincial rights." It remained for King to implement much of the same legislation by the end of the decade, once the necessary constitutional amendment was made. The Conservatives disappeared as a major political force for two decades. Bennett retired to England in 1938 and in 1941 became a member of the House of Lords, Viscount Bennett. Some underlying causes were sought by a royal commission.

NEW DEMOCRATIC PARTY (NDP). Established in 1961 out of the old Co-operative Commonwealth Federation (CCF). In 1932 in Calgary, labour interests, farmers, churchmen, and others met to plan a socialist party. The new party was the CCF. In Regina in 1933, the convention adopted the "Regina Manifesto," which called for economic planning, centralized fiscal control, price stabilization, and public control over communications and natural resources. The manifesto also called for a welfare state and an emergency program of relief to combat the general effects of the Depression. The party rose to opposition status in British Columbia and Saskatchewan, but was late to start in the Maritimes and Québec. The CCF became the official opposition in Ontario in 1943. In 1944, under the leadership of T. C. Douglas, the CCF triumphed in Saskatchewan, where the first state Medicare plan in Canada was introduced. The CCF pushed the Liberal party (q.v.) farther to the left and obliged them to adopt various social welfare measures more fully and more quickly.

Similarly, the CCF faced internal divisions, and Liberal policies forced the CCF to abandon its most doctrinaire elements of its manifesto in 1956. In 1961 the party was renamed the New Democratic Party with Douglas as the leader. The new party contained representation from the Canadian Labour Congress. In 1969 the NDP was elected in Manitoba. In 1972 a group of radicals called "the Waffle" were expelled from the party ranks, and in the same year, the NDP kept the federal Liberal minority in power. In the 1980s, the party became more centralist under the leadership of Ed Broadbent and Audrey McLaughlin. Provincial governments were won in British Columbia and Ontario. In the 1993 federal election, the NDP suffered a major setback at the polls.

NEWFOUNDLAND. Newfoundland and Labrador holds the distinction of being the last province to join the confederation, in 1949. Newfoundland is Canada's easternmost province. It is made of two parts—the island of the same name (10th largest island in the world) and a larger area on the mainland called Labrador (q.v.). The land surface of the province is noted for its rocky surface and heavily forested areas.

The province has a long, rich history. The Norse (q.v.) Vikings settled the area briefly in the 10th century. In 1497, the explorer John Cabot (q.v.) was the first European to rediscover the area. In 1558, the first settlers arrived in Newfoundland aboard the brig *Hawke*. On 5 August 1583 Sir Humphrey Gilbert (q.v.) claimed the land of Newfoundland for England. This land would become the first colony of England in America. Like Acadia, the British and French fought repeatedly over this land until 1763. The Treaty of Paris (q.v.) in 1763 gave Britain full control of Newfoundland. The small islands of St. Pierre and Miquelon off the south coast of Newfoundland were ceded to France and still remain under French control.

In 1855, Newfoundland became a full British colony with responsible government (q.v.) and later had dominion status. This lasted until the depression of the 1930s. The colony could not sustain itself economically, which resulted in the British government's decision to appoint a commission to govern the colony until 1949. In 1948, the Newfoundland people held a referendum to decide whether or not to join Canada. The vote favoured joining Canada. In 1949 Newfoundland gained full provincial status.

Large air bases were built at Gander and Goose Bay in World War II (q.v.). Newfoundland acquired great strategic significance during that war.

The Beothuk (q.v.) were the original inhabitants of the island of Newfoundland. The Beothuk remained on the island, but fought diligently against the invasion of the white man. In 1829 the Beothuk became extinct. In Labrador, many different native groups inhabited the area, such as the Inuit (q.v.), Mi'kmaq (q.v.), Naskapi, and the Montagnais.

Newfoundland has an abundance of natural resources. Wild rivers provide for hydroelectricity, minerals are mined from the pre-Cambrian rock, the forests provide much wood, and a fishing industry has been established from the supplies of the Atlantic. In the past the province relied on the fishing industry to stimulate the economy; in the last few decades, the province has experienced growth in the mineral and wood industries.

The capital of Newfoundland and Labrador is St. John's. The provincial assembly has 52 members. Federally, the province is represented by seven members of Parliament and six senators. The population of the province is 577,300 as of 1999. *See* Hibernia.

NEW FRANCE. A name given, technically speaking, to all French territories in America, but more specifically applied to Canada, including Acadia, Québec, and the Western interior. In 1534 Jacques Cartier (q.v.), at Gaspé, formally claimed Canada for the king of France. Québec was founded in 1608 by Samuel de Champlain (q.v.). In 1663 New France became a royal province, succeeding variously held corporate monopolies. Regulated by a sovereign council headed by a governor, an intendant, and a bishop, New France had a centralized, oligarchic government. Under metropolitan regulation and local direction, the latter mainly owing to the enterprises of Jean Talon (q.v.), economic diversification and self-sufficiency were promoted in fishing, farming, foresting, shipbuilding, and the production of tar and potash. New France was succeeded by the British colony known as Québec (q.v.) in 1763 by the Treaty of Paris.

Champlain, the Jesuits (q.v.), and the French Court wanted more than just good relations with the Indians. And they sought to make Canada more than merely an outpost for the fur trade (q.v.). They wanted to colonize the St. Lawrence Valley and thus make it a jewel in the French crown. They asked how this could be done when monopolists in the trade failed to keep their obligations of sending out settlers in order to protect the Indian trade.

The French government took this matter into consideration in 1627. In that year, Cardinal Richelieu, the chief minister to Louis XIII and a man dedicated to rivalling Spanish, Dutch, and English power by building up a strong marine and colonial system, established a company of 100 shareholders. Known as the Compagnie des Cent-Associés (q.v.), it possessed the fur trade monopoly for 15 years. In return, it was required to establish over 4,000 settlers in Acadia and Canada over the same period, was held responsible for the costs of administration, and was compelled to support the clergy. The fact that the majority of associates were wealthy nobles indicates Richelieu's desire to keep the scheme out of the hands of merchants who hitherto had been interested in the fur trade to the neglect of settlement. The nobles could be expected to take a keen interest in land holding, and the prospects for the expansion of the Canadian population beyond the 100 souls of 1627 looked bright.

Richelieu's design faced great problems, however. In May 1628 four ships with 400 settlers left for Québec. Off Gaspé they were captured by an expedition led by David Kirke, an Englishman commissioned by Charles I to seize Canada and set up trade and plantations in the St. Lawrence region for a group of London merchants. Kirke then aided a Scottish project under Sir William Alexander (q.v.) to settle Port Royal and cut off the associates' supply ships from France. In July 1629, they finally forced Champlain to surrender a Québec that was on the point of starvation. Had the English captured Québec a year earlier, it seems possible that they might have kept Canada at peace in April 1629. King Charles found Canada a useful bargaining point to get the remainder of a dowry owed him, and on the strength of Richelieu's diplomacy, France regained Québec and Port Royal by the Treaty of Saint-Germain-en-Laye in 1632, to the disappointment of English and Scottish commercial and colonizing interests. Kirke later became governor of Newfoundland where Sir George Calvert had founded a fledgling settlement at Avalon. Alexander never lived to see his Nova Scotia (New Scotland) become a reality. As for Champlain, he resumed command at Québec in 1633, rebuilt the fortress, and died there in 1635.

To stimulate emigration from France the Company of New France, beginning in 1627, granted property *en seigneurie et fief* to landholders (*seigneurs*) who to their own advantage would settle it with colonists (*censitaires* or *habitants*). The aim was regulated land control for the purpose of stimulating colonization.

The seigneuries, long and narrow, extended in parallel lines back from the river. This geometric pattern would be repeated within a seigneury itself, with strips of land running parallel to the boundaries and divided into concession rows (*rangs*) with unceded lands in the hinterland. This allowed habitants a variety of soil conditions and access to the river for purposes of water supply, fishing, and transportation. The seigneuries varied in size but the state preferred smaller divisions because they prevented subdivisions and discouraged the building of great landed estates. The grants were not confined to laity. After 1663 the Ursulines (q.v.), Suplicans, Recollets, the Bishop and Seminary of Québec, and especially the Jesuits were awarded lands which, by 1780, totalled 26 percent of all seigneurial lands. This percentage may seem high, but it was probably justifiable in view of the social services in education (q.v.) and hospitalization provided by the Church. At the time of the British conquest in 1760, there were some 250 seigneuries containing nearly eight million acres.

The seigneurial system appears to have been hierarchical in nature and to have reflected the theoretical absolutism and paternalism of French colonial policy. It was not feudal: the seigneur was the king's land agent and not a liege lord. He had duties to perform within the law. He was bound to pay fealty and homage to the governor and to subject himself to the Crown's inquiries. He could not sell his lands without paying tax of a fifth of the selling price. To the *habitant* he had other duties. He was obliged to maintain a manor house, a step designed to prevent absentee landlordism. He was also required to cede lands to applicants, to operate a flour mill, to hold court, to support the church, and to do road work (*corvée*) with the *censitaires*. He had, of course, honours owing him and "burdensome rights" payable by the *habitant*. The latter, burdensome but not oppressive, were designed to discourage land transfer and keep the *habitant* on the soil. They were also intended to protect the *habitant* against seigneurial abuses, and, in this connection, the *habitant* had rights of appeal to the intendant. The seigneurial system, far from being feudal then, was actually a system of checks and balances designed for the mutual benefit of landlord and settler.

The wilderness posed as an "escape valve" to those who sought to profit by the fur trade or to escape the pressures of urban or even agricultural society. In France there was competition for land. In New France there was competition for labour. Indeed, to prevent too many young men from taking to the woods, the government instituted a system of licensing canoes and traders. By this method it was hoped *habitants* would be kept on the land, cultivating crops important to colonial self-sufficiency. The frontier offered freedoms. The fur trade that became increasingly profitable as the 17th century progressed drew *habitants* to the wilderness. In the forests, the flamboyant, gaudy *coureurs-de-bois* adopted native styles of living and frontier values. They thus concerned the colony's authorities, both civil and ecclesiastical.

The frontier (q.v.) was an ameliorating feature on French institutions transported into Canada; it was also the source of danger. In the mid-17th century, the eyes of New France were fixed on the southern frontier, where the Iroquois (q.v.) threat reached decisive proportions. The French, allied with the Algonkians and Huron (q.v.), were in bitter conflict with the Iroquois who traded with the Dutch at Fort Orange (Albany). Between 1640 and 1660 the Iroquois attacked French settlements along the St. Lawrence, intercepted furs coming downriver from Ottawa, and terrorized the Jesuit missions and Indian villages in Huronia (q.v.). The horrors of this war in terms of its effect on both Indian and Jesuit defy description. The Iroquois gained control of the western fur trade, their ultimate aim. As for the Hurons, they ceased to exist as a nation capable of waging war. Moreover, the Jesuits withdrew from Huronia and kept priests only at a few scattered and strategic points on the Great Lakes. The future of French empire in the West was therefore in question.

French power was equally in doubt in settled areas. Near the new towns of Montréal and Trois Rivières, founded in 1634 and 1642, respectively, Iroquois warriors took scalps with ease. This pressure reached a high point in 1660 but was relieved at Long Sault by Adam Dollard des Ormeaux (q.v.), the garrison commander of Montréal, a Canadian legend. The Indian frontier was momentarily stabilized. Meanwhile, Acadia had fallen to Massachusetts expansionists. In 1654 a fleet from Boston captured Port Royal and Fort St. John, and in 1662 an English governor was commissioned for the area. French power in North America, confined to the empire of the St. Lawrence, tottered ominously. Reports from Québec—variously charged with emotion and fear and telling of the untapped prospects of the colony—reached Versailles. Their message was direct: the fate of New France was sealed unless France would send support.

The French Crown heard these clear and desperate appeals for assistance. In March 1661, following the death of the dominating Cardinal Mazaran, the young Louis XIV had dramatically assumed control of affairs with the ambition of making France the strongest European power. The Sun King's minister, the great mercantilist Jean-Baptiste Colbert, had similar intentions. He knew that a strong navy and colonies were necessary for the rise of French national power. They recognized colonial administration and in 1665 created the Ministry of Marine, which directed colonial and naval finances and administration. Colbert, as minister of Marine, now dictated affairs of the French empire as he and his monarch wished.

In May 1663 the king decreed that New France was to be a royal province. At the same time, the charter of the defunct Company of New France was cancelled and with it the fur-trade monopoly. Chartered companies were founded to develop French interests in such places as San Domingo and Louisiana; and in Canada a Crown corporation, the Compagnie de l'Occident, founded in 1664, was a means of infusing royal control and monies into the colony. The Crown assumed responsibility for the administration and defence of the colony.

The new regime called for the establishing of a sovereign or superior council. This would consist of a governor, responsible for relations with the French administration and for defence of the colony; an intendant, responsible for the justice, economy, policy, and finance of the colony; and a bishop, responsible for the ecclesiastical affairs (and, at his own discretion, moral guardianship). Other council members included an attorney general, a clerk of the records, and five councillors, usually representing the merchant class. The resulting conciliar government was rife with conflicts. Yet periodically it gave the colony the local direction lacking under full company auspices. Certainly, the personality and character of the individuals holding office were reflected in the colonial administration, and periodically, graft worked assiduously to the disadvantage of the colony's military preparedness. But the coming of royal government to Canada marked the end of the era: new government institutions, designed to reshape New France in the image of the Old World, were to change forever the social fabric of the colony.

The French government saw that the immediate need of the colony in 1663 was protection from the Iroquois. Several companies of troops, including the famous Carignan-Salières regiment of some 1,100 men, were dispatched to Québec after 1665. They first erected several forts on the southern frontier. Then, in a series of raids and displays of power led by Governor Courcelle and the Marquis de Tracy, the army checked the Mohawk danger. They put four Mohawk villages to the torch, destroyed food supplies, and erected a large cross and a post bearing the French arms at the site of the principal village. They were establishing a *cordon sanitaire*. In July 1667, the Iroquois Confederacy was compelled to treat with the French at Québec. This ended their hostilities with both the French and Algonkians until 1682. As for the soldiers, about 400 officers and men remained at the end of their tour of duty to settle near Montréal and the Richelieu River and form the core of a militia (q.v.) established in 1673 and responsible for the defence of that vulnerable back door to Canada. Elsewhere in the colony, militia captains, chosen from the *habitants,* assumed responsibility for local defence.

The resident royal bureaucracy undertook numerous steps to make the colony self-supporting and populous. When the great Jean Talon (q.v.) was commissioned intendant of all French possessions in North America in 1665, the colony had only some 3,000 residents. He would have to satisfy Colbert's demand that Canada be self-sufficient and thus develop adequate agriculture (q.v.), trade, and industry. He encouraged experimentation in crop production, brewing, and shipbuilding. He also took steps to people the country. From 1665 to 1672, about 1,500 state-aided immigrants and indentured employees landed in Canada and were given land, implements, and supplies. Some 900 *filles de roi,* or "king's daughters," orphans raised by nuns at the Crown's expense, were imported as wives for the soldiers. It is reported that the "fattest went off best, upon the apprehension that these being less active, would keep truer to their Ingagements, and hold out better against the nipping cold of the Winter." The Crown also sent some 1,000 criminals, mainly poachers and salt smugglers, in the 18th century. In 1668 a ship arrived with Portuguese, German, and Dutch settlers. Huguenots, though generally debarred, came to New France intermittently, where they caused the bishop concern. Talon, on Colbert's advice, issued regulations to encourage early marriages and large families. He also imposed heavy penalties on reluctant bachelors and fathers of would-be brides. The very Canadian system of baby bonus and family allowance was born. The Church also encouraged marriage: marriage beds were blessed and exorcised, and the betrothed well understood that the chief purpose of matrimonial state was procreation.

In the family-centred society of New France, marriage was a popular state. Widows and widowers frequently remarried; few women went into holy orders; illegitimacy was low. The family was engaged in a collective enterprise for survival, self-sufficiency, and upward advancement, and marriages were invariably contractual arrangements in which large dowries were significant. In this healthy and productive society low infant mortality rates existed: twice as much of the population reached marriageable age in New as in Old France.

All these factors resulted in phenomenal population growth. In the period from 1666 to 1673, the population doubled from 3,200 to 6,700. By 1713, it was 18,000; by 1730, 34,000; and at the conquest, 76,000. This amazing growth was almost wholly indigenous: only 10,000 immigrated from Europe during the whole French colonial period. Of these, the composition was 3,500 soldiers, 1,100 girls, 3,900 indentured workers, 500 independent males and 1,000 condemned criminals. Colbert did not want to populate New France at the expense of Old France, and French immigration to the New World was a trifling portion of that of the English. Nonetheless, for the reasons given, the French Canadian experienced a fecundity that numbered them 340,000 in 1820, 650,000 in 1850, and 6.5 million in 1970.

As the population grew in the early years of the 18th century, the economy advanced. Bridges and canals were built. New seigneuries were granted and a few ships laid down, ironworks founded, and fishing and sealing occupied a few colonists. French mercantilism aimed at colonial self-sufficiency, which was not to be at the expense of the metropolitan power. For this reason New France remained essentially a colony in which fur was the most important article of trade. Because New France did not have a flourishing commerce with the outside world, its society reflected its basic dependence on the fur staple. Thus, while New France produced various agricultural products for trade on the fishing banks, at Cape Breton, and in the French West Indies, while it had a seemingly inexhaustible fishing ground, and while it had excellent forests and mineral reserves, it lacked—in its dependent position—a society capable of exploiting that potential.

In its spiritual and intellectual growth, its society remained within confines defined by clergy and Crown. Books were of French rather than local manufacture. There is no record of a printing press in New France, and there was no book trade. The grand sum of books in the colony was probably 20,000; and of these, religious works were in the majority. New France had no public library.

In education, as well, growth was slow. Various religious orders kept schools. Many but not all parishes had a *petite école*, but illiteracy remained extensive. Québec and Montréal each had a trade school. In 1635 the Jesuits established a college in Québec for the purpose of preparing students to be priests, navigators, and surveyors. Students of medicine or the law were trained in France. Local cultural developments were not entirely lacking. New France had its men of science and letters, its wood sculptors, silversmiths, and painters, its musicians and actors. But the French Enlightenment had few effusions on the west side of the Atlantic. And, as the 18th century progressed, the intellectual gap between Old and New France widened.

New France, with its society of essentially needy lower-class origin, had a limited intellectual life. The French colonist possessed a social ethic quite different from that of his New England Protestant counterpart. Born of different linguistic and religious stock, living under different institutions of land control and authoritarian government, he developed a unique posture concerning his earth, *terre Québec*. The French Canadian adopted no "puritanical" outlook in the American sense. Yet he came under close Jesuit surveillance, for church codes of social behaviour were by no means lacking in Canada in the late 17th century. His attitude toward the North American Indian contrasted with that of his English or Spanish counterpart. As an *emigré* of France, he tended to be of rural, military, or clerical background. His colonial attitudes underwent little change. By contrast, those of his Massachusetts or Virginia counterparts were nurtured by changing economic and political conditions and hence developed revolutionary overtones and expansionistic tendencies at a much faster rate.

French Canadian society, rooted in land and Catholicism, was not outward-looking. Rather, it had the deficiencies of an unnurtured society far from metropolitan France. Be that as it may, French Canadian society was of such stability and tradition that its legacies remained well after the British conquest.

The fate of New France was not determined by the characteristics of the populace or economy but by the state of international relations and British naval and military paramountcy. Four wars—beginning in 1689 and ending in 1763—were fought by France and England, and the end result in North America, as signified by the Treaty of Paris (q.v.) of 1763, was that the French empire there was at an end. Only the islands of St. Pierre and Miquelon, off the south of Newfoundland coast, remained French, as shelters and drying places for French fishermen.

French imperial efforts of no small merit had failed to hold the colony. The colonization of New Orleans in 1718 and the building of the great fortress port of Louisbourg (q.v.) at Cape Breton in 1720 to secure both ends of a vast and fragile network of forts along the great interconnecting empires of the St. Lawrence and the Mississippi had not been enough. The growth of English settlement in New England, New York, and the Middle Colonies was a force that threatened French settlements both in Acadia and, in time, on the banks of the St. Lawrence. In 1760 Canada had 76,000 colonists as compared with the Thirteen Colonies' 1,599,000. On the shores of Hudson Bay, also, the vigorous growth of the English fur trade under Hudson's Bay Company (q.v.) auspices after 1668 (ironically with the know-how of the *coureurs* Radisson and Groseilliers) threatened the interior appendages of trade and empire of the St. Lawrence. The British victory at Québec on 13 September 1759 was but a climax to an ongoing process which historians have called the Second Hundred Years' War.

Geography and British sea hegemony had told the tale: New France, confined to the great river and unable to be assisted from overseas, now became a British province in a North American empire stretching from the Arctic islands to the Gulf of Mexico and from the Atlantic shore to the Mississippi. Its extent to the north and west of the Great Lakes had yet to be defined. The continuance of the French Canadian race and culture would depend very largely on the deep roots of its colonial society and on the new order of British rule. It was somewhat characteristic of the remote, paternalistic, and to some degree primitive society of Québec that Canon Briand, the grand vicar of Québec, ordered prayers to be said for the new king of the province, George III, and this in advance of the formal recognition of British sovereignty in the Treaty of Paris. In Briand's opinion, the British were "our masters; and we owe to them what we owed to the French when they ruled." Thus, the kingdom of Canada passed from the hands of one European power to another.

NINETY-TWO RESOLUTIONS, THE. A list of complaints or grievances against the government of Upper Canada (q.v.), the Ninety-Two Resolutions were drawn up in 1834 by a committee of reformers led by William Lyon Mackenzie (q.v.). The list included complaints against the system of patronage, the dispensation of clergy reserves, and various economic polices. The document called for an elected legislature.

NISGA'A. "People of the Nass." The Nisga'a tribe inhabits the long, mountainous and, in some places, lava-bedded valley of their great river. The river, deriving from the Tlingit word meaning stomach, or cache, was in prehistoric and early historic times a great food depot. The Nass River rises in the Skeena Mountains, and it runs 236 miles to the Pacific at Portland Canal. River navigation is dangerous. Charles Bishop, a maritime fur trader (q.v.), was the first European to visit the river entrance, in the 1790s. Then as now, the Nisga'a were passionate defenders of their concept of property, and they guarded zealously their valley's resources, which gave them reason for their being, their items of trade and strength, and their precious independence. The *oolachen,* or "candlefish," was one of their principal sources of wealth, and each year (late February/early March to May) the catch (and the extraction of oil or grease) brought them their means of wealth. Coastal and interior natives traded for this oil.

From the 1820s the Hudson's Bay Company (q.v.) traded with the Nisga'a; in 1864 the Church Missionary Society sent R. R. A. Doolan and Robert Cunningham as missionaries (they established schools). Whisky traders were there, too; in 1865 and 1866, British gunboats (*Clio* and *Forward*) made calls at the Nass to stop the whisky traffic, but without complete success. Other vessels entered the river to provide protection to the Nisga'a, or to seek redress for murders (*Sparrowhawk* in 1868). The Methodists established a mission in 1877 (Alfred Green and Thomas Crosby), aided by William Henry Pierce (q.v.), interpreter and guide.

The main Nisga'a settlements are Kincolith, Lakalzap, Gitwinksihlkw, and New Aiyansh.

The Nisga'a never signed a treaty to relinquish territory or define their land, rights and relationship with non-aboriginal people. But they were restricted to small parcels of land: Indian reserves. A major champion for Nisga'a rights was the firebrand Anglican missionary Rev. James McCullagh, an Irishman. He was a social engineer to the Nisga'a. He opposed the potlatch, which he saw as wasteful and inequitable. Their search for compensation was long, and it includes the following highlights: 1887, Nisga'a chiefs travelled to Victoria to demand recognition of title, negotiation of treaties, and provision for self-government; 1913, the Nisga'a petitioned the Privy Council, seeking to resolve the land question; 1968, the Nisga'a launched their challenge in British Columbia (q.v.) supreme court on the land question; 1976, negotiations began with the Government of Canada; 1991, the British Columbia government joined the talks, to ensure British Columbia interests were protected; 1996, British Columbia, Canada, and the Nisga'a reached an agreement in principle; 1998, the final agreement was initiated by the three parties, and the Nisga'a voted to accept. This marked the first "made-in-British Columbia" treaty involving the federal government; it may be noted that Governor James Douglas (q.v.) had signed various treaties with various natives in the 1850s (Salish, Kwagiulth [q.v.], Nanaimo, and others) but these did not involve the federal government. Significant in this long process was the British Columbia recognition of aboriginal title, so long denied. In 1997 the Supreme Court of Canada in *Delgamuuk v. the Queen* affirmed that oral testimony ought to be considered in native title to ancestral lands.

The 1998 Nisga'a arrangement was overseen by the British Columbia Treaty Commission, an independent body of five commissioners appointed by Canada, British Columbia, and the First Nations Summit. The treaty calls for various compensations ($312 million over 15 years), municipal government of a self-governing nature, and the making of the Nisga'a subject to federal and provincial laws relating to the environment, resources, and conservation, and the laws that generally apply to British Columbians today. Ratification of the agreement in principle continued as a major public subject of dispute in 1999.

NOOTKA. *See* Nuu'chah'nulth.

NORAD. *See* North American Air Defence Command.

NORMANDY CAMPAIGN. On 6 June 1944, Canadian forces landed on "Juno" Beach as part of Operation Overlord, the invasion to liberate Western Europe from Nazi German occupation. Canadians penetrated nine kilometres inland on the first day, facing heavy SS Panzer forces at Verrières Ridge.

The Normandy campaign which followed the D-Day landings was not far removed from the Western Front of 1914–18 in terms of the scale of casualties. Though trench warfare did not develop, the fear of such a stalemate was ever-present, and the fighting which took place in Normandy was very much attritional warfare. The Allies mounted numerous large-scale operations designed to break through the main line of German resistance and begin the push for Germany itself.

Operation Spring was the Canadian assault on Verrières Ridge 24–25 July 1944. Lt. Gen. Guy Simonds (1903–74), commander of II Canadian

Corps for Europe, devised a three-phase battle involving the 2nd and 3rd Canadian Infantry Divisions, 2nd Canadian Armoured Brigade, and two British armoured divisions. The first phase, a night attack, involved moves by 3rd Division to capture Tilly-la-Campagne and by 2nd Division to seize May-sur-Orne and Verrières village. The second phase would see these units, plus 7th Armoured Division, capture the remaining high ground of Verrières Ridge, while the third phase involved exploitation of the breech by the Guards Armoured Division.

Like most battles, the operation did not go according to plan. On the night of 24 July, units of 2nd Division attempted to secure St. André-sur-Orne and May-sur-Orne but met only limited success. The one outstanding success of this operation occurred when the Royal Hamilton Light Infantry, commanded by Lt. Col. J. M. "Rocky" Rockingham, captured Verrières village and held it against repeated German counterattacks. The second phase of the operation witnessed one of the blackest days in Canadian military history. On the morning of 25 July the Black Watch (Royal Highland Regiment) of Canada bravely attempted to carry out its assigned mission in the face of overwhelming odds but was virtually wiped out on the western slope of Verrières Ridge. The regiment suffered 322 casualties that day, including 120 killed. Late on the 25th, Simonds called off Operation Spring when it became apparent that no further ground could be gained. It had been a costly battle for the Canadians—it is estimated that over 1,500 casualties were suffered, including 450 dead. This made it the second-costliest day of the war for Canada, behind only the Dieppe Raid (q.v.).

There has been considerable debate over Field Marshal B. L. M. Montgomery's intentions for the attack. Some say Spring was a failure because it failed to break through to Falaise. Others say it was a success because it accomplished its goal of holding the bulk of the German armour in the area south of Caen. In many ways the question is moot because whether it was the former or the latter, Spring kept the attention of the Germans during the crucial period of 24–26 July when the Americans were breaking through in the west. By the time the German armoured divisions were released to head west, it was too late to contain the American breakout. Spring, however costly, was an important contribution to the Allied victory. Falaise was seized 16 August, and Canadians and Poles met American forces to complete a pincer movement. This ended the Normandy Campaign. Canadian forces suffered 18,444 casualties in the campaign. *See also* Canadian Army; World War II.

NORMAN WELLS. Oil was discovered at Norman Wells, Northwest Territories (q.v.), on the Mackenzie River, in 1916. Imperial Oil's drilling team's 1920 well led to the building of a small refinery, the first north of the 60th parallel, to produce gasoline and diesel for the local market. As mining activity grew, a larger refinery was built in 1939. The Norman Wells field supplied the wartime Canol (q.v.) (short for Canadian oil) pipeline, and in the 1980s increased southern Canadian demands led to a further expansion of the plant. Many of the well heads are serviced from production islands lying in the river, which is five kilometres wide. Currently Norman Wells is owned by Imperial Oil Resources Limited (ESSO Resources) and markets its products in Edmonton, beginning in 1985, via Interprovincial Pipe Line Limited.

NORSE. The Norse, or Vikings, are credited with the first known European settlements in North America. Around 985 an Icelandic trading ship was blown off course en route to Greenland, and sailors aboard reported new lands to the west which they called Vinland (q.v.). Fifteen years later, Leif Ericsson wintered at a settlement called Straumfiord—"Leif's Camp"—a grassy terrace near present-day L'Anse aux Meadows, Newfoundland. In following years the Norse ventured farther southwest towards New Brunswick and Acadia.

Conflict with aboriginal peoples is one of the probable reasons for Norse withdrawal from North America and their return to Greenland within a decade. Norse contacts with America continued off and on until at least the mid-14th century. Knowledge provided by the Norse was kept alive by sailors, who facilitated, through discovery and fishing, the reopening of contact in the era of John Cabot (q.v.). The English, Portuguese, Basques, and others replaced the Norse in America. Canada's first European connection was a northern, maritime frontier (q.v.).

Who was the first European to discover America, and was that person Norse? The most likely claim to primacy goes to Biarni Heriulfson, a Norwegian shipowner trading with Iceland. The date was 985 or 986, and the event is said to involve a bit of chance, for Heriulfson went looking for his father, who is said to have left Iceland for Greenland: Heriulfson reached America, or Canada, and found an unknown land "level and covered with woods"—obviously not Greenland.

From Newfoundland and northern waters, the Norse exported the following products, via Greenland, and marketed them in Europe: walrus ivory; ropes made of walrus hide; narwhal horns; polar bear; furs; white gyrfalcon, the prize sporting bird; and eider-duck, from which comes eiderdown.

The end of Norse intermittent occupation in America may also relate to the effect of the Black Death in Norway after 1349, the rise of the Hanseatic League, which gradually controlled Norwegian commerce, and inroads made by Bristol merchants in the trade and economy of the North Atlantic.

L'Anse aux Meadows is on UNESCO's World Heritage List. Here the Vikings built three timber-and-sod longhouses and five smaller buildings. Here too was the first iron-working in the New World. In 1960 Norwegians Helge Ingstad and Anne Stine Ingstad, using Viking sagas, located the ruins of Straumfiord. Excavations by them, and subsequently by Parks Canada, have unearthed various buildings and Viking artifacts.

NORTH AMERICAN AIR DEFENCE COMMAND (NORAD). NORAD was established between Canada and the United States in 1957 to oversee and coordinate the air defence of North America. NORAD is a complex system of early detection defences that make both countries aware of impending attacks. Both Canada and the United States have aircraft and bases situated in strategic positions to intercept attacking missiles or aircraft.

NORTH ATLANTIC TREATY ORGANIZATION (NATO). Canada was an original signatory on 4 April 1949 to this military organization of Western and Atlantic security. Designed to deter Soviet aggression during the long Cold War, after 1989 it redefined its goals in keeping with assorted security and peace-keeping obligations. In 1999 it had 19 member countries.

NORTH WEST COMPANY (NWC). A Montréal-based confederation or association of fur-trading merchants, mainly Scots, generally believed to have been established after the British conquest of Canada and officially proclaimed 1779. The Montréal partners met the "wintering partners" at the annual rendezvous at Grand Portage in present-day Minnesota and, after 1807, at Fort William, Ontario. Under Peter Pond and Sir Alexander Mackenzie (q.v.) the "Nor'Westers" extended their trade to Athabasca and promoted early Canadian trade to China. Their exploration (q.v.) feats were remarkable, and they established the first transcontinental Canadian business. Locked in a life-and-death struggle with the Hudson's Bay Company (q.v.), the Nor'Westers fought an armed campaign against Earl Selkirk's (q.v.) settlement of Red River. In 1821, the Nor'Westers merged with the HBC under the chartered company's name. *See also* Fraser, Simon.

NORTHWEST REBELLION. Food shortages and failed treaty promises among natives and Métis (q.v.) in the Upper Saskatchewan River valley led to the native rebellion against the North West Mounted Police in 1885. The violence continued for four months but was crushed by the Canadian Militia (q.v.). Plains Cree (q.v.) leaders, Big Bear and Poundmaker (qq.v.), featured prominently in the rebellion; Louis Riel and Gabriel Dumont (qq.v.) did likewise for the Métis. The availability of the railroad and steam navigation allowed the Canadian government to send troops to the resistance effectively. Riel was tried and hanged. However, a general amnesty for natives was proclaimed shortly after the rebellion ended. Not all natives joined the revolt; Crowfoot, a Blackfoot Confederacy (q.v.) chief, was a notable opponent to the uprising. Although it is commonly assumed that the natives of the Plains joined the Métis in the resistance, each revolted for distinct reasons, and the amount of native resistance was lower than previously assumed. The Canadian government used the Northwest Rebellion as a means of breaking the power of the Plains Cree and Blackfoot nation and forcing the natives into a submissive role on the Prairies.

NORTHWEST TERRITORIES. Located in the northern part of Canada, the Northwest Territories (NWT) makes up one-third of Canada and is bounded by the Yukon Territory, British Columbia, Alberta, Saskatchewan, Manitoba, and the natural boundaries of Hudson Bay, Baffin Bay, the Arctic Ocean, and the Beaufort Sea. The NWT includes 18 islands in the Arctic, the largest being Baffin Island. The capital of the NWT is Yellowknife, the only city in the territory.

The Canadian government acquired the NWT from the British in 1870. At that time the territory included present-day Alberta, Saskatchewan, Manitoba, the Yukon, and parts of Québec and Ontario. In 1880, the Arctic archipelago was added to the NWT when the British ceded it to Canada. The Inuit (q.v.) constitute a majority of the population. In the sub-Arctic areas, the Dene and Métis (q.v.) also populate the region.

The NWT is governed by an elected 24-member territorial council. A commissioner is appointed by the federal government and reports to the minister of Indian affairs and Northern development. Federally, the NWT has two seats in the House of Commons and one senator. The population of the NWT is 57,100 in 1999. Nunavut (q.v.) became a separate territory in 1999.

NOVA SCOTIA. One of the Canadian Atlantic provinces. Nova Scotia is the most easterly part of mainland North America. The province is surrounded by the ocean, except for a 22-kilometre land boundary with New Brunswick. Cape Breton Island (q.v.) is a part of the province and is connected to mainland by the Canso Causeway.

William Alexander (q.v.) was a Scot sent to the area to establish a colony under a royal charter in 1621. The colony was named Nova Scotia, which means New Scotland. Originally, the capital of Nova Scotia, Halifax, was called Chebucto. This is a Mi'kmaq (q.v.) word meaning "great, long harbour." The name is appropriate because the harbour at Halifax is one of the best and most strategically placed natural harbours in the world.

In 1605, the French, led by Samuel de Champlain (q.v.) and Sieur de Monts, built Port Royal in present-day Nova Scotia. The English first attacked Port Royal in 1613 from Virginia. The long battle between the British and French saw the colony of Port Royal change affiliations many times until it became British to stay in 1713 and was renamed Annapolis Royal. Finally, in 1763 the Treaty of Paris (q.v.) gave Britain control over all the land that is now Nova Scotia. Nova Scotia received an influx of American Loyalists (q.v.) after the American Revolution (q.v.) and New Brunswick (q.v.) was created from Nova Scotia's western lands. This created a population that was predominantly British. In 1773 Highlanders arrived in the *Hector* and established the community of Pictou (q.v.). Nova Scotia was one of the four original provinces to join the confederation in 1867.

Nova Scotia's good harbours have been important militarily and economically. Halifax was a major naval port for the Royal Navy. The Annapolis Valley is the agricultural (q.v.) centre of the province. The economy is resource-based. The fishing industry is a major contributor to the province. The forest and coal mines play a lesser role in terms of economic contributions. As well, Nova Scotia is the largest producer of gypsum in Canada and has the only North American tin mine.

The capital of Nova Scotia is Halifax. The provincial legislative assembly has 52 members. Federally, the province has 11 members in the House of Commons and 10 senators. The population of Nova Scotia is 909,800 as of 1999. *See also* Halifax Explosion.

NUNAVUT. Nunavut is a territory created in 1999 in the eastern Canadian Arctic through an agreement with the federal government and the local Inuit (q.v.). Nunavut comprises 3.5 million square kilometres of land that include the entire eastern area of the Northwest Territories (q.v.) and the Canadian Arctic archipelago.

The creation of Nunavut represents the culmination of more than two decades of efforts by the Inuit of the eastern Arctic and the Canadian government. The agreement, ratified 25 May 1993, was implemented 1 April 1999. It is the combination of a land claim agreement and a political agreement. The land claim is an exchange between the Inuit (under the Tungavik Federation of Nunavut) and the Crown in Right of Canada (federal government). By this agreement, the Inuit agreed to give the government their aboriginal title to both the lands and waters of the area in exchange for certain rights and privileges as defined in the agreement. These include: title to 350,000 square kilometres of land with mineral rights to 36,000 square kilometres; the rights to harvest lands and waters within the Nunavut settlement areas; a share of the royalties that the federal government receives from oil, gas, and mineral development on Crown lands; and capital transfer payments of $1.14 billion over 14 years. The political agreement includes the creation of a new public government and legislature within Nunavut that ensures equal Inuit membership within the new institutions to be established. These include boards to oversee land management, wildlife management, and development impact projects. By election (February 1999), Paul Okiak became Nunavet's premier. The Nunavut government is slated to take over full powers of the new territory in 2007.

NUU'CHAH'NULTH. A native people—previously known as Nootka—who lived on the coast of Vancouver Island from Cape Cook to Port San Juan. The Nuu'chah'nulth were possibly the only whale hunters in British Columbia. Like the Haida (q.v.), they were great sea voyagers. A unique aspect of this tribe was that the chief of a clan was the only man allowed to harpoon a whale. They experienced the same fate that met other tribes: smallpox and other diseases greatly reduced their numbers.

-O-

OCTOBER CRISIS. In the province of Québec terrorists known as the Front de Libération de Québec (FLQ) (q.v.) promoted general anarchy in 1970. The FLQ consisted of a number of left-wing inspired "cells." Two of their leaders, Pierre Vallières and Charles Gagnon, were arrested by Québec authorities. Subsequently, the FLQ changed its tactics from bombings to kidnapping. Not all their plans worked, but on 5 October the FLQ kidnapped James Cross, the British trade commissioner in

Québec. The FLQ demanded payment of $500,000 ransom and the release of "political prisoners." They also called for freedom from police pursuit and for safe transport out of the country. Also, the FLQ manifesto was to be broadcast on the radio and television. Robert Bourassa's (q.v.) Liberal government was pressured (unsuccessfully) by the Parti Québecois (q.v.) to establish a coalition government. On 10 October the FLQ kidnapped Pierre Laporte, the Québec minister of labour and immigration. Laporte was murdered on the 17th. Student rallies and sit-ins were widespread. The provincial government requested that the Canadian Army (q.v.) be brought in to aid the civil power (q.v.). Prime Minister Pierre Trudeau (q.v.) evoked the War Measures Act (q.v.) by an order-in-council, thus declaring martial law. Subsequently 450 persons were detained; 62 cases were brought to trial; and 20 were convicted. Protest against the War Measures Act died down after Laporte's murder. Cross was discovered and then he was released after safe passage was arranged for his kidnappers. In late October, Laporte's kidnappers and murderers were imprisoned.

OFFICIAL LANGUAGES ACT OF 1969. An act passed by the federal government to give official status to the French language in all federal departments and services in Canada and to guarantee service in both official languages, English and French. *See also* Bilingualism and Biculturalism, Royal Commission on.

OKA. A 78-day standoff took place between the members of the Mohawk Warrior Society from the Kansesatake Reserve, in Québec near the town of Oka, and the Surété de Québec in the summer of 1990. The dispute was over a barricade that the Mohawks had erected to prevent the town from building a golf course on land that the Mohawks claimed as sacred territory. The local police stormed the barricade and in the ensuing chaos, a police officer was killed. The Mohawks were highly organized and heavily armed. As barricades were erected by other Mohawks, Québec Premier Robert Bourassa (q.v.) asked the federal government for support. The army besieged the barricades and succeeded in dismantling them. The Mohawks moved into an isolated building and emerged peacefully 24 September 1990, ending the standoff. The local, provincial, and federal governments met with the Mohawk Society and negotiated the land agreement.

ONTARIO. One of the four original provinces to join the confederation in 1867, Ontario is bordered by Québec, Manitoba, the Great Lakes, and the James Bay. The name is Iroquoian for "beautiful water." The province is the second largest in area size. About 90 percent of the population lives within 160 kilometres of the southern border. Prior to European contact, the Iroquois and Huron (qq.v.) were the dominating natives in the area. With the arrival of the French fur traders (q.v.) to the area, the Huron nation became military allies and trading middlemen for the French. Jesuit (q.v.) missionaries attempted to build a settlement in Huronia (q.v.), but the Iroquois attacked the settlement in 1649, effectively destroying the Huron nation. The end of the American Revolution (q.v.) created an influx of settlers from the United States that were loyal to the British crown. Thousands of United Empire Loyalists (q.v.) emigrated to the Ontario region and began to colonize. The Constitutional Act of 1791 named this area Upper Canada (q.v.). The name was changed to Canada West in 1840 under the Act of Union that combined Upper and Lower Canada into one colony. The name Ontario was adopted in 1867 with the passing of the British North America Act (*see* Constitution Act of 1867).

The majority of the Ontario population is English-speaking, but the province also has the largest number of French-speaking people outside of Québec. The native population is largely of Algonkian and Iroquoian descent.

Economically, Ontario is the richest province in Canada. The northern part of Ontario holds an abundance of natural resources, and the southern part is highly industrialised. The primary industries in the province range from agriculture (q.v.) to mining to forestry. Although a majority of the agricultural output is produced in a small part of southern Ontario, Ontario is one of Canada's main producers of agricultural products. The primary industries provided the foundation for the economic development of Ontario, but the manufacturing and service industries have also become large contributors. The province accounts for more than 50 percent of the manufactured goods in Canada, the automobile industry being the largest sector in the province. The service industry, including tourism, is the largest element of the economy of Ontario.

The Ontario provincial parliament, in Toronto, has 125 members. Ontario is represented by 98 members in the House of Commons and 24 senators, the largest representation of any province. The population is 10,259,200 as of 1999.

ORANGE ORDER (CANADA). In 1830 the First Grand Lodge of the Orange Order was established by Irish Protestants in Canada. Its growth (to 2,000 lodges and 100,000 members in the 1880s) made it a powerful pressure group, reinforcing pro-British and Tory sympathies and opposing French Canadian "papists." In 1848 Louis Lafontaine (q.v.) introduced a Secret Societies Bill, designed to check such actions. In the 1860s the Order sought a relationship with the monarchy, but this was declined. Orangeman Thomas Scott (q.v.) was killed during the Red River Rebellion (q.v.), leading the Order to campaign for protection of rights. D'Alton McCarthy's (q.v.) Equal Rights Association was one such group; the Manitoba Schools Act (q.v.) was an indirect result. Sectarian strife continued in Canada, and in 1877 during a parade in Montréal an Orangeman was murdered. Rising resentment, exploited by Sir John A. Macdonald (q.v.) , allowed for a Conservative victory in 1878. In return, Macdonald included the grand master, Mackenzie Bowell, in his Cabinet.

ORDER OF CANADA. Created 1 July 1967, the Order of Canada is the centrepiece of the Canadian national honours system, which includes orders, decorations, medals, and heraldic devices. The Order is a fraternity of merit that recognizes significant achievement in important fields of human endeavour. There are three levels of membership: the Companion level recognizes international service or achievement, or national preeminence; the Officer level recognizes national service or achievement; and the Member level recognizes outstanding contributions at the local or regional level or in a specialized field of activity. Each level of the Order has the corresponding post-nominal letters: C.C., O.C., and M.C., respectively.

The queen of Canada is the sovereign of the Order. The governor general is the chancellor and principal Companion of the Order of Canada and presides over its affairs, in accordance with the terms of its constitution. An advisory council, chaired by the chief justice of Canada, recommends to the chancellor the names of those considered to be the most worthy of appointment. Federal and provincial politicians and judges are not eligible for appointment while holding office. There are no posthumous appointments to the Order, and the number of persons who can be appointed is limited by its constitution. Officers and Members may be elevated within the Order in recognition of further achievement.

The badge of the Order is a stylized snowflake bearing the crown, a maple leaf, and a Latin motto. Descriptions for wearing the insignia, which vary for each level, can be obtained from the Chancellery. The Latin motto, *desiderantes meliorem patriam,* proclaims the aspirations of members of the Order of Canada who, in their lives and work, have demonstrated that "they desire a better country."

OREGON TREATY. Officially the Treaty of Washington, this Anglo-American treaty divided the farthest West between the two powers along the 49th parallel to the middle of the straits leading to the Pacific, leaving Vancouver Island in British hands. The Oregon Treaty gave Britain navigation rights in the Columbia River, which were later abandoned. The water boundary was confused and led to the San Juan Boundary Dispute (q.v.), eventually resolved in 1872 in the United States's favour by arbitration. Oregon as a term now refers to the state of that name in the United States, but in the 1820s through 1840s it referred to a much larger area west of the Rocky Mountains. Historians sometimes refer to it in that time as Old Oregon. Canadian historians note in particular the unrivalled dominance of the Hudson's Bay Company (q.v.) in Old Oregon, until American settlers arriving overland established communities and provisional government and called for U.S. annexation of land. Peaceful resolution of these difficulties was effected by the Oregon Treaty. HBC possessory rights south of the boundary were the subject of protracted, successful negotiations.

OTTAWA CONFERENCES. In 1894 a colonial conference was held in Ottawa to promote communication between portions of the British Empire. In 1932, the Ottawa Economic Conference, chaired by Prime Minister R. B. Bennett (q.v.), considered multilateral tariffs but ended with certain bilateral arrangements. The conference adopted limited imperial preference as the result of a new protective tariff adopted by the British earlier that same year. *See also* Commonwealth of Nations.

-P-

PACIFIC SCANDAL. It has been said that Canada was the creation of the railway age, and in many ways this is true. The completion of the transcontinental railway on Canadian soil in 1885 (regular service established 1886) marked the material link of communication from Atlantic to Pacific. Along the way, there were many physical and technical difficulties. There were also political and financial difficulties, as shown by the particulars of the Pacific Scandal.

By 1876 the Intercolonial Railway linked the Atlantic seaboard and St. Lawrence waterways (essentially Halifax to Montréal, with links to Toronto and Chicago). But British Columbians were calling for a Canadian link to the Pacific (rather than via the Union Pacific–Central Pacific route in the United States). In fact, in the Terms of Union (1871) Ottawa guaranteed the completion of a railroad from central Canada to the Pacific within 10 years. The major question was how to finance this grand design, and this brought government and private capital into a special relationship. The key date was 1872, when the railway charter for a Canadian Pacific Railway (q.v.) line was granted to Sir Hugh Allan (q.v.), a Montréal shipping magnate and investor.

Information leaks revealed that Allan had contributed $300,000 to Conservative party coffers and to the personal bankrolls of Sir John A. Macdonald (q.v.), the prime minister, and Sir George Étienne Cartier (q.v.). A telegram from Macdonald to Allan read: "I must have another ten thousand; will be the last time of calling; do not fail me." These revelations forced Macdonald to resign in November 1873.

An election was held in 1874, and the Liberal party (q.v.) and its leader, Alexander Mackenzie (q.v.), were swept into power. Macdonald was put into opposition for four years; his party, the Conservatives, were discredited. Although the Liberals attempted to pacify British Columbia (called by some at the time "the spoilt child of confederation") various delays ensued, owing to construction, surveying, and engineering requirements or other difficulties. There was also a depression in the late 1870s.

In 1878 the Conservatives were reelected. Under the Canadian Pacific Railway Act (1880) the national enterprise was given new life. This biggest corporate arrangement in 19th-century Canadian history required various cash subsidies (originally $25,000,000), land grants (25,000,000 acres "fit for settlement"), 700 miles of existing track, a 20-year holiday from paying corporate taxes, and 20 years to complete the project. Another $27,000,000 was required to complete the railway, and this came from the public purse. On 7 November 1885, the last spike (q.v.) was driven at Craigellachie, near Golden, in the heart of British Columbia's mountain wilderness — bringing to an end the saga of the Pacific Scandal. This was the biggest, most significant issue in public policy making in the 1800s in Canada, but Macdonald and the Conservatives survived it, and the Liberals did not make sufficient gains at the expense of their rivals.

PADLOCK LAW. Québec province's anti-communist legislation, enacted in 1937 by the Union Natíonale (q.v.) led by Maurice Duplessis. The Padlock Law authorized closure of premises suspected of producing communist propaganda. Inasmuch as "communist" was not defined, or limited, the government hindered growth of the Co-operative Commonwealth Federation (*see* New Democratic Party) and used it against unions. In 1957 the Supreme Court of Canada declared it unconstitutional.

PALLISER EXPEDITION. The British geographical examination, under Capt. John Palliser of the Royal Engineers, of three significant regions: the Canadian shield between Lake Superior and Lake Winnipeg, the prairies of South Saskatchewan, and the passes of the Rocky Mountains. Palliser kept a journal and made comprehensive reports. In the southwest of the Western interior, north of the 49th parallel, he found abundant good soil but decried the extensive sandy wastelands that became known as Palliser's Triangle.

PAPINEAU, LOUIS JOSEPH (1786–1871). French Canadian lawyer, politician, and theorist. As speaker of Lower Canada's (q.v.) House of Assembly, Papineau championed independence from Great Britain, more self-government, and separateness from Upper Canada (q.v.). As one of the most remarkable and serious republican theorists of Canadian history, he led the Patriotes during the Rebellions of 1837 (q.v.) and was charged with treason. Escaping to the United States, he returned to his homeland after the General Amnesty of 1844.

PARIS, TREATY OF. The Treaty of Paris of 1763 ended the Seven Years' War (q.v.). By it, France surrendered claims to Canada, retaining only St. Pierre and Miquelon Islands and some residual fishing rights off the coast of North America. France ceded Canada, all territories east of the Mississippi River, Cape Breton Island (q.v.), the St. Lawrence Islands, Dominica, Tobago, the Grenadines, and Senegal to Britain. Britain thereby established preeminence in North America. Spain surrendered Florida to Britain but received by secret arrangement the Louisiana Territory and New Orleans from France.

PARLIAMENT. Canada's parliament has inherited much of the British traditions as exhibited in the Houses of Parliament, Westminster, England (sometimes called "the Mother of Parliaments"). In fact, Canada's parliament represents Canadian institutions in public decision making and democracy. The Parliament of Canada resides in Ottawa, Ontario; the Government of Canada is headquartered in the National Capital Commission's domain, which embraces Ottawa and Hull, Québec. Parliament Hill, on a bluff jutting into the Ottawa River, puts its buildings into spectacular relief.

The Parliament Buildings are evocative symbols of Canada. Flanked by the East and West Blocks, the Centre Block of Parliament—with its distinctive Peace Tower and Library—is familiar to Canadians and many people around the world. These buildings represent, too, the echoes of past times and personalities; and around Parliament Hill are many statues of great personages of yesteryear: Champlain, Macdonald, Laurier, and Mackenzie King, to name a few.

In the 1840s the government of the Province of Canada could not agree on a site for the capital—Montréal, Québec, Kingston, and Toronto were considered. In 1857 Queen Victoria, whose opinion was requested, chose Ottawa (previously Bytown) as the permanent capital. Ottawa was then a rough-and-tumble lumber town. The choice of Ottawa was a political compromise; it also lay a more secure distance from the American border.

The Centre, East, and West Blocks of the Parliament Buildings were built 1859–66 (excluding the Peace Tower and Library). When the Dominion of Canada (q.v.) was created in 1867, the buildings were immediately chosen as seat of government for the new federation, which assembled there for the first time on 6 November 1867. The library was completed in 1876.

On 3 February 1916 a fire started in the Parliamentary Reading Room in the Centre Block. The fire claimed seven lives and reduced all but the northwest wing and the library to a charred shell; the library was saved by its closed iron doors. Rebuilding immediately began, despite the war, and the new structure embraced the Gothic Revival style of the original. The new building was opened 26 February 1920 and completed in 1922. Architectural features include stateliness and vibrancy: vaulted ceilings, marble floors, dramatic lighting (giving an atmosphere of solemnity), bright detail, gargoyles, bird and animal sculptures, and stone friezes recounting events of Canadian history.

The Library of Parliament, showpiece of Gothic Revival architecture, is the jewel of national architecture. A white marble statue of young Queen Victoria is to be found there. The Library of Parliament services parliamentarians and their staffs. Rising above the Parliament Buildings is the distinctive, massive Peace Tower (built to commemorate the end of World War I, q.v.). On its third floor is the Memorial Chamber, a tribute to Canadians who died in armed conflicts of the nation. In front of the Peace Tower, and inside the central gates, is the Centennial Flame, first lit 1 January 1967 to mark the second century of Canadian confederation.

The East Block's rooms have been restored to appear as in Sir John A. Macdonald's (q.v.) time. Other government buildings nearby include the Confederation Building, Wellington Building, Langevin Building, and Victoria Building.

Parliament consists of the House of Commons Chamber, where elected representatives known as members of Parliament gather to debate legislation, move financial motions, and conduct the nation's legislative business, and the Senate Chamber, where senators review bills passed in the House of Commons and introduce their own legislation (other than money bills). The Senate is the upper house of Parliament through which all legislation must pass before it becomes law. Its members, chosen in all 10 provinces and territories, are appointed by the governor general on recommendation of the prime minister. The throne in the centre of the Senate's dais is used by the queen or the governor general on ceremonial occasions such as the Opening of Parliament. *See also* Parliamentary System.

PARLIAMENTARY SYSTEM. The parliamentary structure in Canada consists of the British Monarch, represented by the governor general (q.v.), the Senate; and the House of Commons. The governor general summons Parliament, brings its sessions to an end by prorogation, and formally assents to every bill before it can become law. In practice, the Governor General exercises all these powers on the advice of the prime minister and the Cabinet.

All Senators are appointed by the governor general on the advice of the prime minister. Members of Parliament in the House of Commons are elected by the people. The House of Commons plays the important part in the parliamentary process. A bill must be agreed to by both houses and receive the Royal Assent before it can become an Act of Parliament. The powers of the Senate and the House of Commons are constitutionally equal except that financial legislation may not be introduced in the Senate. English and French enjoy equal status in both Houses of Parliament; members of both houses are allowed to deliver speeches in either language.

The Senate consists of 104 members, appointed by the government. At the time of Confederation, Québec and the Maritime provinces insisted on equality in the Upper House to counterbalance the weight of Ontario in the Lower House, where representation is based on population. The numbers are based on regional location: 24 from Québec (q.v.); 24 from Ontario (q.v.); 24 from the Maritime provinces (10 each from Nova Scotia and New Brunswick, four from Prince Edward Island); 24 from the Western provinces (six each from Manitoba, Saskatchewan,

Alberta and British Columbia); six from Newfoundland; and one each from Northwest Territory and Yukon Territory.

All bills must be passed by the Senate before they can become law, and the upper chamber has the constitutional right to reject any bill and to keep rejecting it as often as it sees fit. As well, it can amend bills, although it cannot initiate or increase the amount of any bill dealing with taxation or expenditure. Senators represent provinces. In recent years there has been much discussion about having senators voted in by the region they represent so as to make their actions more accountable to the people.

The Canadian House of Commons was modelled after that of the British Parliament; the rules and procedures stem directly from Westminster. The House of Commons is the centre of parliamentary activity and public attention. It is here that the prime minister and the leader of the opposition regularly confront one another and where the nation's business is freely and openly transacted. By law a general election must be held at least once every five years. A parliament may be dissolved and an election called before five years has elapsed. The power to dissolve Parliament resides with the governor general, but only on the advice of the prime minister.

PARTI QUÉBECOIS (PQ) was formed by René Levesque (q.v.) after the defeat of the Liberal party (q.v.) in Québec in 1968, essentially for being insufficiently nationalistic. Members, sometimes called *Pequistes*, gained widespread support from business and labour and formed a government in 1976; it was reelected in 1981. Urging various forms of independence such as "sovereignty association" and now complete independence, the PQ lost the 1980 provincial referendum that asked the people of Québec if they wanted to remain within Canada. In 1995 the leader, Jacques Parizeau, introduced a bill into the National Assembly of Québec calling for public ratification of independence, to be proclaimed.

PEARSON, LESTER BOWLES (1897–1972). History lecturer, diplomat, and politician. Pearson was born in Aurora, Ontario, son of a Methodist minister. He was educated at Toronto and Oxford. After teaching in the University of Toronto, he joined the Department of External Affairs and served as Canada's ambassador to the United States in 1945–46. Elected to Parliament as a Liberal for Algoma, Ontario, Pearson entered the Cabinet as secretary of state for external affairs (1948–57). His plans for the resolution of the Suez Crisis (q.v.) through peacekeeping attracted widespread acclaim. He was awarded the Nobel peace prize in 1957. Becoming leader of the Liberal party (q.v.) in succession to Louis St. Laurent (q.v.) he fought several elections but never succeeded in commanding a majority in the House of Commons. As prime minister (1963–68), he introduced the Canada Pension Plan and the Canadian Health Act (universal medical care) and sought to counter separatism in Québec. He introduced the Canada flag (designed by historian George Stanley), led Canada's Confederation Centennial Celebrations, and launched the Royal Commission on Bilingualism and Biculturalism (q.v.). An activist politician right for the times, his achievements, in a short period of time, were many and fundamental to the nature of modern Canada.

PEMMICAN. The essential portable provision of fur traders (q.v.) and Western travellers, pemmican (the Cree word is *Pimikan,* roughly meaning "manufactured grease") was made from buffalo meat, cut with the grain in strips and dried, then pounded and covered with melted fat in a sewn-up bag the size of a flour sack (each weighing 90 pounds). Kept in a seam-greased bag, it would keep for years. Berries could be added; three-quarters of a pound was a reasonable daily ration. As bison are nowadays a protected species, modern recipes begin with the requirement "to procure a moose, or other large animal."

PERSIAN GULF WAR. Canadian armed forces (q.v.) participated in the Persian Gulf War between United Nations forces, led by the United States, and Iraq in 1991. The Canadian government sent a hospital unit to attend to wounded coalition personnel during the build-up leading to Operation Desert Storm. Also, a three-unit naval task force was dispatched to the Gulf with a destroyer tender. The hurried re-equipping of these ships showed glaring inadequacies in available defensive systems. These ships were used to enforce the embargo on Iraqi shipping and to support the land-based forces. Two squadrons of CF-18 fighters were deployed from Germany to give air support to Coalition shipping in the Gulf. After the war ended, Canadian forces helped in the cleanup of Kuwait and aided in clearing some of the millions of mines laid down.

"PERSONS CASE." The popular name for *Henrietta Muir Edwards and Others v. Attorney General for Canada and Others,* in which the Supreme Court of Canada ruled that the word "persons" in Section 24 of the Constitution Act of 1867 (q.v.) could not be understood to include women and therefore women were ineligible for Senate membership. On appeal, the Judicial Committee of the Privy Council (in favour of "a large and liberal interpretation," rather than "a narrow and technical construction") concluded that "persons" applied to both the male and female sexes. Cairine Wilson became the first female senator, selected by Prime Minister Mackenzie King (q.v.) in 1930 to the Upper Chamber. Joining Edwards in the challenge were Nellie Mooney McClung (q.v.), Irene Marryat Parlby, Louis Crummy McKinney, and Emily Ferguson Murphy (q.v.) .

PICTOU, NOVA SCOTIA. One of many towns of Atlantic Canada and the Maritime Provinces with a unique history, and this entry is given as an example of such diverse heritage. On Northumberland Strait and the Gulf of St. Lawrence, Pictou Harbour was first occupied by the Mi'qmak (q.v.), then by French traders and missionaries. In 1762 the Philadelphia Company obtained a grant for settlement purposes. In 1773 the brig *Hector* brought 200 Highlanders (mainly from Ross-shire) to Pictou, most of them boarding at Ullapool in western Scotland. Their memorable departure, recorded by oral testimony, was reminiscent of that of the *Mayflower's* party leaving Leiden with Puritans aboard. It was a nightmare voyage: crowded hold, dysentery, hurricane, bad food and water; 18 died on the passage. The *Hector* arrived at Pictou 15 September 1773. Too late to plant crops, the immigrants were dependent on settlers living there and in nearby villages such as Truro. They gathered clams, fished, hunted, and developed farms.

In the early 19th century, Pictou exported lumber and timber to Great Britain. The town had sawmills, foundries, biscuit-making establishments, and flour mills. Railways and highways bypassed the town. In the late 20th century, the town has under 5,000 inhabitants. This traditional centre of Highland settlement has become a locus for tourism based on its Scottish heritage. *See also* Nova Scotia.

PIERCE, WILLIAM HENRY (1856–1948). Missionary to the Indians and author. Born at Prince Rupert, British Columbia, to a Scottish father in the service of the Hudson's Bay Company (q.v.) and to an Indian woman of the Port Simpson tribe, Pierce was brought up by the Port Simpson peoples upon his return there. He was much influenced by the zeal of the Anglican lay minister Father William Duncan (q.v.) and by the kindness of Captain Lewis of the HBC steamer *Otter* (on which he served as a sailor for more than two years). Pierce became an interpreter to Anglican missionaries. He was a strong temperance supporter and founder of many such societies for the Methodists. He went to the new station at Fort Wrangel, Alaska, in 1877. He also worked at Port Essington, then at a Nisga'a (q.v.) mission station, at Bella Bella, and at

Bella Coola. In 1895 he was appointed to Rev. Thomas Crosby's steamboat *Glad Tidings* mission. He worked on the Upper Skeena River for a time. He recounted his experiences in his memoir *From Potlatch to Pulpit* (1933), a vital source for the study of the history of these early missions.

PITCHER, HARRIET BROOKS (1876–1933). Nuclear physicist. Born in Exeter, Ontario, Pitcher attended McGill University in 1894 and won a number of scholarships and awards that assisted in financing the cost of her education. She graduated with an honours degree in mathematics and natural philosophy. Pitcher's most significant contribution to the field of physics has gone almost unnoticed. While studying under the direction of Dr. Ernest Rutherford, she concentrated her research on radioactivity. Her work provided to be very important, as it assisted Rutherford and Frederick Soddy, who discovered the secret to radioactivity in 1902. Although not receiving the recognition she deserves, Pitcher was one of the pioneers of modern nuclear science.

PLAINS CREE. Prior to European contact, the Plains Cree comprised a few small bands in northern Saskatchewan and Manitoba. They allied themselves with the Assiniboine (q.v.) against the Blackfoot Confederacy (q.v.) and the Sarcee. After contact with the Europeans, the Cree population swelled as bands with firearms and horses joined the Cree. Plains Cree spread over northern Alberta to the Peace River. Smallpox in the 18th century drastically reduced the population of Cree, and the decline of buffalo further reduced their numbers.

PLANTERS. Between 1759 and 1774, some 8,000 Planters—an old English term for colonists—arrived in Nova Scotia (q.v.) from the colonies of Connecticut, Massachusetts, Rhode Island, and New Hampshire. Their purpose was to establish an English Protestant community. The British had begun deporting Acadians (q.v.) from Nova Scotia in 1755 and encouraged the settlement of Nova Scotia with loyal subjects. At that time France was the most likely enemy, and subsequently the Seven Years' War (1756–63, q.v.) was fought, in part for the control of Nova Scotia. Planters settled much of the Annapolis Valley—Liverpool, Yarmouth, Cumberland, and also places in New Brunswick. The Planters replaced the Acadians and shaped the cultural history of the area in a different way. Settlers also arrived from other jurisdictions: in 1772–75 over 20 ships carrying more than 1,000 settlers from Yorkshire reached Nova Scotia. Most settled in the Chignecto region, soon to be the border counties straddling Nova Scotia and the newly formed New Brunswick.

Acadian culture did not disappear altogether, and the relationships between Acadians and Planters is a subject for important historical inquiry. Acadia University, Wolfville, Nova Scotia, beginning in 1993, developed a curriculum in Planter Studies; the leader for this was John Victor Duncanson (1919–1999), foremost expert on the documentation of Planter history. The Friends of Planter Studies, headquartered at Acadia University, has a newsletter, *Planter Notes,* and a society for the promotion of these matters.

PONTIAC'S WAR. Chief Pontiac (1720?–1729) of the Ottawa nation led a series of attacks against fur trading posts (q.v.). He organized the Ottawa, Potawatomi, and Ojibwa into an alliance in 1763 and led these people to attack Fort Detroit, killing 46 British soldiers. As the alliance grew, British settlers and additional posts were attacked. Within a short period of time, 2,000 settlers had been killed and eight garrisons captured. As French assistance failed to materialize, the alliances disintegrated, and Pontiac signed a number of treaties in the summer of 1766.

POUNDMAKER (1826–1886). A Stoney native, Poundmaker was the adopted son of Crowfoot, a Blackfoot (q.v.) chief. In 1878, Poundmaker became a band chief of the Cree (q.v.) and was instrumental in signing Treaty Six. In the Northwest Rebellion (q.v.), he attempted to restrain his band from violence. He was ignored and his band raided Battleford, Northwest Territory. Although seen as an agitator by police, Poundmaker prevented the massacre of Col. William Otter's troops on Cut Knife Hill by allowing the force to retreat. Poundmaker was forced to surrender and served a three-year sentence. The sentence was not due to deviant behaviour but a fear by the Canadian government of native uprisings in the West.

PRINCE EDWARD ISLAND. Located in eastern Canada, off the north shores of Nova Scotia and New Brunswick, Prince Edward Island holds the distinction as being the smallest Canadian province. Jacques Cartier (q.v.), there 29 June 1534, described it as "the fairest land that may possibly be seen." The province joined the confederation 1 July 1873.

Prior to European contact, the province was inhabited by the Mi'kmaq (q.v.). The Europeans to first settle on the island were French, who called the island Île St. Jean. The British changed the name to Prince Edward Island in 1799 in honour of Prince Edward, Duke of Kent. Charlottetown, the capital, hosted the first conference to consider confederation of British North America, in 1864. The majority of the present-day inhabitants are of British origin. The small size of the island and the economic conditions there have resulted in few immigrants.

The coast of Prince Edward Island is dotted with small harbours that are suitable for inshore fishing vessels. Deep-water ports are located at Charlottetown and Summerside. The resources of the province are the soil and the sea. Agriculture (q.v.) is the strength of the economy, the most important product being potatoes. Tourism and fishing also contribute to the economy of the province. Electricity is mostly imported from New Brunswick by undersea cable.

The capital of the province is Charlottetown. The province has a 32-member legislative assembly. The province has four members of Parliament and four senators. The population of Prince Edward Island is 131,700 as of 1999.

PROCLAMATION OF 1763 was issued by King George III on 7 October 1763 after the conclusion of the Seven Years' War (q.v.). It extended British laws and institutions to the British colony of Québec, contracted the boundaries of the colony, and provided some protection for the rights of native peoples. It announced a prohibition of settlement beyond the western "line." The proclamation established four colonial governments for the regions of Québec, East Florida, West Florida, and Grenada. It gave Québec its first civil government under British rule; civil government in Québec was effected 10 August 1764. Executive authority was placed in the hands of a governor and council. Of special significance in aboriginal history, the proclamation set forth principles of treaty-making, forbidding natives to sell lands directly to any other than constituted governments, through Crown agents.

PROGRESSIVE PARTY. Founded in 1920 by agrarian interests, especially in the Prairies and Ontario, this reform-minded movement sought lower tariffs, reciprocity (q.v.) with the United States, reduced freight rates, nationalized railways, and more accountable members of Parliament. In the 1921 election, Progressives returned an astonishing 65 members, making them the second largest party in the Commons. Leader Thomas Crerar, an ex-Liberal, declined being named leader of the opposition. In subsequent years, the Liberal party (q.v.) under Mackenzie King (q.v.) drew away disaffected Progressives. Numbers of Progressives in the Commons dropped in the election of 1925 and again in 1926. Some radical members joined the Co-operative Commonwealth Federation (*see* New Democratic Party) in 1932. The remnant linked with the Conservatives in 1942, giving it the name Progressive Conservative party. Agrarian discontent of this era transformed Canadian politics. It broke the two-party mould and institutionalized Western disaffection.

-Q-

QUÉBEC. The province of Québec is the largest province in landmass in Canada and second largest in population. In 1534, explorer Jacques Cartier (q.v.) claimed the land for France. The area became a frequent point of return for fur traders (q.v.) during the summer months. In 1608, Samuel de Champlain (q.v.) built the Habitation at Québec. The colony began to flourish, and the area became known as Nouvelle France (New France, q.v.). On 13 September 1759 during the Seven Years' War (q.v.), Québec fell to British control in the famous Battle of the Plains of Abraham. The Treaty of Paris (q.v.) in 1763 placed Britain in control of New France. With the Constitution Act of 1791, Québec became Lower Canada (q.v.). In 1840, it was renamed Canada East. Upon confederation in 1867, the province reclaimed its name, Québec.

The Québec economy is based on agriculture (q.v.) and forestry, but it has strong mining and shipping industries. Manufacturing also has been traditionally strong, especially in the textile area. The powerful rivers that drain the Canadian Shield make Québec the largest producer of hydro-electricity in Canada.

The population of Québec is predominantly French-speaking, but there is a large contingent of native people and a minority of English-speaking people. Prior to the arrival of Europeans, the Iroquois (q.v.), Naskapi, Montagnais, Cree (q.v.), Huron (q.v.), Algonquin, Malecite, Mi'kmaq (q.v.), and Inuit (q.v.) were all living within the vast area of Québec. Today the native population is significantly reduced, but they still remain an important part of Québec society.

Québec's legal system does not follow the common law of British tradition like the rest of Canada, but that of the civil code of French tradition (*see* Québec Act of 1774). The provincial government of Québec is the 122-member National Assembly. Federally, Québec is represented by 75 members in the House of Commons and 24 senators. The population of Québec is 6,985,400 as of 1999.

QUÉBEC ACT OF 1774. Designed to give Québec a new colonial constitution, the Québec Act established the use of French civil law in Québec (British criminal law applied universally elsewhere in British colonies). It revised the oath of holders of public office so that it was acceptable of Roman Catholics. The rights of the Catholic Church to tithe, or tax, were enshrined. Government was to be appointed, and the promise of an assembly, as given in the royal Proclamation of 1763 (q.v.), was suspended. The use of French is not mentioned in this act. The "architect of the Québec Act" was Sir Guy Carleton (q.v.), Lord Dorchester.

QUÉBEC CONFERENCES. U.S. President Franklin Roosevelt and British Prime Minister Sir Winston Churchill held two conferences in Québec during World War II (q.v.) to discuss Allied strategy. Canada hosted, but was not a participant in, the meetings held 17–24 August 1943 and 10–15 September 1944.

QUEENSTON HEIGHTS, BATTLE OF. On 13 October 1812, a battle took place between American militia crossing the Niagara River at Queenston Heights and a combined force of British regulars and Canadian militia (q.v.). British general Sir Isaac Brock (q.v.) led the attack against the invading Americans and was killed. Nevertheless, the British circled the American force and forced their surrender. The battle was a significant victory for Canada, as it prevented American forces from occupying Canadian territory and gaining a hold in the area.

-R-

RADIO. *See* Canadian Broadcasting Corporation.

REBELLIONS OF 1837. In Lower Canada (q.v.) and Upper Canada (q.v.) rebellions occurred that are integral to that process, or historical story, called the fight for responsible government (q.v.). The causes, as explained herein, were different for the two colonies or provinces, but had significant effects—and long after the fact advanced the causes of colonial self-government. After 1791 each of the colonies was ruled by a governor and executive council, and each had a legislative assembly whose political power was severely constrained by virtue of executive power.

Lower Canada. The assembly was dominated by middle-class, nationally conscious French Catholics who were largely excluded from policymaking, for the governor and executive council were controlled by English-speaking persons or French otherwise in partnership with this oligarchy. Reform-minded champions for democratization, with ties to the press, called for protection of French rights against English dominance. These same persons called for the reform of government, for what became known as responsible government (that the Legislative Assembly would control policy and that the executive would be responsible to the legislative arm).

In Lower Canada the executive was dominated by the Château Clique, an unflattering reference to those close to the governor's residence. This urban group had powerful influence in political appointments, Crown land grants, banking, business, public works contracts, and education (q.v.). Against this Tory (or Blue) group stood the reformers, particularly Louis Joseph Papineau (q.v), eloquent leader of the Patriote Party (1826) in the Legislative Assembly. In 1834 a list of grievances, the Ninety-two Resolutions (q.v.), was issued. A key issue was control over the provincial civil service and, related to this, the right to determine how revenues raised in the colony were spent.

In the 1830s there was depression, agricultural failure, cholera, and an electoral riot. These fuelled dissension. The governor held firm against this rising tide of resentment. In 1837 Papineau and the Patriotes led an armed rebellion. It began as a street fight in Montreal. On 23 November a small British army force attacked poorly armed and trained Patriotes (led by Wolfred Nelson) at St. Denis, Richelieu River, but after an attack of five hours was obliged to withdraw. On 25 November, at St. Charles, south of St. Denis, the Patriotes were defeated by British regulars, giving them control of the Richelieu River valley. Papineau fled to the United States. In December a fierce battle was fought at St. Eustache, northwest of Montreal. British forces (1,200 regulars under Sir John Colborne) attacked the Patriotes headed by Amury Girod and Dr. Jean-Olivier Chenier, and the rebellion was put down. Chenier and 70 Patriotes were killed; 118 were taken prisoner. The rebellion disrupted trade, caused widespread migration to the United States, and indicated to the British government that reform ought to be taken serious. In consequence Durham (q.v.) was sent out as governor general and special commissioner to investigate the causes of the rebellion, and was charged with making recommendations.

The second phase of the rebellion came after Durham's departure from Canada in early November 1838. There were incidents at Napierville and Odelletown; rebels were captured at Caughnawaga by the Iroquois (q.v.) allied to the British; and at Beauharnois the Patriotes won the day but then were scattered. One hundred and eight men were convicted by court-martials; of 99 condemned to death, 12 went to the gallows and 58 were transported to Bermuda and Australian colonies. The six battles of the two campaigns left 325 dead, 27 of whom were soldiers and the rest rebels. For a time, therefore, the power of the oligarchy was reinforced, and the reform processes curtailed. The racial divisions—English–French—continued unabated.

Upper Canada. If the differences in Lower Canada were racial, in Upper Canada they were related to denominational differences on the one hand, and urban–rural differences on the other. Upper Canada's founding had been on Anglican expectations, and Crown lands known as Clergy Reserves were set aside for an established church. The politics, institutions and administration of Upper Canada were run by the erroneously named Family Compact (q.v.). Rule was by patronage. In the 1820s Methodists complained of their disadvantages, and particularly control of the Clergy Reserves; and by the mid-1830s William Lyon Mackenzie (q.v.) was championing radical reform. In 1835 he published his *Seventh Report on Grievances*, which listed the demands of the extreme Reformers. One such was that the Legislative Council be elected (and not chosen by the governor). In 1836 the new lieutenant-governor, Sir Francis Bond Head (q.v.), dissolved the Legislative Assembly on grounds that it would not vote funds for government monies. Bond Head actually led the Tory party to victory in the general election that followed. Mackenzie continued to promote rebellion and was encouraged by Patriote activities. He advocated American democratic institutions instead of British moderate changes. On 7 December Bond Head sent a militia (q.v.) force against 1,000 mustering rebels at Montgomery's Tavern, and it routed a mob of rebels. Many of the protesters came from the Home District north of Toronto and represented the agrarian sector of the populace that Mackenzie drew his strength from. Mackenzie promptly fled to Navy Island, Niagara River, in the United States, and there proclaimed a Canadian republic in exile. He was arrested by American authorities and briefly imprisoned. He was later granted amnesty by Canadian officials and was allowed to return to Toronto. He was reelected to the Assembly.

Meanwhile at Brantford 500 men under Charles Duncombe were dispersed by a force under Sir Allan MacNab (q.v.). Other rural disturbances fizzled out. Many of the Patriotes and Rebels were aided in the United States by Hunters Lodges, and in 1838 these groups were engaged in actions against Pelee Island, Lake Erie; Prescott (Battle of the Windmill) on the St. Lawrence; and Windsor. These raids were poorly arranged and were unsuccessful; but they made the Canadian–American border a place of turbulence during those years and immediately after. *See also* Marshall Spring Bidwell.

RECIPROCITY. A concept and movement begun in British North American colonies to facilitate trade with the United States along free trade (q.v.) lines. Reciprocity called for bilateral reduction of tariffs. In 1854 the governor general, Lord Elgin (q.v.), negotiated the Reciprocity Treaty with the United States, bringing unrivalled prosperity. In 1866 Washington abrogated the arrangement. Sir John A. Macdonald's (q.v.) national policy and tariff were designed to provide protection for the Canadian economy and build up a manufacturing base. Reciprocity was encouraged by the Liberal party (q.v.) and argued strongly by them in the 1911 election (which they lost because of it). Free trade, however, returned in 1989 under the Progressive Conservatives and expanded to embrace Mexico and the North American Free Trade Agreement in 1994.

RED RIVER REBELLION. An 1869–70 uprising by the Métis (q.v.) National Committee, of which Louis Riel (q.v.) was secretary, against what it saw as an unauthorized Canadian takeover of Assiniboia and Manitoba (q.v.) upon the demise of the Hudson's Bay Company (q.v.) as a land-holding power. The rebellion was caused by Canadian blunders, specifically failure to advise the Métis and other residents of Assiniboia of the change in status from HBC to Canadian sovereignty.

Lt.-Gov.William McDougall (q.v.) was prevented from entering Red River. The Métis declared martial law and tried and executed Thomas Scott (q.v.), an Ontario member of the Orange Order (q.v.). This sparked a Canadian official response. A Canadian armed force was sent in aid of the civil power (q.v.).

Meanwhile, Riel, leading a provisional government, issued a "Declaration of the People of Rupert's Land and the North West." Sir John A. Macdonald (q.v.), the prime minister, also sent Donald Smith (later Lord Strathcona) to negotiate. Eventually Riel's government fixed on some demands for Manitoba's provincial status. Canada then passed the Manitoba Act, creating a new province in 1871. Riel was elected as MP but was denied taking his seat in Parliament (q.v.), and he went in exile into the United States.

REFORM PARTY OF CANADA. Founded in 1987, the Reform party has as one of its central tenets grassroots populism. Interested in promoting changes to Canada's system of representative democracy, party policies include potential recall of parliamentarians, recall rules, and citizens initiatives. The founding leader is Preston Manning, an Alberta member of Parliament. In 1997, upon the election, he became leader of the opposition.

REFUGEES. Canada resettled a quarter of a million refugees in the years 1947 to 1967, 95 percent of whom were from Eastern Europe. In November 1946 Prime Minister Mackenzie King (q.v.) announced emergency measures to bring some refugees and displaced persons in camps from Europe. In 1956–57 Canada received 37,500 Hungarians fleeing Soviet repression, and in 1968, 8,800 from Czechoslovakia, for similar reasons. In the 1970s refugees came from Uganda (after the 1972 expulsion of Asians), Chile (after the 1973 coup d'état), Vietnam (after the fall of Saigon in 1975), and Lebanon (after the civil war in 1975). Since 1979, refugees have been accepted under humanitarian immigration policies if designated political prisoners or oppressed persons. Poland, Argentina, Chile, Uruguay, El Salvador, Guatemala, Iraq, Iran, former Yugoslavia, and Afghanistan are examples of the source countries of such refugees.

REPRESENTATION BY POPULATION. The British North America Act (*see* Constitution Act of 1867) accorded 65 seats in the House of Commons to Québec and assigned seats to the rest of the federation in relation to Québec's population:seat ratio. Though designed to guarantee "rep-by-pop" and ensure Québec's representation irrespective of its population, it additionally stipulated that no province could lose a seat unless its population lessened by more than 5 percent relative to the national population of the previous census.

The subsequent decline of population in the Maritimes and in Saskatchewan brought political pressure from these regions to avoid anticipated electoral losses. In 1915, a constitutional amendment established the so-called senatorial floor rule. Under this, a province's number of seats in the Commons could never fall below its number in the Senate. Within a century, New Brunswick, Prince Edward Island, and Nova Scotia were at or near this equivalency. In 1946, the 5-percent decline rule was abandoned. *See also* Parliamentary System.

RESPONSIBLE GOVERNMENT. A born-in-British North America doctrine or policy, with implications for government liberalization in other parts of the British Empire, its adherents (specifically Robert Baldwin and L. H. Lafontaine [qq.v.]) argued for local controls on matters of local responsibility, including patronage (control over the civil list). Central to their argument was that the legislature should decide upon the ministry to take control of the affairs of the government. The executive required the confidence of the legislature. The concept was recommended by Lord Durham (q.v.) in his *Report* and advanced by Joseph Howe (q.v.).

In 1846 the Colonial Office issued instructions that the governors of British North American provinces were to accede to the will of the assembly. This was first done in Nova Scotia, and later in Lower and Upper Canada, effective 1848. Prince Edward Island acquired responsible government in 1851, New Brunswick in 1854, and Newfoundland in 1855.

RIEL, LOUIS (1844–1885). Considered by many to be "Father of Manitoba," Riel led the Métis (q.v.) during the risings known as the Red River Rebellion and the Northwest Rebellion (qq.v.). He remains one of the most controversial of historical figures. He has been styled a martyr, hero, saint, traitor, lunatic, madman, and other descriptions. He was born at Red River.

A studious youth, Riel was sent to Québec for further education in the law and for the priesthood. He completed no formal education or training in these fields. He returned to Assiniboia, where his father was a leading advocate of local and Métis rights. A fiery orator, he was secretary of the Métis National Committee that denied Canadian attempts to exert sovereignty. He drafted declarations of (1) independence, (2) Métis rights, and (3) compromise—intended demands for Manitoba as a Canadian province. He fled to the United States to escape capture after the Red River Rebellion.

Although elected as a member of Parliament (q.v.) for a federal riding in the new province of Manitoba, in 1873 and 1874 he was denied his seat. He went to live in Montana, where he became a school teacher. In 1875 he was granted amnesty on a condition of a further five years of exile. In his exile, he suffered a nervous breakdown and experienced delusions about being a messiah. He planned to set up an independent republic in the North American West with its own pope.

In 1884, Riel returned to lead the Métis rising in 1885. He was caught by Canadian authorities and tried for high treason. At his trial he would not let his lawyer make a plea on the grounds of insanity. He was found guilty and sentenced to death. Although the jury recommended clemency, after reprieves and a mental examination, Riel was hanged 16 November 1885 in Regina, the Northwest Territories capital. He was buried in the St. Boniface Cathedral graveyard.

In his time, English Canadians remembered him for his implication in the martial law that brought about the death of Orangeman Thomas Scott (q.v.). French Canadians tended to view his life as that of a martyr, and outrage at his execution brought nationalist and provincial rights activists Honoré Mercier (q.v.) to power in Québec in 1886. Riel remains the most complicated, enigmatic personality in Canadian history. In 1998, in a controversial move, the Government of Canada offered a pardon to Riel as part of its "offer of reconciliation" to Canada's aboriginal peoples.

ROBINSON, JOHN BEVERLEY (1791–1863). Lawyer, politician, and jurist; coined the term "Family Compact" ([q.v.], of which he was a member). In the wake of the War of 1812 (q.v.), Robinson became attorney general of Upper Canada (q.v.) and later chief justice. He tightened regulations, thereby classifying Americans as aliens to deprive them of property and civil rights. President of the Executive Council in 1830 he was, during the 1837 rebellions, instrumental for the execution of two rebels and the banishment of 25 others.

ROUGES. Epithet for the Reform party (q.v.) of Canada East that emerged from the late 1840s; known as the Institut Canadien. Influenced by American republicanism and French radicalism, the Rouges were led successively by Louis Joseph Papineau and A. A. Dorion (qq.v.). They opposed confederation. Later they allied with the Clear Grits (q.v.) to form the federal Liberal party (q.v.). In Québec they were opposed by Conservative and Roman Catholic forces.

ROYAL CANADIAN AIR FORCE. See Canadian Air Force.

ROYAL CANADIAN NAVY. See Canadian Navy.

ROYAL MILITARY COLLEGE OF CANADA (RMC). Established in Kingston, Ontario, in 1874 to train Canadian officers. The training and education reflected the British military schools, as the RMC was originally staffed by British officers. In the early years, RMC graduates were sent to Britain to serve with the British Army. After 1919, RMC graduates were required to join the permanent force or the militia (q.v.). In 1979, the RMC began admitting female cadets. In 1995 upon the closure of College Militaire Royale (St. Jean, Québec) and Royal Roads Military College (Victoria, British Columbia) it again became Canada's only military college. See also Canadian Army.

RUPERT'S LAND. See Hudson's Bay Company; Manitoba; Northwest Territories.

RUSH-BAGOT CONVENTION (1817). After the War of 1812 (q.v.), Britain and the United States agreed to establish limits on the number of naval vessels in the Great Lakes and Lake Champlain. The limit was two ships each on the upper lakes and one each on Lake Champlain. This was the first arms limitation treaty in history.

RYERSON, ADOLPHUS EGERTON (1803–1882). Educator and reformer. Ryerson was born in Norfolk County, Upper Canada (q.v.), of a Loyalist (q.v.) family. In 1825 he became a Methodist preacher, and in 1829 editor of the *Christian Guardian*, organ of the Wesleyan Methodists. He attacked the exclusive claims of the Church of England, led by Rev. John Strachan (q.v.), to the Clergy Reserves. He strongly opposed, as a Loyalist, William Lyon Mackenzie (q.v.) and the rebels of the 1830s. He supported the administration's electoral victory under Governor Sir Charles Metcalfe (q.v.) in 1844.

Ryerson's powerful, reforming, and Methodist personality and character led to further significant contributions: first president of University of Victoria College (then at Cobourg) in 1841, chief superintendent of education for Upper Canada in 1844 (held to 1876), and founding editor of the *Journal of Education*. He was the architect of the public school system of Ontario, and he had wide influence across Canada, mainly in Western provinces and the territories. Ryerson Press became the imprint for the United Church of Canada but was later purchased by McGraw-Hill. He wrote a history of the Loyalists (1882) and a history of Canadian Methodism (also 1882).

-S-

SABLE ISLAND. Canada's "Graveyard of the Atlantic." At the edge of the continental shelf, Sable Island has been the centre of intensive exploration for oil and natural gas. Uninhabited except for lighthouse keepers and seasonal Coast Guard members (and horses), it has an important maritime heritage in ship casualties. A natural gas pipeline commenced moving the commodity to market (destination Portland, Maine) in 1999.

SACHS HARBOUR (IKAAHUK). One of many Inuit (q.v.) communities, Sachs Harbour is on Banks Island in the Arctic archipelago. Thule house ruins indicate Inuit occupation about 500 years ago. Visited by Royal Navy explorers Frederick Beechey (1820) and Sir Robert McClure (1851), it became a permanent Inuit community in 1929 when three Delta Inuit families sailed in their own schooners to Sachs Harbour, where they trapped white fox. This prosperous trading and trapping community became the site of an RCMP detachment post in 1953.

SAGARD, GABRIEL (?–1650). Missionary, traveller, and historian. Sagard came to Canada in 1623 as a friar in the Recollet order. He travelled to Huron (q.v.) county, living there for a year or so (1623–24). He returned to France and wrote two fine books: *Le Grand voyage au pays des Hurons* (1632) and *L'Histoire du Canada* (1636), both published in Paris. The former is a valuable ethnology of the Huron and recounts the demanding lives of the missionaries. The latter incorporates the former book but adds considerable detail on the arrival of the Jesuits (q.v.) in Canada, the capture of Québec by the English (1629), and France's temporary abandonment of the colony. He was the first religious historian of Canada. Sagard left the Recollets sometime shortly after 1632 and may have joined the Franciscans. The Recollets were excluded from Canada when France regained control from the English in 1632.

SAILING SHIPS. Much of Canada's early history occurred during the great age of sail, when sailors "under canvas" crossed the Atlantic on expeditions of trade, colonization, and exploration. However, by the mid-19th century, Canada had become a principal seaborne nation. Canada's ports were crowded with sailing vessels, and its shipbuilding yards flourished. Canada's ships sailed every major ocean and visited every major port doing the world's business. Over 4,000 ships, each exceeding 500 tons burthen, were built in Canada. In 1878 Canadian-registered ships numbered 7,196 and totalled 1,333,015 tons. Among the nations, Canada stood fourth in seagoing tonnage. Canada had an abundance of good timber—tamarack, spruce, and especially pine—near to shipyards, which were established in secure harbours and river mouths. Canada also possessed good ship designers and shipwrights, and builders were able to sell their vessels to U.S., British, Norwegian, and other seaborne traders. Canadian vessels were given the highest quality rating—14 years A.1—by the marine insurer Lloyd's of London.

Canadian ships were built at numerous locations. The coastal trader *Northwest America*, built by John Meares, was launched at Friendly Cove, Nootka Sound, Vancouver Island, in 1788. The first lumber carrier, the *Columbus*, 3,690 tons, was built at Île d'Orleans in 1824. The 2,459-ton *William D. Lawrence*, launched at Maitland, Nova Scotia, in 1874, was the largest wooden full-rigger built in Canada. Other famous ships of this period include the *Marco Polo*, launched at Saint John, New Brunswick, in 1851, which made her name trading to Australia during the gold rush; the square-rigger *Canada*, 2,137 tons, launched at Kingsport, Nova Scotia, in 1891, which ended her worldwide trading career in 1926; and the square-rigger *City of Toronto*, built in the Great Lakes. Canadian ports constructed a variety of smaller commercial craft. Victoria, for instance, built sealing vessels; ports on the St. Lawrence built one- or two-masted traders. Atlantic yards built whalers and sealers and fishing and trading schooners such as the *Bluenose* (q.v.); York and Mackinaw boats were built for specific needs determined by geography. Canada also built naval ships. The three-decker HMS *St. Lawrence*, launched at Kingston, Ontario, in 1814, displaced 2,304 tons and was intended to carry 119 guns and 1,000 men. HMCS *Venture*, built in Nova Scotia in 1937, was a three-masted schooner for officer training. At important centres from Halifax to the lower Great Lakes, smaller naval vessels were built, maintaining shipbuilding traditions dating from René La Salle's *Griffon*, launched on the Great Lakes in 1679, and the British brig *Ontario*, launched at Oswego, New York, in 1755.

The age of sail came to an end gradually with the introduction of steam propulsion and iron hulls, masts, and yards. Paddle steamers came first to the St. Lawrence in 1809, to the Great Lakes in 1817, and to the Pacific Coast in 1835. In 1831 the Québec-built *Royal William* became the first merchant ship to cross the Atlantic primarily under steam. Canada's shipbuilding industry made the transition to steam and iron, but the 200-year age of Canadian ships under canvas was rapidly coming to an end, and with it came the nostalgia of an age when Canada was known for its great sailing ships.

ST.-GERMAIN-EN-LAYE, TREATY OF. This treaty returned the settlements at Port Royal and Québec in New France (q.v.), as well as ships and cargo seized from Samuel de Champlain (q.v.), to France on 29 March 1632. Québec had been occupied for three years following its conquest by English pirates led by David Kirke.

ST. LAURENT, LOUIS (1882–1973). Lawyer, prime minister, law professor at Laval University, president of the Canadian Bar Association, and counsel to the Rowell–Sirois Commission on Dominion–Provincial Relations. Born in Compton, Québec, St. Laurent was appointed minister of justice in Mackenzie King's (q.v.) government in 1941. He was elected for Québec East the following year. St. Laurent supported conscription in 1944 and became secretary of state for external affairs in 1946. Chosen by King as his successor, "Uncle Louis" became prime minister 15 November 1948. He won increasing majorities in 1949 and 1953. His government extended old-age pensions, enacted hospital insurance and equalization payments to provinces, and brought Canada in as a signatory member of NATO (q.v.). He was a strong advocate of the United Nations and sent forces to the Korean Conflict (q.v.). His government was defeated by John G. Diefenbaker's (q.v.) Progressive Conservatives in June 1957. He retired from politics in 1958.

ST. LAWRENCE RIVER. The St. Lawrence River figures prominently in Canada's early history. It was the route of exploration (q.v.), the centre of New France's (q.v.) development, and a commercial highway that aided in the economic growth of Canada. The river is still a major transportation route and provides electric power.

The St. Lawrence was a focal point for native, French, and English settlers. Sedentary native groups, such as the Iroquois (q.v.), were settled on the future sites of Québec (Stadacona) and Montréal (Hochelaga) at the time the first explorers ventured into the St. Lawrence. Jacques Cartier (q.v.) founded the river with the aid of natives in 1535. The French explorers and traders developed settlements around the native areas on the lower St. Lawrence, eventually forcing the natives from the land. By 1760, the length of river bank between Montréal and Québec was patterned with long seigneurial strips. The St. Lawrence River was used for various commercial enterprises from lumber, wheat, and the fur trade (q.v.). The prosperity of Québec and Montréal stem from the importance that the St. Lawrence played in Canada's economic growth.

Historian Donald Creighton contends that the St. Lawrence created an empire—"the empire of the St. Lawrence"—that reached to the Mackenzie River of the Western provinces. This is called "the Laurentian thesis." The east–west axis that reaches 3,790 kilometres into North America facilitated the growth of Canada as a nation. Cartier called it "the great river of Canada," a description that stands the test of time. The great mountain rim that lies to the north and west of the river is called the Laurentian (or Canadian) Shield.

STE.-MARIE AMONG THE HURONS. Now a celebrated historic tourist attraction near Martyrs' Shrine, Midland, Ontario, Ste.-Marie among the Hurons was a Roman Catholic mission to the Huron (q.v.) Indians, commenced in 1615 by Recollets and renewed in 1634 by the Jesuits (q.v.). Superior Jean de Brébeuf (q.v.) established the mission to the *Wendat,* or Huron, people. In 1638 Jerome Lalemant, another Jesuit, arrived as the new superior. By 1639 (the date usually specified as the founding date of Ste.-Marie), 13 fathers were active in the mission, which served as a base for a cluster of outstations. It was a place of rest and repair for the Jesuits. In 1648, at its highest position of prominence, Ste.-Marie among the Hurons housed 19 priests and various assistants. The French planted gardens and imported livestock from Québec.

From this post, the influence of the Jesuits spread among other natives, including Petun, Nipissing, Ottawa, and various Algonquin bands. The geographical site was superb but also a source of weakness. Situated on or near the river route from Montréal via the Ottawa and French Rivers, with rich agricultural soil, the Huronia (q.v.) missions became a key to French expansion in Georgian Bay, Lake Huron, and to the southwest and northwest. The Huron were great traders as well as farmers; their prominence in the Great Lakes area increased.

The Iroquois (q.v.), ambitious for greater fur trading (q.v.) wealth in the lands north and west of Huronia, had designs on the Huron. With the Huron–Iroquois wars that commenced in 1648, Huron power collapsed. Disease (influenza, measles, smallpox) and internal dissension had also caused a crisis. Five priests lost their lives: Brébeuf, Antoine Daniel, Gabriel Lalemant, Charles Garnier, and Noel Chabanel. They were canonized by Pope Pius XI in 1930. The Jesuits withdrew the mission 15 May 1649. Survivors scattered. The Jesuits burned Ste.-Marie on purpose, thus keeping it out of the hands of the Iroquois and avoiding desecration.

For a year the mission was transferred to Christian Island, Lake Huron, but because of starvation and winter hardship was removed altogether to Québec, 10 June 1650. Beginning in 1855 archaeological investigations occurred, and these were completed in the mid-20th century by K. E. Kidd for the Royal Ontario Museum and Wilfrid Jury of the University of Western Ontario. In 1964 the Government of Ontario began the reconstruction of the mission as a historical treasure. *See also* Carhagouha.

SAN JUAN BOUNDARY DISPUTE. One of several contentious border problems in Canadian history, this one erupted in 1859 at the height of the British Columbia gold rush. The issue was control and sovereignty of San Juan Island. U.S. authorities in Whatcom County, Washington Territory, claimed taxing powers on U.S. soil. Hudson's Bay Company (q.v.) authorities, headquartered at Victoria, Vancouver Island (q.v.), and dominated by James (later Sir James) Douglas (q.v.) fought for British control.

The "Pig War," as it is sometimes called, was sparked when a HBC boar was shot 15 June 1859 by American squatter Lyman Cutler on company land. On 18 July 1859, General Harney, U.S. Army, ordered 60 soldiers under Capt. George Pickett from Fort Bellingham to San Juan Island. Douglas wanted the Royal Navy to intervene, but although there was some show of British naval force, no violence occurred. San Juan Island was placed under joint Anglo-American occupation until 1872, when the kaiser of Germany ruled, on hydrographical (and not historical) evidence, that Haro Strait (nearest Vancouver Island) was the main channel separating Vancouver Island from the mainland. Historical data also revealed, in discussions preceding the Oregon Treaty (q.v.), that the British Foreign Office and Lord Aberdeen, the secretary of state, merely wanted to preserve Vancouver Island—and not the adjacent islands—for Britain. The entire San Juan archipelago thus became U.S. territory.

SASKATCHEWAN. This province is the only one in Canada to have no natural boundaries. The boundaries are lines of latitude and longitude. The name Saskatchewan stems from a Cree (q.v.) word *Kisiskatchawan*, meaning "swiftly flowing water."

Cree, Blackfoot (q.v.), Assiniboine (q.v.) and Chipewyan tribes were inhabitants of the area prior to immigrant settlement. The first settlers of the area were the Métis (q.v.), descendants of European fur traders (q.v.) and native wives. Saskatchewan joined the confederation in 1905. The promise of free or cheap land created a wave of European immigrants in the early 1900s.

The province has more farmland that any other province in Canada. Saskatchewan produces a large portion of Canada's wheat. The province is also rich in minerals. Saskatchewan is the world's leading exporter of uranium and the world's largest producer of potash. It has oil and natural gas. Although agriculture (q.v.) is the base of the economy, the mining and manufacturing industries are expanding.

The capital of Saskatchewan is Regina. The provincial legislative assembly has 64 seats. Saskatchewan holds 64 seats in the House of Commons and has six senators. The population of the province is 992,400 as of 1999.

SASKATCHEWAN RIVER. Called *Kisiskatchewani Sipi*, "swift-flowing river," by the natives, Henry Kelsey (1690) and Pierre La Vérendrye and his sons (c.1741) were the first Europeans to see it. The river was a transportation route used by both the Hudson's Bay Company (q.v.) and the North West Company (q.v.). The Saskatchewan also provided a east–west highway that linked the Western provinces to the English commercial enterprise during a period of question about sovereignty over land in the west.

SCHUBERT, CATHERINE O'HARE (1835–1918). Strong-willed and determined, O'Hare was born in Rathfriland, County Down, Ireland. She was married at Springfield, Massachusetts, to August Schubert. Together they ran a beer hall in St. Paul, Minnesota, before moving to Fort Garry in 1862 with their three children. When her husband wanted to leave her and the family behind to seek his fortune in the Cariboo with the Overland Party of 1862, she would hear nothing of it. The only woman Overlander, Mrs. Schubert was pregnant with her fourth child when she undertook the journey. The baby, Rose, was born at Kamloops a few hours after her mother's arrival there in October 1862. Mr. Schubert mined in the Cariboo for 11 years, beginning in 1863, while the family stayed at Lillooet. They then lived in various places before settling in Spallumcheen, British Columbia.

SCOTT, FRANCIS REGINALD (1899–1985). F. R. Scott was born in Québec City, son of a poet and archdeacon. This renaissance man went to Oxford as a Rhodes scholar, returning to Montréal and McGill University, where he became a professor of law with a specialty in constitutional law. He later became dean of law. Scott served as national chairman for the Co-operative Commonwealth Federation (later New Democratic Party, q.v.) and was active in the Penal Association. An expert on law, economics, and international relations, he wrote widely on that subject, more particularly assessing the constitutional issues of his time (e.g., the constitutionality of the Bennett New Deal). He edited several scholarly and learned journals. He was a poet of note.

It has been said of F. R. Scott that he was his own blasted pine. He started to teach constitutional law the year before the Great Depression, when, as he put it, the whole North American economy collapsed—and the world seemed turned upside down. As a teacher he was also a social activist. No one, he believed, could live through that Depression and be unaffected by it. Canadian institutions, he believed, needed reform. His poetry, marked by epigrammatic expression, had a strong sarcastic note to it and much irony. He was a strong supporter of bilingualism and the free development of Canada's two principal cultures alongside other ethnic groups. He fought racial intolerance and was a committed civil libertarian. In his time, he stood for the idea of Canada. His creed was: "The world is my country/The human race is my race/The spirit of man is my God/The future of man is my heaven."

SCOTT, THOMAS (1842?–1870). An Ontario member of the Orange Order (q.v.), Scott was executed by a firing squad by order of the Métis (q.v.) Provisional Government in Assiniboia, Manitoba. A martyr for English-speaking, Protestant causes, his death brought calls for revenge. Sir John A. Macdonald's (q.v.) government put down the rebellion by show of force; Louis Riel (q.v.) went into exile or was banished from Canada. It is said that Scott's ghost was in the courtroom when Riel was found guilty in 1885. D'Alton McCarthy's (q.v.) agitation and the Manitoba

Schools Act (q.v.) represented attempts to secure English, Protestant rights, agitation which split the country.

SECORD, LAURA INGERSOLL (1775–1868). Born in Massachusetts, Secord's family emigrated to Upper Canada (q.v.) after the American Revolution (q.v.). In June 1813, during the War of 1812 (q.v.), Secord overheard a number of American officers discussing an attack on a nearby British outpost. Upon hearing this, Secord moved to inform the British of the attack, aided by natives. She arrived at the British encampment on 22 June 1813. Two days later, natives ambushed the Americans as they approached the post. She became a hero after it was discovered that she had been the person who had forewarned the British.

SECRET SERVICE. Canada's first secret service and counter espionage organization was the "Mounties," the RCMP. It was concerned with internal security and only incidentally with intelligence gained from outside. Highly effective before and during World War II (q.v.), its gleanings were largely ignored by Canadian and British governments.

Gen. Walter Kirvitsky (a.k.a. Walter Thompson) defected from the Soviet Union and was followed by unidentified foreigners all the time he was in Canada. The RCMP advised authorities, including the British, about this, but this information was ignored. However, when Igor Gouzenko (q.v) defected in 1945 the RCMP used his evidence to round up the whole Soviet ring in Canada, including such people as Fred Rose, MP; P. F. P. Smith of the National Research Council in Ottawa; Kathleen Willsher, a registrar in the British High Commission in Ottawa; and D. G. Lunan, editor of *Canadian Affairs*. In the 1960s the RCMP targeted the Front de Libération de Québec, a terrorist campaign organized apparently with Soviet involvement. The campaign climaxed in the Cross-Laporte kidnappings in 1970 and played a positive role in René Levesque's Parti Québecois (qq.v.) coming to power.

In 1977 the Commission of Inquiry, probing allegations into RCMP wrongdoings, concentrated on operations against FLQ terrorists. Various RCMP personnel were convicted of illegal wire-tapping and breaking and entering. Mr. Justice David C. McDonald, who conducted the inquiry, found that the RCMP had made surreptitious entries "without consent or warrant" and exhibited "a willingness on the part of some members to deceive those outside the Force who have some sort of constitutional authority." In consequence, government established a new agency in 1993, the Canadian Security Intelligence Service (CSIS). Its role is to look after internal security and counter espionage; it was given broad powers under stringent controls.

SEIGNEURIAL SYSTEM. *See* New France.

SELKIRK, EARL OF [THOMAS DOUGLAS]. Scottish philanthropist and idealist. In 1811, Douglas, the fifth earl of Selkirk, acquired from the Hudson's Bay Company (q.v.) (by buying up its shares) a grant to 116,000 square miles of land in what is now southern Manitoba, North Dakota, and Minnesota. Selkirk hoped to relieve the distress of Scottish and Irish peasants at home and keep them in the British Empire by giving them arable land in Rupert's Land. These settlers, he argued, would provide food for the company and thereby save it money. And positioned along the North West Company's (q.v.) thoroughfare to the Athabasca country, they were strategically situated to cut off the rival's trade and provoke the Métis (q.v.), who claimed the area (and its hunting territories) as their own.

Canadian fur traders (q.v.) called the settlers "oatmeal eaters." Sir Alexander Mackenzie (q.v.) had engaged in a stock-buying war against Selkirk and had failed to stop the settlement. Terribly cold winters, pestilence, killing frosts, recurring spring floods, and hostility from the North West Company all combined to make the early years of the settlers trying ones. On 8 January 1814 Governor Miles Macdonnel issued a proclamation (the "Pemmican Proclamation") forbidding the trappers to take provisions in the territory. By 1815 conflict between the two companies had reached decisive proportions. In June of the following year in the Battle of Seven Oaks, near the forks of the Red and Assiniboine Rivers, the Nor'Westers defeated Hudson's Bay Company forces and drove the settlers from Red River. Meanwhile, Selkirk, acting without legal right, decided to retaliate and seize the North West Company's Fort William. This proved to be a costly mistake. Various court cases went against him. Mackenzie and Selkirk settled out of court. Selkirk returned to Europe a broken man and died in France in 1820. Mackenzie died the same year in Scotland. They had fought an interesting war between the fur trade and settlement. The rivalry had been violent, and the Colonial Office in London was anxious to end frontier warfare: they therefore encouraged the union of the two corporations under the heading of the Hudson's Bay Company in 1821. Selkirk Settlers reached the territory as follows: in 1812, 18; in 1813, 120; in 1814, 83.

SELKIRK SETTLERS. *See* Selkirk, Earl of.

SENATE. *See* Parliament; Parliamentary System.

SEPARATISM. In various forms and expressions this Québec-based pragmatic ideology proposes a separate status—and even independence or sovereignty—for Québec. Of indeterminate though ancient roots, it may be said to express itself in Louis Papineau (q.v.) and Jean-Olivier Chénier's rebellions of 1837, in the Front de Libération de Québec (q.v.) violence of the October Crisis (q.v.) in 1970, in the election of the Parti Québecois (q.v.) in 1976 (and the unsuccessful referendum of 1980), and in the return to power of the PQ in 1994. At times vibrant at other times muted, separatism has attracted many Québecois of all classes. To date, however, federal forces and internal Québec influences and constituencies have made independence but a dream for its adherents.

SEVEN YEARS' WAR. The Seven Years' War (1756–1763) was fought between Britain and its colonies on one side and France and its colonies on the other. It was fought around the globe. In North America the war began in 1754, as British colonists led by Maj. George Washington tried to force the French out of the Ohio Valley. The French sent reinforcements to Louisbourg (q.v.) to strengthen its position in the St. Lawrence Valley. Until 1757, the French tallied numerous victories in North America. In 1757, however, more than 20,000 British regulars arrived in North America. This essentially turned the tide. In 1758, native allies of the French signed a peace pact with the British, leaving the French to battle alone. In 1759 Britain recorded a number of victories, the most noted was on the Plains of Abraham at Québec City. With the fall of Louisbourg, Québec, and Montréal, the French were all but lost in North America. The war was ended by the Treaty of Paris (q.v.), which confirmed Britain's conquest of virtually all of New France (q.v.). *See also* Carleton, Sir Guy; Wolfe, James.

SHAWNADITHIT (1800–1829). Known also as Nancy, Shawnadithit was the last member of the Beothuk (q.v.) nation. She was captured and worked as an unpaid slave for a British settler, who called her Nancy. In April 1828, concern about loss of the Beothuk nation led to finding Shawnadithit. She was brought to St. John's and taught William Cormack about the Beothuk culture and language. She died of tuberculosis in 1829, but her teachings to Cormack preserved a record of the once-vibrant Beothuk.

SIFTON, SIR CLIFFORD (1861–1929). Defender of the Manitoba Schools Act (q.v.), Sifton later became minister of the interior under Wilfrid Laurier (q.v.) and promoted immigration from central and eastern Europe, bringing Ukrainians and Doukhobors (qq.v.) to Canada. He resigned in 1905 when separate schools were restored in the Northwest Territories and again when his defection helped the Conservatives to victory in 1911.

SIX NATIONS IROQUOIS CONFEDERACY. *See* Iroquois.

SKELTON, OSCAR DOUGLAS (1878–1941). Civil servant and historian. Skelton was born in Orangeville, Ontario, and attended Queen's University, where he studied Latin and English, and the University of Chicago. After working for four years on the staff of a Philadelphia literary magazine, he became a professor of political and economic science at Queen's in 1908.

Skelton's first book was *Socialism: A Critical Analysis* (1911), which caught V. I. Lenin's attention. Most of his work was on Canadian history, including: *The Railway Builders* (1916); *The Canadian Dominion* (1919), an early history of Canada written specifically for Americans; *Life and Times of A. T. Galt* (1920); and his classic *Life and Letters of Sir Wilfrid Laurier* (1921), a sympathetic defence of its subject, and thus a contribution to the Liberal party (q.v.) perspective in Canadian historical traditions.

Skelton's second career began almost immediately after the publication of his biography of Laurier. Skelton was long interested in Canada's role in the British Empire. He was unsympathetic to England's constant worries, and he was equally anxious to defend Canada's interests and promote its autonomy. In many ways, then, Skelton became an architect of the British Commonwealth of Nations (q.v.). Indeed, he led, with his political master William Lyon Mackenzie King (q.v.), the quest for a separate Canadian external or foreign policy. Skelton joined the Department of External Affairs in 1923, accompanied the prime minister to London for the Imperial Conferences, and promoted the idea of an independent responsibility for Canada in external affairs, of which intra-imperial affairs were the first requirement. In July 1924 he resigned from Queen's and became a permanent civil servant. In 1925, on Sir Joseph Pope's retirement, Skelton became under-secretary of state for external affairs. He brought in a group of able young persons: Hume Wrong, Norman Robertson and Lester Pearson (q.v.).

SKYDOME. Toronto's multiuse sports and entertainment complex. Opened 3 June 1989, SkyDome is arguably the most significant achievement in engineering and civic pride in the world. It has the world's first fully retractable roof, uncovering 100 percent of the field area and 91 percent of the seats. Some 280 events minimum are held in the facility every year. Most prominent among these events is Major League Baseball, for SkyDome is home to the American League Toronto Blue Jays (originated 1977), World Series champions in 1992 and 1993 (the later championship being the first time Major League Baseball's championship was won on a field outside of the United States). The Blue Jays played their first game in SkyDome on 5 June 1989 and hosted the Major League Baseball All-Star game in 1991. SkyDome is also home of the Toronto Argonaut Football Club (founded 1873), one of the oldest professional sports teams in North America, with more Grey Cup Championships to its credit (13) than any other team in the Canadian Football League. The Vanier Cup, Canada's university football championship, is held here annually. Its origin dates from the College Bowl of 1965.

SkyDome contains the Sony JumboTron, for many years the largest video display board in the world. Besides its stadium, SkyDome is a complex of hotel, restaurants, cinemas, and shops. The electronically controlled roof, which runs on steel tracks and bogies, can be opened in 20 minutes. A weather data centre and a radar and climate headquarters advises operators of the need to close the roof if a storm is approaching. SkyDome is one of the modern marvels of the world in another sense, for Toronto has been accentuated by SkyDome, allowing games and other events to go on year-round.

The history of SkyDome reflects public demands of the 1980s that old railway lands be reused but that heritage requirements be observed. Thus the old railroad roundhouse was preserved (for redevelopment) and the adjacent lands redeveloped. SkyDome sits on old rail lands and an early garbage dump. Archaeologists recovered many valuable artifacts, now on display in the facility. These include a French cannon, a mustard jar (with contents), and various glass, porcelain, and metal objects of note of colonial and aboriginal times. At the grand opening various labour unions employed in construction were celebratory participants; they are recognized permanently in a celebratory wall of honour. Just west of SkyDome is a remarkable statue/sculpture dedicated to the memory of Chinese (q.v.) labourers employed in the construction of Canadian railways.

SLAVERY. Slavery was declared legal in New France in 1709. Slavery existed in New France (q.v.) legally or illegally, from 1632 until 1763, when slavery was given new life under British law. Both *panis* (Indians, q.v.) and Blacks were slaves in Canada, and in 1760 there were some 4,000. The economy of Canada required little plantation or mining labour, so slavery was primarily domestic.

In 1793 Governor John Graves Simcoe of Upper Canada (q.v.) had legislation passed to say that any slave who reached the province would become free. Slaves who had come with Loyalists (q.v.) were freed. In

1807 the British Parliament abolished the trade in slaves and in 1833, by the Abolition Act, abolished slavery throughout the British Empire. Black Loyalists moved to Nova Scotia in 1775, although many migrated to Sierra Leone.

In 1826, Upper Canada formally refused to return runaway slaves to the United States. The "underground railroad" (q.v.) commenced. Josiah Henson, a slave, escaped to Canada and in 1849 wrote the story of his life. From this book and conversations with him, Harriet Beecher Stowe wrote her best-selling *Uncle Tom's Cabin* (1852).

In British Columbia, Governor James Douglas would not countenance slavery. Accordingly, Black slaves found refuge in Victoria and on Saltspring Island and elsewhere. However, native or Indian slavery was more extensive and was a conspicuous feature of Northwest Coast tribes until abolished by British diplomacy, coercion, and gunboats in the 1860s.

Many ex-slaves and their descendants, who had become Jamaicans or Bahamians, or other nationalities, moved to Canada. This process began after the easing of Canadian immigration regulations in 1967. *See* Blacks.

SMALLWOOD, JOSEPH ROBERTS (1900–1991). Politician, journalist, union organizer, farmer, and broadcaster. Smallwood was the driving force that led Newfoundland into confederation in 1949. After two referenda to decide Newfoundland's course, he was named its first premier in 1949. He held the position under the Liberal party (q.v.) until 1972. Smallwood integrated Newfoundland into Canada. He became a popular figure in Newfoundland. After his retirement from politics in 1977, he prepared a multivolume Newfoundland encyclopaedia.

SOCIAL CREDIT PARTY. Based, technically speaking, on monetarist policy developed by British engineer Maj. C. H. Douglas, the Social Credit party evolved in Alberta under radio evangelist William ("Bible Bill") Aberhart. Backed by disaffected farmers suffering continuing effects of the Depression of 1929 and vested Eastern interests, Social Credit won all seats in the 1935 Alberta election. Monetarist legislation was declared *ultra vires*. In 1952, W. A. C. Bennett forged a Social Credit government in British Columbia. His son, Bill Bennett, was a later British Columbia Social Credit premier. A Québec right-wing group known as *Creditistes* existed for a time and was influential in bringing down Joe Clark's (q.v.) 1979 government when they refused to back his budget. In the 1990s Social Credit was succeeded by the Reform party (q.v.).

SOCIAL GOSPEL. Certain late 19th- and early 20th-century Christian social practices and enthusiasms were precursors of the modern welfare state. Particularly prevalent among Congregationalists, Baptists, and Methodists, the Social Gospel promoted the cause for liquor control, prohibition and temperance (q.v.), protection for the disadvantaged, and equality before the law. The Social Gospel had profound effects on creating in Canada egalitarianism and social improvement, including universal rights to education (q.v.), to health care, and to pensions and unemployment insurance. Leaders included Salem Bland, Emily Ferguson Murphy (q.v.), and James Shaver Woodsworth (q.v.). Social Gospel is not to be confused with its parallel socialism, which is similar in many respects but is heavily union-based. Social Gospel was based primarily in church and volunteer organizations.

SOUTH AFRICAN WAR. War for the defence of British imperial interest in southern Africa, it was fought from 11 October 1899 to 31 May 1902. The war was fought between the Boer republics in South Africa (Orange Free State and Transvaal) and the British.

Canada was divided in terms of support for the British; imperialists pushed to participate, but many French Canadians were opposed. Prime Minister Sir Wilfrid Laurier (q.v.) authorized a force of 1,000 men to be formed on a voluntary basis. Units were raised from 12 military districts in Canada. Companies numbered 125 men each. The men came from both the permanent force and militia (q.v.). The first ship to carry Canadian troops was the *Sardinia*, a converted cattle transport. She left Québec City 31 October 1899. The first contingent was eventually augmented by some 6,000 other volunteers. The Canadians' first action was 31 December 1899, when one company of the Royal Canadian Regiment (RCR) took part in action with British and Australian troops at Sunnyside Kopje.

The first significant battle for the Canadians was Paardeburg, which took place 18 to 27 February 1900. The elements of weather took a heavy toll on the Canadians as they endured heat, sand, and especially disease. As the Boers continued to lose, they shifted to guerrilla tactics. The RCR sustained heavy casualties in ambushes, and the Boer tactics caused the war to drag on. By the end of the war, Canada had sent 8,372 men to the field; 244 were either killed in action or succumbed to disease, 252 were wounded, and four were awarded the Victoria Cross. *See also* Canadian Army.

SPORT. In all ages of modern Canada's history, sport has played an important role. Not only is sport a national preoccupation, it is a national pastime (and a daily subject of discussion). In addition, the organization of sport competitions has had a profound impact on the physical infrastructures of Montréal, Toronto, Ottawa, Québec City, Winnipeg, Calgary, Edmonton, Vancouver, and Victoria—as well as many other cities and towns.

How sport developed in Canada is also of importance to the study of the national history. Sport was a force in the building of the national ethos. Championships acquired became national achievements, especially against rival nation-states and even ideologies. Games and sport generally are forces of social integration and community building; in consequence, Canadian schools, colleges, and universities (q.v.) have stressed athletic and sport events, and prided themselves on great teams of the past and present.

Canada's sport is not generally indigenous; however, the national game is lacrosse, a native (or aboriginal) invention, noted in the various fur trade (q.v.) and traveller narratives. It is pleasing to note that Canada (itself a native name of community, or houses clustered together) should have adopted a native game for its national sport. On the other hand, a national sport may not be necessarily the most well-known national athletic or sporting activity. Hockey, generally regarded as *the* Canadian game of choice, has flourished in Canada and has as its period of great growth the 20th century.

Having been a part of the British Empire for many years, it is natural that British games have taken root in Canada. The most prominent of these is rugby, played variously across the country, but less so than Canadian football (that is, the Canadian variant of American football). Rugby in Canada conforms to the classic rules of British and international rugby and has never followed Australian or Rugby League (an English variant) rules. Rugby was instituted in Canada by military and naval forces and was developed by public and private schoolteachers. In some cities of Canada, school superintendents (such as John Gough of the Greater Victoria School Board) refused as late as 1960 to introduce Canadian football (again the variant of American football) in public schools on the grounds of its expense, or its more dangerous format (leading to more numerous injuries). By contrast, in some communities such as Vancouver, rugby and Canadian football developed side by side. Another sport introduced from England was cricket, which had in the early years of colonial development a great following—but one which lessened with the growing popularity of softball and baseball. West Indian and Indian/Pakistani immigration helped give cricket a new lease on life in the 1960s and 1970s. In short, rugby and cricket have long histories in Canada, even though these sports are the preoccupation of a devoted few. Much the same could be said of what is known in Canada as field grass hockey (thus differentiating it from hockey, which is played on ice—and which the English call ice hockey). Soccer (the English "football") has a wider following and a longer history.

Beginning in the 1970s, baseball became a national spectator preoccupation, and Canada's two Major League Baseball franchises (the Montréal Expos, who play in the National League, and the Toronto Blue Jays, in the American League) have brought a Canadian essence to the game. Long before such premier professional teams came to Canada, excellent baseball and softball teams, whether amateur, semiprofessional, or professional, existed in Canada. Softball, for instance, is a major preoccupation in some cities; Victoria is an example. Little League Baseball, introduced in the 1950s, has had a strong following in most Canadian cities. There are other examples.

Football, especially the Canadian variant of American football, which has a wider and longer field and a 12th player on each side, has a large professional and amateur following. It is characterized by a strong aerial game, owing to the fact that there are only three "downs" rather than four (the ball must be advanced 10 yards without penalty to get, again, a first down).

Other sports of prominence include curling, golf, and tennis. In addition, there are skating, skiing, bobsledding, and numerous other individual (and team) activities of competition. Each has a history all of its own. It is not possible here to recount these several histories.

When Canadians think sport they think hockey. Harshness of climate, availability of outdoor ice, and the ethos of the game all contributed to national possession, even obsession, of the sport. It has no rival for affection, from young or old, male or female. Lord Stanley, the governor general, 1888–93, donated a cup for the national championship—and it has since become emblematic of professional hockey's highest prize. The Stanley Cup was first played for in 1893 and the Allan Cup, emblematic of the amateur championship, in 1908.

Social disorder and riots have occurred over certain matters related to hockey. When superstar Maurice "Rocket" Richard of the Montréal Canadiens was ejected from a critically important game in 1955 and suspended by National Hockey League (NHL) president Clarence Campbell, a general riot occurred in Montréal. In international hockey, Canada's history has been central to national identification. Team Canada's victory over the Soviet Union in the 1972 eight-game series (with games divided between North America and the Soviet Union) remains the stuff of legend, bringing Canadian collective passions from the state of despair to total triumph. This Cold War struggle had overtones of irregular warfare, fought for high stakes.

How professional hockey has been broadcast and telecast has been important in the shaping of Canadian consciousness of the game. Foster Hewitt ("Hello Canada"; "He shoots! He scores!") reported regularly from Toronto's Mutual Street Arena and later Maple Leaf Gardens and became legendary as an integrating force on the Canadian Broadcasting Corporation's (q.v.) radio network Hockey Night in Canada. Saturday nights became synonymous with Canadian hockey. Similarly, Danny Gallivan had a wide following from the Montréal Forum. Other commentators of note include Howie Meeker, one-time player for the Toronto Maple Leafs, and Don Cherry, one-time coach of the Boston Bruins.

In the early 20th century the Stanley Cup was a Canadian championship and was won by such unlikely teams as the Victoria Cougars. In later years, hockey went "north and south," including American teams in the major league, the NHL. Throughout the 1950s and 1960s the Stanley Cup was fought for by Toronto, Montréal, Chicago, Detroit, New York, and Boston. Later, with league expansion, new teams were given franchises in St. Louis and Los Angeles, for example; in Canada, new NHL teams such as Vancouver, Calgary, and Edmonton were established. Québec City and Winnipeg once had NHL teams; eventually the franchises shifted south of the border to American cities. Another factor influencing hockey's change was the introduction of outstanding European players, principally from Sweden, Finland, Czechoslovakia (as was), and when they could escape the Iron Curtain outward bound, the Soviet Union.

Canadian hockey rests on amateur hockey clubs and leagues. Among outstanding "Junior" leagues is the Ontario Hockey League, which, like its other parallel organizations, is the cradle of the NHL for Canadian talents. In addition, other professional leagues have made hockey history, including the World Hockey Association, the Pacific Coast League, and the Eastern Hockey League, to give a few examples.

Track and field holds a special place in Canadian athletic history. Prominent among early athletes of historical note are: Percy Williams, who won gold for the 100 and 200 metres at the 1928 Olympics (Gen. Douglas MacArthur said that Williams, the shy Vancouver athlete, was the greatest sprinter the world had ever seen); steroid-user Ben Johnson, winner in Seoul in 1988 after his record-shattering 100 metres and then disqualified (and suspended indefinitely); and Donovan Bailey, who won gold with his record-breaking 1996 Atlanta Olympic 100-metre dash. Abby Hoffman, the middle-distance runner, represented Canada at four Olympics and later became a prominent supervisor of sports services for the Ontario Ministry of Culture and Recreation and also director general of Sports Canada. She actively campaigned for women's and girls' sports, particularly athletics and, above all, for fitness programs. She was, too, champion for gender equity in sports. Why Canadians are less successful in longer-distance races is a subject for speculation, though in relays (both male and female) great successes have been achieved.

Canada has hosted the British Empire Games (Vancouver, 1954—at which the "miracle mile" was run by Roger Bannister of England) and the Commonwealth Games (Victoria, 1994). Canada has hosted the Olympic Winter Games in Calgary (1988) and the Summer Games in Montréal (1976). Over the years primacy of "medal gathering" has gone to swimmers, skiers, rowers, and canoeists.

Golf remains one of Canada's great sports or recreations. The game is regulated by the Royal Canadian Golf Association, headquartered in Oakville, Ontario, at Glen Abbey Golf Club, a public course where the Canadian Open is frequently but not always played. Older courses in Canada include Royal Montréal, Royal Ottawa, and Victoria Golf Club. Included in the greats of golf architecture are Stanley Thompson, who designed Kitchener Westmount (for instance), and A. Maccan (Victoria Golf Club). Golf clubs were sometimes established by garrison social societies (e.g., the Royal United Services Club of Victoria established Uplands Golf Club). Prominent golf champions of Canadian history are Vancouver's Stan Leonard (professional) and Kitchener's Gary Cowan (amateur, senior professional).

The greatest female golf legend of Canada—who is really Canada's greatest golf legend—is Marlene Stewart Streit, many-time winner of the Canadian and U.S. amateur championships. Of an earlier time is Ada Mackenzie (1918–71), regarded by many as the first woman of Canadian golf, who for half a century dominated Ontario and Canadian women's golf.

Other prominent female figures in Canadian sport are: Barbara Ann Scott, figure skating champion; Marilyn Bell, long-distance swimmer (Lake Ontario and Strait of Juan de Fuca crossings completed); and Nancy Greene, downhill skier (and the first to profit widely from financial investments and business, endorsements, and public appearances).

Historians use sport in Canada as an important means of showing community pride and development, national aspirations, and international perspectives. Sports historians also are able to analyze class relations, gender relations, and broadcasting/telecasting. Once considered a sideline of historians and publishers, sport in Canada is a vital prism through which to see so many varied aspects of Canada's history. Sport runs deeply through Canadian history. *See also* SkyDome.

STACEY, CHARLES PERRY (1906–1989). Historian and soldier. Educated at Toronto, Oxford, and Princeton universities, Stacey wrote many articles on the War of 1812 (q.v.). Colonel Stacey became the army's official historian and director of the Canadian Army Historical Section in 1945. In his time he was considered the foremost practitioner in the field of Canadian military history in Canada. His trenchant, well-researched works include *Canada and the British Army* (1939) and *Canada and the Age of Conflict* in two volumes (1977, 1981). His memoirs are entitled *A Date with History* (1983).

STANTON, SIR AMBROSE THOMAS (1875–1938). At the time of his death, Stanton was chief medical advisor to the secretary of state for the colonies and had his offices in Downing Street, London. Born in Kendal, Durham County, Ontario, he attended local schools, Port Hope High School and the University of Toronto. He took various courses in London, England, where he was associated with the Institute of Tropical Medicine. He served with distinction in the British Malay States and found cures for beriberi and melioidosis, two debilitating and fatal diseases. Later, in London, he was at the Centre of Tropical Medical Research, mainly in advisory and administrative capacities. He was knighted (K.C.M.G.) for his distinguished contributions to medical science. His work was recognized in Canada, and the University of Toronto awarded him a D.Sc. in 1934. He was one of Canada's sons who went outwards into the services of the British Empire, and he brought great credit to his home communities, his province, and his country.

STATUTE OF WESTMINSTER. An act of the British government passed in 1931, which proclaimed that no law passed by Westminster should apply to a dominion without the dominion government's request and consent. The statute also preserved the British North America Act as a British statute, to be amended only at Westminster, when asked to do so by Canada's parliament. It declared Britain, Canada, and other self-governing dominions to be linked by common allegiance to the Crown, though in no way subordinate to one another in any aspect of their internal or external affairs. *See also* Constitution Act of 1867.

STEELE, SIR SAMUEL BENFIELD (1851–1919). Born at Purbrook, Simcoe County, Ontario, Sam Steele enlisted in the militia (q.v.) at the age of 15 to fight the Fenian Raids (q.v.) (Irish nationalists in the United States who were threatening to invade Canada in 1866). In 1870, he again joined the militia to put down the Red River Rebellion (q.v.) led by Louis Riel (q.v.). In 1873, Steele joined the newly formed North West Mounted Police and became superintendent of this force in 1885. He commanded the cavalry during the Northwest Rebellion (q.v.) that year. Two years later he was sent to the Kootenay district of British Columbia, where he helped bring peace between the settlers and the local Indians (q.v.). In 1898, Steele was ordered to the Yukon and put in charge of the North West Mounted Police posts on the Chilkoot and White Passes. He then became commander of all police in the newly established Yukon Territory and gained much respect for establishing law and order among the unruly miners.

Steele left the Yukon in 1899. He later fought in the South African War (q.v.) and served in World War I (q.v.) with the rank of major general. Knighted in 1918, he died in London, England.

STEFANSSON, VILHJALMUR (1879–1962). Explorer, lecturer, and publicist of the Arctic regions. Stefansson was born in Arnes, near Gimli, Manitoba, the son of Icelandic immigrants who shortly thereafter moved to North Dakota. He studied at the Universities of North Dakota, Iowa, and Harvard. In 1904 he went to Iceland to study anthropology and archaeology.

Stefansson made three expeditions of note. In 1906–07 he went to Mackenzie River Delta of northwestern Arctic Canada with the expedition led by Ernest Leffingwell and Ejnar Mikklesen and learned to live, speak, eat, and hunt like the Inuit (q.v.). Between 1908 and 1912 he conducted an ethnological survey of the central Arctic coast for the American Museum of Natural History and the Geological Survey of Canada (q.v.). Between 1913 and 1918, under Canadian government auspices, he commanded the Canadian Arctic Expedition, using sleds in his explorations after the loss of the supply ship *Karluk* in 1914. Stefansson extended contemporary knowledge of the Arctic archipelago. He mapped large regions of coastline and gained increased knowledge of Inuit life. He developed a thesis that the Arctic was a habitable zone where life could be sustained even on the ice floes without supplies. By rejecting the idea that Arctic exploration was difficult or venturesome, he invited the censure of other explorers, such as Roald Amundsen. He believed that the North was rich in natural resources and could serve as a shortcut between major centres of commerce and civilization. He also developed a theme of human history, now largely discredited, that great empires in northern climes had supplanted lesser empires in more southerly latitudes.

Realizing that future exploration of the north could be conducted by aeroplane, Stefansson retired in 1919 to write and lecture. Among his 24 books and numerous articles are the following volumes, which enjoyed a wide reading public: *My Life with the Eskimo* (1913), *Friendly Arctic* (1921), *The Northward Course of Empire* (1922), *Hunters of the Great North* (1922), *Ultima Thule* (1940), and his autobiography, *Discovery* (1964). He died in Hanover, New Hampshire.

STOWE, EMILY JENNINGS (1831–1903). Educator and doctor. Stowe was born in Norwich, Ontario, attended teachers' college in Toronto, and became the first woman principal in Canada. With the illness of her husband, she decided to attend medical school to obtain a better job to offset the cost of hospital bills. She was not admitted by the University of Toronto and instead attended the New York Medical College for Women. In 1867 she received her degree, moved to Toronto, and became the first Canadian woman doctor to practice medicine in Canada. In 1877, Emily organized the first women's rights group in Canada to lobby for unfair laws against women. The group became the Toronto Women's Suffrage Association. In 1883 her daughter, Augusta, became the first woman to receive a degree in medicine in Canada. Today, many rights of Canadian women were a result of the efforts of Dr. Emily Jennings Stowe.

STRACHAN, JOHN (1778–1867). First Anglican bishop of Toronto (1839–67). Strachan was born in Aberdeen, Scotland, and educated at Aberdeen and St. Andrews Universities, arriving in Upper Canada (q.v.) in 1799 to take charge of a school projected but stillborn by Governor J. G. Simcoe. He took orders in the Church of England in 1803. His high-church leanings were suitably Tory and shaped establishment thinking. He became one of the pillars of the Executive Council and Legislative Assembly of Upper Canada. He left both bodies by 1841. Meanwhile he had become one of the "Family Compact" (q.v.), the dominant clique running the Province of Upper Canada.

In 1827 Strachan became the first president of King's College, Toronto. When this was reorganized as the University of Toronto (1850), he ceased his connection, founding the University of Trinity College, Toronto (1851).

SUEZ CRISIS. A major event in the history of Canadian external, or foreign relations, history, the Suez Crisis was an international crisis that emerged when Egypt (under its president, Gamal Abdel Nasser) expropriated and nationalized the Suez Canal Company, hitherto an Anglo-French company. When diplomacy failed, France and Britain launched a secret plan with Israel in which Israel attacked Egypt to regain the Canal, and then France and Britain intervened to "stabilize" the situation. At first Canada did not "condemn" the intervention, only "regretted" it. The reason for this was that Canadian public opinion was greatly divided by the event. In fact, the event severely split Commonwealth opinion on the matter, for hitherto consultation in advance of action (an understood technique of intra-imperial diplomacy) had been the rule.

At the United Nations, the Anglo-French intervention was looked on as a violation of the UN Charter. Canada voted with the United States against Britain and Russia in condemning the British and French governments. Under the leadership of Lester B. Pearson (q.v.), secretary of state for external affairs of Canada, and of Canadian diplomats at the UN, the UN reached a settlement and introduced a peacekeeping force. Under command of Maj. Gen. E. L. M. Burns of Canada, the UN Emergency Force supervised the evacuation of the Canal Zone. This it did successfully, and the Middle East situation had been defused, if temporarily. Pearson's leadership was much lauded at the time: he was awarded the Nobel prize for peace (1957). It is less possible to judge the political consequences of the Suez Crisis to Canadian national politics. Not unlikely, however, is the fact that the Liberals' position against Britain (which provoked much complaint in Britain and in Canada) reduced national trust in that party as the ruling party. In 1957, at the general election, the Liberal party (q.v.) lost power to the Progressive Conservative party under John George Diefenbaker (q.v.).

Canada had acted out of self-interest in the Suez Crisis. A "middle power," Canada backed the United States and the United Nations against her imperial ally and against France and Israel. The event may therefore be considered a declaration of independence in foreign affairs policymaking for Canada.

SUPREME COURT OF CANADA. Created by the Dominion Act of 1875, promoted by Edward Blake (q.v.). Until 1949, however, the court of last resort was the Judicial Committee of the Privy Council (JCPC) in London. By the 1949 Supreme Court Amendment Act, the Court was reaffirmed as the final arbiter over the British North America Act, thus ending appeals to the JCPC.

-T-

"TAINTED-BLOOD" INVESTIGATION. *See* Krever Inquiry and Report.

TALON, JEAN-BAPTISTE [COMTE D'ORSAINVILLE] (1625?–1694). First intendant of New France (q.v.), 1665–68 and 1670–72. Talon was responsible for justice, administration, and finance in the colony.

TECUMSEH (1768–1813). Shawnee chief and orator. Tecumseh joined his brother Tenskwatawa, "The Prophet," in an armed resistance against American arms at the Battle of Tippecanoe in 1811. An ally of the British in the War of 1812 (q.v.), he commanded native forces and fell fighting at the Battle of the Thames in Upper Canada (q.v.).

TELEVISION. *See* Canadian Broadcasting Corporation.

TEMPERANCE. A movement, with parallels in Britain, the United States, and elsewhere, urging society to control or cease consumption of alcoholic beverages. The temperance movement was an organized response to the social disruption caused by alcoholism. Legal prohibition was made possible by the Canada Temperance Act of 1878, giving local governments the right to prohibit, by vote, retail sale of alcohol. The first temperance societies were founded in Pictou, Nova Scotia, and Montréal. A Canadian counterpart of the Women's Christian Temperance Union was founded by Letitia Youmans of Picton, Ontario, in 1874. Prohibition was instituted in Prince Edward Island, Québec, and elsewhere, but bootlegging and exports of Canadian spirituous liquors to the United States continued. Government control of liquor sales was introduced, and prohibition was suspended.

THANADELTHUR (1697–1717). Interpreter, guide, consultant, and peace negotiator. A member of the Chipewyan nation, in 1713 Thanadelthur was captured by some Crees. She managed to escape with another Chipewyan woman, who eventually died, and she reached York Factory, a Hudson's Bay Company (q.v.) trading post. There, Thanadelthur learned English and became an interpreter between the Chipewyan and the fur traders (q.v.). She joined a peace expedition into Chipewyan territory with fur traders and Cree members. After failing to find the Chipewyan tribe, Thanadelthur left the group and travelled alone to find her people. She managed to persuade her people to talk peace with the Cree. Thanadelthur brought peace between the Chipewyan and Cree tribes. As well, she encouraged fur trading between the Chipewyan nation and the HBC.

THOMPSON, DAVID (1770–1857). Fur trader (q.v.), explorer, surveyor, and geographer. Thompson was born in London, England. He was apprenticed to the Hudson's Bay Company (q.v.) in 1784 and sent to Churchill. He surveyed territory between Cumberland House and York Factory and, in particular, to Lake Athabasca.

In 1797 Thompson entered the service of the North West Company (q.v.). He discovered the headwaters of the Saskatchewan River (q.v.). In 1804 he became a partner in the North West Company, and in 1807 he crossed the Rockies and built Kootenay House, the first fur trading post on the Columbia River. His surveying of the Columbia and Kootenay Rivers for North West Company trade delayed his arrival at his ultimate objective, the mouth of the Columbia. Thus, when he reached the Pacific, he found Americans at Astoria. He was the first man to travel the full length of the great river of the West and the first to map its course with any accuracy. Thompson River, a large, southern tributary of the Fraser River, was named after him by his friend Simon Fraser (q.v.).

In 1812 Thompson left the fur trading interior forever. He settled near Montréal and prepared for the North West Company a great map of western Canada (now in the Ontario Archives). He surveyed for the International Boundary Commission (q.v.) the Canada–United States boundary from Saint-Regis, Québec, to the northwest corner of Lake of the Woods. He died in poverty at Longueuil, near Montréal. In 1799 he had married Charlotte Small, a half-native or Métis (q.v.) woman, by whom he had 16 children.

Thompson ranks among the great geographer-explorers of the world. His North American Western travels covered 80,460 kilometres by canoe, horse, and foot. He mapped routes through 2,735,800 kilometres of Canada and the United States. His maps were precise, reflecting his persistent and methodical surveys. Through his labours, he unlocked to science and cartography the secrets of two great river systems, the Saskatchewan and the Columbia. *See also* Mackenzie, Sir Alexander.

TILLEY, SIR SAMUEL LEONARD (1818–1896). New Brunswick supporter of confederation and subsequently lieutenant-governor of the province. As Canadian minister of finance, he brought in the National Policy tariff.

TORONTO. Capital of the Province of Ontario, its name is derived from Mohawk *tkaronto,* that is, "trees standing in the water," referring to native fish weirs. It is incorrectly said to mean "place of meeting." The French had a post there, and in 1793, Lt.-Governor John Graves Simcoe called the place York. It was renamed Toronto when it was incorporated as a city (1834). Metropolitan Toronto includes Toronto, North York, Scarborough, York, Etobicoke, and East York and does not include Mississauga.

Location gave it its role in the developing economy of Upper Canada (q.v). From the beginning Simcoe recognized its military value and strategic focus, important in the Province's defence against American aggression. In 1794 Toronto was named (as York) capital of Upper Canada. Major arterial roads ran to and from Toronto, prominent among which were Dundas Street and Yonge Street, the latter said to be the longest in the world (it runs north, with links to Lake Simcoe and Georgian Bay). By 1812 only 700 persons lived in York, but its political and administrative importance was ensured. During the War of 1812 (q.v.) York was twice raided and pillaged by U.S. forces, leaving anti-American viewpoints in the populace most important to the further direction of Canadian national attitudes. Immigration from the United Kingdom spurred Toronto's growth, and by 1834 it had over 9,000 inhabitants. William Lyon Mackenzie (q.v.) was its first mayor. Banking, industrial development, government administration, collegiate and higher education (q.v.), publishing and ecclesiastical affairs all were central to its rise to prominence. Toronto was also home of some of Canada's early unions and its radicalism. Farm machinery and railway-related industries were particularly prominent. In 1911 hydroelectricity from Niagara Falls provided cheap energy, further stimulating economic growth. World War I (q.v.) necessitated great growth of meat packing and bacon production; it also encouraged clothes and munitions production. In World War II (q.v.), aircraft production increased dramatically, and by 1951 Toronto had over one million residents.

Toronto's transportation links were key to its rise to Canadian prominence. All major freight and passenger railways served it, and all Canadian transcontinental passenger trains called at Union Station (1927). Today VIA and AMTRAK service Toronto. Similarly, being near the evolving St. Lawrence Seaway merchant shipping, especially relating to grains and milling, called at Toronto Port, regulated by a commission. The Toronto Transit Commission (1953) developed tram and underground services, later exporting some of these innovative technologies. GO Transit developed urban-outlying communities rail/bus commuter traffic services. Toronto's financial primacy in Canada was aided by the establishment of the Toronto Stock Exchange.

Highlights of the population history of Toronto include: large Irish immigration in the 1850s, both Protestant and Roman Catholic; continuing English and Scottish immigration in the late 19th century (and after); Jews, Italians and Ukrainians at the turn of the century; Italians in the 1960s; Germans, Poles, Hungarians, Balkan Slavs, Greeks and Portuguese in the 1970s and after. Throughout, Chinese and other Asians arrived. Throughout, the Anglo-Celtic element remained prominent. By 1991 the population of Greater Toronto neared 2.5 million.

Institutional and cultural institutions of prominence include: Archives of Ontario, Legislative Library of the Province of Ontario, Royal Ontario Museum, Royal Canadian Military Institute, Upper Canada Law Society's Osgoode Hall, University of Toronto and its affiliates, York University, Ontario College of Art, Art Gallery of Ontario, Roy Thomson Hall, Hockey Hall of Fame, and SkyDome (q.v.). Toronto is headquarters of the Canadian Broadcasting Corporation (q.v.), many churches including the Anglican Church of Canada and the United Church of Canada, and the principal Canadian banks. Prominent national newspapers published in Toronto are *Globe and Mail* and the *National Post*. Ontario Place is an amusement mecca, and Canada's most famous warship (and now a museum) HMCS *Haida* (q.v.) is berthed there. *See also* Universities, Sports.

TREATY OF PARIS. *See* Paris, Treaty of.

TREATY OF UTRECHT. *See* Utrecht, Treaty of.

TRUDEAU, PIERRE ELLIOTT (1919–). Prime minister of Canada (1968–79, 1980–84). Born in Montréal, Trudeau was educated at College Jean de Brébeuf, the University of Montréal, Harvard University, and the London School of Economics. He travelled extensively. He was first elected to the House of Commons in 1965 for the riding of Mount Royal. In 1968, he was elected leader of the Liberal party (q.v.) of Canada. He became prime minister of Canada in 1968 and held the position until 1979. In 1980, the Liberals were returned to power and Trudeau again was prime minister until 1984 when he resigned.

Trudeau helped found *Cité Libre*, an intellectual journal that challenged the Union Nationale (q.v.) government of Maurice Duplessis in Québec. In 1965, with Jean Marchand and Gérard Pelletier (the "three wise men" so-called), Trudeau ran for the federal Liberals, won and was named parliamentary secretary to Prime Minister Lester Pearson (q.v.). In 1967, Trudeau became minister of justice. He pushed through a major reform of the Criminal Code. For a new Divorce Act, he won national attention for his now-famous remark, "the state has no place in the bedrooms of the nation."

With the retirement of Pearson in 1968, Trudeau was elected leader of the Liberal party. His style, urbanity, and intelligence captivated the nation. In the election, he was awarded a majority. In his first term, his government passed the Official Languages Act and began, among other efforts, to give Canada a truly bilingual public service. During the October Crisis (q.v.) in 1970, Trudeau implemented the War Measures Act (q.v.) after the Front de Libération de Québec (q.v.) kidnapped James Cross and Pierre Laporte and murdered the latter. His actions during the event illustrated his toughness when dealing with separatists.

In 1972, Trudeau won a minority and relied on the New Democratic party (q.v.) for support in the House of Commons. Between 1972 and 1974, he passed popular legislation that encouraged free spending within the government. In 1974, he won a majority due to his free-spending legislation. Soaring inflation forced Trudeau's government to impose wage and price controls. The economic crisis was compounded by the election of René Levesque's Parti Québecois (qq.v.) over Robert Bourassa's (q.v.) Liberals in Québec in 1976. Levesque's separatist (q.v.) government was a direct challenge to Trudeau.

In 1979, Trudeau's government lost to Joe Clark's (q.v.) Progressive Conservatives. Trudeau resigned from politics, but before a leadership convention could be held, Clark's government was defeated in the House of Commons. Trudeau led the Liberals to victory in 1980 with a majority. In office, Trudeau intervened in the Québec Referendum of May 1980 and contributed largely to the defeat of the PQ's sovereignty-association proposals. In 1982, he managed to secure provincial consent, except for Québec, for the Canadian Charter of Rights and Freedoms and the patriation of the constitution in the Constitution Act of 1982 (q.v.). In 1984, Trudeau retired from office.

Trudeau has been portrayed as enigmatic. His flamboyance and stunts have been said to have been staged and rehearsed. He stands out as a loner, a gunslinger. His *Memoir*, published 1993, revealed little of his inner self; critics regarded it as crass commercial opportunism. Marshall McLuhan (q.v.) saw Trudeau's mask as that of warrior chief. His legacy is that he was the architect of federal bilingualism, father of the Charter of Rights and Freedoms, fixer of the patriation of the Canadian constitution (that is, from Westminster to Ottawa), and spokesperson for his unique view of a strong Canadian nationalism under a federal structure (and thus a strong central government).

TSIMSHIAN. The Tsimshian ("people inside of the Skeena River") were divided into three groups: the Tsimshian proper, located around the mouth of the Skeena River, British Columbia; the Gitxsan, located farther up the Skeena River; and the Nisga'a (q.v.) who inhabited the basin of the Nass River. All three groups spoke dialects of the Tsimshian language. The Tsimshian were quick to adapt to the fur trade (q.v.). In this respect, the Tsimshian society changed after contact with the European fur traders. In 1862, the tribe experienced a severe smallpox epidemic. This epidemic, coupled with the challenge to the social balance that the fur trade was inflicting upon the tribe, almost destroyed the Tsimshian. Many became Christian under Anglican lay missionary William Duncan (q.v.) at Metlakatla, and some sought refuge in Alaska in 1887.

TUPPER, SIR CHARLES (1821–1915). Halifax-born physician and Nova Scotia premier (1864–67). Tupper promoted confederation against the opposition of Joseph Howe (q.v.). He became the prime minister, briefly in 1896, committed the Conservatives to remedial legislation in the Manitoba Schools Act (q.v.) (not effected), and was leader of the opposition until 1900.

TYRRELL, JOSEPH BURR (1858–1957). Geologist, historian, and mining engineer. Tyrrell conducted studies during several expeditions in northwestern Canada that aided the development of the Canadian mining industry. Born in Weston, Ontario, near Toronto (qq.v.), he graduated from the University of Toronto and joined the Geological Survey of Canada (q.v.). Near Drumheller, Alberta, Tyrrell discovered the first dinosaur bones ever found in Canada. Shortly afterward, he discovered one of the nation's largest coal deposits nearby.

During 1893 and 1894, Tyrrell travelled from Lake Athabasca across the barren lands of the Northwest Territories to Hudson Bay. Tyrrell mapped the region and predicted correctly that minerals there would greatly increase Canada's wealth.

Tyrrell left the Geological Survey of Canada in 1898 and became a mining engineer and manager. He joined the Kirkland Lake Gold Mining Company in 1924 and served as president of the firm from 1931 until his death. Tyrrell wrote many articles about geology and exploration (q.v.) in Canada and edited the journals of fur trader Samuel Hearne (q.v.), surveyor Philip Turnor, and geographer David Thompson (q.v.), all published by the Champlain Society.

-U-

UKRAINIANS. The Ukrainian community is one of the largest ethnic groups in Canada. Originating from old Slavic peasant stock, they settled mainly in the Prairie provinces. Large Ukrainian immigration to Canada began in the late 1890s. Overpopulation, excessive land subdivision, hopeless economic conditions, and political, social, and religious oppression were mainly responsible for the migration to Canada. Ukrainians were encouraged by Clifford Sifton's (q.v.) immigration policy promising free land. A second wave of Ukrainian immigrants came to Canada in the 1920s and 1930s as political refugees. A third movement occurred following World War II (q.v.), beginning in 1946. Although there have been numerous achievements by individual Ukrainian Canadians, the most important contribution made by Ukrainian Canadians was their pioneer work in opening up the Canadian West. Many settled on poor land and persevered in the struggle to make the land productive. They struggled through many years of drought and frigid temperatures, living in sod houses. In a period of less than 100 years, they have established their own religion and cultural life and contributed to the main stream of Canadian life. The first Ukrainian to be elected to the House of Commons was Michael Luchkovich in 1926. In 1991, 406,645 Ukrainians were living in Canada.

UNDERGROUND RAILROAD. The "underground railroad" freedom movement was a network of refuges and routes for fugitive slaves into the North or to Canada, especially Chatham, in southwest Ontario. Dating from 1786, it was strongest in the 1850s and 1860s. Freedom-seekers travelled from one secret safe house to another. It has been estimated that of 4,000,000 slaves in the United States before the end of the Civil War, 40,000 made it to Canada (after the Civil War, 20,000 returned to the United States). *See also* Slavery.

UNION NATIONALE. The Conservative and Action Liberale Nationale parties allied in 1935 as the Union Nationale to fight the Québec election. Originally the union was reformist and rural. In 1936 under leader Maurice Duplessis, it formed a government which was defeated in 1939 but returned in 1944. Duplessis died in 1959. The party lost the 1960 election. It returned to power in 1968 under Daniel Johnson but lost the mantle to the nationalistic Parti Québecois (q.v.). Union Nationale lost the 1970 election to the Liberals and virtually disappeared. *See also* Padlock Law.

UNITED CHURCH OF CANADA. Formed 10 June 1925 by union of the Presbyterian Church in Canada, the Methodist Church (Canada, Newfoundland, and Bermuda), the Congregational Churches of Canada, and the General Council of Local Union Churches. In 1968 the eastern Canada Conference of the Evangelical United Brethren Church joined;

the western conference remained outside. The largest Protestant church in Canada, its membership is about one million though since the 1960s has declined. Discussion with the Anglican Church of Canada, for union, broke down in 1975 and with the Disciples of Christ in 1984. Mid-Canada's church, the United Church of Canada has confronted many leading issues and was first to recognize gay/lesbian rights of ordination or church membership. Its powerful United Church Women forms the largest women's organization in Canada. The United Church maintains connections with various universities (q.v.) and colleges. The Church has campaigned on labour issues, prisoners' rights, amnesty, anti-gambling, anti-pornography, and social justice issues. It has provided a prophetic critique of society.

UNITED FARMERS. The United Farmers of Alberta (UFA), established 1909, was interested in rural economic issues. Pressures led to organization of the Alberta Farmers' Cooperative Elevator Company—eventually United Grain Growers. United Farm Women (1915) promoted women's suffrage (gained in Alberta in 1916). UFA was elected in 1921 and held office until 1935; it promoted education (q.v.), health, and farmers' needs, but did not cope well with the Depression. Charismatic Henry Wise Wood was one notable leader. Eventually UFA grew into United Farmers of Alberta Cooperative Limited.

Other United Farmers were founded: in Manitoba (1920), in Saskatchewan (1926 as United Farmers of Canada [Saskatchewan Section]), in Ontario (1914), and in Québec (1920). In Ontario in 1919 the United Farmers of Ontario under E. C. Drury, a Barrie, Ontario, farmer, held the reigns of office. Agnes MacPhail (q.v.) was prominent in this organization, which in the 1940s grew into United Cooperatives of Ontario. The Women's Institute, the Grange, and 4-H clubs were features of their work. The influence of these groups on the Liberals, Progressives, and Co-operative Commonwealth Federation was significant. The Co-operative movement survives, an important legacy of these reform-minded Canadians.

UNIVERSITIES. Educational systems of Canada represent, in large degree, extensions or adaptations of the civilizations from which Canada derives. France, Britain, and the United States all have made significant influences on the course of Canadian higher education (q.v.). The French brought the conviction that faith and education were closely bound together. The British, more especially the Scots who had a profound impact on the founding of universities and colleges, brought a more secular bent. The Americans, who saw as necessary a division between church and state, urged nonaligned education systems. The great public universities of the Prairie West were yet again a diffusion of some of these older models and ideas. The British North America Act (Constitution Act of 1867, q.v.) made education a specific provincial realm of authority. However, in training and job development, the federal government has had influential tasks. Indeed federal funding for provincially run universities was a prominent feature of the history of the 1950s and 1960s, during the remarkable growth of higher education (in terms of student numbers and physical plants).

Some highlights of this long history are as follows. In 1635 the College des Jésuites was founded in Québec (it closed in 1775). This was the root from which sprang two branches. In 1663 Bishop Laval (q.v.) founded a seminary, which became, by charter (1852), Laval University and the Université de Montréal (1878, charter 1920). These then can claim to come from the oldest university in Canada.

In 1821 McGill College (later University), Montréal, was founded. It became in time the wealthiest university in Canada, with a large group of alumni, many of whom are American. McGill had predominant Anglican and then Presbyterian links; its soul was wrestled with by both, but it is a secular institution. Engineering, medicine, law and the arts and sciences became McGill's predominant subjects, and its postgraduate programs were among the first in Canada.

Outside the province of Quebec, Roman Catholic universities have developed variously: Ottawa (1849); St. Francis Xavier, Antigonish, Nova Scotia (1866); Assumption College, Windsor, Ontario; Kings College, London, Ontario; Mount St. Vincent, Halifax; and St. Thomas More College, Saskatchewan, are only a few of the numerous institutions that owe connection to the Roman Catholics.

The Church of England took an early lead in establishing colleges on the Oxford or Cambridge model (colleges forming a central university) or on the (later) London University model, with stronger central powers. In order of foundations these were: King's College, Windsor, Nova Scotia (1788); King's College, Fredericton, New Brunswick (1800); and King's College, Toronto (1827). Bishop's College, Lennoxville, Québec, was founded 1843, and Trinity College, Toronto, in 1852, after the secularization of the University of Toronto. Huron College, London, Ontario (1863), and St. John's College, Winnipeg (1871), were other important additions. These colleges became prime movers or foundation stones in the larger universities that grew up around them. Huron College, for instance, became part of the University of Western Ontario.

The Church of Scotland, the Presbyterian Church, likewise took a role. The early histories of Dalhousie University, Halifax; Queen's University, Kingston, Ontario; and Manitoba College, Winnipeg, have Presbyterian origins.

Other denominations made contributions as follows: Methodists established Mount Allison University (1858), Sackville, New Brunswick, and Victoria University (1836), Cobourg, Ontario (later moved to Toronto, where it became a unit of the federal University of Toronto). Wesley (later United) College, Winnipeg, was for a time an affiliate of the University of Manitoba and became a separate University of Winnipeg. The Baptist institution in Wolfville, Nova Scotia, became Acadia University (1841), and McMaster University was founded in Toronto in 1887, moving to Hamilton in 1930. Lutherans established Waterloo Lutheran Seminary in 1911 in Waterloo, Ontario, from whence grew Waterloo College, or after 1973, Wilfrid Laurier University.

Many larger universities of Canada derive from earlier colleges or institutes; others derive from direct government planning to deal with rising student numbers, particularly after 1945 (returning veterans) and subsequent baby booms. In the 20th century, the following are noteworthy: the University of British Columbia (UBC, 1908) and, in the 1960s, the University of Victoria and Simon Fraser University; the University of Alberta and the University of Calgary; the University of Saskatchewan and the University of Regina; and Manitoba and Winnipeg, already mentioned, and Brandon University. In Ontario new universities include Guelph, derived from Ontario Agricultural College and the Home Economics Institute, and the University of Waterloo (a federated university). Lakehead University at Thunder Bay and Laurentian University in Sudbury are northern examples (there are others: Algoma, Hearst, Nipissing).

In Quebec the secularization of the province in the era known as the Quiet Revolution brought the establishment of a new university system with branches in various cities, including Montréal and Québec.

By the end of the 20th century, there were about 66 degree-granting universities in Canada. Many of them are small colleges, often with religious roots and identifications. Many of these colleges are connected to others of other denominations in federal universities. Most scientific and research activities go on at the large universities; Toronto, McGill,

UBC, and Alberta being noteworthy. At one time student tuition was very low, approximating 10 percent of cost, but by the end of this century it had risen to nearly 40 percent. Similarly the progress of universities by the end of the century was depending increasingly on gifts, or donations, from the private sector. Alumni affairs therefore became more important than ever in the running of good institutions. Faculty associations grew into powerful entities in Canada, giving rise to numerous unionized faculties. In comparison to other countries, Canada has the highest percentage of its population who hold university degrees (about 10 percent). This is a remarkable number and speaks to the long history of higher education in the country, the contribution of churches and their denominations, and the funding from the government sector. This history is remarkably different from that of the United States, where private funding has been a fact from the beginning; it is also different from that of the United Kingdom, where privilege and controlled access were aspects of higher education. Thus the university system of Canada reflects the more democratic, state-engineered nature of the Canadian populace. *See* United Church of Canada.

UPPER CANADA. By the Constitutional (or Canada) Act of 1791, the province of Upper Canada came into existence. Different in social composition from Lower Canada (q.v.), Upper Canada contained many Loyalists (q.v.) and American settlers. Struggles over land and patronage led to the rebellions of 1837, a much smaller affair than the one in Lower Canada. Upper Canada became Canada West in the united Province of Canada in 1841. In 1867 Canada West became the province of Ontario (q.v.). *See* Rebellions of 1837.

URSULINES. The Company of Saint Ursula (founded 1536 in Italy and made an order in 1612) became established in Québec in 1639 by Marie Guyart de l'Incarnation, who arrived from Tours with Madame de la Petrie, lay benefactrice, and two other Ursulines. Together they founded the first Ursuline monastery and girls school in North America. They taught European and native women and made profound contributions to education (q.v.) and social development in Canada. The Ursulines maintain a superb museum in Québec City.

UTRECHT, TREATY OF. Signed 11 April 1713 by Britain and France, the Treaty of Utrecht ended the War of the Spanish Succession. The treaty gave Britain the Hudson Bay drainage area, Acadia, and sole claim to Newfoundland. France kept Cape Breton Island (q.v.), as well as parts of New Brunswick and Prince Edward Island.

-V-

VANCOUVER. British Columbia's largest city, it has an excellent deep-sea port and is adjacent to the Fraser River, with access to the Fraser River and the interior and the adjacent Washington State. Coastal Indians are known to have lived there since 500 B.C., and the area was explored by George Vancouver (q.v.) and Spain's Galiano and Valdez in 1792. In the 1860s English settlers preempted land, and various sawmills were in operation in the 1870s. Not until the Canadian Pacific Railway (q.v.) arrived, with an extension westward from Port Moody, its statuary terminus, was Vancouver established (incorporated 6 April 1886). The name was suggested by Sir William Van Horne, CPR manager, in honour of the English mariner. The CPR was the biggest landholder in the city's history and its most prominent developer.

The development of Vancouver was aided by the Klondike gold rush, the establishment of the CPR's trans-Pacific services (first under sail, later all steam, including the Empress vessels), and the CPR's coast steamship services. Vancouver also profited from the trade of the Panama Canal and the opening of mining, forestry, and fishing (also canning). The Vancouver Stock Exchange was founded in 1907, listing mainly mining stocks. In early days Vancouver exported timber, foodstuffs and above all grain, and by the 1920s Vancouver had replaced Winnipeg (q.v.) as the principal western city. Later sulphur, low grade coal, and potash were to become large export commodities. Containerization allowed for the increase in volume of imports, with rail links to Seattle and Portland making Vancouver the port of choice. Vancouver is the largest port for volume of traffic on the west coast of North America.

Vancouver is the air travel nexus of British Columbia. Canadian Airlines (est. 1949) is headquartered there, as is BC Forest Products, Cominco, and Macmillan Bloedel. Until recently industries relating to forestry and wood products flourished in the East Vancouver port and on the lower Fraser River, but these have given way to residential development and relocations.

Vancouver's history is reflected in its neighbourhoods: Strathcona, working class and ethnic; the West End, high rise apartments and middle class; Kerrisdale, suburban middle class and Chinese; Shaughnessy, established money; and Point Grey, university lands (University of British Columbia, est. 1908). Also of note are East Vancouver (east of Cambie Street), North Vancouver and West Vancouver. Outlying municipalities include Burnaby, Surrey and Delta. Urban redevelopment has occurred on False Creek (former industrial lands, and later Expo '86 properties) and in Kitsilano.

Architectural highlights include Vancouver Art Gallery (1983), Simon Fraser University (Burnaby 1963), and the Vancouver Maritime Museum and a Planetarium (1958; as British Columbia Centennial projects). A recreational paradise, noted for its skiing and water sports, Vancouver is home to the British Columbia Lions football club, Vancouver Canucks, and Vancouver Grizzlies. At the Pacific National Exhibition grounds is the Hastings Race Track, principal horse-racing venue of western Canada.

Vancouver is a multiracial city in which race has had significant roles. Its essential roots are English and Scottish, and it became home to many from Ontario. It had strong identification, until 1939, with the British Empire. Anti-Asiatic riots occurred in 1887 and 1907; and in 1914, in conformity with Canadian law, Sikhs aboard the *Komagata Maru* were denied entry on the grounds that they did not have immigration papers. In 1942, in conformity with Federal regulations, all Japanese (8,600 Vancouver residents) were evacuated and resettled and their property confiscated. In the 1980s Asian immigration to Canada, particularly from Hong Kong, escalated, so that 40 percent of students of elementary school age did not speak English as a first tongue.

Vancouver's park system is prominent in the city's development, the highlights of which are Stanley Park (with its celebrated cricket pitch, which Rudyard Kipling said was the most beautiful in the British Empire), Queen Elizabeth Park, and the beach parks at English Bay and Kitsilano. Local politics are dominated by groups such as the Non-Partisan Association and the Electors Action Movement, which vie for control of municipal government and City Hall.

Canada's window on the Pacific world, Vancouver was once called the Constantinople of the Pacific. It is a world-class seaport and a regular port of call for Alaska cruise ships. Vancouver is prone to shifts of world trade, including depression of trade, and is a place of great wealth and poverty—and a place of politically conscious citizens.

VANCOUVER, GEORGE (1757–1798). Naval surveyor and explorer. Vancouver sailed on Capt. James Cook's (q.v.) second voyage to the Pacific. In 1789 Captain Vancouver was ordered to sail in HMS *Discovery* on a voyage to plant a small British settlement on the northwest coast of North America to aid British maritime fur traders (q.v.), then anxious for government support in a new branch of commerce. However, a crisis stemming from the Spanish seizure of several British ships at Nootka Sound forced the British to employ different measures to stop Spanish pretensions in an area they did not occupy solely. The settlement was never effected. When the government decided to send an officer to Nootka Sound to receive back the land and property seized by the Spanish and to make an accurate survey of the northwest coast north of 30 degrees north, Vancouver was detailed for the task. Before arriving at Nootka Sound in 1792, he charted the Strait of Juan de Fuca, Puget Sound, and the Strait of Georgia. He then circumnavigated the large island which bears his name. Vancouver reported the nonexistence of a Northwest Passage south of the Arctic Sea, confirming the discoveries of Sir Alexander Mackenzie (q.v.). He also visited the Hawaiian Islands. In retirement, he prepared his journals for publication but died, at Petersham, Surrey, on 12 May 1798, a few months before his book *A Voyage of Discovery to the North Pacific Ocean and Round the World* appeared in print.

VANCOUVER ISLAND, COLONY OF. Created by Royal Charter dated 13 January 1849, as a consequence of British government decision to offset American political and settlement pressures northward from Oregon Territory, Vancouver Island was not a Crown colony but rather a corporate colony (in keeping with prevailing political theory). The Hudson's Bay Company (q.v.) was awarded the Charter of Grant to administer the colony. The first governor, theoretically independent of the HBC (though in fact at the mercy of the firm), was Richard Blanshard. The second governor (James [later Sir James] Douglas) was entirely a company man. The HBC held Vancouver Island by lease, for seven shillings rent a year, became lords and proprietors, and was obliged to turn 90 percent of all land sales into public benefit, for developing the colony. HBC exclusive right to trade with the Indians was to expire, in any event, on 30 May 1859, at which time the Crown would resume title and compensate HBC for its expenses and investment.

The Queen Charlotte Islands were annexed to Vancouver Island in 1853. The Colony of British Columbia (q.v.) was created in 1858. In 1866 the United Colony of British Columbia was established, with the colonial capital at Victoria.

VANIER, GEORGES-PHILEAS (1888–1967). Sometimes claimed to be the most outstanding Canadian of the modern era, Vanier was educated at Université Laval. He joined the Royal 22E Regiment in 1915 and served in France, where he lost a leg. He won both the Distinguished Service Order and the Military Cross. Vanier was a brilliant soldier and leader. He was also a superb diplomat. He joined the Department of

External Affairs and served in London during World War II (q.v.) as Canadian minister to the French Government. He was appointed governor general of Canada in 1959. He died in office and was memorialized in the regimental crypt of the Québec Citadel.

VIMY MEMORIAL. On the site of "Hill 145" and designed by Canadian architect and sculptor Walter Seymour Allward, the Vimy Memorial marks the location of the Battle of Vimy Ridge (q.v.) and stands as a tribute to those who risked or gave their lives for the sake of Canada's armed effort during World War I (q.v.). The monument took 11 years and $1.5 million to build. It rests on a huge bed of concrete, reinforced with steel. The nearby ground is pockmarked with shell holes from the artillery bombardment before the taking of the ridge. The towering pylons and 20 sculptured figures are made of limestone. The largest figure is that of a saddened woman who represents Canada, a young nation mourning her fallen sons. In addition, twin white pylons, one bearing maple leaves, the other the fleur-de-lis of France, symbolize the sacrifices of both countries. Carved on the walls are the names of 11,285 Canadians who were killed in France and whose final resting place is unknown. More than 7,000 Canadians are buried in 30 war cemeteries within a 16-kilometre radius of the Vimy Memorial. The memorial is also a commemorative park, administered by the government of Canada. The park surrounding the memorial has been planted with Canadian trees and shrubs, and trenches have been restored. It is altogether a remarkable tribute to the Canadian Corps and the difficulties it faced.

VIMY RIDGE. Located in northeastern France on the road from Lens to Arras, 14-kilometre-long Vimy Ridge had been held by the Imperial German army from fall 1914, forming a salient in the Allied lines. The ridge enabled the Germans to keep watch over allied movement for miles around. Between 1914 and 1917, several attempts were made by French and British troops to take the ridge; each time they had failed and casualties were heavy.

In early 1917, the Canadian Corps was sent to Vimy. Under the leadership of corps commander Lt. Gen. Julian Byng (q.v.), an assault of the ridge was prepared. All four Canadian divisions were to be used in the assault.

On 9 April 1917, Easter Monday, the battle opened with a massive creeping barrage. The Canadian strategy was to fight a classic set-piece battle, with heavy reliance on the artillery. The Canadian counterbattery, which utilized sound locators, was effective in silencing the German guns. Under heavy artillery cover, the infantry progressed rapidly to the ridge. The Canadians succeeded in capturing and holding the greater part of the ridge on the first day of the assault. By midafternoon, the Canadians had taken the ridge. They did so at great cost. Three days later the Canadians held the ridge against German counterattack. The Canadian Corps lost 3,598, and 7,004 were wounded. The victory at Vimy was considered Canada's greatest military victory of World War I (q.v.). *See also* Canadian Army; Canadian Expeditionary Force; Vimy Memorial.

VINLAND. The name early Scandinavian explorers gave to a region on the eastern coast of North America. Many historians believe that Norse (q.v.) Vikings visited this coastal area almost 500 years before Christopher Columbus sailed to America in 1492. Some historians believe Vinland was probably in the region of Cape Cod, others believe it was Newfoundland (q.v.). In 1961, an archaeologist found the remains of a Viking settlement at L'Anse aux Meadows, near St. Luaire, Newfoundland.

Early Norse sagas tell of the explorers' voyages. These tales describe a fertile land with mild climate. The Norsemen called the region Vinland (also spelled Vineland or Wineland) because of the grapes that grew there or because it was a fine land of meadows. The sagas tell that Leif Ericsson, son of Eric the Red, wintered in Vinland about A.D.1000. Historians believe the Norsemen had to abandon Vinland because they could not defend their settlements against hostile natives.

-W-

WALSH, JAMES MORROW (1843–1905). James Walsh was born in Prescott, Ontario. He joined the militia (q.v.) and fought in the Fenian Raid (q.v.) of 1866. In 1873, he became an inspector in the newly formed North West Mounted Police. He served with the force until 1883 and was famous for his handling of Sitting Bull, the Lakota Sioux chief, who crossed the border from the United States after defeating Gen. George Custer at the Battle of the Little Big Horn. In 1883, Walsh resigned and established the Dominion Coke, Coal, and Transportation Company. Fourteen years later, the discovery of gold in the Yukon brought him back to the North West Mounted Police. He became the first commissioner of the Yukon District in 1897. He retired the following year and died at Brockville, Ontario.

WAR MEASURES ACT (1914). Gave the Privy Council in Ottawa extraordinary powers under Section 91 of the British North America Act (*see* Constitution Act of 1867) including full economic controls for nationalization of the economy, war production, and transportation. It also gave the government executive powers to deal with potential enemies of the state. Invoked in 1945 it was also employed in 1970 during the October Crisis (q.v.). The legislation was subsequently modified.

WAR OF 1812. A conflict between the United States and Britain, involving Nova Scotia, Lower Canada and Upper Canada, and many tribes of Indians. War was declared by the United States for two reasons: maritime rights and control of the Old Northwest. American politicians found irritating the commercial ambitions of the empire of the St. Lawrence (q.v.) south of the boundary. Loyalist (q.v.) claims for compensation were not being paid by the United States, and consequently Britain kept control of the southwestern posts until Jay's Treaty of 1794. This agreement ceded the posts to the Americans but permitted Canadian commerce south of the line. The Indians in such areas as the Wabash Valley, who had nothing to say in these matters, tried to keep up the Canadian trade and to resist the encroachment of American settlers. The Battle of Tippecanoe (1811) in which Tecumseh (q.v.), his brother "The Prophet," and others fought for the Shawnee cause marked the decline of the Canadian–Indian trading alliance and the rise of American military influence in the Indiana Territory. American politicians then looked for a permanent solution to the interrelated questions of Canadian trade with such tribes as the Shawnee and of land control in the Midwest. The Americans also objected to British treatment of American ships, commerce, and seamen and British political activities in Florida and Texas. The result was that expansionists, both in and out of Congress, sought a military campaign that would strengthen their position in relation to Great Britain. Why not invade Canada, they argued, expel the British from the continent, and make the United States safe, peaceful, and secure?

In deciding to send an army to invade Canada in 1812 the American Congress underestimated both British power in North America and British determination not to abandon their North American colonies to the Americans. Congress believed that the Ontario Peninsula, so heavily populated with American settlers, would be an easy conquest, or, as Thomas Jefferson put it, "a mere matter of marching."

To Canadians and Americans alike, the War of 1812 was a renewal of an old encounter, and most theatres of war were familiar ones: the Atlantic Seaboard, the Great Lakes, and Louisiana. In the Atlantic, despite the early frigate victories that left the American public reeling with success, the British navy acquired command of the sea and by 1813 had enforced a blockade of the coast from Boston to New Orleans. Now the British could press their advantage and in 1813 they gave convoy support to a North West Company (q.v.) expedition to secure the Far Western fur trade (q.v.) at the mouth of the Columbia River, where Americans had been since 1811. The coastal blockade meant that the Americans would have to attack the British at inland points, and they determined to undertake a three-pronged, simultaneous attack on Canada. By the Champlain–Richelieu access, by the Niagara Peninsula, and by Detroit, the American army was to attack and then march on Montréal and Québec. But the British and Canadians enjoyed a high degree of success on the battlefield. Control of the lakes was sometimes in doubt (the Battle of Lake Erie, 1813, gave the U.S. ascendancy on that lake) but never the total control of the Ontario Peninsula. Imperial forces conquered Michilimackinac in 1812 and kept it for the duration. The brilliant feats of Gen. Sir Isaac Brock (q.v.) at Queenston Heights (q.v.) had other parallels along the Canadian border. At the same time the ill-trained, badly led American forces suffered some embarrassing defeats. Only at New Orleans, where 10,000 British veterans of European campaigns led by Sir Edward Pakenham were repulsed by Andrew Jackson and his frontiersmen in January 1815, did Americans enjoy a splendid victory. Even so, in the irony of circumstances, the battle occurred 15 days after the Peace of Ghent had been signed in Belgium.

The war begun for control of North America ended in the maintenance of the *status quo ante bellum*. The Peace failed to resolve the maritime rights question. But it did allow that a joint commission would resolve several issues, including the boundary from the Saint Croix River to the Lake of the Woods, the question of British navigation of the Mississippi, and American rights to fish. Subsequently, the Convention of 1818 provided for a boundary along the 49th parallel from the Lake of the Woods to the Rocky Mountains. The New Brunswick–Maine boundary controversy was not considered, but that of Oregon was discussed and there joint control agreed on. On the fisheries question, the Americans were barred from the inshore fisheries of the British colonies.

Canadians did not view the War of 1812 as an exercise in frustration or an unsuccessful military venture. They regarded it as a great victory for themselves and for the British Empire. More important, the war coloured their basic outlook toward the American republic. It shaped their national identity. Loyalists became Canadians. Heavy fighting occurred on the Niagara Peninsula, Lake Champlain, and Upper Canada. *See also* Lundy's Lane, Battle of; Secord, Laura; Rush–Bagot Convention.

WASHINGTON, TREATY OF. At the negotiations for the Anglo-American Treaty of Washington (1871), Canada was represented by its premier, Sir John A. Macdonald (q.v.), as a member of the British negotiators. Under the treaty, arbitration was set for the Alabama Claims and for the San Juan Islands boundary. Numerous fishing and navigation provisions were part of the treaty significant to Canadian–American joint use of water and fish resources. *See also* San Juan Boundary Dispute.

WILLIAMS, EUNICE (1696–1785). Eunice Williams was born in Deerfield, Massachusetts, to a Puritan family. Her father was John Williams, a Puritan minister. Living in a hostile environment that was harsh and cruel, Puritans in New England were in constant threat of attack from enemy First Nations. The village where the Williamses lived was attacked in winter of 1704 by a group of Mohawk and French forces. Eunice was kidnapped and taken back to Mohawk territory.

By 1713, she was married to a Mohawk named Arosen. She adopted the language and way of life and refused to return to Deerfield to see her father. Although Eunice and her Mohawk family paid visits to her Puritan family, she always refused to stay. She lived until the age of 89 in Kahnawake. Eunice Williams was Puritan by birth but Mohawk by choice.

WINNIPEG. Indigenous people first gathered at the future site of Winnipeg about 4000 B.C. In 1738, Fort Rouge, the first trading post, built by the French, was erected at the Forks of the Red River (running northward toward Hudson Bay) and the Assiniboine (q.v.) (the traders' route to the Western Plains). The North West Company (q.v.) built Fort Gibraltar on the same site in 1810. In 1812, agents of the Earl of Selkirk (q.v.) established an agricultural colony at Red River. "Nor' Westers," dependent on pemmican (q.v.) for foodstuffs in their trade, opposed the introduction of settlers (who were Scots and were called derisively "oatmeal eaters" by their opponents). Tension led to violence. In 1816, following the Battle of Seven Oaks, Jean-Baptiste Lagimodière journeyed from Red River to Montréal to advise Selkirk. With 100 Swiss and German mercenaries, the de Meurons, Selkirk went west. He seized the NWC depot at Fort William and wintered there. The de Meurons pushed on to Red River and recaptured the settlement. Selkirk marched into Red River in June 1817. He awarded Lagimodière land at the junction of the Red and Seine Rivers, now St. Boniface. Lagimodière became a prominent trader and farmer.

The early population of Winnipeg, and of the Red River forks, was multicultural: English, Scots, native peoples, and mixed-bloods or Métis (q.v.). Local political organizations, political assemblies, and colleges (St. John's College, established 1849) promoted local strengths and cultures. The fur trade and agriculture (qq.v.) moved side by side, but gradually, through decline of fur-bearing mammals and the collapse of the beaver-felt hat market, demand for furs diminished. The buffalo, too, faced extinction. In 1869 the Hudson's Bay Company (q.v.) sold Rupert's Land to Canada, by way of the transferring auspices of the British government. This sparked a strong resistance from the Métis and brought to the fore the young, educated, and eloquent Louis Riel (q.v.), grandson of Lagimodière.

The provisional government established by the Métis under Riel's command resulted in the introduction of martial law (unauthorized by Canadian law), the killing of the Orangeman and Protestant Thomas Scott (q.v.), and the necessary and authorized reprisal by the Dominion of Canada (q.v.). Meanwhile, Riel was forced to bring forward political demands (most of which were met) and he is thus referred to as "the Father of Manitoba." He was elected an MP on several occasions but was denied the right of taking his seat in the House of Commons in Ottawa. He travelled widely in the United States, especially in Minnesota and Montana (where at Sun River he taught in a Jesuit [q.v.] school). In 1884 Riel answered an urgent Métis appeal to lead the Indian-Métis rebellion in the upper Saskatchewan River Valley. He was captured, found guilty, and hanged in Regina (16 November 1885). His body was taken to Winnipeg and buried in St. Boniface, now one of the most famous graves in Canada.

Agricultural growth, steamship navigation, and economic diversity characterized the early history of Winnipeg. In 1878 the railway arrived, initiating a phenomenal era of expansion, speculation, and prosperity. Particularly important was the grain trade and Grain Exchange. The immigration boom saw many arrive from Eastern Canada, the British Isles, Iceland, and eastern Europe. Businessmen used American cities as their model of success, especially Chicago. Indeed, Winnipeg has been called the "Chicago of the North," as well as "Gem of the Prairies" and "Bull's Eye of the Dominion."

Winnipeg's population by the 1871 federal census was 241; by the 1911 federal census, 136,000; and in 1996 for Greater Winnipeg, 650,000.

Winnipeg was the location of the famous Winnipeg General Strike (q.v.) of 1919. Winnipeg was also a focal point of Methodist, Baptist,

Congregational, Presbyterian, and other Christian denominations, besides being a locus for Jews and Greek Orthodox–adhering Ukrainians and Russian Mennonites. Winnipeg was a melting pot but, north of the railroad tracks, it also had ethnic and religious diversity. Timothy Eaton's (q.v.) department store was built in 1905 on Portage Avenue, and "Portage and Main" became the most famous crossroads in the Canadian urban landscape. Because Winnipeg was the capital of the province of Manitoba, all major government buildings were built there for conducting provincial and federal business. The commercial headquarters and especially distribution centre for western Canada, Winnipeg's leaders and newspapers adopted transcontinental Canadian perspectives as well as continental perspectives. The first club of Rotary International was founded in Winnipeg. Other notable establishments were the University of Manitoba (esablished 1877) and Wesley College (later University of Winnipeg). In 1970 the Hudson's Bay Company archives were transferred from London to the Manitoba Provincial Archives in Winnipeg. Historical sites, or institutions dedicated to history, include: the Children's Museum, Museum of Man and Nature, St. Boniface Museum, Western Canada Aviation Museum, Forbes National Historic Site, and, north of town, Lower Fort Garry.

In the 1980s and 1990s Winnipeg became an important scientific and communications centre, including computers, and continued its diversifications in manufacturing. It remains a prominent centre for aviation and is headquarters of Canadian Air Command.

WINNIPEG GENERAL STRIKE. Perhaps the largest, most significant labour and public strike in national history, the Winnipeg General Strike of 1919 commenced as a relatively small demand by building and metal trades for collective bargaining procedures and increased wages. The Winnipeg Trade and Labour Council joined the strike in sympathetic solidarity. Federal intervention on behalf of business and industry (in the assumed interests of law and order) led to a rally and march, which was broken up by the official use of violence. One spectator was killed and 30 injured. Strike leaders and backers were arrested and jailed for sedition. In the 1920 Manitoba election, four of the jailed strike leaders were elected as socialists. In 1921, J. S. Woodsworth (q.v.) was elected first socialist of the House of Commons, representing Winnipeg.

WOMEN. The role of women in Canada, past and present, is central to the fortunes of this country. Native women had roles dictated by domestic needs: gathering of foods, cooking, childcare, and so forth. Many became partners for fur traders (q.v.) and soldiers (*see* Métis). Several female religious orders came to Canada, most notably the Ursulines (q.v.). Jeanne Mance was co-founder of Montréal. Many heroines lived in Canada's early history (*see* Marie Jacqueline de la Tour, Laura Secord, Thanadelthur), but many such are lost to the annals of history.

To increase European marriages in Canada, the King's Daughters were introduced under auspices of Church and State during the era of New France (q.v.). Meanwhile, miscegenation resulted in the evolution of the Métis.

Females have become prominent politicians (*see* Kim Campbell), have fought for political rights and recognition (*see* "Persons Case") and for temperance (q.v.), and have become prominent writers (*see* the early examples Emily Shaw Beavan, Lucy Maud Montgomery). They have served in the Canadian Army, Air Force, and Navy and in the Coast Guard (qq.v.). Their roles in nursing and medicine, law, education, home economics (domestic science), science, and numerous other fields have shaped the character of Canada in innumerable ways (*see*, for example, Adelaide Hunter Hoodless, Emily Ferguson Murphy, Nellie Mooney McClung, Agnes MacPhail. *See also* United Church of Canada).

WOLFE, JAMES (1727–1759). British commander at the Battle of the Plains of Abraham in the Seven Years' War (q.v.) and excellent practitioner of combined operations. Placed in command of the charge by William Pitt after his creditable performance during the capture of Louisbourg (q.v.) in 1758. Maj. Gen. Wolfe's troops defeated the French, capturing Québec for the English (13 September 1759), but he died in the battle.

WOODSWORTH, JAMES SHAVER (1874–1942). Ontario-born, MP for Winnipeg (q.v.), Christian Socialist, ordained Methodist and circuit rider, and proponent of the Social Gospel (q.v.). Woodsworoth, a radical in his times, was concerned with many causes, including urban missions, and worried about Mormon and non-Christian immigration into Canada. He also worked for longshoreman's rights in British Columbia. He was a progressive reformer who left a profound legacy in the style as well as content of social welfare legislation. First leader of the Co-operative Commonwealth Federation, he remained an MP from 1921 to 1942 (Winnipeg North Centre riding). He was the father of Grace MacInnis, a well-known progressive politician. He died in Vancouver.

WORLD WAR I. When Great Britain declared war on Germany and Austria-Hungary on 6 August 1914, the entire Empire, including Canada, was automatically at war. Immediately, the minister of the militia, Col. Sir Samuel Hughes (q.v.), called for volunteers to fight in the European war. The first contingent sailed to England in October 1914. By the end of 1914, the Canadian Expeditionary Force (CEF, q.v.) numbered 50,000 officers and men and by the summer of 1915, 150,000. By the end of 1916, the CEF was to full strength of four divisions. In the middle of 1916, Prime Minister Sir Robert Borden (q.v.) pledged to the Allied cause over 500,000 men for overseas service. However, only 330,000 were recruited voluntarily. The conscription issue thus came up.

The demands for labour made it profitable for many to stay home. The old English–French conflict came to a head and threatened to pull the country apart. Many in English Canada thought that Québec was not doing its share by sending its sons overseas. However, in Québec there was a feeling that the war was a British war and that they should not be forced to fight and die on the European continent.

At first, the untried Canadian forces suffered severe losses. At the Second Battle of Ypres in April 1915, the 1st Canadian Division suffered over 6,000 dead in facing German gas attacks, but it held its ground. The Canadian Corps took part in other battles at Arras and Passchendaele.

In April 1917, the Canadian Corps took Vimy Ridge (q.v.) from its German defenders during the Nivelle offensive. Two other attempts to take the ridge by British and French forces had resulted in severe losses and failure. Vimy proved an important point of attention for Canadian pride and prestige, since the CEF took the hill alone. The ridge was taken in five days and at great cost. After Vimy, the Canadian Corps was placed under the command of a Canadian, Gen. Sir Arthur Currie (q.v.). The Canadian Corps also took part in the final offensive of the war at Amiens, which cracked German resistance on the Western front and forced the November 1918 armistice.

WORLD WAR II. Having won the right to declare war independently in the 1931 Statute of Westminster (q.v.), Canada did not declare war on Nazi Germany until 10 September 1939, a full week after Great Britain. Canada mobilized rapidly after the fall of France in June 1940, however, and sent a number of infantry divisions to the British Isles. Massive shipbuilding programs were implemented and national resources were channelled to the war effort.

At the end of 1941, two battalions of Canadian infantry were dispatched to reinforce the garrison of Hong Kong in order to deter Japanese (q.v.) aggression. However, when the Japanese struck in December

1941, British defences were paralyzed and reinforcements and supplies could not be sent to the Crown colony. After a bloody struggle, the garrison surrendered and was placed in Japanese prison camps. Many Canadians died in the Japanese camps, which did not follow accepted international practices in regard to the treatment of prisoners.

In August 1942, the 2nd Canadian Infantry Division, together with British Royal Marine Commandos and American Rangers, raided the French port of Dieppe (*see* Dieppe Raid). Planning and preparation problems and lack of air and naval support thrust the Canadians into the teeth of German defences. Only a very few of those who went returned to England; the rest were either killed on the lines or were captured and spent the rest of the war in a prison camp. The raid, though only a small part of the war, had a large impact on Canada. Over 900 Canadian soldiers were killed and 1,874 taken prisoner out of 5,000 landed.

The Canadian government sent the 1st Canadian Infantry Division to the Mediterranean theatre for the invasion of Sicily and Italy. Eventually, the 5th Armoured Division was also sent with a corps headquarters. The Canadians faced extremely hard conditions and took heavy losses. They faced hard fighting at Ortona and aided in the smashing of the German defences in northern Italy. Over 92,000 Canadians served in the Italian campaign, and nearly 6,000 were killed.

In the Normandy campaign (q.v.) the remaining elements of the First Canadian Army were dispatched to the French coast and landed on "Juno" Beach on 6 June 1944. Canadian formations took part in many of the battles on the Normandy beachhead and helped the Allied armies break out in August. Canadian forces fought along the Channel coast and liberated much of Belgium and the Netherlands and had crossed into German territory by the time of the armistice in May 1945. Over 230,000 Canadians served in Northwest Europe at the cost of over 11,000 killed.

Canadians also took part in the strategic air offensive over Germany. By the end of the war, 48 Canadian Air Force squadrons were deployed overseas and one entire Bomber Command group (No. 6) was made up of RCAF squadrons. Also, many Canadians flew in Royal Air Force squadrons. Furthermore, the RCAF managed the British Commonwealth Air Training Plan (q.v.), which turned out thousands of aircrew for war service. Over 17,000 Canadians were killed in the skies over Europe out of a total force of nearly 250,000 men and women. Also, RCAF aircraft took part in the Battle of the Atlantic (q.v.) and were responsible for the destruction of 23 U-boats. The RCN was active in Murmansk convoys,

English Channel work and convoy protection, among other duties (*see* HMCS *Haida*).

Economically, Canada grew by leaps and bounds. In order to fulfill war orders, many new factories were built. Thousands of aircraft, armoured vehicles, trucks, and ships were constructed in Canadian factories to aid the Allied war effort. "War-time housing" and the Veterans Administration (and hospitals) were significant consequences in Canada.

-Y-

YUKON RIVER. The Yukon River basin is believed to be the migration route of America's original settlers. The name Yukon is derived from the Loucheux natives word *Yu-kun-ah*, meaning "great river." Russian fur traders (q.v.) knew of the river basin by 1831. The upper parts of the river were explored by Hudson's Bay Company (q.v.) trader Robert Campbell. Campbell established Fort Selkirk on the Yukon in 1848. At the height of the Klondike Gold Rush in the late 1890s and early 1900s, the Yukon was used as a transportation route for gold seekers.

YUKON TERRITORY. The Yukon Territory is located in the northwest corner of Canada. It is bounded by Alaska on the west, the Northwest Territories on the east, British Columbia on the south, and the Arctic Ocean on the north. The terrain of the Yukon Territory is rugged and covered with mountains, high plateaus, and fast-flowing rivers. The Kutchin natives inhabited the land of the Yukon prior to European contact. In 1847, Alexander Murray Hunter of the Hudson's Bay Company (q.v.) established a fur trading (q.v.) post, Fort Yukon, on the Yukon River (q.v.). The Yukon Territory is most noted for the Klondike Gold Rush that occurred in early August 1896 when gold was discovered on Bonanza Creek. The influx of gold prospectors led to the establishment of the Yukon Territory in 1898. In 1942, the Americans built the Alaska Highway (q.v.) through the Yukon.

The Yukon economy is based on natural resources. Minerals, such as gold, silver, lead, and zinc, and furs are the main resources. The fluctuations of this type of economy has led to periods of economic hardship, but tourism in the area is rapidly growing.

The territory is governed by an elected 16-member legislative assembly and a federally appointed commissioner. The assembly has the power to deal with all local matters, but the signature of the commissioner is required on all legislation. Federally, the Yukon is represented by one member in the House of Commons and one senator. The population of the Yukon is 29,400 as of 1999. *See also* Carmack, George Washington; Dawson.

Appendix A
Governors General of Canada

The Viscount Monck	1 July 1867
Lord Lisgar	2 February 1869
The Earl of Dufferin	25 June 1872
The Marquess of Lorne	25 November 1878
The Marquess of Lansdowne	23 October 1883
Lord Stanley of Preston	11 June 1888
The Earl of Aberdeen	18 September 1893
The Earl of Minto	12 November 1898
The Earl of Grey	10 December 1904
Field Marshal H.R.H. The Duke of Connaught	13 October 1911
The Duke of Devonshire	11 November 1916
Gen. The Lord Byng of Vimy	11 August 1921
Viscount Willingdon of Ratton	2 October 1926
The Earl of Bessborough	4 April 1931
Lord Tweedsmuir of Elsfield	2 November 1935
Maj. Gen. The Earl of Athlone	21 June 1940
Field Marshal Rt. Hon. Viscount Alexander of Tunis	2 April 1946
The Rt. Hon. Vincent Massey	28 February 1952
Maj. Gen. Rt. Hon. Georges-Philias Vanier	15 September 1959
The Rt. Hon. Daniel Roland Michener	17 April 1967
The Rt. Hon. Jules Leger	14 January 1974
The Rt. Hon. Edward Richard Schreyer	22 January 1979
The Rt. Hon. Jeanne Sauvé	14 May 1984
The Rt. Hon. Ramon John Hnatyshyn	29 January 1990
The Rt. Hon. Romeno Leblanc	22 November 1994

Appendix B
Prime Ministers of Canada

Sir John A. Macdonald	1 July 1867–5 November 1873
Alexander Mackenzie	7 November 1873–8 October 1878
Sir John A. Macdonald	17 October 1878–6 June 1891
Sir John Abbott	16 June 1891–24 November 1892
Sir John Thompson	5 December 1892–12 December 1894
Sir Mackenzie Bowell	21 December 1894–27 April 1896
Sir Charles Tupper	1 May 1896–8 July 1896
Sir Wilfrid Laurier	11 July 1896–6 October 1911
Sir Robert Borden	10 October 1911–10 July 1920
Arthur Meighen	10 July 1920–29 December 1921
William Lyon Mackenzie King	29 December 1921–28 June 1926
Arthur Meighen	29 June 1926–25 September 1926
William Lyon Mackenzie King	25 September 1926–7 August 1930
Richard Bennett	7 August 1930–23 October 1935
William Lyon Mackenzie King	23 October 1935–15 November 1948
Louis St. Laurent	15 November 1948–21 June 1957
John Diefenbaker	21 June 1957–22 April 1963
Lester B. Pearson	22 April 1963–20 April 1968
Pierre Elliott Trudeau	20 April 1968–4 June 1979
Joe Clark	4 June 1979–3 March 1980
Pierre Elliott Trudeau	3 March 1980–30 June 1984
John Turner	30 June 1984–17 September 1984
Brian Mulroney	17 September 1984–25 June 1993
Kim Campbell	25 June 1993–4 November 1993
Jean Chrétien	4 November 1993–

Appendix C
Colonial Governors

FRENCH REGIME

Samuel de Champlain	1612–1629, 1633–1635
Charles de Montmagny	1636–1648
Louis d'Ailleboust de Coulonge	1648–1651
Jean de Lauzon	1651–1656
Le vicomte d'Argenson	1658–1661
Le baron d'Avaugour	1661–1663
Sieur de Mésy	1663–1665
Sieur de Courcelle	1665–1672
Le comte de Frontenac	1672–1682
Joseph-Antoine de LaBarre	1682–1685
Le marquis de Denonville	1685–1689
Le comte de Frontenac	1689–1698
Hector de Callière	1699–1705
Le marquis de Vaudreuil	1705–1725
Le marquis de Beauharnois	1726–1747
Le comte de La Galissonière	1747–1749
Le marquis de La Jonquière	1749–1752
Le marquis Duquesne de Menneville	1752–1755
Le marquis de Vaudreuil-Cavagnal	1755–1760

BRITISH REGIME

Jeffrey Amherst	1760–1763
James Murray	1764–1768
Sir Guy Carleton (Lord Dorchester)	1768–1778
Sir Frederick Haldimand	1778–1786
Lord Dorchester	1786–1796
Robert Prescott	1797–1807

Sir James Craig	1807–1811
Sir George Prevost	1812–1815
Sir John Sherbrooke	1816–1818
The Duke of Richmond	1818–1819
The Earl of Dalhousie	1820–1828
Lord Aylmer	1831–1835
Earl Amherst	1835
The Earl of Gosford	1835–1837
The Earl of Durham	1838
Sir John Colborne	1839
Lord Sydenham	1839–1841
Sir Charles Bagot	1841–1843
Lord Metcalfe	1843–1845
The Earl Cathcart	1846–1847
The Earl of Elgin	1847–1854
Sir Edmund Head	1854–1861
The Viscount Monck	1861–1867

Bibliography

A vast bibliography exists on Canadian history. It derives mainly from works published in Canada—principally in the English language but also in French. In addition, numerous works on Canada's history have been published in the United States, the United Kingdom, France, and elsewhere. Increasingly, moreover, as Canadian Studies grows as an international field for study, books and journals concerning themselves with Canadian historical subjects are making their appearance worldwide. A notable example of this is Spain, whose historical connections with British Columbia (Nootka Sound crisis and exploration), Newfoundland (fisheries), and the upper Mississippi Valley are now extended to the world of letters. It may be noted in passing that Canadians themselves have been slow to realize that they are an attractive subject for international study.

The writing of Canadian history is indeed centuries old. The literature of Canadian history dates to the early historians of New France. For the sake of this reference book, however, the sources listed below are chiefly those of the twentieth century and in particular those since 1945. This bibliography is confined to books only and does not include articles, chapters in books, or government reports.

A complete guide to Canadian historical literature would constitute many volumes. What follows, therefore, must be a selection, mainly in English, of some of the best works. These items are intended to lead the student and researcher to other sources. Not included here, principally for want of space, are individual bibliographies on music history; the visual, plastic, and performing arts; culture; gardening and landscaping; urban/rural studies; municipalities; governments; crime and punishment; and medicine. Where possible and convenient, key reference books in these areas are included at the most appropriate spot.

Readers will note that names of publishers have been included for the most recent edition. In every case these are the Canadian imprint.

Some of the sources given below are monographs on set subjects. These indicate the sort of scholarship being undertaken in such fields. They are representative, too, of subareas of interest. They do not necessarily constitute either the only work on the subject or the most recent, although here a necessary preference has been given for the most recent. Multiauthored volumes are listed by title.

The bibliography is organized as follows: from reference works to national history, to regional, provincial, and territorial histories, and then to other subdivisions (topical, regional, and thematic aspects of Canadian history). From category to category, duplication and overlap are unavoidable. Textbooks of a composite nature are not included except in certain circumstances where chapters (or reprinted articles) are otherwise not normally available. Canada's native policies are to be found under Aboriginal History, which includes Indians, Métis, and Inuit (recognized as such in the Canadian Charter of Rights and Freedoms). Canada's external or foreign relations and policy are to be found under External and Foreign Affairs, and on this aspect of Canadian history, the reader is also advised to consult the sections entitled Constitutional Affairs, Military and Naval History, and Prime Ministers. Political history is related to most works in this bibliography; special attention may be given to the entries under Constitutional Affairs and Prime Ministers. Each province and territory has its own concise bibliography, and thus for a regional biography of Western Canada, inquiries should be made under headings for Alberta, Saskatchewan, Manitoba, and possibly British Columbia. Similarly, for Atlantic Canada, inquiries should be made under Nova Scotia, New Brunswick, Prince Edward Island, and Newfoundland and Labrador. Works on individual territories, the Arctic, or the North will be found collectively under Yukon, the Northwest Territories and Nunavut.

Finally, please note that reference works are listed by title, not by author.

OUTLINE OF THIS BIBLIOGRAPHY

I. REFERENCE WORKS

1. Bibliographies and Guides
2. Encyclopaedias and Dictionaries
3. Chronologies
4. Yearbooks
5. Biographical Guides and Biographical Dictionaries
6. Periodicals
7. Historical Atlases

II. CANADA: NATIONAL HISTORY

1. General Works
   a) Texts and Survey Histories
   b) Collected Essays and Approaches
   c) Historiography/Historical Literature
   d) Intellectual History, Political Thought
   e) Pre-Confederation Canada
   f) Post-Confederation Canada
2. Constitutional Affairs
3. External and Foreign Affairs
4. Military and Naval History
5. Prime Ministers
6. Economic and Business History
7. Industry and Development

III. PROVINCIAL AND TERRITORIAL HISTORY

1. Alberta
2. British Columbia
3. Manitoba
4. New Brunswick
5. Newfoundland and Labrador
6. Nova Scotia
7. Ontario
8. Prince Edward Island
9. Québec
10. Saskatchewan
11. Yukon, Northwest Territories, and Nunavut

IV. TOPICAL, REGIONAL, AND THEMATIC ASPECTS

1. Physical Features and Historical Geography
2. Education
3. Aboriginal History (Indian, Métis, and Inuit)
4. Women's History
5. Immigration and Ethnic Groups
6. Labour
7. Literature
8. Science and Technology

I. REFERENCE WORKS

1. Bibliographies And Guides

Bibliographia Canadiana. Claude Thibault. Don Mills, ONT: Longman Canada, 1973.

Canadian History: A Reader's Guide: Beginnings to Confederation. M. Brook Taylor, ed. Toronto: University of Toronto Press, 1994.

Canadian History: A Reader's Guide: Confederation to the Present. Douglas Owram, ed. Toronto: University of Toronto Press, 1994.

Canadian Parliamentary Guide/Guide Parlementaire Canadien. 1873 to date, annual.

Dictionary of Canadian Biography/Dictionaire biographique du Canada. Toronto: University of Toronto Press, and Québec: Laval University Press, 1965 to date.

Guide d'histoire du Canada. André Beaulieu, Jean Hamelin, and Benoit Bernier. New ed. Québec: Presses de l'Université Laval, 1969.

Historical Statistics of Canada. M. C. Urquart, ed. Toronto: Cambridge University Press, 1965.

Introducing Canada: An Annotated Bibliography of Canadian History in English. Brian Gobbott and Robert Irwin. Lanham, MD: Scarecrow Press, 1998.

The Oxford Companion to Canadian History and Literature. Norah Story. Toronto: Oxford University Press, 1967. *Supplement to Oxford Companion to Canadian History and Literature.* William Toye, ed. Toronto: Oxford University Press, 1973.

The Oxford Companion to Canadian Literature. William Toye, ed. Toronto: Oxford University Press, 1983.

A Reader's Guide to Canadian History. D. A. Muise, J. L. Granatstein, and Paul Stevens, eds. 2 vols. Toronto: University of Toronto Press, 1982.

Winners and Losers: The Book of Canadian Political Lists. Derek Black. Toronto: Methuen, 1984.

2. Encyclopaedias And Dictionaries

Canadian Dictionary of Business and Economics. David Crane. Don Mills, ONT: Stoddart, 1993.

The Canadian Encyclopaedia. 2nd ed. 4 vols. Edmonton: Hurtig, 1988.

The Collins Dictionary of Canadian History, 1867 to the Present. Jack Granatstein, and David J. Bercuson. Toronto: Collins, 1988.

Colombo's Canadian References. John R. Colombo. Toronto: Oxford University Press, 1976.

A Dictionary of Canadianisms on Historical Principles. Walter S. Avis. Toronto: Gage, 1967.

Dictionary of Canadian Place Names. Alan Rayburn. Toronto: Oxford University Press, 1997.

Dictionary of Canadian Military History. David J. Bercuson and J. L. Granatstein. Toronto: Oxford University Press, 1992.

Encyclopaedia Canadiana. 10 vols. Toronto: Grolier of Canada, 1975.

Language of Canadian Politics: A Guide to Important Terms and Concepts. John McMenemy. Rev. ed. Waterloo, ONT: Wilfrid Laurier University Press, 1995.

3. Chronologies

Canada, 1875–1973: A Chronology and Fact Book. Brian Hill. Dobbs Ferry, NY: Oceana Publications, 1973.

Canadian Chronology. Glen W. Taplin. Metuchen, NJ: Scarecrow Press, 1970.

Canadian Historical Dates and Events. Francis J. Audet. Ottawa: George Beauregard, 1917.

Dateline: Canada. Bob Bowman. Toronto: Holt, Rinehart and Winston of Canada, 1967.

The Fitzhenry and Whiteside Book of Canadian Facts and Dates. Jay Myers. Markham, ONT: Fitzhenry and Whiteside, 1986.

Handbook of Upper Canadian Chronology. Frederick Henry Armstrong. Rev. ed. Toronto: Dundurn, 1985.

4. Yearbooks

Canada Year Book. Statistics Canada. Ottawa: Government Printer, 1906 to date.

Canadian Almanac and Directory. Toronto: Copp Clark, published since 1848 under various titles.

Canadian Annual Review of Politics and Public Affairs. John Saywell, ed. Toronto: University of Toronto Press, 1960 to date.

The Canadian Annual Review of Public Affairs. J. Castell Hopkins et al., eds. Toronto: Annual Review Publishing Company, 1901–38.

The Dominion Annual Register and Review. Henry J. Morgan, ed. Toronto: Hunter Rose, 1878–86.

5. Biographical Guides And Biographical Dictionaries

The Canadian Who's Who. Toronto: University of Toronto Press, published annually.

Dictionary of Canadian Biography. Toronto: University of Toronto Press, 1965–.

The Macmillian Dictionary of Canadian Biography. William Stewart Wallace, comp. 4th ed. rev. Toronto: Macmillan of Canada, 1978.

Prudential's Book of Canadian Winners and Heroes. Brenna Brown et al. Toronto: Prentice-Hall Canada, 1983.

6. Periodicals

BC Studies. Vancouver: University of British Columbia.
The Beaver. Winnipeg: National History Society.
Bulletin. Ottawa: Canadian Historical Association.
Canada. Washington, DC: Stryker-Post Pub.
Canada. Toronto: Holt, Rinehart and Winston of Canada.
Canadian Defence Quarterly. Toronto and Ottawa.
Canadian Geographic. Ottawa: Royal Canadian Geographical Society.
The Canadian Historical Review. Toronto: University of Toronto Press.
Canadian Horticultural History. Hamilton, ONT: Centre for Canadian Historical Horticultural Studies.
Canadian Journal of History. Toronto.
Canadian Journal of History and Social Science. Toronto.
Canadian Military History. Waterloo, ONT: Laurier Centre for Military Strategic and Disarmament Studies, Wilfrid Laurier University.
Canadian News Facts: The Indexed Digest of Canadian Current Events. Toronto: Canadian News Facts.
Canadian Oral History Association. Ottawa: Canadian Oral History Association.
Histoire Sociale/Social History. Ottawa: University of Ottawa Press.
Journal of Canadian Studies. Peterborough, ONT: Trent University.
Journal of the Canadian Historical Association/Revue de la Société Historique du Canada (previously *Annual Reports and Historical Papers*). Ottawa: Canadian Historical Association.
National History. Mississauga, ONT: Organisation for the Study of the National History of Canada.
Nature Canada. Ottawa: Canadian Nature Federation.
Ontario History. Toronto: Ontario Historical Society.
Revue d'Histoire de l'Amerique Française. Montréal: Institut d'histoire de l'Amerique française.
Urban History Review/Revue d'Histoire Urbaine. Ottawa: History Division, National Museum of Man.

7. Historical Atlases

Atlas de la nouvelle-France/An Atlas of New France. Marcel Trudel, ed. Québec: Les Presses de l'Université Laval, 1973.
A Historical Atlas of Canada. Donald G. G. Kerr, ed. Toronto: Nelson, 1960.
Historical Atlas of Canada. William Dean et al., eds. 3 vols. Toronto: University of Toronto Press, 1987–93.
Philip's Historical Atlas of Canada. John W. Chalmers et al., eds. London: G. Philip, 1966.

II. CANADA: NATIONAL HISTORY

1. General Works

A. Texts And Survey Histories

Berton, Pierre. *My Country: The Remarkable Past.* Toronto: McClelland and Stewart, 1976.

Brown, Robert Craig. *The Illustrated History of Canada.* Toronto: Lester Publishing, 1991.

Bumstead, J. M. *The Peoples of Canada.* 2 vols. Toronto: Oxford University Press, 1992.

Careless, James M. S. *Canada: A Story of Challenge.* Toronto: Macmillan of Canada, 1977.

Cook, Ramsay, John C. Ricker, and John T. Saywell. *Canada: A Modern Study.* Toronto: Clarke, Irwin, 1977.

Creighton, Donald G. *Canada: The Heroic Beginnings.* Toronto: Macmillan of Canada, 1974.

―――. *Canada's First Century, 1867–1967.* Toronto: Macmillan of Canada, 1970.

―――. *Dominion of the North: A History of Canada.* New ed. Toronto: Macmillan of Canada, 1966.

―――. *Empire of the St. Lawrence.* New ed. Toronto: Macmillan of Canada, 1956.

Gough, Barry. *Canada.* Englewood Cliffs, NJ: Prentice-Hall, 1975.

Lamb, W. Kaye. *Canada's Five Centuries: From Discovery to Present Day.* Toronto: McGraw Hill of Canada, 1971.

Lower, Arthur R. M. *Colony to Nation: A History of Canada.* 4th ed. Toronto: Longmans, 1964.

McInnis, Edgar. *Canada: A Political and Social History.* 4th ed. Toronto: Holt, Rinehart and Winston of Canada, 1982.

McNaught, Kenneth. *The Pelican History of Canada.* London: Allen Lane, 1978; paperback ed., Harmondsworth: Penguin, 1995.

Malcolm, Andrew H. *The Canadians.* New York: Time Books, 1985.

Morton, Desmond. *A Short History of Canada.* New ed. Toronto: McClelland and Stewart, 1995.

Morton, William L. *The Kingdom of Canada: A General History from Earliest Time.* Toronto: McClelland and Stewart, 1963.

Woodcock, George. *The Canadians.* Toronto: Fitzhenry and Whiteside, 1979.

B. Collected Essays And Approaches

Berger, Carl. *Approaches to Canadian History.* Toronto: University of Toronto Press, 1967.

Cook, Ramsay. *The Maple Leaf Forever: Essays on Nationalism and Politics in Canada.* Toronto: Macmillan, 1986.

Eccles, William J. *Essays on New France.* Toronto: Oxford University Press, 1987.

Heick, Welf H. *History and Myth: Arthur Lower and the Making of Canadian Nationalism.* Vancouver: University of British Columbia Press, 1975.

Moir, John S. *Character and Circumstance: Essays in Honour of Donald Grant Creighton.* Toronto: Macmillan of Canada, 1970.

Morton, William L. *The Canadian Identity.* Toronto: University of Toronto Press, 1972.

_____. *Contexts of Canada's Past: Selected Essays.* Toronto: Macmillan of Canada, 1980.

_____. *Shield of Achilles: Aspects of Canada in the Victorian Age.* Toronto: McClelland and Stewart, 1968.

Pryke, Kenneth G., and Walter C. Soderlund, eds. *Profiles of Canada,* 2nd ed. Toronto: Urwin, 1998.

C. Historiography/Historical Literature

Berger, Carl. *The Writing of Canadian History: Aspects of English-Canadian Historical Writing since 1900.* 2nd ed. Toronto: University of Toronto Press, 1986.

_____, ed. *Contemporary Approaches to Canadian History.* Toronto: Copp Clark Pitman, 1987.

Gagnon, Serge. *Québec and Its Historians, 1840–1940.* Montréal: Harvest, 1982.

_____. *Québec and Its Historians: The Twentieth Century.* Montréal: Harvest, 1985.

Writing about Canada: A Handbook for Modern Canadian History. John Schultz, ed. Scarborough: Prentice-Hall Canada, 1990.

D. Intellectual History, Political Thought

Cook, Ramsay. *The Regenerators: Social Criticism in Late Victorian English Canada.* Toronto: University of Toronto Press, 1985.

_____. *Science, God, and Nature in Victorian Canada.* Toronto: University of Toronto Press, 1983.

Errington, Jane. *The Lion and Eagle and Upper Canada: A Developing Colonial Ideology.* Montréal: McGill-Queen's University Press, 1987.

Ferguson, Barry. *Remaking Liberalism: Intellectual Legacy of Adam Shortt, W. C. Clark, and W. A. Mackintosh.* Montréal: McGill-Queen's University Press, 1993.

Francis, Daniel. *National Dreams: Myth, Memory, and National History.* Toronto: Arsenal Pulp Press, 1997.

Francis, R. Douglas. *Frank H. Underhill: Intellectual Provocateur.* Toronto: University of Toronto Press, 1986.

McKillop, A. B. *A Disciplined Intelligence: Critical Inquiry and Canadian Thought in the Victorian Era.* Montréal: McGill-Queen's University Press, 1979.

Mills, David. *The Idea of Loyalty in Upper Canada, 1784–1850.* Kingston, ONT: McGill-Queen's University Press, 1988.

Owram, Doug. *The Government Generation: Canadian Intellectuals and the State, 1900–1945*. Toronto: University of Toronto Press, 1986.

Radwanski, George, and Julia Lattrell. *Will of a Nation: Awakening the Canadian Spirit*. Ottawa: General Distribution Services, 1992.

Shortt, Samuel E. D. *The Search for an Ideal: Six Canadian Intellectuals and Their Convictions in an Age of Transition, 1890–1930*. Toronto: University of Toronto Press, 1976.

Socknat, Thomas P. *Witness against War: Pacifism in Canada, 1900–1945*. Toronto: University of Toronto Press, 1985.

Trofimenkoff, Susan Mann. *The Dream of Nation: A Social and Intellectual History of Québec*. Toronto: Gage, 1983.

E. Pre-confederation Canada

Craig, Gerald M. *Upper Canada: The Formative Years, 1784–1841*. Toronto: McClelland and Stewart, 1963.

Creighton, Donald. *The Road to Confederation: The Emergence of Canada, 1863–1867*. Toronto: Macmillan of Canada, 1964.

Eccles, W. J. *Canada under Louis XIV, 1663–1701*. Toronto: McClelland and Stewart, 1964.

MacNutt, Walter S. *The Atlantic Provinces: The Emergence of Colonial Society, 1712–1857*. Toronto: McClelland and Stewart, 1965.

Miquelon, Dale. *New France, 1701–1744: "A Supplement to Europe."* Toronto: McClelland and Stewart, 1987.

Morton, William L. *The Critical Years: The Union of British North America, 1857–1873*. Toronto: McClelland and Stewart, 1964.

Ouellet, Fernand. *Lower Canada, 1791–1840: Social Change and Nationalism*. Toronto: McClelland and Stewart, 1980.

Waite, Peter B. *The Life and Times of Confederation, 1864–1867*. Toronto: University of Toronto Press, 1962.

Winks, Robin W. *Canada and the United States: The Civil War Years*. 4th rev. ed. Montréal: McGill-Queen's University Press, 1998.

F. Post-confederation Canada

Brown, Robert Craig, and Ramsay Cook. *Canada, 1896–1921: A Nation Transformed*. Toronto: McClelland and Stewart, 1974.

Creighton, Donald. *The Forked Road: Canada, 1939–1954*. Toronto: McClelland and Stewart, 1976.

Granatstein, J. L. *Canada, 1957–1967: The Years of Uncertainty and Innovation*. Toronto: McClelland and Stewart, 1986.

Thompson, John Herd, and Allen Seager. *Canada, 1922–1939: Decades of Discord*. Toronto: McClelland and Stewart, 1985.

Waite, Peter B. *Canada, 1874–1896: Arduous Destiny*. Toronto: McClelland and Stewart, 1971.

2. Constitutional Affairs

Cairns, Alan C. *Disruptions: Constitutional Struggles, from the Charter to Meech Lake.* Toronto: McClelland and Stewart, 1991.

Cook, Curtis, ed. *Constitutional Predicament: Canada after the Referendum of 1992.* Montréal: McGill-Queen's University Press, 1995.

Dawson, Robert MacGregor. *Democratic Government in Canada.* Toronto: University of Toronto Press, 1965.

———. *The Development of Dominion Status, 1900–1936.* London: Cass, 1965.

Gagnon, Alain. *Allaire, Belanger, Campeau, et les autres: Les Québecois s'interrogent sur leur avenir.* Montréal: Éditions Québec-Amerique, 1991.

Gerin-Lajoie, Paul. *Constitutional Amendment in Canada.* Toronto: University of Toronto Press, 1950.

Hawkes, David C. *Aboriginal Peoples and Constitutional Reform: What Have We Learned?* Kingston, ONT: Institute of Intergovernmental Relations, Queen's University, 1989.

McRoberts, Kenneth, and Patrick J. Monahan, eds. *Charlotte Accord: The Referendum and the Future of Canada.* Toronto: University of Toronto Press, 1993.

Milne, David. *The Canadian Constitution: From Patriation to Meech Lake.* Toronto: J. Lorimer, 1989.

Monahan, Patrick J. *Meech Lake: The Inside Story.* Toronto: University of Toronto Press, 1990.

Ollivier, Maurice. *Problems of Canadian Sovereignty from the British North America Act, 1867, to the Statute of Westminster, 1931.* Toronto: Canada Law Book Co., 1945.

Pentney, William F. *The Aboriginal Rights Provisions in the Constitution Act, 1982.* Saskatoon: University of Saskatchewan, Native Law Centre, 1987.

Robertson, Gordon. *A House Divided: Meech Lake, Senate Reform, and the Canadian Union.* Halifax: Institute for Research on Public Policy, 1989.

Smith, David E. *The Invisible Crown: The First Principle of Canadian Government.* Toronto: University of Toronto Press, 1995.

Stein, Michael B. *Canadian Constitutional Renewal, 1968–1981: A Case Study in Integrative Bargaining.* Kingston, ONT: Institute of Intergovernmental Relations, Queen's University, 1989.

Symonds, Hilda, and H. Peter Oberlander, eds. *Meech Lake, from Centre to Periphery: The Impact of the 1987 Constitutional Accord on Canadian Settlements: A Speculation.* Toronto: Micromedia, 1990.

Vipond, Robert. *Liberty and Community: Canadian Federation and the Failure of the Constitution.* New York: State University of New York Press, 1990.

3. External And Foreign Affairs

Black, J. L. *Canada in the Soviet Mirror: Ideology and Perception in Soviet Foreign Affairs, 1917–1991.* Ottawa: Carleton, 1998.

Bothwell, Robert. *Canada and the United States: The Politics of Partnership.* Toronto: University of Toronto Press, 1993.

Canada in World Affairs. 14 vols. Toronto: Canadian Institute of International Affairs, 1935–73.

Charlton, Mark. *The Making of Canadian Food Aid Policy.* Toronto: University of Toronto Press, 1993.

Clarkson, Stephen. *Canada and the Reagan Challenge: Crisis and Adjustment, 1981–1985.* Toronto: Lorimer, 1985.

Dewitt, David. *Canada's International Security Policy.* Toronto: Prentice-Hall, 1996.

Dewitt, David, and John Kirton. *Canada as a Principal Power.* Toronto: Wiley, 1983.

Doran, Charles. *Forgotten Partnership: U.S.–Canada Relations Today.* Baltimore: Johns Hopkins University Press, 1983.

Drache, Daniel, and Meric S. Gettler, eds. *New Era of Global Competition: State Policy and Market Power.* Toronto: University of Toronto Press, 1990.

Eayrs, James. *In Defence of Canada.* 5 vols. to date. Toronto: University of Toronto Press, 1965– .

Glazebrook, George P. de T. *A History of Canadian External Relations.* Rev. ed. 2 vols. Toronto: McClelland and Stewart, 1966.

Granatstein, J. L. *A Man of Influence: Norman Robertson and Canadian Statecraft, 1929–1968.* Ottawa: Deveau, 1981.

Granatstein, J. L., and Robert Bothwell. *Pirouette: Pierre Trudeau and Canadian Foreign Policy.* Toronto: University of Toronto Press, 1990.

Hilliker, John. *Canada's Department of External Affairs.* Vol. 1: *The Early Years, 1909–1946.* Montréal: McGill-Queen's University Press, Institute of Public Administration of Canada, 1990.

Hilliker, John, and Donald Barry. *Canada's Department of External Affairs.* Vol. 2. *Coming of Age, 1946–1968.* Montréal: McGill-Queen's University Press, Institute of Public Administration of Canada, 1995.

Hillmer, Norman, and J. L. Granatstein. *Empire to Umpire: Canada and the World to the 1990s.* Toronto: Copp Clark Longman, 1994.

Holmes, John W. *The Shaping of Peace: Canada and the Search for World Order, 1943–1957.* 2 vols. Toronto: University of Toronto Press, 1979.

Keating, Tom. *Canada and World Order: Canadian Foreign Policy and Multi-lateralist Tradition in Canadian Foreign Policy.* Toronto: McClelland and Stewart, 1993.

Keenleyside, Hugh L., et al. *The Growth of Canadian Policies in External Affairs.* Durham, NC: Duke University Press, 1960.

Lemco, Jonathan, ed. *Canada–United States Relationship: The Policies of Energy and Environmental Coordination.* Westport, CT: Praeger, 1993.

Lyon, Peyton V., and Brian W. Tomlin. *Canada as an International Actor.* Toronto: Macmillan of Canada, 1979.

Masters, Donald C. *The Reciprocity Treaty of 1854*. London: Longmans Green, 1939; Toronto: McClelland and Stewart, 1963.

Nossal, Kim R. *The Politics of Canadian Foreign Policy*. Scarborough, ONT: Prentice-Hall, 1997.

Robinson, H. Basil. *Diefenbaker's World: A Populist in Foreign Affairs*. Toronto: University of Toronto Press, 1989.

Ross, Douglas A. *In the Interests of Peace: Canada and Vietnam, 1954–1973*. Toronto: University of Toronto Press, 1984.

Smith, Denis. *Diplomacy of Fear: Canada and the Cold War, 1941–1948*. Toronto: University of Toronto Press, 1988.

Stacey, Charles P. *Canada and the Age of Conflict: A History of Canadian External Relations*, Vol. 1: *1867–1921*. Toronto: Macmillan of Canada, 1977. Vol. 2: *1921–1948*. Toronto: University of Toronto Press, 1981.

Swanson, Roger F. *Intergovernmental Perspectives on the Canada–U.S. Relationship*. New York: New York University Press, 1978.

Taylor, Charles. *Snow Job: Canada, the United States, and Vietnam, 1954–1973*. Toronto: Anansi, 1974.

Tucker, Michael. *Canadian Foreign Policy: Contemporary Issues and Themes*. Toronto: McGraw-Hill Ryerson, 1980.

Whitaker, Reg, and Gary Marcuse. *Cold War Canada: The Making of a National Security State, 1945–1957*. Toronto: University of Toronto Press, 1996.

4. Military And Naval History

Antal, Sandy. *A Wampum Denied: Procter's War of 1812*. Ottawa: Carleton University Press, 1997.

Bass, George, ed. *Ships and Shipwrecks of the Americas: A History Based on Underwater Archaeology*. London: Thames and Hudson, 1988.

Bercuson, David J. *Maple Leaf against the Axis: Canada's Second World War*. Toronto: Stoddart, 1995.

A Bibliography of Works on Canadian Foreign Relations. Toronto: Canadian Institute of International Affairs, 1973.

Bland, Douglas. *Administration of Defence Policy in Canada, 1947–1985*. Kingston, ONT: Frye, 1987.

Byers, R. B. *Canadian Security and Defence: The Legacy and the Challenge*. London: International Institute for Strategic Studies, 1986.

Canada and NATO. Nils Orvik, ed. Kingston, ONT: Centre for International Relations, Queen's University, 1982.

Canada's Defence: Perspectives on Policy in the Twentieth Century. B. D. Hunt, and R. G. Haycock, eds. Toronto: Copp Clark Pitman, 1993.

Copp, J. Terry. *The Brigade: The Fifth Canadian Infantry Brigade, 1939–1945*. Stoney Creek, ONT: Fortress, 1992.

Copp, J. Terry, and Bill McAndrew. *Battle Exhaustion: Soldiers and Psychiatrists in the Canadian Army, 1939–1945*. Montréal: McGill-Queen's University Press, 1990.

Copp, J. Terry, and Robert Vogel. *Maple Leaf Route.* 5 vols. *Caen; Falaise; Antwerp; Scheldt; Victory.* Alma, ONT: Maple Leaf Route, 1983–88.

Douglas, W. A. B. *The Creation of a National Air Force: The Official History of the Royal Canadian Air Force.* 3 vols. Toronto: University of Toronto Press, 1980– .

Dyer, Gwynne. *The Defence of Canada.* Toronto: McClelland and Stewart, 1990.

Eayrs, James. *In Defence of Canada.* 5 vols. to date. Toronto: University of Toronto Press, 1965– .

English, John A. *The Canadian Army and the Normandy Campaign: A Study of Failure in High Command.* New York: Praeger, 1991.

Eustace, Marilyn. *Canada's European Force, 1964–1971: Canada's Commitment to Europe.* Kingston, ONT: Centre for International Relations, Queen's University, 1982.

Granatstein, J. L. *Broken Promises: A History of Conscription in Canada.* Toronto: Oxford University Press, 1977.

_____. *The Generals: The Canadian Army's Senior Commanders in the Second World War.* Toronto: Stoddart, 1993.

_____. *War and Peacekeeping: From South Africa to the Gulf: Canada's Limited Wars.* Toronto: Key Porter Books, 1991.

Gravel, Jean-Yves. *Le Québec et la guerre, 1867–1960.* Montréal: Éditions du boreal Express, 1974.

Gray, Colin S. *Canada's Maritime Forces.* Toronto: Canadian Institute of International Affairs, 1973.

Gwyn, Sandra. *Tapestry of War: A Private View of Canadians in the Great War.* Toronto: Harper Collins, 1992.

Hadley, Michael L. *U-Boats against Canada: German Submarines in Canadian Waters.* Kingston, ONT: McGill-Queen's University Press, 1985.

Hitsman, J. Mackay. *Safeguarding Canada, 1763–1871.* Toronto: University of Toronto Press, 1968.

Hyatt, A. M. J. *General Sir Arthur Currie: A Military Biography.* Toronto: University of Toronto Press, 1980.

Kostenuk, Samuel. *RCAF: Squadron Histories and Aircraft, 1924–1968.* Sarasota, FL: S. Stevens, 1977.

Leach, Douglas Edward. *Arms for Empire: A Military History of the British Colonies in North America, 1607–1763.* New York: Macmillan, 1973.

Legget, Robert F. *Ottawa River Canals and the Defence of British North America.* Toronto: University of Toronto Press, 1988.

MacLaren, Roy. *Canadians in Russia, 1918–1919.* Toronto: Macmillan of Canada, 1976.

Malcomson, Robert. *Lords of the Lake: The Naval War on Lake Ontario, 1812–1814.* Toronto: Robin Bass Studio, 1998.

Meyers, Edward C. *Thunder in the Morning Calm: The Royal Canadian Navy in Korea, 1950–1955.* St. Catharines, ONT: Vanwell Publishing, 1992.

Middlemiss, D. W., and J. J. Sokolsky. *Canadian Defence: Decisions and Determinants.* Toronto: Harcourt Brace Jovanovich, 1989.

Milner, Marc. *North Atlantic Run: The Royal Canadian Navy and the Battle for the Convoys, 1939–1943*. Toronto: University of Toronto Press, 1985.

_____. *The U-Boat Hunters: The Royal Canadian Navy and the Offensive against Germany's Submarines, 1943–1945*. Toronto: University of Toronto Press, 1994.

Morton, Desmond. *Canada and War: A Military and Political History*. Toronto: Butterworths, 1981.

_____. *A Military History of Canada: From Champlain to the Gulf War*. 3rd ed. Toronto: McClelland and Stewart, 1992.

_____. *A Peculiar Kind of Politics: Canada's Overseas Ministry in the First World War*. Toronto: University of Toronto Press, 1982.

Newman, Peter Charles. *True North, Not Strong and Free: Defending the Peaceable Kingdom in the Nuclear Age*. Toronto: McClelland and Stewart, 1983.

Preston, Richard Arthur. *Canadian Defence Policy and the Development of the Canadian Nation, 1867–1917*. Ottawa: Canadian Historical Association, 1970.

Raudzens, George. *The British Ordnance Department and Canada's Canals*. Waterloo, ONT: Wilfrid Laurier University Press, 1979.

RCN in Retrospect. James A. Boutilier, ed. Vancouver: University of British Columbia Press, 1982.

RCN in Transition. W. A. B. Douglas, ed. Vancouver: University of British Columbia Press, 1988.

Roy, Reginald. *1944: The Canadians in Normandy*. Toronto: Macmillan of Canada, 1984.

Sarty, Roger. *Canada and the Battle of the Atlantic*. Montréal: Art Global, 1998.

Sokolsky, Joel J. *Defending Canada: U.S–Canadian Defence Policies*. New York: Priority Press Publications, 1989.

_____. *Ogdensburg Plus Fifty and Still Counting: Canada–U.S. Defence Relations in the Post–Cold War Era*. Orono, ME: Canadian-American Center, 1991.

Sokolsky, Joel J., and Joseph T. Jockel, eds. *Fifty Years of Canada–United States Defence Cooperation: The Road from Ogdensburg*. Lewiston, NY: Mellen Press, 1992.

Stacey, Charles P. *Arms, Men, and Governments: The War Policies of Canada, 1939–1945*. Ottawa: Information Canada, 1974.

_____. *The Canadian Army, 1939–1945: An Official Historical Summary*. Ottawa: Ministry of National Defence, 1948.

_____. *The Military Problems of Canada: A Survey of Defence Policies and Strategic Conditions Past and Present*. Toronto: Issued for the Canadian Institute of International Affairs by Ryerson, 1940.

Stanley, George Francis Gilman. *Canada's Soldiers: The Military History of an Unmilitary People*. Toronto: Macmillan of Canada, 1974.

_____. *Toil and Trouble: Military Expeditions to Red River*. Toronto: Dundurn Press, 1989.

_____. *War of 1812: Land Operations*. Toronto: Macmillan of Canada, 1983.

Sugden, John. *Tecumseh's Last Stand*. Norman: University of Oklahoma Press, 1985.

Tippett, Maria. *Art at the Service of War: Canada, Art, and the Great War*. Toronto: University of Toronto Press, 1984.

5. Prime Ministers

Bliss, Michael. *Right Honourable Men: The Descent of Canadian Politics from Macdonald to Mulroney*. Toronto: Harper Collins, 1994.

Clippingdale, Richard. *Laurier: His Life and World*. Toronto: McGraw-Hill Ryerson, 1979.

Creighton, Donald G. *John A. Macdonald: The Old Chieftain*. Toronto: Macmillan of Canada, 1955.

———. *John A. Macdonald: The Young Politician*. Toronto: Macmillan of Canada, 1952.

Dobbin, Murray. *The Politics of Kim Campbell: From School Trustee to Prime Minister*. Toronto: J. Lorimer, 1993.

English, John. *The Life of Lester Pearson, 1897–1948, 1949–1972*. 2 vols. Toronto: Lester and Orpen Dennys, 1989– .

Esberey, Joy E. *Knight of the Holy Spirit: A Study of William Lyon Mackenzie King*. Toronto: University of Toronto Press, 1980.

Graham, Ron. *One-Eyed Kings: Promise and Illusion in Canadian Politics*. Toronto: Collins, 1986.

Gray, James J. *R. B. Bennett: The Calgary Years*. Toronto: University of Toronto Press, 1980.

Gwyn, Richard J. *The Northern Magus: Pierre Trudeau and Canadians*. Toronto: McClelland and Stewart, 1980.

Hutchison, Bruce. *Mr. Prime Minister, 1867–1964*. Don Mills, ONT: Longmans Canada, 1964.

Matheson, William A. *The Prime Minister and the Cabinet*. Toronto: Methuen, 1976.

Ondaatje, Christopher. *The Prime Ministers of Canada: Macdonald to Mulroney, 1867–1985*. Toronto: Pagurian Press, 1985.

Pal, Leslie, and David Taras, eds. *Prime Ministers and Premiers: Political Leadership and Public Policy in Canada*. Scarborough, ONT: Prentice-Hall Canada, 1988.

Pearson, Geoffrey. *Seize the Day: Lester B. Pearson and Crisis Diplomacy*. Ottawa: Carleton University Press, 1993.

Punnett, R. M. *The Prime Minister in Canadian Government and Politics*. Toronto: Macmillan of Canada, 1977.

Robertson, Heather. *More than a Rose: Prime Ministers, Wives, and Other Women*. Toronto: Seal, 1991.

Sawatsky, John. *Mulroney: The Politics of Ambition*. Toronto: Macfarlane Walter and Ross, 1991.

Stacey, Charles P. *Mackenzie King and the Atlantic Triangle*. Toronto: Macmillan of Canada, 1976.

Stursberg, Peter. *Lester Pearson and the Dream of Unity*. Toronto: Doubleday Canada, 1978.

Thomson, Dale C. *Alexander Mackenzie: Clear Grit*. Toronto: Macmillan, 1960.

Trudeau, Pierre Elliott. *Memoirs*. Toronto: McClelland and Stewart, 1993.

Vastel, Michel. *The Outsider: The Life of Pierre Elliott Trudeau*. Toronto: Macmillan of Canada, 1990.

Waite, Peter B. *The Loner: Three Sketches of the Personal Life and Ideas of R. B. Bennett, 1870–1947*. Toronto: University of Toronto Press, 1992.

_____. *The Man from Halifax: Sir John Thompson, Prime Minister*. Toronto: University of Toronto Press, 1984.

Wilson, Garrett. *Diefenbaker for the Defence*. Toronto: J. Lorimer, 1988.

6. Economic And Business History

Armstrong, Christopher, and H. V. Nelles. *Monopoly's Moment: Organization and Regulation of Canada's Utilities, 1830–1930*. Philadelphia: Temple University Press, 1986.

Baskerville, Peter, ed. *The Bank of Upper Canada: A Collection of Documents*. Toronto: Champlain Society, 1987.

Bosher, John F. *The Canada Merchants, 1713–1763*. Oxford: Clarendon Press, 1987.

Bothwell, Robert. *Eldorado: Canada's National Uranium Company*. Toronto: University of Toronto Press, 1984.

Eagle, John Andrew. *The Canadian Pacific Railway and the Development of Western Canada, 1896–1914*. Kingston, ONT: McGill-Queen's University Press, 1989.

Freeman, Neil. *Politics of Power: Ontario Hydro and Its Government, 1906–1995*. Toronto: University of Toronto Press, 1996.

Gray, James Henry. *The Winter Years: The Depression on the Prairies*. Toronto: Macmillan of Canada, 1966.

Greer, Alan, and Ian Radforth. *Colonial Leviathan: State Formation in Nineteenth-Century Canada*. Toronto: University of Toronto Press, 1992.

Innis, Harold Adams. *The Fur Trade in Canada: An Introduction to Canadian Economic History*. Reprint. Toronto: University of Toronto Press, 1962.

Inwood, Kris. *Farm, Factory, and Fortune: New Studies in the Economic History of the Maritime Provinces*. Fredericton, NB: Acadiensis Press, 1993.

McCalla, Douglas. *Planting the Province: The Economic History of Upper Canada, 1784–1870*. Toronto: University of Toronto Press, 1993.

McDowall, Duncan. *The Light: Brazilian Traction, Light and Power Co. Ltd*. Toronto: University of Toronto Press, 1988.

Myers, Gustavus. *A History of Canadian Wealth*. 1914. Reprint with introduction by Stanley Ryerson. Toronto: J. Lewis and Samuel, 1972.

Norrie, Kenneth H., and Doug Owram. *A History of the Canadian Economy*. Toronto: Harcourt Brace Jovanovich, 1991.

Picard, Robert G., ed. *Press Concentration and Monopoly: New Perspectives on Newspaper Ownership and Operation.* Norwood, NJ: Ablex, 1988.

Rich, Edwin E. *The Fur Trade and the Northwest to 1857.* Toronto: McClelland and Stewart, 1967.

Stevens, G. R. *History of the Canadian National Railways.* New York: Macmillan, 1973.

Taylor, Graham, and Peter Baskerville. *A Concise History of Business in Canada.* Toronto: Oxford University Press, 1994.

Wuttunee, Wanda A. *In Business for Ourselves: Northern Entrepreneurs.* Montréal: McGill-Queen's University Press, 1992.

7. Industry And Development

Craven, Paul. *An Impartial Umpire: Industrial Relations and the Canadian State, 1900–1911.* Toronto: University of Toronto Press, 1980.

Forsey, Eugene Alfred. *Trade Unions in Canada, 1812–1902.* Toronto: University of Toronto Press, 1981.

Millerd, Frank W. *Canadian Urban Industrial Growth, 1961–1971.* Waterloo, ONT: School of Business and Economics, Wilfrid Laurier University, 1981.

Porter, Glenn, ed. *Enterprise and National Development: Essays in Canadian Business and Economic History.* Toronto: Hakkert, 1973.

Smucker, Joseph. *Industrialisation in Canada.* Scarborough, ONT: Prentice-Hall of Canada, 1980.

Taylor, Don. *The Rise of Industrial Unionism in Canada: A History of the CIO.* Kingston, ONT: Industrial Relations Centre, Queen's University, 1988.

Traves, Tom. *The State and Enterprise: Canadian Manufacturers and the Federal Government, 1917–1931.* Toronto: University of Toronto Press, 1979.

III. PROVINCIAL AND TERRITORIAL HISTORY

1. Alberta

Barr, John J. *The Dynasty: The Rise and Fall of Social Credit in Alberta.* Toronto: McClelland and Stewart, 1974.

Dempsey, Hugh Aylmer. *Indian Tribes of Alberta.* Calgary: Glenbow-Museum, 1979.

Driben, Paul. *We Are Métis: The Ethnography of a Halfbreed Community in Northern Alberta.* New York: AMS Press, 1985.

Dunn, Jack. *The Alberta Field Force of 1885.* Calgary: Jack Dunn, 1994.

Finkel, Alvin. *The Social Credit Phenomenon in Alberta.* Toronto: University of Toronto Press, 1989.

MacGregor, James Grierson. *A History of Alberta.* Edmonton: Hurtig Publishers, 1972.

Owram, Douglas R., ed. *The Formation of Alberta: A Documentary History.* Alberta Records Publication Board, Historical Society of Alberta, 1979

Palmer, Howard, and Tamara Palmer. *Alberta: A New History.* Edmonton: Hurtig, 1990.

Palmer, Howard, and Donald Smith, eds. *The New Provinces: Alberta and Saskatchewan, 1905–1980.* Vancouver: Tantalus Research, 1980.

Pratt, Larry, ed. *Essays in Honour of Grant Notley: Socialism and Democracy in Alberta.* Edmonton: NeWest Press, 1986.

Silverman, Elaine Leslau. *The Last Best West: Women on the Alberta Frontier, 1880–1930.* Montréal: Eden Press, 1984.

Snow, John. *These Mountains Are Our Sacred Places: The Story of the Stoney Indians.* Toronto: S. Stevens, 1977.

2. British Columbia

Barman, Jean. *The West beyond the West: A History of British Columbia.* Toronto: University of Toronto Press, 1991.

Begg, Alexander. *History of British Columbia from Its Earliest Discovery to the Present Time.* Toronto: W. Briggs, 1894.

Carstens, Peter. *The Queen's People: A Study of Hegemony, Coercion, and Accommodation among the Okanagan of Canada.* Toronto: University of Toronto Press, 1991.

Creese, Gillian, and Veronica Strong-Boag, eds. *British Columbia Reconsidered: Essays on Women.* Vancouver: Press Gang Publishers, 1992.

Fisher, Robin. *Contact and Conflict: Indian–European Relations in British Columbia, 1774–1890.* 2nd ed. Vancouver: University of British Columbia Press, 1992.

_____. *Duff Pattullo of British Columbia.* Toronto: University of Toronto Press, 1991.

Friesen, J., and H. K. Ralston, eds. *Historical Essays on British Columbia.* Toronto: McClelland and Stewart, in association with the Institute of Canadian Studies, Carleton University, 1976.

Gibson, James R. *Lifeline of the Oregon Country: The Fraser-Columbia Brigade System, 1811–1847.* Vancouver: University of British Columbia Press, 1997.

Gough, Barry M. *Gunboat Frontier: British Maritime Authority and Northwest Coast Indians, 1846–1890.* Vancouver: University of British Columbia Press, 1984.

_____. *The Northwest Coast: British Navigation, Trade, and Discoveries to 1812.* Vancouver: University of British Columbia Press, 1992.

Gould, Jan. *Women of British Columbia.* Saanichton, BC: Hancock House Publishers, 1975.

Mackie, Richard Somerset. *Trading beyond the Mountains: The British Fur Trade on the Pacific.* Vancouver: University of British Columbia Press, 1997.

Ormsby, Margaret Anchoretta. *British Columbia: A History.* 2nd ed. Toronto: Macmillan of Canada, 1971.

Paterson, Thomas William. *British Columbia: The Pioneer Years.* Langley, BC: Stagecoach, 1977.

_____. *Vancouver: An Illustrated History.* Toronto: J. Lorimer, 1980.

Roy, Patricia. *A White Man's Province: British Columbia Politicians and Chinese and Japanese Immigrants, 1858–1914.* Vancouver: University of British Columbia Press, 1989.

Social Science Research Centre. *A Bibliography of British Columbia.* Victoria: University of Victoria, 1968– .

Ward, W. Peter, and Robert A. J. McDonald, eds. *British Columbia: Historical Readings.* Vancouver: Douglas and McIntyre, 1981.

Woodcock, George. *British Columbia: A History of the Province.* Vancouver: Douglas and McIntyre, 1990.

3. Manitoba

Bercuson, David Jay. *Confrontation at Winnipeg: Labour, Industrial Relations, and the General Strike.* Montréal: McGill-Queen's University Press, 1990.

Coates, Kenneth. *Manitoba: The Province and the People.* Edmonton: Hurtig, 1987.

Jackson, James A. *The Centennial History of Manitoba.* Toronto: McClelland and Stewart, 1970.

Morton, William Lewis. *Manitoba: A History.* Toronto: University of Toronto Press, 1967.

_____. *Manitoba: The Birth of a Province.* Altona, MAN: D. W. Friesen, 1965.

Wood, Louis Aubrey. *The Red River Colony: A Chronicle of the Beginnings of Manitoba.* Toronto: Brook and Co., 1915.

4. New Brunswick

Bailey, Alfred Goldsworthy. *Culture and Nationality: Essays.* Toronto: McClelland and Stewart, 1972.

Fisher, Peter. *The First History of New Brunswick.* Woodstock, NB: Non-Entity Press, 1980.

Hannay, James. *History of New Brunswick.* St. John, NB: J. A. Bowes, 1909.

MacNutt, William S. *New Brunswick: A History, 1784–1867.* Toronto: Macmillan of Canada, 1963.

Trueman, Stuart. *An Intimate History of New Brunswick.* Toronto: McClelland and Stewart, 1972.

5. Newfoundland And Labrador

Chadwick, Gerald William St. John. *Newfoundland: Island into Province.* Cambridge: Cambridge University Press, 1967.

Goudie, Elizabeth. *Woman of Labrador.* Toronto: P. Martin Associates, 1979.

Neary, Peter F. *Newfoundland in the North Atlantic World, 1929–1949*. Kingston, ONT: McGill-Queen's University Press, 1988.

Rompkey, Ronald. *Grenfell of Labrador: A Biography*. Toronto: University of Toronto Press, 1991.

Rothney, G. O. *Newfoundland: A History*. Ottawa: Canadian Historical Association, 1964.

Rowe, Frederick William. *Education and Culture in Newfoundland*. Toronto: McGraw-Hill Ryerson, 1976.

_____. *A History of Newfoundland and Labrador*. Toronto: McGraw-Hill Ryerson, 1980.

Story, G. M., ed. *Early European Settlement and Exploitation in Atlantic Canada: Selected Papers*. St. John's: Memorial University of Newfoundland, 1982.

6. Nova Scotia

Balcom, B. A. *The Cod Fishery of Isle Royale, 1713–1758*. Ottawa: Parks Canada, 1984.

Bell, David. *Henry Alline and Maritime Religion*. Ottawa: Canadian Historical Association, 1993.

Clark, Andrew Hill. *Acadia: The Early Geography of Nova Scotia to 1760*. Madison: University of Wisconsin Press, 1968.

Clarke, George Frederick. *Someone before Us: Our Maritime Indians*. Fredericton, NB: Brunswick Press, 1968.

Crowley, Terry. *Louisbourg: Atlantic Fortress and Seaport*. Ottawa: Canadian Historical Association, 1990.

Fergusson, Charles Bruce. *Glimpses into Nova Scotia History*. Windsor, NS: Lancelot Press, 1975.

Griffiths, Naomi E. S. *The Acadian Deportation*. Toronto: Copp Clark, 1969.

Gwyn, Julian, ed. *The Royal Navy and North America: The Warren Papers, 1736–1752*. London: Navy Records Society, 1973.

Haliburton, Thomas Chandler. *History of Nova Scotia*. Reprint, Belleville, ONT: Mika, 1973.

Rawlyk, George. *Nova Scotia's Massachusetts: A Study of Relations, 1630–1784*. Montréal: McGill-Queen's University Press, 1973.

_____. *Yankees at Louisbourg*. Orono: University of Maine Press, 1967.

Stewart, Gordon T. *A People Highly Favoured of God: The Nova Scotia Yankees and the American Revolution*. Toronto: Macmillan of Canada, 1972.

7. Ontario

Akenson, Donald H. *The Irish in Ontario: A Study in Rural History*. Kingston, ONT: McGill-Queen's University Press, 1984.

Avison, Margaret. *History of Ontario*. Toronto: W. J. Gage, 1951.

Bothwell, Robert. *A Short History of Ontario*. Edmonton: Hurtig, 1986.

Burnet, Jean R. *Ethnic Groups in Upper Canada*. Toronto: Ontario Historical Society, 1972.

Cohen, Marjorie Griffin. *Women's Work, Markets, and Economic Development in Nineteenth-Century Ontario*. Toronto: University of Toronto Press, 1988.

Cooper, John Irwin. *Ontario's First Century, 1610–1713*. Montréal: Lawrence Land Foundation, McGill University, 1978.

Curtis, Bruce. *True Government by Choice Men?: Inspection, Education, and State Formation in Canada West*. Toronto: University of Toronto Press, 1992.

Drummond, Ian M. *Progress without Planning:The Economic History of Ontario from Confederation to the Second World War*. Toronto: University of Toronto Press, 1987.

Errington, Jane. *The Lion, the Eagle, and Upper Canada: A Developing Colonial Ideology*. Kingston, ONT: McGill-Queen's University Press, 1987.

Gervais, Gaetan, comp. *The Bibliography of Ontario History, 1976–1986*. Toronto: Dundurn Press, 1989.

Godfrey, Charles M. *Medicine for Ontario: A History*. Belleville, ONT: Mika, 1979.

Heap, Ruby, and Alison Prentice, eds. *Gender and Education in Ontario: An Historical Reader*. Toronto: Canadian Scholars' Press, 1991.

Hiller, James, and Peter Neary, eds. *Newfoundland in the Nineteenth and Twentieth Centuries: Essays in Interpretation*. Toronto: University of Toronto Press, 1980.

Johnson, J. K., and Bruce G. Wilson, eds. *Historical Essays on Upper Canada: New Perspectives*. Ottawa: Carleton University Press, 1989.

Keane, David, Colin Read, and Frederick H. Armstrong, eds. *Old Ontario: Essays in Honour of J. M. S. Careless*. Toronto: Dundurn Press, 1990.

McLean, Marianne. *The People of Glengarry: Highlanders in Transition, 1745–1820*. Montréal: McGill-Queen's University Press, 1991.

Middleton, Jesse Edgar. *The Province of Ontario: A History, 1615–1927*. Toronto: Dominion Publishing, 1927–28.

Naylor, James. *The New Democracy: Challenging the Social Order in Industrial Ontario, 1914–1925*. Toronto: University of Toronto Press, 1991.

Noel, Sidney John Roderick. *Patrons, Clients, Brokers: Ontario Society and Politics, 1791–1896*. Toronto: University of Toronto Press, 1990.

Piva, Michael J., ed. *A History of Ontario: Selected Readings*. Toronto: Copp Clark Pitman, 1988.

Reaman, George Elmore. *A History of Agriculture in Ontario*. Don Mills, ONT: Saunders of Toronto, 1970.

Schmalz, Peter S. *The Ojibwa of Southern Ontario*. Toronto: University of Toronto Press, 1991.

Schull, Joseph. *Ontario since 1867*. Toronto: McClelland and Stewart, 1978.

Smith, Philip. *Harvest from the Rock: A History of Mining in Ontario*. Toronto: Macmillan of Canada, 1986.

Splane, Richard B. *Social Welfare in Ontario, 1791–1893: A Study of Public*

Welfare Administration. Toronto: University of Toronto Press, 1965.

Sylvestre, Paul François. *Les journaux de l'Ontario français, 1858–1983.* Sudbury, ONT: Société historique du Nouvel-Ontario, Université de Sudbury, 1984.

Wise, Sydney Francis. *God's Peculiar Peoples: Essays on Political Culture in Nineteenth-Century Canada.* Ottawa: Carleton University Press, 1993.

8. Prince Edward Island

Bolger, Francis W. P. *Canada's Smallest Province: A History of Prince Edward Island.* Charlottetown: Prince Edward Island Centennial Commission, 1973.

Bumsted, J. M. *Land, Settlement, and Politics on Eighteenth-Century Prince Edward Island.* Kingston, ONT: McGill-Queen's University Press, 1987.

Graham, Robert J. *The Currency and Medals of Prince Edward Island.* Willowdale, ONT: Published on behalf of J. Douglas Ferguson Historical Research Foundation by the Numismatic Education Society of Canada, 1988.

Henry, Daniel Cobb. *The French Régime in Prince Edward Island.* New Haven: Yale University Press, 1926.

MacKinnon, Frank. *The Government of Prince Edward Island.* Toronto: University of Toronto Press, 1951.

Pineau, J. Wilfrid. *Le Clergé français dans l'île du Prince Edouard, 1721–1821.* Québec: Éditions Ferland, 1967.

Sharpe, Errol. *A People's History of Prince Edward Island.* Toronto: Steel Rail, 1976.

Smitheram, Verner, David Milne, and Satadal Dasgupta, eds. *The Garden Transformed: Prince Edward Island, 1945–1980.* Charlottetown, PEI: Ragweed Press, 1982.

9. Québec

Aube, Jacques. *Chanson et politique au Québec, 1960–1980.* Montréal: Triptyque, 1990.

Aubin, Paul, comp. *Bibliography of the History of Québec and Canada, 1946–1965.* Québec: Institut Québecois de Recherche sur la Culture, 1987.

———. *Bibliographie de l'histoire du Québec et du Canada, 1966–1975.* UE Institut Québecois de Recherche sur la Culture, 1981.

Balthazar, Louis. *Bilan du nationalisme au Québec.* Montréal: L'Hexagone, 1986.

Baum, Gregory. *The Church in Québec.* Outremont, QUE: Novalis, 1991.

Beaulieu, André. *La province de Québec.* Toronto: University of Toronto Press, 1971.

Behiels, Michael D., ed. *Québec since 1945: Selected Readings.* Toronto: Copp Clark Pitman, 1987.

Bercuson, David Jay. *Deconfederation: Canada without Québec.* Toronto: Key Porter Books, 1991.

Bergeron, Gerard. *Syndrome Québecois et mal Canadien.* Québec: Presses de l'Université Laval, 1981.

Bernier, Gerald. *The Shaping of Québec Politics and Society: Colonialism, Power, and the Transition to Capitalism in the 19th Century.* Washington, DC: C. Russak, 1992.

Bourque, Gilles. *Le Québec: La question nationale.* Paris: F. Maspero, 1979.

Cameron, David R. *Nationalism, Self-Determination, and the Québec Question.* Toronto: Macmillan of Canada, 1974.

Coleman, William D. *The Independence Movement in Québec, 1945–1980.* Toronto: University of Toronto Press, 1984.

Conway, John Frederick. *Debts to Pay: English Canada and Québec from the Conquest to the Referendum.* Toronto: J. Lorimer, 1992.

Cook, Ramsay. *French-Canadian Nationalism: An Anthology.* Toronto: Macmillan of Canada, 1969.

Copp, Terry. *The Anatomy of Poverty: The Condition of the Working Class in Montréal, 1897–1929.* Toronto: McClelland and Stewart, 1974.

Daniels, Dan, ed. *Québec, Canada, and the October Crisis.* Montréal: Black Rose Books, 1973.

Dirks, Patricia G. *The Failure of l'Action Liberale Nationale.* Montréal: McGill-Queen's University Press, 1991.

Dumont, Fernand. *The Vigil of Québec.* Toronto: University of Toronto Press, 1974.

Dumont, Micheline, et al., eds. *Québec Women: A History.* Toronto: Women's Press, 1987.

Durocher, René. *Histoire du Québec: Bibliographie selective, 1867–1970.* Trois-Rivières, QUE: Éditions Boreal Express, 1970.

Dussault, Gabriel. *Le cure labelle: Messianisme, utopie et colonisation au Québec, 1850–1900.* Montréal: Hurtubise HMH, 1983.

Fortin, Marcel. *Guide de la literature québecoise.* Montréal: Boreal, 1988.

Frechette, Louis Honoré. *Satires et polemiques, ou, l'Ecole clericale au Canada.* Montréal: Presses de l'Université de Montréal, 1993.

Gagnon, Alain. *Allaire, Belanger, Campeau, et les autres: les Québecois s'interrogent sur leur avenir.* Montréal: Éditions Québec-Amerique, 1991.

_____. *Québec: Beyond the Quiet Revolution.* Scarborough, ONT: Nelson, 1990.

Gagnon, Serge. *Québec and Its Historians, 1840 to 1920.* Montréal: Harvest House, 1982.

Gougeon, Gilles. *Histoire du nationalisme québecois: Entrevues avec sept specialistes.* Montréal: VLB: Société Radio-Canada, 1993.

Gravel, Jean-Yves. *Le Québec et la guerre, 1867–1960.* Montréal: Éditions du Boreal Express, 1974.

Griffin, Anne. *Québec: The Challenge of Independence.* Rutherford, NJ: Fairleigh Dickinson University Press, 1983.

Hebert, Robert. *L'amerique française devant l'opinion étrangere, 1756–1960: Anthologie.* Montréal: L'Hexagone, 1989.

Lamarche, Jacques. *L'Éte des mohawks: bilan des 78 jours.* Montréal: Stanke, 1990.

Lambert, Ronald D. *The Sociology of Contemporary Québec Nationalism: An Annotated Bibliography and Review.* New York: Garland, 1981.

Latouche, Daniel. *Canada and Québec, Past and Future: An Essay.* Toronto: University of Toronto Press, 1986.

Lemieux, Vincent, and Harold M. Angell, eds. *Personnel et partis politiques au Québec: aspects historiques.* Montréal: Éditions du Boreal Express, 1982.

Levesque, René. *La passion du Québec.* Toronto: Methuen, 1979.

Levine, Marc. *The Reconquest of Montréal: Language Policy and Social Change in a Bilingual City.* Philadelphia: Temple University Press, 1990.

Little, John Irvine. *Nationalism, Capitalism, and Colonisation in Nineteenth-Century Québec: The Upper St. Francis District.* Kingston, ONT: McGill-Queen's University Press, 1989.

McWhinney, Edward. *Québec and the Constitution, 1960–1978.* Toronto: University of Toronto Press, 1979.

Maille, Chantal. *Les Québecoises et la conquête du pouvoir politique: Enquete sur l'emergence d'une élite politique feminine au Québec.* Montréal: Éditions Saint-Martin, 1990.

Manning, Helen Taft. *The Revolt of French Canada: A Chapter in the History of the British Commonwealth.* London: Macmillan, 1962.

Mellouki, M'Hammed. *Savoir enseignant et ideologie reformiste: La formation des maîtres, 1930–1964.* Québec: Institut Québecois de Recherche sur la Culture, 1989.

Milner, Henry. *The Decolonisation of Québec: An Analysis of Left-Wing Nationalism.* Toronto: McClelland and Stewart, 1973.

Ministère des Affaires Culturelles. *Histoire des communautés religieuses au Québec: bibliographie.* Montréal: Bibliothèque Nationale du Québec, 1984.

Moniere, Denis. *Le developpement des ideologies au Québec: des origines à nos jours.* Montréal: Éditions Québec-Amerique, 1977.

Oliver, Michael. *The Passionate Debate: The Social and Political Ideas of Québec Nationalism, 1920–1945.* Montréal: Vehicule Press, 1991.

Ouellet, Fernand, ed. *Constitutionalism and Nationalism in Lower Canada: Essays.* Toronto: University of Toronto Press, 1969.

Pelletier, Gerard. *The October Crisis.* Toronto: McClelland and Stewart, 1971.

Proulx, Bernard. *Le roman du territoire.* Montréal: Université du Québec à Montréal, 1987.

Provencher, Jean. *Chronologie du Québec.* Montréal: Boreal, 1991.

Raboy, Marc. *Movements and Messages: Media and Radical Politics in Québec.* Toronto: Between the Lines, 1984.

Richler, Mordecai. *Oh Canada! Oh Québec!: Requiem for a Divided Country.* Toronto: Penguin, 1992.

Rioux, Marcel. *La question du Québec.* Toronto: J. Lorimer, 1978.

Rumilly, Robert. *Histoire de la province de Québec.* Montréal: Valiquette, 1940.

Seguin, Maurice K. *L'idée d'independance au Québec: Genese et historique.* Montréal: Éditions Boreal Express, 1971.

Serant, Paul. *Les enfants de Jacques Cartier: Du grand nord au Mississippi, les americains de langue française.* Paris: R. Laffont, 1991.

Simard, Francis. *Talking It Out: The October Crisis from Inside.* Montréal: Guernica, 1987.

Trofimenkoff, Susan Mann. *The Dream of Nation: A Social and Intellectual History of Québec.* Toronto: Gage, 1983.

Vincenthier, Georges, ed. *Histoire des idées au Québec: des troubles de 1837 au referendum de 1980.* Montréal: VLB, 1983.

Wade, Mason. *The French Canadians: 1760–1967.* 2 vols. Toronto: Macmillan of Canada, 1968.

Young, Brian J. *A Short History of Québec: A Socio-Economic Perspective.* Toronto: Copp Clark Pitman, 1988.

10. Saskatchewan

Archer, John H. *Saskatchewan: A History.* Saskatoon, SASK: Western Producer Prairie Books, 1980.

Beal, Bob, and Rod Macleod. *Prairie Fire: The 1885 North-West Rebellion.* Toronto: McClelland and Stewart, 1994.

Lapointe, Richard. *The Francophones of Saskatchewan: A History.* Regina: Campion College, 1988.

Lipset, Seymour Martin. *Agrarian Socialism: The Cooperative Commonwealth Federation in Saskatchewan.* Rev. ed. Berkeley and Los Angeles: University of California Press, 1971.

Palmer, Howard, and Donald Smith, eds. *The New Provinces: Alberta and Saskatchewan, 1905–1980.* Vancouver: Tantalus Research, 1980.

Smith, David E., ed. *Building a Province: A History of Saskatchewan in Documents.* Saskatoon, SASK: Fifth House Publishers, 1992.

Wright, James Frederick Church. *Saskatchewan: The History of a Province.* Toronto: McClelland and Stewart, 1955.

11. Yukon, Northwest Territories, and Nunavut

Coates, Kenneth. *Canada's Colonies: A History of the Yukon and Northwest Territories.* Toronto: Lorimer, 1985.

Dacks, Gurston, ed. *The Forgotten North: A History of Canada's Provincial Norths: Devolution and Constitutional Development in the Canadian North.* Ottawa: Carleton University Press, 1990.

Duffy, R. Quinn. *The Road to Nunavut.* Montréal: McGill-Queens University Press, 1988.

Hamilton, John David. *Arctic Revolution: Social Change in the Northwest Territories, 1935–1994.* Toronto: Dundurn, 1994.

Zaslow, Morris. *The North and Expansion of Canada, 1914–1967*. Toronto: McClelland and Stewart, 1988.
_____. *The Opening of the Canadian North, 1870–1914*. Toronto: McClelland and Stewart, 1971.

IV. TOPICAL, REGIONAL, AND THEMATIC ASPECTS

1. Physical Features And Historical Geography

Falconer, Allan. *Physical Geography: The Canadian Context*. Toronto: McGraw-Hill Ryerson, 1974.
LeBourdais, Donat Marc. *Canada's Century*. Toronto: McClelland and Stewart, 1956.
Robinson, J. Lewis. *The Physical Environment of Canada and the Evolution of Settlement Patterns*. Vancouver: Talonbooks, 1982.
Swatridge, Leonard A. *Canada: Exploring New Directions*. Markham, ONT: Fitzhenry and Whiteside, 1990.

2. Education

Adams, Howard. *The Education of Canadians, 1800–1967: The Roots of Separatism*. Montréal: Harvest House, 1968.
Auster, Ethel. *Reference Sources on Canadian Education: An Annotated Bibliography*. Toronto: Ontario Institute for Studies in Education, 1978.
Axelrod, Paul, and John G. Reid, eds. *Youth, University, and Canadian Society: Essays in the Social History of Higher Education*. Kingston, ONT: McGill-Queen's University Press, 1989.
Finley, E. Gault. *Education in Canada: A Bibliography*. Toronto: Dundurn in co-operation with the National Library of Canada and the Canadian Government Publishing Centre, Supply and Services Canada, 1989.
Harris, Robin Sutton. *A History of Higher Education in Canada, 1663–1960*. Toronto: University of Toronto Press, 1976.
Magnuson, Roger. *Education in New France*. Montréal: McGill-Queen's University Press, 1992.
McDonald, Neil, and Alf Chaiton, eds. *Egerton Ryerson and His Times*. Toronto: Macmillan of Canada, 1978.
Nock, David A. *A Victorian Missionary and Canadian Indian Policy: Cultural Synthesis vs Cultural Replacement*. Waterloo, ONT: Printed for the Canadian Corporation for Studies in Religion by Wilfrid Laurier University Press, 1988.
Phillips, Charles Edward. *The Development of Education in Canada*. Toronto: W. J. Gage, 1957.
Prentice, Alison L., and Susan E. Houston, eds. *Family, School, and Society in Nineteenth-Century Canada*. Toronto: Oxford University Press, 1975.

Sheehan, Nancy M., J. Donald Wilson, and David C. Jones, eds. *Schools in the West: Essays in Canadian Educational History.* Calgary: Detselig Enterprises, 1986.

Sissons, Charles Bruce. *Church and State in Canadian Education on Historical Study.* Toronto: Ryerson Press, 1959.

Titley, E. Brian, and Peter J. Miller, eds. *Education in Canada: An Interpretation.* Calgary: Detselig Enterprises, 1982.

Wilson, J. Donald. *Canadian Education: A History.* Scarborough, ONT: Prentice-Hall, 1970.

———, ed. *An Imperfect Past: Education and Society in Canadian History.* Vancouver: Centre for the Study of Curriculum and Instruction, University of British Columbia, 1984.

3. Aboriginal History (Indian, Métis, and Inuit)

Ash, Michael. *Home and Native Land: Aboriginal Rights and the Canadian Constitution.* Toronto: Methuen, 1984.

Barron, F. Laurie, and James B. Waldram, eds. *1885 and After: Native Society in Transition.* Regina, SASK: Canadian Plains Research Centre, University of Regina, 1986.

Beardy, Flora, and Robert Coutts. *Voices from Hudson Bay: Cree Stories from York Factory.* Montréal: McGill-Queen's University Press, 1996.

Buckley, Helen. *From Wooden Ploughs to Welfare: Why Indian Policy Failed in the Prairie Provinces.* Montréal: McGill-Queen's University Press, 1992.

Carter, Sarah. *Lost Harvests: Prairie Indian Reserve Farmers and Government Policy.* Montréal: McGill-Queen's University Press, 1990.

Clark, Bruce A. *Native Liberty, Crown Sovereignty: The Existing Aboriginal Right of Self-Government in Canada.* Montréal: McGill-Queen's University Press, 1990.

Cole, Douglas. *Captured Heritage: The Scramble for Northwest Coast Artifacts.* Vancouver: Douglas and McIntyre, 1985.

Cole, Douglas, and Ira Chaikin. *An Iran Hand Upon the People: The Law Against the Potlatch on the Northwest Coast.* Vancouver: Douglas and McIntyre, 1990.

Dickason, Olive Patricia. *Canada's First Nations: A History of Founding Peoples from Earliest Times.* Toronto: McClelland and Stewart, 1992.

Dyck, Noel, and James B. Waldram, eds. *Anthropology, Public Policy, and Native Peoples in Canada.* Montréal: McGill-Queen's University Press, 1993.

Getty, Ian A. L., and Antoine S. Lussier, eds. *As Long as the Sun Shines and Water Flows: A Reader in Canadian Native Studies.* Vancouver: University of British Columbia Press, 1983.

Giraud, Marcel. *The Métis in the Canadian West.* 1945. 1st English ed., trans. by George Woodcock. Edmonton: University of Alberta Press, 1986.

Godard, Barbara. *Talking about Ourselves: The Literary Productions of Native*

Women of Canada. Ottawa: Canadian Research Institute for the Advancement of Women, 1985.

Goddard, John. *Last Stand of the Lubicon Cree.* Vancouver: Douglas and McIntyre, 1991.

Goldie, Terry. *Fear and Temptation: The Image of the Indigene in Canadian, Australian, and New Zealand Literatures.* Montréal: McGill-Queen's University Press, 1989.

Gough, Barry M. *Gunboat Frontier: British Maritime Authority and Northwest Coast Indians, 1846–1890.* Vancouver: University of British Columbia Press, 1984.

Greene, Alma (gah-wonh-nos-doh). *Forbidden Voice: Reflections of a Mohawk Indian.* New ed. Toronto: Green Dragon Press, 1997.

McMillan, Alan D. *Native Peoples and Cultures of Canada: An Anthropological Overview.* Vancouver: Douglas and McIntyre, 1988.

Miller, James Rodger. *Skyscrapers Hide the Heavens: A History of Indian–White Relations in Canada.* Toronto: University of Toronto Press, 1989.

———, ed. *Sweet Promises: A Reader on Indian–White Relations in Canada.* Toronto: University of Toronto Press, 1991.

Morrison, R. Bruce, and C. Roderick Wilson. *Native Peoples: The Canadian Experience.* 2nd ed. Toronto: McClelland and Stewart, 1995.

Morse, Brad. *Aboriginal Peoples and the Law: Indian, Métis, and Inuit Rights in Canada.* Ottawa: Carleton University Press, 1985.

New, W. H., ed. *Native Writers and Canadian Writing.* Vancouver: University of British Columbia Press, 1991.

Pathways to Self-Determination: Canadian Indians and the Canadian State. Toronto: University of Toronto Press, 1984.

Patterson, E. Palmer. *The Canadian Indian: A History since 1500.* Don Mills, ONT: Collier-Macmillan Canada, 1971.

Petrone, Penny, ed. *First People, First Voices.* Toronto: University of Toronto Press, 1983.

Petrone, Penny, ed. *Northern Voices: Inuit Writing in English.* Toronto: University of Toronto Press, 1988.

Pitseolak, Peter, and Dorothy Harley Eber. *People from Our Side: A Life Story with Photographs and Oral Biography.* Montréal: McGill-Queen's University Press, 1993.

Purich, Donald J. *Our Land: Native Rights in Canada.* Toronto: Lorimer, 1986.

Ray, Arthur. *Indians in the Fur Trade: Their Role as Hunters, Trappers, and Middlemen in the Lands Southwest of Hudson Bay, 1660–1870.* Toronto: University of Toronto Press, 1974.

Sioui, Georges E. *For an Amerindian Autohistory: An Essay on the Foundations of a Social Ethic.* Montréal: McGill-Queen's University Press, 1992.

Tennant, Paul. *Aboriginal Peoples and Politics: The Indian Land Question in British Columbia.* Vancouver: University of British Columbia Press, 1990.

Trigger, Bruce G. *Natives and Newcomers: Canada's "Heroic Age" Reconsidered.* Kingston, ONT: McGill-Queen's University Press, 1985.

Waldram, James. *As Long as the Rivers Run: Hydroelectric Development and Native Communities in Western Canada.* Winnipeg: University of Manitoba Press, 1988.

Weaver, Sally. *Making Canadian Indian Policy: The Hidden Agenda, 1968–1970.* Toronto: University of Toronto Press, 1981.

Woodward, Jack. *Native Law.* Toronto: Carswell, 1990.

Wuttunee, Wanda A. *In Business for Ourselves: Northern Entrepreneurs.* Montréal: McGill-Queen's University Press, 1992.

4. Women's History

Armour, Moira. *Canadian Women in History: A Chronology.* Toronto: Green Dragon Press, 1992.

Buss, Helen M. *Mapping Ourselves: Canadian Women's Autobiography in English.* Montréal: McGill-Queen's University Press, 1993.

Danylewycz, Marta. *Taking the Veil: An Alternative to Marriage, Motherhood, and Spinsterhood in Québec, 1840–1920.* Toronto: McClelland and Stewart, 1987.

Devens, Carol. *Countering Colonisation: Native American Women and Great Lakes Missions, 1630–1900.* Berkeley, CA: University of California Press, 1992.

Fulford, Margaret, ed. *The Canadian Women's Movement, 1960–1990: A Guide to Archival Resources.* Toronto: ECW Press, 1992.

Iacovetta, Franca, and Mariana Valverde, eds. *Gender Conflicts: New Essays in Women's History.* Toronto: University of Toronto Press, 1992.

Lévesque, Andrée. *Making and Breaking the Rules: Women in Québec, 1919–1939.* Toronto: McClelland and Stewart, 1994.

Light, Beth. *True Daughters of the North: Canadian Women's History: An Annotated Bibliography.* Toronto: Ontario Institute for Studies in Education Press, 1980.

Matheson, Gwen, ed. *Women in the Canadian Mosaic.* Toronto: P. Martin, 1976.

Prentice, Alison, ed. *Canadian Women: A History.* Toronto: Harcourt Brace Jovanovich, 1988.

Roach Pierson, Ruth. *"They're Still Women After All": The Second World War and Canadian Womanhood.* Toronto: McClelland and Stewart, 1986.

Sangster, Joan. *Dreams of Equality: Women on the Canadian Left, 1920–1950.* Toronto: McClelland and Stewart, 1989.

Strong-Boag, Veronica, and Anita Clair, eds. *Rethinking Canada: The Promise of Women's History.* Toronto: Copp Clark Pitman, 1986.

Trofimenkoff, Susan Mann, and Alison Prentice, eds. *The Neglected Majority: Essays in Canadian Women's History.* Toronto: McClelland and Stewart, 1977–85.

Zaremba, Eve, ed. *Privilege of Sex: A Century of Canadian Women.* Toronto: Anansi, 1974.

5. Immigration And Ethnic Groups

Andracki, Stanislaw. *Immigration of Orientals into Canada, with Special Reference to Chinese.* New York: Arno Press, 1978.

Avery, Donald H. *Reluctant Host: Canada's Response to Immigrant Workers, 1896–1994.* Toronto: McClelland and Stewart, 1995.

Berton, Pierre. *The Promised Land: Settling the West, 1896–1914.* Toronto: McClelland and Stewart, 1984.

Broadfoot, Barry. *The Immigrant Years: From Europe to Canada, 1945–1967.* Vancouver: Douglas and McIntyre, 1986.

Bumsted, J. M. *The People's Clearance: Highland Emigration to British North America, 1770–1815.* Winnipeg: University of Manitoba Press, 1982.

Burnet, Jean R., ed. *Coming Canadians: An Introduction to a History of Canada's Peoples.* Toronto: McClelland and Stewart, 1988.

Charon, Milly, ed. *Between Two Worlds: The Canadian Immigration Experience.* Dunvegan, ONT: Quadrant Editions, 1983.

Chiswick, Barry R., ed. *Immigration, Language, and Ethnicity: Canada and the United States.* Washington, DC: American Enterprise Institute Press, 1992.

Cowan, Helen I. *British Immigration before Confederation.* Ottawa: Canadian Historical Association, 1968.

England, Robert. *The Central European Immigrant in Canada.* Toronto: Macmillan of Canada, 1929.

Epp, Frank H. *Mennonites in Canada.* 2 vols. Toronto: Macmillan of Canada, 1974–82.

Ferguson, Edith. *Immigrants in Canada.* Toronto: University of Toronto, 1977.

Guillet, Edwin Clarence. *The Great Migration: The Atlantic Crossing by Sailing-Ship since 1770.* New York: J. S. Ozer, 1971.

Harvey, Daniel Cobb. *The Colonisation of Canada.* Toronto: Clarke Irwin, 1936.

Harvey, David D. *Americans in Canada: Migration and Settlement since 1840.* Lewiston, NY: E. Mellen Press, 1991.

Johnson, Stanley Currie. *A History of Emigration from the United Kingdom to North America, 1763–1912.* London: Cass, 1966.

Kage, Joseph. *With Faith and Thanksgiving: The Story of Two Hundred Years of Jewish Immigration and Immigrant Aid Effort in Canada, 1760–1960.* Montréal: Eagle, 1962.

Knowles, Valerie. *Strangers at Our Gates: Canadian Immigration and Immigration Policy, 1540–1990.* Toronto: Dundurn, 1992.

Lindstrom-Best, Varpu, ed. *Defiant Sisters: A Social History of Finnish Immigrant Women in Canada.* Toronto: Multicultural History Society of Ontario, 1988.

MacKay, Donald. *Flight from Famine: The Coming of the Irish to Canada.* Toronto: McClelland and Stewart, 1990.

Macleod, Betty. *A History of Canadian Economic Development, with Special Reference to Immigration.* Durham, NC: Duke University Press, 1967.

Montero, Gloria. *The Immigrants.* Toronto: J. Lorimer, 1977.

Overbeek, Johannes. *Population and Canadian Society*. Toronto: Butterworths, 1980.

Petryshyn, Jaroslav. *Peasants in the Promised Land: Canada and the Ukrainians, 1891–1914*. Toronto: J. Lorimer, 1985.

Ramirez, Bruno. *On the Move: French-Canadian and Italian Immigrants in the North Atlantic Economy, 1860–1914*. Toronto: McClelland and Stewart, 1991.

Roy, Patricia, et al. *Mutual Hostages: Canadian and Japanese during the Second World War*. Toronto: University of Toronto Press, 1990.

Seward, Shirley B. *Immigrants in the Canadian Labour Force: Their Role in Structural Change*. Ottawa: Studies in Social Policy, 1989.

––––––. *The Relationship between Immigration and the Canadian Economy*: *Studies in Social Policy*. Ottawa: Institute for Research on Public Policy, 1987.

Sharma, Satya P., Alexander M. Ervin, and Deirdre Meintel, eds. *Immigrants and Refugees in Canada: A National Perspective on Ethnicity, Multiculturalism, and Cross-Cultural Adjustment*. Saskatoon: University of Saskatchewan, 1991.

Sturhahn, William J. H. *They Came from East and West: A History of Immigration in Canada*. Winnipeg: North American Baptist Immigration and Colonisation Society, 1976.

Whitaker, Reginald. *Canadian Immigration Policy since Confederation*. Ottawa: Canadian Historical Association, 1991.

Winks, Robin W. *The Blacks in Canada: A History*. 2nd ed. Montréal: McGill-Queen's University Press, 1997.

Yard, Brigham, ed. *The Mormon Presence in Canada*. Edmonton, ed. University of Alberta Press, 1990.

6. Labour

Babcock, Robert H. *Gompers in Canada: A Study in American Continentalism before the First World War*. Toronto: University of Toronto Press, 1974.

Forsey, Eugene. *History of Trade Unions in Canada, 1812–1902*. Toronto: University of Toronto Press, 1981.

Kealey, Gregory S. *Toronto Workers Respond to Industrial Capitalism, 1867–1892*. Toronto: University of Toronto Press, 1980.

Kealey, Gregory S., and Bryan D. Palmer. *Dreaming of What Might Be: The Knights of Labour in Ontario, 1890–1900*. New York: Cambridge University Press, 1982.

Logan, Harold A. *History of Trade-Union Organization in Canada*. Chicago: University of Chicago Press, 1928.

Palmer, Bryan D. *Working Class Experience: Rethinking the History of Canadian Labour, 1800–1990*. Toronto: McClelland and Stewart, 1992.

7. Literature

Buss, Helen M. *Mapping Our Selves: Canadian Women's Autobiography in English*. Montréal: McGill-Queen's University Press, 1993.

Cameron, Elspeth. *Hugh MacLennan: A Writer's Life*. Toronto: University of Toronto Press, 1980.

Davies, Robertson. *The Well-Tempered Critic: One Man's View of Theatre and Letters in Canada*. Toronto: McClelland and Stewart, 1981.

Davis, Geoffrey, ed. *Kanada: gesellschaft, landeskunde, literatur*. Wurzburg: Konigshausen and Neumann, 1991.

Denham, Robert D., and Thomas Willard, eds. *Visionary Poetics: Essays on Northrop Frye's Criticism*. New York: P. Lang, 1991.

D'haen, Theo, and Hans Bertens, eds. *Postmodern Fiction in Canada*. Amsterdam: Rodopi, 1992.

Duffy, Dennis. *Sounding the Iceberg: An Essay on Canadian Historical Novels*. Toronto, ONT: ECW Press, 1986.

Easingwood, Peter, Konrad Gross, and Wolfgang Klooss, eds. *Probing Canadian Culture*. Augsburg, Germany: AV-Verlag, 1991.

Fraser, Wayne. *The Dominion of Women: The Personal and the Political in Canadian Women's Literature*. New York: Greenwood Press, 1991.

Guttenberg, A. Ch. de. *Early Canadian Art and Literature*. Vaduz, Liechtenstein: Europe Print, 1969.

Hathorn, Ramon, and Patrick Holland, eds. *Images of Louis Riel in Canadian Culture*. Lewiston, NY: E. Mellen Press, 1992.

Itwaru, Arnold. *The Invention of Canada: Literary Text and the Immigrant Imaginary*. Toronto: TSAR Publications, 1990.

McCourt, Edward A. *The Canadian West in Fiction*. Toronto: Ryerson Press, 1970.

MacDonald, Mary Lu. *Literature and Society in the Canadas, 1817–1850*. Lewiston, NY: E. Mellen Press, 1992.

McDougall, Robert L. *Totems: Essays on the Cultural History of Canada*. Ottawa: Tecumseh Press, 1990.

Mandryka, M. I. *History of Ukrainian Literature in Canada*. Winnipeg: Ukrainian Free Academy of Sciences, 1968.

Moritz, Albert Frank. *The Oxford Illustrated Literary Guide to Canada*. Toronto: Oxford University Press, 1987.

New, W. H., ed. *Native Writers and Canadian Writing*. Vancouver: University of British Columbia Press, 1990.

Pearlman, Mickey, ed. *Canadian Women Writing Fiction*. Jackson: University Press of Mississippi, 1993.

Petrone, Penny, ed. *First People, First Voices*. Toronto: University of Toronto Press, 1983.

Petrone, Penny. *Native Literature in Canada: From the Oral Tradition to the Present*. Toronto: Oxford University Press, 1990.

Petrone, Penny, ed. *Northern Voices: Inuit Writing in English*. Toronto: University of Toronto Press, 1988.

Poff, Deborah C., ed. *Literatures in Canada*. Montréal: Association for Canadian Studies, 1989.

Relke, Diana A. M. *Literary Mothers and Daughters: A Review of Twentieth-Century Poetry by Canadian Women.* Ottawa: Canadian Research Institute for the Advancement of Women, 1987.

Ross, Frances Aileen. *The Land and People of Canada.* Philadelphia: Lippincott, 1960.

Simpson-Housley, Paul, and Glen Norcliffe, eds. *A Few Acres of Snow: Literary and Artistic Images of Canada.* Toronto: Dundurn Press, 1992.

Staines, David. *Beyond the Provinces: Literary Canada at Century's End.* Toronto: University of Toronto Press, 1995.

Steele, Apollonia. *Theses on English-Canadian Literature: A Bibliography of Research Produced in Canada and Elsewhere from 1903 Forward.* Calgary: University of Calgary Press, 1988.

Stich, K. P., ed. *Reflections: Autobiography and Canadian Literature.* Ottawa: University of Ottawa Press, 1988.

Vassanji, M. G., ed. *A Meeting of Streams: South Asian Canadian Literature.* Toronto: TSAR Publications, 1985.

Vigneault, Robert, ed. *Langue, littérature, culture au Canada français.* Ottawa: Éditions de l'Université d'Ottawa, 1977.

Waterston, Elizabeth. *Children's Literature in Canada.* New York: Twayne Publishers, 1992.

Woodcock, George. *The Meeting of Time and Space: Regionalism in Canadian Literature.* Edmonton: NeWest Institute for Western Canadian Studies, 1981.

8. Science And Technology

Martyn, Katharine. *J. B. Tyrrell: Explorer and Adventurer: The Geological Survey Years, 1881–1898.* Toronto: University of Toronto Press, 1993.

Waiser, William A. *The Field Naturalist: John Macoun, the Geological Survey and Natural Science.* Toronto: University of Toronto Press, 1989.

Zaslow, Morris. *Reading the Rocks: The Story of the Geological Survey of Canada, 1842–1972.* Toronto: Macmillan of Canada, 1975.

Zeller, Suzanne. *Inventing Canada: Early Victorian Science and the Idea of a Transcontinental Nation.* Toronto: University of Toronto Press, 1987.

About the Author

BARRY M. GOUGH (B.Ed., University of British Columbia; M.A., Montana; Ph.D. and D.Lit., King's College, London University; Fellow of the Royal Historical Society) is a professor of history at Wilfrid Laurier University, Waterloo, Ontario, Canada. He has served for many years as coordinator of Canadian studies at this university. A founding member of the Association of Canadian Studies in the United States, he is also a life member of the Association for Canadian Studies. Dr. Gough has been a visiting professor at Duke, Maine, and Otago Universities and has lectured abroad on Canadian history and politics. His articles on Canadian history have appeared in various journals, including *Alberta, Arctic, BC Studies, The Beaver, Canadian Geographical Journal, Canadian Journal of Native Studies*, and *The Journal of Canadian Studies*. His *Canada* (1975) was published in the Modern Nations in Historical Perspective Series (Prentice-Hall), edited by Robin W. Winks. Dr. Gough has been a European Commission Official Visitor, NATO Research Fellow, and University Research Professor, Wilfrid Laurier University. He serves on a number of scholarly journal boards, including *Polar Record* and *Pacific Historical Review*. Dr. Gough is editor-in-chief of *The American Neptune: Maritime History and Arts*. He is a past president of the Canadian Nautical Research Society and also the North American Society for Oceanic History. He is the author of several books on the history of Canada, including *Royal Navy and the Northwest Coast* (1971), *Distant Dominion* (1980), *Gold Rush!* (1983), *Gunboat Frontier* (1984), *The Northwest Coast* (1992), and *First across the Continent: Sir Alexander Mackenzie* (1997).